ENGINES OF THE BLACK
POWER MOVEMENT

ALSO EDITED BY JAMES L. CONYERS, JR.

Africana Studies:
A Disciplinary Quest for Both Theory and Method
(McFarland, 1997; softcover 2005)

Afrocentricity and the Academy:
Essays on Theory and Practice
(McFarland, 2003)

African American Jazz and Rap:
Social and Philosophical Examinations of Black Expressive Behavior
(McFarland, 2001)

ENGINES OF THE BLACK POWER MOVEMENT

Essays on the Influence of Civil Rights Actions, Arts, and Islam

Edited by James L. Conyers, Jr.

McFarland & Company, Inc., Publishers
Jefferson, North Carolina, and London

Library of Congress Cataloguing-in-Publication Data

Engines of the Black power movement: essays on the influence of
    civil rights actions, arts, and Islam / edited by James L. Conyers, Jr.
        p.   cm.
    Includes bibliographical references and index.

    ISBN-13: 978-0-7864-2540-2
    softcover : 50# alkaline paper ∞

    1. Black power—United States—History—20th century.
    2. African Americans—Civil rights—History—20th century.
    3. Civil rights movements—United States—History—20th
    century.   4. African Americans—Politics and government—
    20th century.   5. African Americans—Intellectual life—20th
    century.   6. Black Arts movement.   7. Black Muslims—
    History.   8. Nation of Islam (Chicago, Ill.)—History.
    I. Conyers, James L.
    E185.615.E54   2007
    305.896'073—dc22   2006029823

British Library cataloguing data are available

Cover image ©2006 SuperStock

Manufactured in the United States of America

McFarland & Company, Inc., Publishers
    Box 611, Jefferson, North Carolina 28640
    www.mcfarlandpub.com

To the memory and spirit
of my beautiful and loving wife of 21 years,
Jacqueline I. Conyers, 1961–2006.
We miss you everyday.

Acknowledgments

Writing the first word is the beginning. One of my mentors often shares this favorite phrase with me. True, thought begins with writing and continues through redrafting, reflecting, and transmitting information from an idea to a document on paper. Now, as I celebrate another published volume, I often think of how to phrase my gratitude and appreciation for the people who provide continued support and guidance. Of course my mother, Agnes Conyers, and my wife, Jacqueline I. Conyers, are my foundation of strength and continue to offer prayers, provide nourishment, maintain a protective covenant, and dispense indubitable love. My sons, Sekou Conyers, Kamau Conyers, and Chad Hawkins, are the young warriors of our household, and I bear the responsibility for their initiation, their rites of passage, and their transition from maleness to manhood.

Of course, mentors are valuable and have assisted in my career development. Dr. Julius E. Thompson stands out as a professor, mentor, brother, and friend who consistently challenges me to be a better human. Others such as Drs. Delores Aldridge, James B. Stewart, Jerry Ward Jr., and the late Gerald Davis are pivotal resources to my continued learning.

Friends are an important ingredient in the operation and development of successful endeavors. Fortunately, now in my early forties, I have friends who are supportive and continue to listen, respect, and offer me critique from substance and not jealously. These men are Qawi Jamison, Anthony Robinson, Zane Corbin, Henry B. Robinson, Gregory Mainor, Abdul Mainor, Mustafa Aziz Rasool, Mustafa Harper, James Bullock, Andrew Smallwood, and Ahati N.N. Toure.

Still others must be acknowledged for their research productivity, personal engagement, and support: Dr. Molefi K. Asante, Dr. Abu Abarry, Dr. Anthony Pinn, Dr. Tyrone Tillery, Dr. Russell Jackson, Dr. Christel Temple, Russell and Betty Jackson, Dr. Arvah Strickland, Mr. Malcolm Champion, Dr. Mekada Graham, Dr. Irving Horowitz, the Sankofa Student Organization at the University of Houston, Dr. Jay Gogue, Dr. John Antel, and Dr. Tatcho Mindiola. I would also like thank Mrs. Jackie Lynch and Mrs. Sylvia Macey for their typing and indexing assistance in organizing this volume.

Contents

IV : AFRICAN AMERICANS AND ISLAM 157

V : CIVIL RIGHTS AND REDEMPTION 207

Preface

Considered a pivotal awakening of social conscience in America, the period of protest in the 1960s left a turbulent legacy. The era's Civil Rights movement, which began as a movement organized to address issues of segregation, voting rights, and racial equality, became a larger cultural force encompassing campaigns for free speech and gender equity, antiwar sentiments, and continuous questioning of authoritarian structures.

Despite the significant gains of this social movement, it appears that four decades later, America fails to remember, and perhaps even dismisses, the achievements of the 1960s. It is difficult to explain how and why people struggled to attain civil rights and then failed to remember the struggle.

We must not lose the moral ground that we—meaning all Americans—have gained. We must not forget how that ground was won, and who brought us to it.

To spur our will to remember, and to fix the achievements of the 1960s into our cultural memory, this study considers from an interdisciplinary perspective the lasting contributions of the Black Power movement. It looks at how Black Power was influenced, and its success supported, by potent forces in society: the Civil Rights movement, the arts, and Islam.

The book is divided into five parts, each part including essays on a particular theme. The essays in the first part, "Cultural Analysis," consider how specific movements and figures in Black art and music influenced society and spurred an interest in the Black Power movement. Part II, "Black Power Analysis," looks at the artistic and educational impetus for social policy, that is, how such policy is affected by cultural education. Part III, "Black Arts Movement Analysis," examines the interplay of aesthetic and political imperatives that made Black Power a force in America. Part IV, "African Americans and Islam," offers perspectives on black culture through the lens of a religion that has proved attractive to many African Americans seeking new spiritual paths. Finally, Part V considers what it means to be black in the United States—and, at a deeper level, what it means to be human. This part, "Civil Rights and Redemption," also addresses the loss of historical memory and warns against its consequences.

It is my hope, and the hope of all the contributors to this volume, that

1

the essays will inspire thought and provoke readers to reflect on their civil rights—perhaps even to propose social change. Certainly, readers will have the opportunity to critique, review, and advance the ideas presented in this book, and to connect the phenomenology of Africana past and present to possible outcomes in the future. Above all, readers should come away from this book aware that from the faith to persevere, and a belief in human possibility, comes the chance for resurrection.

I

CULTURAL ANALYSIS

As the topic of the Black Arts movement is engaged, critical dialogue permeates the contextual boundaries of cultural aesthetics. The two essays in Part I consider art history and music centered on Africana phenomena and culture. Sharon Pruitt's assessment of cohesiveness of the Spiral Group and the dynamics for the reclamation and recovery of Black Art is an appropriate beginning for a survey approach to the Civil Rights movement. This continues with Larry Ross examining the consequences of African American jazz musicians' voluntary migration to Europe from 1919 to 1945. Culture can be defined by four descriptive variables: history, mythology, motif, and ethos. Culture in many ways can be referred to as the spirit of a people. Without it, they function in a state of immobility.

1. The Spiral Group: Defining African American Art During the Civil Rights Movement

SHARON PRUITT

I suggest that Western society, and particularly that of America, is gravely ill and a major symptom is the American treatment of the Negro. The artistic expression of this culture concentrates on themes of "absurdity" and "anti-art" which provide further evidence of its ill health. It is the right of everyone now to re-examine history to see if Western Culture offers the only solutions to man's purpose on this earth.—Romare Bearden (Siegel 1966, p. 49)

Introduction

The Civil Rights Movement of the 1960s spawned the emergence of the Spiral Group, an organization of African American visual artists residing in New York City. The objective of the group was to define the role of art and the artists' relationship to the movement. Under the leadership of Romare Bearden, Norman Lewis, and Hale Woodruff, group members mobilized to establish collective visions. They examined their cultural identity and explored the possibility of defining a "black aesthetic." As purveyors of black cultural life, the artists sought to empower themselves through self-examination and self-discovery. In an attempt to understand the Spiralists' response to the turbulent decade of the 1960s, this essay will examine the art philosophy of the group as well as the artistic career of Bearden.

The Spiral Group members' perspectives were diverse. In 1966, when fourteen of the sixteen members were interviewed for a review of a group exhibition, each Spiralist expressed different opinions about his or her contribution (Siegel 1966). The philosophy of one of the founding members, Romare Bearden (b. 1912; d. 1988), exemplifies the objectives of the group to the movement. Bearden's promotion of the power of the visuality[1] of African American artists included establishing group solidarity and activities. Ever since 1935, Bearden knew there existed a substantial number of active African American visual artists. He had met and befriended many of them in the Harlem Artists Guild and the 306 Group.[2] In these organizations, he also encountered other artists who were formerly members of the Works Progress Administration (WPA) Federal Art Project.

Before the 1960s, Bearden's own artwork received limited but impressive visuality. He held major exhibitions at the Samuel Kootz Gallery, a mainstream New York gallery. Also, he received positive reviews from such acclaimed publications as *The New York Times*, *Art Digest*, and *Art News*. Despite Bearden's successes prior to his membership in the Spiral Group, his fame was augmented later when he drastically transformed his artwork.

According to Bearden, his oeuvres are not invitations to social protest. They do not depict violent mistreatment of African Americans (Schwartzman 1990, pp. 131–32). Nevertheless, after careful scrutiny of his art and philosophy, it is apparent that Bearden's approach to the creative process and his artistic images reflect reactions to social maladies. As a socially and politically conscious artist, Bearden created images that may be perceived as didactic lectures on Black Power.

This essay begins with an explanation of the Spiral Group's evolution and objectives. It proceeds by examining the changes in Bearden's medium, aesthetics, and subject matter. The essay explores Bearden's role as a visual, political activist who produced revolutionary art. It postulates that his solution to aesthetic representation in the 1960s was inspired by a radical, modern European aesthetic philosophy, which was based on traditional African art.[3]

The Formation of the Spiral Group

Visual artists are frequently marginalized in African American political activities. However, the Spiral Group seized the opportunity to participate in the Civil Rights Movement. According to Gelburd (1997, p. 18), the formation of the Spiral Group was in response to a request made by A. Philip Randolph, a prominent civil rights labor leader. Randolph wanted artists to devise "a new visual order" in the movement. Although he resided in New York City, the specifics of Randolph's relationship to the New York–based artists is unclear and is undocumented in the literature. Perhaps Randolph reflected upon the important role that the federal government played for African American artists during the Depression: the WPA provided jobs for unemployed artists, while artists were able to express social and cultural statements in their artworks. Randolph's interest in the artists' participation demonstrates a policy of inclusion of a variety of voices that might help further the civil rights cause for African Americans.

On July 5, 1963, the group met at Bearden's studio loft on Canal Street[4] "for the purpose of discussing the commitment of the Negro artist in the present struggle for civil liberties, and as [*sic*] [to form] a discussion group to consider common aesthetic problems" (Bearden and Henderson 1993, p. 400). The organization comprised an older generation of established artists as well as a younger generation of relatively-unknown artists. The group served as a catalyst for the artists' increased visibility among themselves as well as among both the black and white communities at large. Prior to participating in the Spiral Group, some members were aware of neither the others' existence nor their artworks (p. 402, 474).

Besides Bearden, Lewis, and Woodruff, other Spiral members included Charles Alston, James Yeargans, Felrath Hines, Richard Mayhew, William Pritchard, Emma Amos, Reginald Gammon, Alvin Hollingsworth, Calvin Douglass, Perry Ferguson, William Majors, Earl Miller, and Merton Simpson.[5] Bearden, Lewis, Woodruff, Alston, and Yeargans were among the older, accomplished members who assumed a leadership role. Woodruff and Alston were Harlem Renaissance artists in the 1920s and WPA artists in the 1930s. The members were primarily male painters; Pritchard was the only sculptor and Amos was the only female artist. The Spiralists were educated intellectuals who sought to change their position of isolation and alienation from each other and from their community.

At first, the members did not consider using their artistry in the movement but rather felt compelled to participate in the upcoming March on Washington on August 28. They contemplated chartering a bus to Washington, D.C., but ultimately abandoned the idea. Their focus turned to defining and discussing aesthetics and philosophical problems which were unique to African American artists. The group met regularly for informal discussions on visuality, assimilation, and civil rights.

Questions about identity were central to the discussions of the Spiral Group. Defining a black identity in a white-dominated society was not a new discourse. It was discussed by artists in the 1920s during the Harlem Renaissance period and was restated in the 1930s in the discussions of the Harlem Artists Guild (Bearden and Henderson 1993, p. 400). For the Spiral Group, the inquiry about the artistic representation of "blackness" was met with a variety of solutions. One was the investigation of an African legacy which the Harlem Renaissance artists had explored before them. Bearden suggested that "identity" be addressed by examining the philosophy of African writers such as Alioune Diop and Léopold Senghor, Senegalese cultural theorists. In 1940, Bearden had already befriended Claude McKay, whose writings inspired Senghor's concepts about the Négritude movement. Another approach was to study African art. Although some Spiralists had previously viewed African art in venues such as the Schomburg Center for Research in Black Culture and the Museum of Modern Art,[6] they all were further enlightened by lectures on African art presented by Simpson, a Spiralist who was also an African art dealer (Siegel 1966, p. 50).

In the group's discussions about universal themes of human suffering, Alston cited Pablo Picasso's *Guernica* (1937) as a possible reference for the members. Picasso's Post-Cubist painting had universal implications and moved beyond the representation of a locale (Bearden and Henderson 1993, p. 400). Its large scale (11'6" x 25'8") is replete with black, white, and gray images that simulate photojournalism. The painting brought international attention to an event that occurred during the Spanish Civil War (1936–39)— the bombing of an ancient Spanish Basque city by German forces acting on behalf of the fascist leader Francisco Franco. The painting suggests human brutality and man's inhumanity to man, a universal socio-political theme. The Spiralists queried the possibility of representing black peoples' plight in America in terms of a similar universal construct.

The group's concern for universality was not only confined to social politics in art but extended to the social politics of identity in a society that disparaged their achievements. They saw themselves as artists existing in a universal scheme. Their philosophical position developed from an "identity of self," which was conceived from experiences of cultural hybridizations. Also, they had a world-view about races of people and interracial relationships. These issues were particularly germane to Bearden's experiences. Throughout his career and before the 1960s, he had already met and befriended a diverse array of prominent artists including visual, literary, and performing artists of different heritages. In 1950, he traveled to Paris, France,[7] and throughout Italy and met renowned European artists. Bearden stated his feelings in the following manner:

> The Negro artist must come to think of himself not primarily as a Negro artist, but as an artist.... There is only one art ... and it belongs to all mankind.... Examine the art forms of any culture and one becomes aware of the patterns that link it to other cultures and peoples [Schwartzman 1990, p. 131].

Regardless of the artists' individual solutions to art problems, Lewis advocated the need for excellence in the final presentation of artworks and group exhibitions. He believed that the Spiral members would serve as future leaders for other artists and, therefore, were obligated to establish high standards for their productions. The members' artworks were critiqued. However, some of the younger artists vehemently opposed the harsh criticisms their work received from older members.

Upon reflecting on the significance of the group discussions, years later Mayhew conceded that each artist was forced to confront two crucial and timeless questions. First, how relevant is the artist's artwork to the struggles of black people? Secondly, how honest is the artist in expressing concepts presented in his or her artwork? The younger artists in the group wanted to portray overt militancy. On the other hand, the older generation rejected these themes because 1) images of violence and death were not considered constructive nor innovative, 2) these types of themes were simply an imitation of life and lacked artistic creativity, and 3) scenes of militancy and violence were already well-known to the black community. Instead, the older generation felt that real protest or constructive painting should be uplifting and stimulating. The majority of the members of the Spiral Group were not inclined to represent a repertoire that was an imitation of life (Bearden and Henderson 1993, pp. 474–75). One exception was Reginald Gammon's *Freedom Now* (1964),[8] a painting that depicts a civil rights march. On this controversial issue, Mayhew's conciliatory role is exemplified as follows:

> He [Mayhew] recalled a young black painter asserting, "I've got to do protest painting?" To which Mayhew responded, "Do protest paintings— not to protest but to be innovative and constructive in relationship to art and your relationship with the community.... Real protest painting or constructive painting should be involved with an uplifting and stimulating element [ibid].

Bearden expressed a similar attitude about social protest art.[9] However, his philosophy about the role of the African American in mainstream society vacillates between supporting the ideas of Dr. Martin Luther King, Jr., and those of Malcolm X. He stated:

> either the Negro, through such figures as Dr. King, will give this country a transfusion it badly needs, or the Negro must reject the values of this society completely [ibid., p. 400].

Overall, the Spiral Group's discussions were extremely beneficial in engaging the artists in a continual self-discovery of inner strength and productive growth. Years after the group dissolved, its members acknowledged this impact by constantly questioning their honesty in the creative process. Bearden realized the significance of periodically returning to "a Spiral discussion moment" to understand the disgust some African Americans had towards the imagery in his work. In May 1985, he stated:

> One painter wrote from the South that my stuff [artwork] was forced and deliberately painted to cater to what the [white] critics think a Negro should paint like. To many of my own people, I learn, my work was very disgusting and morbid—and portrayed a type of Negro that they were trying to get away from. One man bought a painting and brought it back in three days because his wife couldn't stand it in the house.
> So I ask myself, is what I'm doing good or bad, are my paintings an honest and valid statement. Have you ever felt like this?...

I guess to be anything of a painter you need to have the hide of an elephant. There is a lot more to it than just putting the paint on canvas [Schwartzman 1990, p. 121].

The Spiral members' focus on abstract forms and distorted figures rather than representational art guaranteed opposition among some members of the black community. Considered to be elitist blacks, the artists' works were viewed as being divorced from their racial and cultural origins (Coleman 1966, pp. 150–51). However, to approach their work and role in this manner limits one's understanding of the intentions of the artists, who sought to express a reawakening of the black cultural experience. The Spiralists were in search of an aesthetics that rejected the traditional Eurocentric qualifiers of physical beauty, which were grounded in the Greek art tradition.[10] They explored establishing a new paradigm for symbols of beauty. Bearden, in particular, chose to create abstract black figures, influenced by African figural sculpture, to relate to heritage. By doing so, he prescribed a "new" and "African American" aesthetic, which proclaimed that "African art and blackness are beautiful."

The Spiralists were not alone in their pursuit to divert the focus of aesthetics away from a Western illusionistic tradition. They were following a similar path as the nineteenth century modern European artists and the contemporary American artists of the day. Older Spiral members, such as Lewis and Woodruff, produced paintings in the mainstream fashion of the New York School of Abstract Expressionism. Like the New York School of artists, they created large paintings filled with gestural brushstrokes. Their paintings were frequently devoid of any recognizable objects.

Previously, Bearden had experimented with Abstract Expressionism but abandoned it for a Cubist, abstract style. Unlike the Abstract Expressionist painters, he studied the structural relationships of planar spaces, similar to Picasso's Cubist style. Before becoming a Spiralist, Bearden's abstract paintings were reminiscent of the linear exaggeration of figures expressed in Picasso's Synthetic and Post-Cubist styles. Despite their diverse painting styles, the Spiralists remained unified in their commitment to follow the path of a "spiral."

The Archimedean Spiral of Levitation

The name, Spiral Group, was coined by Woodruff. In nature, the spiral is the form found in kinetic energies such as tornados, hurricanes, and smoke. However, the name chosen for the group is specifically derived from a principle theorized by Archimedes, who is considered by modern scholars to be the greatest Greek mathematician and whose numerous mathematical principles are so complex that they are still studied today. The choice of a mathematical construct to apply to the art group appears apropos. The vortex of the spiral suggested for them the freedom to move upward and outward. Moreover, the relationship between the arts and mathematics dates back to the ancient Egyptian and Greek periods.[11] For the artists, mathematical systems used in art allowed for the existence of order.

Archimedes, who studied in ancient Egypt, was one of the first scholars to apply geometry to mechanics and hydrostatics. He proved the law of the lever entirely by geometry and established Archimedes' Principle (*The Concise Columbia Encyclopedia*, "Archimedes"). Archimedes' principle is

> [a] principle that states that a body immersed in a fluid is buoyed up by a force equal to the weight of the displaced fluid. The principle applies to both floating and submerged bodies, and to all fluids. It explains not only the buoyancy of ships but also the rise of a helium-filled balloon and the apparent loss of weight of objects underwater [ibid].

Also known as a physicist and an inventor, Archimedes is alleged to have invented the Archimedean Screw (also called Archimedes' Screw), which was used for irrigation in ancient Egypt. The Archimedean Screw is

> An ancient apparatus for raising water, consisting of either a spiral tube around an inclined axis or an inclined tube containing a tight-fitting, broad-threaded screw [*The American Heritage Dictionary*, "Archimedean Screw"].

Thus, the name Spiral Group relates to both Archimedes' Principle and Screw. It symbolizes the philosophy of the art group who felt a moral obligation to communicate to the community through their art. The Spiral Group's art was intended to provide hope and renewed energy by constantly moving forward. In spite of the turbulent social climate, their mission entailed uplifting and keeping afloat the spirits of their people and themselves. As Mayhew contends, "The name 'spiral' embodied this extending concept of evolving and unifying, bonding and constructively supportive relationships with one another, which was an art of Afro-American sensibility" (Coleman 1996, p. 149).

The Evolution of Bearden's Collages: Deconstruction, Fragmentation, Improvisation

Probably no one in the group could understand the concept of the spiral as it relates to the Greek mathematician Archimedes better than Bearden, who received a bachelor's degree in mathematics from New York University in 1935. Perhaps in an attempt to symbolize the solidarity of his people both as an extension of the spiral and as the impending March on Washington would demonstrate, Bearden suggested that the Spiral artists create a collaborative work. He had collected a bag full of cut-out photographs from *Life*, *Look*, and *Ebony* magazines[12] and explained to the group the concepts for creating a photomontage. However, group members quickly lost interest and resumed working individually on their own projects. Bearden was compelled to complete the photomontage alone. Upon the suggestion of Gammon, Bearden created an enlargement of five or six of his small photomontages by photostating them. The size increased from the small 8½" × 11½" photomontage to a 3' × 4' or 6' x 8' photostat (Schwartzman 1990, p. 210).

Bearden was reluctant to show the work to Arne Ekstrom, one of the dealers of the co-owned gallery Cordier and Ekstrom,[13] when he visited Bearden's studio to discuss his next exhibition. Apparently, Bearden felt the content of the work was too strong and bold. He only discussed the enlargement (the photostat photomontages) upon the request of Ekstrom, who saw the work wrapped up alongside the studio wall. Much to Bearden's surprise, Ekstrom was fascinated by the enlarged photomontage and suggested that, along with twenty more, they could be Bearden's next one-man show. This was a pivotal moment for Bearden, who used collages as his primary medium for the rest of his career (ibid., pp. 210–211).

The twenty-one enlarged photomontages debuted in an exhibition titled "Projections," which opened first at Cordier and Ekstrom in October 1964 and a year later at the Corcoran Gallery in Washington, D.C. The works were well received by the art community. In 1971, when the "Projection" series was exhibited at the Museum of Modern Art, the works were described as having "a starkness more akin to *cinéma verité* than to painting" (Allen 1971, p. 28). The photomontages, such as *Evening, 9:10, 461 Lenox Avenue* structured powerful messages like a documentary film. They were the works of a visionary because during the "twentieth-century movie, video, and other imaging [had] so far outdistanced sculpture and painting in mimetic power as to render their [painting's and sculpture's] traditional mission obsolete" (Stewart 1997, p. 45).

Technically, the photomontages were collages (French, *papier collé*), which is a "technique in art consisting of cutting natural or manufactured materials and pasting them to a painted or unpainted surface" (*The Concise Columbia Encyclopedia*). Bearden's magazine photographs were not only manufactured, but represented a new medium for him. Whereas before he was painting abstractly on canvas, now he was using "found" objects, or readymades, for his works.

The technique of collage was first introduced by Picasso in a work entitled *Still Life with Chair Caning* (1912) in which a piece of commercially printed oilcloth was pasted to a surface. In subsequent collages such as *Gui-*

tar, Sheet-Music and Wineglass (1912), Picasso not only pasted pieces of sheet music to the surface but also added a section from the French newspaper, *Le Journal*. For Picasso, words become an important part of the message of the collage. In the collage entitled *Bottle of Suze* (1912), Picasso's newspaper collage chronicles the anarchists' position and, therefore, becomes a direct reference to Picasso's own political identity.[14]

The multi-media assemblage of collage deconstructs the illusionistic space that is standard in the tradition of Western art. Almost by definition, collage is a method that deconstructs, fragments, improvises, and reconstructs forms and meaning in the pictorial space. During the early twentieth century, collage elements were the basic medium for European Dada and Surrealist painters, who sought to create a "new art" that deconstructed European traditions. Scholars (e.g., Patton, Gelburd, and Powell) indicate that Bearden's collages were inspired by Dada and Surrealist collages.[15] However, they do not provide a specific explanation of the medium nor of other Dada inspirations for Bearden.

The photographic collage was the artistic contribution of the Berlin Dadaists. It was conceived in 1918 by Raoul Hausmann, who was inspired by the photographic tricks used by German army photographers. The latter made oleolithograph mounts, from which the faces were cut out, showing groups of soldiers in idealized settings. In the mounts, they inserted the photographed heads of their clients (Rubin 1968, p. 83).[16]

In his criticism of American mainstream art and its social ills, Bearden used terms such as "absurdity" and "anti-art" — terms which are couched in both French and German Dada semantics (see Bearden's quote at the beginning of this essay) and were voiced as an element of social change in those countries.[17] Bearden indicated that Dada art philosophy resonated in the United States in 1966 in the destruction of its moral fiber — the mistreatment of African Americans. One may query: Besides the medium, what are other aspects of Dada that resonant in Bearden's artwork?

There are elements of the Dada movement that Bearden renounced and others which he retained. Besides the concepts of "absurdity" and "anti-art," Bearden relinquishes the humor, frivolity, and triviality in Dada art. Instead, his photomontages capture the graveness of the black people's survival. While Dada artists repudiated Picasso, Paul Cézanne, and the Renaissance artists, Bearden ultimately revered them.[18] Bearden was a voracious reader of history, literature, and philosophy (Schwartzman 1990, p. 207). He infused into his art the teachings of world art histories — Asian, African, ancient, medieval, Renaissance, Dutch Baroque, Impressionism, Post-Impressionism, and the modern and contemporary movements in both Europe and America.

Nevertheless, there are components of Dada art that are not only apparent in Bearden's art but also occur in both Cubist and Surrealist art. Close scrutiny of characteristics of the three art movements—Cubism (begun c. 1910),[19] Dada (begun c. 1917), and Surrealism (begun c. 1924)—reveals similarities. Cubism, Dada, and Surrealism employ typography and mass-produced objects as an aspect of their media. In all three movements, oeuvres depict forms and pictorial space that are deconstructed, then reconstructed to create an improvisational feeling. These works exemplify the cerebral arts and constantly challenge the viewer to deconstruct known paradigms regarding art, beauty, and social constructs. By so doing, art forms empower the viewer to look anew at art, cultural values, and social disorder. Finally, all three art movements were revolutionary and members in each movement became associated with political programs. Members used art to protest the doctrines of aesthetic realism that sustained the European art academies from the fifteenth through the nineteenth centuries. Also, their art displayed, although sometimes subtly, opposition to the modern bourgeois society.[20]

Bearden was an eclectic intellectual who astutely perceived the interrelationships in the arts. He was energized by all the arts: classical music, old and new jazz music, dance, and film (Schwartzman 1990, p. 128). For his visual deconstruction of structures, defragmentation of imageries, and improvisionation, Bearden does not rely only on the twentieth century European art movements but also on the African American expressive art form of jazz. In the 1950s, Bearden was so familiar with jazz that he wrote and published music for such luminaries as Billy Eckstine and Billie Holiday (Gelburd and Golden 1997, p. 77). Ralph Ellison, a friend of Bearden, correlates jazz and surrealism in Bearden's collages. Ellison saw similarities with "the sharp breaks, leaps in consciousness, distortions, paradoxes, reversals, telescoping of time and *surreal* [italics, my own] blending of styles, value, hopes and dreams which characterize much of Negro American History" (Aaron Myers, "Bearden, Romare," *Africana*, p. 207). Thus, because the constructs of jazz as well as Cubism are derivative of the arts of Africa, their similarities are not surprising. It is against this extensive background of artistic knowledge that Bearden was able to change his artwork in reaction to the social ills of the 1960s.

Bearden's Collages and Southern Memories

Black people were the major subject matter for Bearden's collages, and remained so throughout his artistic career. He had produced political cartoons dealing with race issues for the *Baltimore Afro-American* in the 1930s, Social Realist paintings of black life in the 1940s, and Abstract paintings, often depicting biblical subject matter with obscure figures, in the 1930s and 1940s.

Although his photomontages in the 1960s continued the use of black subject matter, the figures became more pronounced and contorted. In *Evening, 9:10, 461 Lenox Avenue*, the faces comprise features from many images and project enormous eyes. Their stark directness provides an "in-your-face" confrontation with the viewer. The colossal heads in Bearden's work may reflect the lessons he learned from two influential sources: 1) George Grosz, his teacher at the Arts Student League in New York, and 2) African art.

Grosz taught Bearden to concentrate on his drawing style. He introduced Bearden to political cartoons and to drawings by Europeans portraying the pain and sufferings resulting from political wars and opposition movements.[21] Moreover, Grosz was a former Berlin Dada artist. He participated in the Dada movement in Berlin, Germany, during the early period of its inception in 1918. In Grosz's career, Dada was only a passing phase; he separated from it after the 1920s. However, while a Dadaist, his provocative, anti-militaristic, anti-bourgeois visual satires portrayed caricatures of individuals.[22] Like other Dadaists, Grosz used Hausmann's photographic collage technique in which heads could be emphasized.

Also, Bearden probably incorporated the proportions of traditional African sculpture, which he had the opportunity to observe in various museums and private collections in America as well as while in Paris in the 1950s. Traditional African figural sculpture exaggerates the head, often in a ratio, in relation to the size of the rest of the body, of 1:3 or 1:4. This enlargement occurs because the head is considered the "seat of power"; it is the body part that identifies a human being and allows for spiritual connections to occur.

African imagery is also present in *Prevalence of Ritual: Baptism*. The mask-like images recall ritual performances. An African ritual performance is a practice in which a performer uses some combination of facial disguise, costume, body decoration, props, movement, vocalization, drumming, and music to create the illusion of the spirit world. A masquerader can attain what one in ordinary life cannot—a reversal of roles: men into women, old into young, human into animals, mortals into gods, dead into living, or the reverse of these. In the new persona, the masquerader is a mediator between humans and the spiritual realm. As the embodiment of spiritual powers, the masquerader represents the spirit(s) who restructure social maladies.

In depicting African proportion and black images in his collages, Bearden does not deny his African heritage in order to participate in mainstream society. This is a particular honest statement for the artist, whose racial identify was not always discernible because of his fair skin and blue eyes. In Paris upon his first meeting with Bearden, Albert Murray, the African American novelist and jazz historian, thought Bearden was Russian "or what[ever]" until he laughed. Then, Murray identified Bearden's laughter as that of a black man (Schwartzman 1990, p. 168).

Bearden used the collage "to literally piece together his memories of the past" (Campbell 1985). For the subject matter in many of his collages, he derived images from his childhood memories of the South and North. They include experiences in Charlotte, Mecklenburg County, North Carolina, where Bearden was born; Pittsburgh, where he stayed with his paternal grandmother for a year; and New York City, where his parents ultimately moved. To capture the power of the memories, one must construct three interrelated mental activities: Bearden reached beyond the photographs to the human qualities they illustrated, he reconstructed the original in his mind's eye, and he recreated images in an unusual, striking manner. By portraying these memories, he recalled images that helped sustain the historical culture of African Americans.

In the top of Bearden's *Prevalence of Ritual: Baptism*, a train projects from an elevated space in a surreal manner reminiscent of the Surrealist artist René Magritte's *Time Transfixed* (1939). As a child, Bearden frequently visited the train depot to watch arriving and departing trains. The train provided hope for blacks as they traveled from the South to the North for better jobs and education. The train tracks became a dividing line, separating black and white communities and defining the social, political, and economic division of communities. For Bearden, it is a cultural symbol:

> I use the train as a symbol of the other civilization—the white civilization and its encroachment upon the lives of blacks. The train was always something that could take you away and could also bring you to where you were. And in the little town it's the black people who live near the trains [Patton 1991, p. 39].

Bearden represents the train, fracturing the picture plane in the distance while the black figures are lined up in the foreground. It fractures social relationships. The collage represents a layering of images. Bearden is like an African American *griot*.[23] However, each time the story is told, it changes slightly.

Bearden's layering of events and imagery is an element which influenced August Wilson, an African American playwright. Bearden's *Piano Lesson* Series (1983–84) inspired Wilson to write a play by the same name,[24] which won him a Pulitzer Prize, and was made into a screen-play.[25] The theme of the play revolves around a piano, which was inherited by Berniece and her brother Boy Willie. They are equal owners of their parents' piano, which was stolen from their family's slave master. For Berniece, the piano represents the heritage of their family, the carvings on it carries the Charles' family story from their days as slaves. Boy Willie views the piano in terms of its market value for purchasing a piece of their heritage. He wants to sell the piano to buy farmland—the same land on which their family worked as slaves. Stern and steadfast, Berniece refuses to part with it. She views the piano as the soul of the family; it symbolizes the pride and struggle of the survival of the family. The conflict is ultimately resolved. In the end, Boy Willie agrees with Berniece but not before they both deal with a tragic and painful past. The scene at the beginning and the end of Wilson's play portrays Berniece watching over her own daughter's shoulder as the youngster plays the piano (Wilson 1995).

Wilson believes Bearden's significance is not only in memories and passing traditions or rituals from one generation to another, but also exists in his depiction of Southern scenes. For Wilson, the South represents Africa and is the African's and African American's symbol for persistence and endurance.

The Spiraling of the Spiralists

The Spiral Group was short-lived (1963–65). It disbanded in 1965 when the group lost their lease at their meeting place—Christopher Street Gallery. Although they were criticized by later members of the Black Arts Movement, their significance in the 1960s cannot be ignored. As Floyd Coleman stated, the Spiralists "paved the way for those African American artists who followed, if not in their footsteps, at least in the broad paths they cleared. Thus, the legacy of Spiral will expand and remain secure for generations to come" (Coleman 1996, p. 157).

Bearden, concerned about the visibility of black artists in major American museums, participated with other demonstrators in a picket at the Whitney Museum in New York in 1968. The protest was about the exclusion of "Negro" artists from the Whitney's then-current exhibition, "The 1930s: Painting and Sculpture in America" (Glueck 1968, p. 31). Bearden's works were shown posthumously at the Whitney in 1997 in an exhibition titled "Romare Bearden in Black-and-White: Photomontage Projections, 1964." He is among the three or four African American artists whose artworks appear in current World Art History textbooks.

Bearden attempted to place his work and his feelings about the social conditions of blacks within a European, African, and African American construct. He depicted concepts about memories (oral traditions) and individual accountability of the Southern black culture. He embraced slave ancestry, rituals, and the past because they provide strength. The resiliency of these cultural elements had sustained African Americans in the past and, like an Archimedean spiral, was the buoyancy for the Spiral Group during the Civil Rights Movement.

Notes

1. The term visuality is used here in the same manner that it is defined by Andrew Stewart. "Visuality—the definition and critique of the way societies see, of what some call their 'scopic regimes'" (Stewart 1997, p. 13).

2. Named after the address of the artists' studio loft, 306 West 141st Street, where

the first meeting was held. The loft was the art space which was shared jointly by painter Charles "Spinky" Alston, a former WPA artist and cousin of Bearden, and sculptor Henry ("Mike") Bannarn (Patton and Campbell 1991, pp. 20–21).

3. For examples of some of the Spiralists' art, see Lewis (1990). For examples of mainstream American and European art and art movements, see Stokstad (1999).

4. By mid–October 1963, meetings were moved to the 147 Christopher Street in the Village (Bearden and Henderson 1990, p. 401).

5. In Siegel's (1966) article on the Spiral Group's exhibition in 1966, Mayhew and Pritchard are not mentioned. Mayhew joined a year after the group was originally formed. It is uncertain if the same is true of Pritchard.

6. The Museum of Modern Art held an exhibition of African Negro art in 1935. Bearden and Lewis attended the exhibit with Wylie Seyfert and Jacob Lawrence (Schwartzman 1990, p. 84).

7. After serving in the US Army from 1942 to 1945, Bearden received GI Bill funds to study philosophy at the Sorbonne in Paris. There he befriended such eminent European visual artists as Constantin Brancusi and Georges Braque as well as American expatriates: novelists Albert Murray and James Baldwin, poet Samuel Allen, and painters William Rivers and Paul Keene (Gelburd and Golden 1997, p. 77).

8. This painting was exhibited in the Spiral exhibition in 1964. See Siegel (1966, p. 50).

9. For a discussion, see Schwartzman (1990, pp. 131–32).

10. The Spiralists abandoned the Western ideal of beauty in human forms that originally appeared in Greek sculpture and paintings—the perfect Greek male nude athlete, Greek god, and Greek goddess—and was appropriated in later Western art traditions.

11. The Greeks were the first Western culture to write theories placing arts and mathematics in separate categories.

12. Powell (1992, p. 66) identifies the magazine sources.

13. Cordier and Ekstrom, a colossal and expansive space at 978 Madison Avenue, was the gallery where Bearden exhibited from the early 1960s to his death in 1968. The gallery was run by Daniel Cordier, Arne Ekstrom, and Michel Warren. Besides Bearden, it exhibited works by eminent European artists, such as Dubuffet, Matta, Michaux, Duchamp, Lindner, and Noguchi (Schwartzman 1990, p. 206).

14. For a discussion of Picasso's *Bottle of Suze* as a political artwork, representing Picasso's anarchist position, see Leighten (1989).

15. Dada art began in Germany and France and was brought to New York City by French artist Marcel Duchamp during the early part of the twentieth century.

16. Hausmann's *Head* (1923) illustrates his elaboration upon the technique, which was also implemented in the works by other Berlin Dadaists (Rubin 1968, pp. 83, 85).

17. For a brief discussion of Dada art in the United States, see Goldwin (1965).

18. Bearden spent a great deal of time "struggling to understand the structure and composition of Cézanne's work. In the end [in works after the 1960s], Cézanne had as much or more influence on Bearden's handling of the picture plane than Picasso" (Schwartzman 1990, p. 128).

19. Although Picasso is most known for developing Cubist abstraction, it was technically the joint invention of Picasso and his artist friend Georges Braque. The style was built upon the foundation of Picasso's early work.

20. For a discussion of the Surrealists' political protest against the French government for the civil rights of African Americans in Paris, particularly the exploitation of Al Brown in a boxing championship, see Jules-Rosette (1998, pp. 26–30). Also, for Picasso's association with the Surrealists and the impact of Surrealism on his paintings *Guernica*, see Rubin (1968, pp. 279–309).

21. Grosz introduced Bearden to European artists who portrayed the theme of "man's

inhumanity to man" in black-and-white prints and drawings. These artists include Honoré Daumier (French), Francisco Goya (Spanish), and Kathë Kollowitz (German). These artists use black-and-white imagery as if mimicking the photo-journalist style and as if reporting in print a newsworthy documentary on societal ills.

22. For a discussion of the Berlin Dada, Grosz's participation in the movement, and Grosz's art, see Rubin (1968, pp. 82–93).

23. See Richard Long's description of Bearden's intellectual talents in Powell (1992, p. 66).

24. Wilson never meant Bearden. For further discussion of Bearden's impact upon August Wilson's work, see Wilson (1992) and the foreword in Schwartzman (1990).

25. In the screen-play, Berniece is portrayed by Alfre Woodard, and Boy Willie is played by Charles S. Dutton.

Bibliography

Allen, Charles. 1971. "Have the Walls Come Tumbling Down?" *The New York Times,* Section 2, April 11: 28–29.

The American Heritage Dictionary of the English Language. 1992. Third edition. Boston, New York, London: Houghton Mifflin Company.

Bearden, Romare and Harry Henderson. 1993. *A History of African-American Artists: From 1792 to the Present.* New York: Pantheon Books.

Campbell, Mary Schmidt. 1985. "Tradition and Conflict: Images of a Turbulent Decade, 1963–1973." In *Tradition and Conflict: Images of a Turbulent Decade, 1963–1973,* pp. 45–67. New York: Studio Museum in Harlem.

Childs, Charles. 1964. "Bearden: Identification and Identity." *Art News* 63 (October): 24–25, 54, 61–62.

Coleman, Floyd. 1996. "The Changing Same: Spiral, the Sixties, and African-American Art." In *A Shared Heritage: Art by Four African Americans,* edited by William E. Taylor and Harriet G. Warkel, pp. 147–157. Bloomington: The Indianapolis Museum of Art; distributed by Indiana University Press.

The Concise Columbia Encyclopedia. 1995. New York: Columbia University Press.

Gelburd, Gail and Thelma Golden. 1997. *Romare Bearden in Black-and-White: Photomontage Projections, 1964.* New York: Whitney Museum of American Art; distributed by Harry N. Abrams, Inc.

Glueck, Grace. 1968. "1930s Show at Whitney Picketed by Negro Artists Who Call It Incomplete." *The New York Times,* Section L, Monday, November 18: 31.

Goldwin, Amy. 1965. "The Dada Legacy." *Arts Magazine* 39, 10 (September–October): 26–28.

Jules-Rosette, Bennetta. 1998. *Black Paris: The African Writers' Landscape.* Urbana and Chicago: University of Illinois Press.

Leighten, Patricia. 1989. *Re-Ordering the Universe: Picasso and Anarchism, 1897–1914.* Princeton: Princeton University Press.

Lewis, Samella. 1990. *African American Art and Artists.* Second edition. Berkeley, Los Angeles, London: University of California Press.

Murray, Albert. 1997. "To Hear Another Language: Alvin Ailey, James Baldwin, Romare Bearden, and Albert Murray." In *Conversations with Albert Murray,* edited by Roberta S. Maguire, pp. 25–45. Jackson: University Press of Mississippi.

Myers, Aaron. 1999. "Bearden, Romare." *Africana: The Encyclopedia of the African and African American Experience,* edited by Anthony Appiah and Louis Gates, 206–7. New York: A Member of the Perseus Group.

Patton, Sharon and Mary Schmidt Campbell. 1991. *Memory and Metaphor: The Art of Romare Bearden, 1940–1987*. New York and Oxford: Studio Museum in Harlem; distributed by Oxford University Press.

Powell, Richard J. 1992. "What Becomes a Legend Most? Reflections on Romare Bearden." *Transition* (Oxford) 55: 63–72.

Rubin, William S. 1968. *Dada and Surrealist Art*. New York: Harry N. Abrams, Inc.

Schwartzman, Myron. 1990. *Romare Bearden: His Life and Art*. Foreword by August Wilson. New York: Harry N. Abrams, Inc.

Siegel, Jeanne. 1966. "Why Spiral?" *Art News* 65, 5 (September): 48–51, 67, 68.

Stewart, Andrew. 1997. *Art, Desire, and the Body in Ancient Greece*. Cambridge: University Press.

Stokstad, Marilyn. 1999. *Art History*. Vol. II. Revised edition. New York: Prentice Hall, Inc., and Harry N. Abrams. Inc.

Taylor, Clyde R. 1998. *The Mask of Art: Breaking the Aesthetic Contract—Film and Literature*. Bloomington and Indianapolis: Indiana University Press.

Wilson, August and Matteo Bellinelli. 1992. *August Wilson: A Conversation with August Wilson*. Videorecording. Swiss Television Production. San Francisco, Cal.: California Newsreel.

Wilson, August. 1995. *The Piano Lesson*. Videorecording. Hallmark Hall of Fame Productions, Inc. Los Angeles: Republic Pictures.

Wilson, Judith. 1992. "Getting Down to Get Over: Romare Bearden's Use of Pornography and the Problem of the Black Female Body in Afro-U.S. Art." In *Black Popular Culture*, edited by Gina Dent, pp. 112–122. Seattle: Bay Press.

2. Jazz Musicians in Europe: 1919 to 1945

LARRY ROSS

Jazz musicians actually shifted the course of World War II in favor of the Allies. They influenced the decisions and behaviors of the Nazi high command, rank, file, and citizens after Sidney Bechet established jazz on the European cultural landscape in 1919. The *Luftwaffe* pilots were listening to African American jazz musicians in their planes on the BBC radio station, and the anti–Nazi propaganda they heard undermined their resolve to fight against the Allies. (Pilot Werner Molders went to Joseph Goebbels to inform him of this fact.) German citizens used a number of smuggling techniques during World War II to obtain African American jazz recordings that had been banned by Goebbels, including putting Johann Sebastian Bach labels on Duke Ellington albums and selling them in local record shops. Goebbels's attempts to suppress and destroy jazz were further impeded by SS member Dr. Johann Wolfgang Schottlander, a musicologist from the Berlin Conservatory whose research was funded by Heinrich Himmler. One of his duties was to develop the German film industry by using American films as a model. According to Michael Kater, "Having become a specialist for film music, he was employed by Goebbels's ministry in the early 1940s to help the minister perfect movie technology, for which he so envied the Americans." Germans who were at odds with the Nazi regime's measures aimed at banning jazz and jazz musicians found refuge in Dr. Schottlander's inner circle, which met to view American films. "The musicologist became a charismatic figure for the sensitive among Berlin's jazz artists and their admirers, who would meet with him to watch those rare originals; there seems to have developed a consensus in this circle of friends about the rights and wrongs of life." Schottlander's group had no designs on overthrowing the Nazi regime; "the group gathered there was not conspiratorial, but they were convinced of the genuine quality of American culture that shone through these films, and they all shared a great admiration for jazz."[1] This paper documents the extent to which African

American jazz musicians influenced world culture and politics from the end of World War I to the end of World War II.

Two of the most notable jazz musicians of the early twentieth century who introduced Europeans to jazz were Sidney Bechet and James Reese Europe. Bechet made his European debut in 1919, and he was immediately embraced by the French public with a passion that transformed his status to a level that is usually reserved for deities. Bechet was born in New Orleans in 1897, and he proved to be a gifted clarinetist, though he is known as a soprano saxophonist by most people today. Bechet's work is of great historical importance to the jazz genre, because he was soloing with abandon long before 1919.

The training that Bechet received in New Orleans prepared him well for the road. He "led from 1914 to 1917 an itinerant life, touring in shows and going as far north as Chicago." Will Marion Cook, who had studied with Antonin Dvorak, "hired Bechet as a soloist for his New York Syncopated Orchestra in 1919," and facilitated Bechet's European debut later that year. The Swiss composer Ernest Ansermet was apparently in awe of what he heard. Ansermet wrote: "There is in the Southern Syncopated Orchestra an extraordinary clarinet virtuoso who is, so it seems, the first of his race to have composed perfectly formed blues on the clarinet. I wish to set down the name of this artist of genius: as for myself, I shall never forget it—it is Sidney Bechet." The reception of Bechet's music in Europe was the opposite of its American reception, evidenced by the comments of the Swiss composer Ansermet upon hearing Bechet play for the first time. Bechet must have been inspired by confirming comments such as these, and "it may have led to his adoption of the instrument with which he is eternally linked, the soprano saxophone; its bore is considerably wider than that of the clarinet, and the bell flares out more, thus the instrument is capable of producing more volume than the clarinet."[2] The soprano saxophone is a very expressive, compact instrument, but it's very difficult to play in tune. Only a few players have mastered the soprano saxophone, though many reed players have used the instrument since it was revived by John Coltrane in the early 1960s.

During his tour of London with Cook's orchestra, the virtues of the soprano sax became clear, and "Bechet soon developed on this difficult instrument one of the most extravagant, and least polite, sounds in jazz." Bechet's European tour ended in 1922, and he returned to New York; in the following year, he recorded with the famous Bessie Smith, pianist Clarence Williams, and Louis Armstrong in 1924. It would seem that such a collaboration between two seasoned, well-traveled virtuosos like Louis Armstrong and Sidney Bechet would have firmly established both of them on the American musical landscape; however, this clearly was not the case. Quite possibly, Bechet's abrasive personality may have been responsible for the demise of his collaboration

2. Jazz Musicians in Europe (Ross)

with Armstrong; he was very competitive, as opposed to being accommodating, with Armstrong during the recording sessions, and Armstrong simply didn't need Bechet anyway. Armstrong was an international jazz star, and he was touring Europe in the 1930s, frequently performing in Copenhagen and other cities. In the late 1930s, Bechet started recording again, and notably, he experimented with a number of musical genres including Haitian merengues; he received harsh criticism from purists who sought to confine him to the New Orleans genre that had made him famous. In 1941, Bechet did some experimental recordings on "Victor—Mezz Mezzrow called them outrages—recording *Sheik of Araby* and *Blues of Bechet* as a one-man band. He plays as many as six instruments himself."[3] Mezzrow was a white jazz musician who had become famous as a bandleader. Thus the white jazz musicians who were having successful careers in America, after appropriating jazz from the negroes, became the aesthetic standard bearers of jazz by owning the methods of production, and artistic criticism.

Bechet played with Bunk Johnson, Johnny Windhurst, Muggsy Spanier, Pops Foster, Baby Dodds, and James P. Johnson during the 1940s on various occasions, but at bottom, he was not particularly successful in America. He became famed, however, in France, "where after successful tours in 1949 and 1950, he emigrated in 1951. He was adored there. The Rue Bechet was named after him, and his wedding in 1951 was covered by the press as if he was royalty." In France, Bechet was not criticized for his compositions; rather, he was revered: "He was greatly respected for what he had produced in the past, and given a free hand to create as he pleased. He recorded prolifically in the fifties." In France, Bechet's compositions became hits, which is in itself a remarkable and telling occurrence. The question becomes, how could a jazz musician, playing the same material, become virtual royalty in France within just two years, and at the same time be ignored in America? The question is somewhat perplexing, but in view of Levine's research, there is substantial evidence that Bechet's skin color, the concomitant segregation, and the denigration of jazz as an expressive musical genre in practice throughout America was, in no small way, responsible for Bechet's fledgling career at home. By the time Bechet's career became a success, he only had about eight more years to live. He learned in 1956 that he had lung cancer. Rather than being robbed of what little time he had left, "Bechet continued to carouse and frequent the nightspots until he died in 1959 on his birthday, May 14th. Bechet's life was a jazz life, and he lived it in that particular way." According to Bechet, playing jazz "took the utmost sensitivity to other musicians and the music itself, for the music will tell you which way to go in your life, and what you can feel."[4] Until his death, Bechet insisted that jazz must continue to expand its scope by including experimental techniques, like overdubbing and borrowing from other musical genres, while still keeping real feeling in the music. His overall contribution to music is recognized around the world.

Though his career never reached the heights that Bechet briefly enjoyed in France, James Reese Europe made a significant contribution to the proliferation of jazz in the diaspora around the turn of the century. Reese was originally from Mobile, Alabama, but he moved to Washington, D.C., as a child. Reese was a student of the violin, "beginning sometime before he was ten-years-old, with the assistant director of the U.S. Marine Band. Obviously, he became a multi-instrumentalist because in 1904, he moved to New York City and took a job as a pianist. By 1910, Reese had organized The Clef Club, which was known as a clearing house for negro musicians."[5] Interestingly, Reese did a concert at Carnegie Hall in 1914 which featured 125 musicians and singers, and he continued to tour the U.S. and perform at clubs around New York City until he joined the U.S. Army, achieving the rank of lieutenant. He formed the 369th Infantry Regiment Band and toured France in 1918; thus he may have been one of the first to take so-called negro jazz musicians abroad, though they were not there to play jazz, per se. Some of Reese's recordings have survived, and they prominently feature the contemporary blues and jazz tunes that were popular.

Trumpeter Freddie Keppard might have been the first, had he accepted an offer from Victor Records in 1916. The American critic Rudi Blesh, "in his book *Combo: USA*, asserts that the Original Dixieland Jazz Band stole *Livery Stable Blues*, one of their most popular numbers, from the black trumpeter Freddie Keppard. Ironically, Keppard refused, in 1916, to record for the Victor label for fear that his rivals would steal his ideas from his records."[6] As a result of Keppard's refusal, the Original Dixieland Jazz Band became the first band to bring jazz to Britain and, ironically, there were no negroes in the band.

Unfortunately, James Reese Europe was stabbed to death in a nightclub brawl in 1919 when he retired from the U.S. Army and returned to the U.S. Thus a promising career ended prematurely, as is too often the case with jazz musicians.

African American jazz pioneers found a myriad of venues in the jazz diaspora. For example, in the mid–1920s, "Sam Wooding's quazi-jazz orchestra toured Europe and the Soviet Union; in 1926 Jack Carter and Teddy Weatherford began leading bands in China, Singapore, India, and other Asian locales; beginning in 1929, Valiada Snow, from Carter's Shanghai band, toured the Middle East and the Soviet Union."[7]

The reasons why musicians traveled abroad varied from escaping family circumstances, to escaping from the castigation that has been mentioned earlier. However, the situation was not altogether rosy. Elliot Carpenter surmised that Americans were not held in high esteem by the French, and "they figured that the black ones were just as bad.... Duke Ellington undoubtedly had mixed feelings in 1931 when a London hotel provided a room only after he proved he was not a West Indian." So, even in other parts of the world, the legacy of discrimination had arrived in advance of the jazz musicians, and it must have been a sickening reminder. In spite of this, "blacks who lived in Europe before 1940 savored various freedoms and the absence of Jim Crow. The adulation jazz received from European admirers had important emotional and intellectual effects on the players. Prominent European art musicians publicly praised black ragtime and jazz and incorporated their properties into their compositions." Europe was especially fertile ground for jazz, because the music incorporated familiar elements, theories, and methods that had been gleaned from European music praxis. "Jazz players drew on the musical cultures of Europe and Africa, as they had been transformed in the first few centuries of democracy and slavery in North America. Africa and Europe thus were the two general traditions upon which jazz drew for its musical identity."[8]

Another jazz great who had a phenomenal career abroad was composer/trumpeter Buck Clayton, who was born in Parsons, Kansas, in 1911. His father played trumpet, bass, and piano, and led the orchestra of his church. Buck's father taught him to play the trumpet and the piano, and "eventually he played in the church orchestra when he was 19-years-old. Buck went to California in 1932 and started playing in a 14-piece band later taken over by Teddy Weatherford, with whom he worked at the Canidrome in Shanghai from 1934 to 1936." He did tours in France in 1949 and 1953, receiving rave reviews, and returned during another European tour in 1959 with his own group. Buck Clayton's tenure abroad and at home was brilliant. Clayton's "vibrato, well-modulated open sound, and highly individual use of the cup mute were some of the vitally distinctive sounds of the great Basie band of the 1930s, and during the same period they were heard on hundreds of recordings under the names of Teddy Wilson and Billy Holiday. Clayton won *Esquire*'s best musician Gold Award '45."[9]

My friend Ed Thigpen, a jazz drummer who moved to Copenhagen, Denmark in 1972, speaks of Buck Clayton's career, and especially the fact that Clayton was playing jazz in China back in the 1930s, as if it's one of his fondest memories.

In 1927, trumpeter "Doc Cheatham landed his opportunity to go to Europe by playing in Sam Wooding's band: three or four of the other guys in the band wanted to stay in New York, so Wooding hired Cheatham, Jerry Blake, and Ted Fields." Wooding recorded one of Cheatham's arrangements in Europe. Cheatham recalls that their boat docked at Cherbourg, and they took a train to Berlin, which became the band's headquarters; they lived at 28 Ranka Strasse. He found Berlin beautiful and later said that his time there was the happiest of his life. The band played in Romania, Czechoslovakia, Holland, France, Spain, Istanbul, and Belgium and "in about every country all over Europe, Sam was recognized as having one of the greatest entertaining bands in the world at the time, a time when jazz and jazz musicians were consistently being denigrated." The band recorded on rare "wax disks" in Barcelona that have now become treasured collectibles, and they played in Nice, France, at the Hotel Negresco, where visiting nobility, like the Prince of Wales and the King of Norway, were in attendance. The band was served publicly with food and drink near the bandstand. This could not have happened in America in 1927: it would have been outrageous, as well as illegal. Cheatham was also able to swim at the beach near the hotel. He lived in Europe until 1930, when the band was playing at the Paris Club Florida during the stock market crash. Although he regretted leaving Europe, he felt that in America he could "play a better type of jazz; he took a job at the Savoy in New York."[10]

Cheatham traveled through the South, where the musicians had to sleep and change clothes on the bus they toured in. They couldn't eat at white restaurants, but had to park the bus out of sight and have a manager go in to pick up orders to go. There were a few hotels in the South that catered to negroes, but they were rat-infested holes. "Cheatham registered at one hotel where the manager gave each musician a baseball bat; they asked what the bat was for, and the manager replied that they may see some rats: they did. The rats were as big as dogs, and there were chinches and bed bugs all over the beds, which were filthy."[11] Thus when musicians finished a tour of this type, their bodies would be covered with insect bites and "crabs."

A telling incident occurred when Cheatham played at an all-white dance in Memphis, Tennessee, with Cab Calloway's band. He recalls that the hall was very crowded, and the people really enjoyed the music to the point that they rushed the stage for autographs of the musicians. One white man, however, upset by the two races mixing, threw bottles at the group. When the musicians started to fight back, a riot broke out and the victims were yet again victimized, arrested for defending themselves, and they were blasted with more projectiles as the trucks took them to jail. "This was typical in the South, and events like this happened so often that bands refused to perform at a number of establishments in Alabama, Mississippi, Florida and Georgia, that were known for such dangers."[12]

In 1934 when Cheatham went to England with Cab Calloway's band, it was evident that winds of change were blowing in Europe. Calloway endured some heckling in England, although not in Scotland. The ugly receptions in England caused Calloway to find solace in the bottle. But "in the last years of his life, when Cab made a tour of Europe, there were lines waiting right around the block wherever he played. In London, Paris, and Japan, Cab was one of the biggest musical stars in the world."[13]

Cheatham was heading for a job in Paris, in 1939, on the SS *United States* just as World War II was about to break out. He heard conflicting news reports during the crossing, and he presumed that the hostilities would cease so he decided to stay when the boat docked at Le Havre. He checked into a hotel, but the situation in France was more desperate than he had imagined. Cheatham decided to return home, but he didn't even have enough money to buy a return ticket. Eventually, a friendly worker at the consulate loaned him enough money to pay his hotel bill and buy a return ticket to America.

Cheatham returned to Paris in 1950, and he played with Coleman Hawkins and Eartha Kitt, also filling in on occasion for Buck Clayton, before returning to New York. In 1958, Cheatham returned to Europe to record and travel extensively through the decade, and into the 1960s, 1970s, and 1980s with a number of distinguished ensembles that included Eddie Lockjaw Davis and Illinois Jacquet. Cheatham's return engagement in Vienna, Austria, "sixty years after his first performance there, was a poignant one. Cheatham appeared at the Moulin Rouge, and the place was packed every night. A lot of elderly people came to hear this old trumpeter in his 80s who'd been there so long ago; professors, teachers, musicians, they all came to hear what it was all about." It was the same when he recently performed in Nice, Barcelona, and London; however, Cheatham was shocked by the reality of America's devaluation of jazz, and jazz musicians, when he returned to New York to do a concert in the park, in the Bronx. According to Cheatham, the band that he played with was a great one, but the audience virtually ignored them. In Europe and Japan, the fans revere jazz musicians and know all of their vital statistics. This includes the children, as well as the adults, so it seems that the parents or the educational systems in the jazz diaspora are committed to the inclusion of jazz musicians among the significant contributors to music as a whole. Cheatham admits that it hurts when he deplanes in New York, "and nobody cares whether you play the saxophone or the telephone.... He believes that playing in Europe makes jazz musicians play better, because they know that they are being listened to carefully."[14]

On June 1, 1997, Doc Cheatham died in Washington, D.C., at the age of 92. His lifespan occurred in tandem with the very origin of jazz, its rise to prominence during World War II, and its demise during the 1960s. Cheatham was one of those rare musicians who continued to improve as they aged, rather than falter: he made an intentional commitment to do so. Doc Cheatham's contributions will not be forgotten by jazz historians, musicians, enthusiasts, or Parisians.

The questions that arise from analyzing the migration of American jazz musicians to the diaspora caught the attention of Bill Moody, who is a jazz musician, author, and English instructor at the University of Nevada, Las Vegas; he wrote *The Jazz Exiles: American Musicians Abroad* in 1993. The book is, essentially, a compilation of first-hand interviews with the most prolific jazz exiles of all time, along with his insights on jazz over the past three decades. Moody believes that *exile*, as opposed to *expatriate*, is the most appropriate term for describing these dislocated artists, based on the reaction to their music in America. Moody was trained at the Berkeley College of Music, and in 1967 he embarked on a three-year European tour that included performances with Jr. Mance and the singer Johnny Hartman. Upon his return to America in 1970, "his reflections on the experience caused him to question when this migration had started, why it had started, and how many of the major names in jazz were spending large portions of their lives in foreign countries performing a music that was uniquely American in origin." American jazz exiles "were accorded respect, sometimes star treatment from European jazz fans, and enjoyed ample opportunities to perform though many of the musicians were forgotten names back home, however much in demand they were in Europe."[15] This migration paralleled the exodus of American writers to Europe in the 1920s.

Reed man Garvin Bushnell, who is unknown to most Americans, was a remarkable jazz exile whose career extended from the origin of jazz to its decline. He was born around 1900, and he began playing in circus sideshows in 1916. Bushnell played saxophone, oboe, and bassoon, and he was one of those rare musicians who could play both jazz and classical music at their highest levels: Bushnell even taught John Coltrane in his New York studio during the late 1940s. Today, we marvel at the ability to negotiate between these two musical genres displayed by Wynton Marsalis, but he was preceded by Garvin Bushnell. Bushnell has worked with major symphonic orchestras, and can be heard on two of John Coltrane's albums: *Africa Brass* and *Trane's Modes*. "Like most American jazz musicians, Bushnell spent considerable time touring and living in foreign countries. He made his first trip abroad with pianist Sam Wooding and the show *Chocolate Kiddies* in 1925 that resulted in a stay of nearly three years in Europe." Bushnell notes that in those days, people cued up to see them in the capitols of Europe, and that the musicians were "invited to dinner after each performance. While in Berlin, Bushnell heard a number of orchestral performances, and it was there that he resolved to forge his career as a jazz and classical musician. He studied with Henry Selmer, the world's most famous saxophone maker, in Paris and bassoon with Eli Carmen."[16]

He returned to America in 1927, where segregation was in full force. Bushnell's wife was a dancer at the Cotton Club, and he was not allowed in, unless he was playing there: their policy was, no negroes allowed. At the Apollo Theater, negroes had to use the back stairs to gain entry. "At the

Roseland Ballroom, where he was performing with Fletcher Henderson, negro musicians were not allowed to walk across the floor, rather, they were forced to walk along the wall and directly to the basement when the band took a break."

Bushnell's experiences were even worse in the South while he was traveling with Cab Calloway's band. They were playing in East Texas, and they had to have a police escort to and from the gigs; one Texan tried to pay the sheriff to let him go up on the stage and hit Cab Calloway in the mouth. Bushnell moved to Puerto Rico in the early 1940s, and on one occasion, he visited Biloxi, Mississippi. He remembers being told by a cop that he didn't have to stay in the negro section of town, and the progressive officer took him to a motel, "told the clerk that he had some niggers from Puerto Rico, and instructed the clerk to give them a room." In 1948, Bushnell received a call to go on tour playing bassoon and oboe with the Paul Whiteman band; however, when Whiteman actually saw him, the name of the game was changed. Whiteman insisted that the double-reed player had to play flute too, though he had not mentioned this to the union previously. Bushnell didn't play flute, and the job was given to one of Bushnell's friends, who was white. "Eventually, Bushnell landed the job as bassoonist of the New York City Ballet Theater. During the first three days of rehearsal, Bushnell recalls, no one spoke to him. He responded with an old jazzman's trick: waiting for a solo to show your stuff. After the solo, they spoke to him."[17] Apparently, the dire expectations of the other orchestra members were not realized.

Although some European countries were "very color-conscious,"[18] black musicians including Bushnell enjoyed more freedom from prejudice there than in America. We now know, as a result of some recent disclosures by the Swedish government, that Sweden was engaged in an aggressive eugenics program, and coercive euthanasia was being practiced during the first half of the twentieth century on a broad scale. These sentiments led to the horrors of World War II, and many jazz musicians were forced to leave the continent and return to America. As the influence of Germany expanded beyond its traditional boundaries, the face and course of jazz in the diaspora changed dramatically.

By far, the country that exerted the most influence upon the development of jazz in Europe was Germany, because Germany eventually occupied most of Europe and implemented its policies in the occupied territories which included France, Romania, Denmark, Norway, Poland, the Balkans, and even a large portion of the Soviet Union. Germany, during the Weimar Republic, was a crucible of the extreme liberalism evidenced by the exploits of Anita Berber, and pervasive racism, according to author Michael Kater. Bushnell, Bechet, and Josephine Baker all performed in Germany in 1925, and Baker concluded that Berlin was the city of lights, rather than Paris at that time.

Anita Berber, a contemporary of Baker from Berlin, "represented a particular kind of culture that defied categorization. This bisexual daughter of a professor of classical music personified the sensuality in which Berlin was awash."[19]
To say that jazz became associated with some excessive behaviors early on in
Berlin is a huge understatement. For example, Berber's favored hangout was
the "White Mouse, where she would perform pornographic dance numbers
and then break champagne bottles on the heads of raunchy male clients.
When she died in November 1928 from a lifelong abuse of alcohol and
cocaine, her funeral was attended by an array of whores, pimps, bartenders,
and transvestites."[20]

The situation and reception of jazz musicians from America became
more complicated. Although the social conditions were thought to be liberal
during the "Weimar democracy, the public and private attitude towards
blacks, including Afro-Americans, was an ambivalent one, and this reflected
on the few black jazz musicians in Germany. The pervading racism of the
day did not countenance blacks, no matter what their social station or where
they originally hailed from." Racist attitudes towards blacks in Germany were
fueled by their ill-fated colonial activities of the late eighteenth and early
nineteenth centuries in Africa, and not by anything connected to African
Americans, per se. Baker surmised that the jovial reception she received was
a cover for the real disdain that Germans actually harbored. The evidence
that this was actually the case is borne out by a comparison of German and
French practices. The French were accepting of black artists, in part because
their colonials were considered citizens. Thus the black jazz pioneers found
in France a welcoming home and "France remains the foremost outpost of
jazz in the diaspora." In Germany only a few black musicians, or foreigners
at all, played jazz, while the genre flourished in neighboring France. Germany
kept blacks in the same relative position that they held in the American South.
In 1926, a hotel advertised for two negroes who could perform silly, stereotypical parts in a band; however, in 1932 the hiring of black musicians was
forbidden altogether by the Nationalist Party. Jazz was denounced as nigger
music, and blamed for the introduction of obscene acts and the like into Germany. Exaggerations were made about the dangers of black sexuality, which
would allegedly undermine the reasoning capabilities of whites if it were
allowed to proliferate. As far as the situation in Germany is concerned, "so
humiliating a view of jazz was a direct consequence of the inability of the losers of World War I to come to terms with a compromising colonial past, especially where native peoples were concerned. Here lay the seeds of a kind of
racism that eventually led, from Negrophobia by way of anti–Semitism, to
the Nazi liquidation camps."[21]

The Germans considered themselves more humane than the French,
as far as their colonial administration technique was concerned, and they

complained that Africans were brutal and lazy, and they lacked the emotions and intelligence found in Europeans. These claims were not new to Germany: they had been made in the 1853 publication of Jacques Arthur de Gobineau's *The Inequality of the Races*, a volume that helped Hitler to shape his racial policies. Another convenient reason for this animosity toward blacks was that many Africans participated in the occupying forces after World War I ended. It must have seemed surreal, and intolerable, to the Germans that their former colonial charges were now in power, as occupying forces. The combination of two forces, that is, Social Darwinism and the occupation of the German home land by outsiders, was indeed perfect for propaganda purposes. Eugenics gained prominence during this time and became, increasingly, a part of Western cultural beliefs and practices. The cutting edge so-called research in Eugenics originated in America, and "Europeans eagerly accepted the findings that blacks were inferior to whites. Simultaneously a link was forged between racially inferior blacks and Jews. The latter were recognized in jazz not just as musicians and composers but also as commercial managers and middlemen of the music." Germans began to make an association between Jews and blacks; this was in accord with the popular Eugenicist views that were spreading around the country after the end of World War I. The so-called sexual hunger of jazz musicians was an underlying theme, and since many of the Jews were in the forefront of the performing arts at the time, they were high-profile individuals who served as easily accessible targets. Both groups were deemed racially inferior, and they became a target of the Eugenicists' propaganda campaigns. In conjunction, many classical musicians in Germany rebelled against the trend of having jazz in the conservatory, mostly on musical grounds. Some of the best known classical composers in Germany, like Richard Strauss and Siegfried Wagner, the son of Richard Wagner, fought against jazz by "castigating it as some Americans had done. Conservative Germans rejected modernity, and jazz, to them, symbolized American democracy, modernity and decadence."[22]

One particularly zealous opponent of jazz was racist Muck Lamberty. Lamberty's campaign was aimed at "rejuvenating the white race for Adolf Hitler, and the defeat of the Jews and blacks who were spreading jazz in Germany. Adolf Hitler himself is not known to have made any specific pronouncements on jazz in the Weimar republic. As a follower of Richard Wagner he did not like modernism in the arts, including music." Hitler frequently referred to the presence of the Senegalese troops on the Rhine as the black shame; therefore his repulsion was based, predominately, on Eugenics. Jazz just happened to be part of the alleged conspiracy being initiated by the Jews and blacks; according to Hitler, the Jews were making German women available to blacks at the dance halls. An amateur pianist named Joseph Goebbels, who happened to be an advisor of Hitler, received an appointment from the

leader to control the arts. The film *The Singing Fool*, in which Al Jolson performed jazz songs in blackface, added fuel to Goebbels' claims of a Jewish-
black conspiracy. Alfred Rosenberg, a rival of Goebbels, founded the Combat
League for German Culture in 1929. The purpose of this group, also known
as the Kampfbund, was to stress the connection between race, art, and scholarship and reinforce the foundations of so-called German culture. To Rosenberg, a pseudo-scholar, "this cretinized American art form symbolized
everything that was insidiously evil in the Jewish-Negro plot." Hans Hinkel
worked with Rosenberg to develop the Kampfbund, and eventually he became
a close associate of Goebbels. With Hinkel in charge as general secretary, the
Kampfbund fought all Jewish cultural activities and promoted Nordic artists.
In 1930, the "National Socialists initiated an ordinance against Negro Culture, though they had not officially taken power. Jazz was prohibited, negro
dances were prohibited, and negro plays were prohibited."[23]

In the 1930s, Germans were suspicious of anything connected with the
Americanism, and jazz happened to be one of the casualties of this association. At the Frankfurt conservatory, jazz was approached with the serious-
ness of the current German harshness; thus the music was executed in a very
clumsy manner, and it lacked the exuberant frivolity that is commonly associated with jazz music. The Nationalist Party clearly intended to eradicate
jazz from Germany; however, they could not have imagined that jazz would
later reemerge with vigor. In 1933, Fritz Stein, who directed the Berlin Conservatory, banned jazz, with the support of the Third Reich. However,
Goebbels paid a backhanded complement to jazz by noting that "America's
only contribution to the world of music was what he called jazzed-up nigger
music not worthy of a single mention."[25]

Then why was he mentioning it? The Nazis experienced difficulties in
their attempts to eradicate jazz, because they really had problems deciding
what it was. German musicologists couldn't agree on whether their scorn
should be directed at America, or at Africa for originating jazz, and as a result
their credibility as musicologists came into question. Another problem was
that they identified rhythmic devices that were supposedly unique to jazz;
however, they found that the same devices had been used by Bach himself.
Then, there was an attempt to blame the saxophone; however, the inventor
of the saxophone had a connection with Germany, and Richard Strauss used
the saxophone quite often in his music. Finally, the Nazis arrived at the argument that the sexual powers of jazz were so profound that it would corrupt
national morality. In spite of all of this, "jazz was never officially banned."[26]
Hitler didn't seem to bother himself with trying to mold the cultural desires
of the public; rather, he left it to his subordinates.

Most people think of the Nazis as a highly efficient organization;
however, recent information has proven otherwise. The leader, Adolf Hitler,

seldom rose before noon, and sometimes he would not appear until 2:00 in the afternoon. Hitler was annoyed by details, and according to his philosophy, things would work themselves out if they were just left alone. His subordinates were careful not to make any decisions without his personal approval, and there was a great deal of bureaucratic inefficiency. Hans Bruckner, who seemed to have hated jazz more than anyone else in the Nazi regime, "persecuted jazz, blacks, and Jews." However despite his dislike of "delays and procedural inefficiency," his own publication listing Jewish musicians contained "so many errors that his plan backfired. Bruckner, who at great cost to himself had published his third edition in 1938, became the laughingstock even of the party."[27] Thus, the bureaucratic shortcomings of the Nazis may have helped jazz slip through the cracks, or shall we say, the gaping administrative holes.

Ultimately, it was the mainstream of Germany's population, during the Nazi regime, that sustained jazz, risking their lives in the process. There was such a demand for jazz music that even Goebbels was rendered defenseless. Real pressure was being exerted on Goebbels's broadcasting monopoly by powerful foreign radio stations that Germans could easily listen to on their Superhet receivers, and by the preexisting agreements with foreign record companies for the distribution of their respective records. German citizens received New Orleans style and swing style broadcasts from the powerful Radio Luxemburg, right in their homes on demand: this posed some staunch competition for the Nazi-sponsored broadcasts of propaganda and marches! This forced Goebbels to program Nazi-sponsored jazz on his stations. Goebbels rationalized this as trivial entertainment for uneducated workers. Apparently, jazz was not as trivial as Goebbels pretended; the demand for jazz music actually dictated to him what his programming agenda must include. Goebbels launched a jazz band on his Duetschlandsender station called the Golden Seven, but they were eventually purged, as the Nazis became more powerful.[28]

In order to keep their war machine going, the Nazis "depended on international commerce for precious foreign currency, and if the German records of Beethoven symphonies conducted by Wilhelm Furtwangler were to be marketed abroad, then British Decca or American Vocalion jazz records featuring the black Louis Armstrong had to be allowed." Germans could purchase jazz recordings from record stores, but it had to be done in a clandestine manner because such an act could be interpreted as a crime by the Nazis. To remedy this, store owners or dealers would exchange the labels on jazz records with classical German labels: a Duke Ellington record might have had a Richard Strauss label on it. Another way that Germans got their hands on coveted jazz records was by mail-order. After the spring of 1938, German jazz record collectors entered a potential crisis. However, the ban on jazz record

imports was inefficient and could sometimes be worked around. Additionally, the Nazis had "considerable difficulties in trying to identify all foreign
blacks." As a result of these difficulties, the Nazis allowed certain black musicians to pass, whereas other black musicians were not allowed to pass: they
couldn't figure out their exact status. Duke Ellington was dropped from
Brunswick's catalogs while his song *Caravan* "remained in their catalogs. *Caravan* was sung the by Mills Brothers, whom the Nazis, apparently, considered to be Aryans. Such Nazi inconsistency might benefit some black artists
for a while, but conversely it could also victimize non–Aryans who were mis-
taken for Jews or blacks."[29] Both Hitler and Goebbels claimed that they hated
jazz, and they were not open to its coexistence, but for all their hatred of jazz,
their inept bureaucracy allowed it to flourish.

The Nazis became increasingly frustrated in their attempt to eradicate
jazz, so they decided to create a "new" musical form that would replace it. A
competition of bands from across Germany yielded no new musical styles.
In fact, to the dismay of the Nazis, some of their own party members were
imitating negro jazz musicians religiously, like "Fritz Schulze who transcribed,
played, and internalized the piano music of Teddy Wilson. Schultz's exploits
were recognized in the December 1937 issue of *Downbeat*, America's premier
jazz magazine." At classy jazz establishments in Berlin, the owners contrived
ways to get around the RMK prohibitions. The doormen admitted high-class
patrons, and turned away the unknown or unfashionable; it was known that
Nazi spies purported themselves in a low-key manner, so they were seldom
well-dressed. The musicians had jazz arrangements on their music stands,
but at the ringing of a certain bell, they would start playing corny, non-
confrontational songs like "*Schwarzer Panther*" that were also included on the
jazz arrangements, in an emergency situation. There was a cost to these upscale
jazz establishments like The Quartier Latin, a real cost: it was so expensive
to go there that only the extremely wealthy and movie stars could afford it.[30]

It is notable that Jack Hylton, a German bandleader with whom Coleman Hawkins was playing in the mid 1930s, had been ordered not to take
Hawkins with the band to Berlin. Hylton was also "instructed by Goebbels's
office that if Hitler and his entourage should attend the performance, any
Jews were to be placed at the back of the band. Allegedly, Hylton disregarded
this order."[31]

Curiously, some blacks had eluded the Nazi purges, and they were still
playing jazz in Germany, including Herb Flemming, who "performed by dint
of an Egyptian passport, but was definitely an American citizen and considered to be 'colored' in the United States." In conjunction with the high-cost
jazz clubs, other significant jazz congregations thrived in many German cities,
showing that jazz was popular throughout Germany.[32]

A perplexing thing happened in Düsseldorf in 1936. Under the auspices of Werner Daniels, the International Swing Rhythm Club was founded. These were young jazz enthusiasts who had heard jazz on the radio and had really been attracted to it. The members met to listen to jazz radio and records, but their interest was in more than just the music. They called themselves by English names "and tried to identify as closely as possible with blacks in Harlem and the rural American South, rather than the Hitler Youth most of them belonged to." Jazz drummer Fritz Brocksieper and all of his friends who were becoming jazz fanatics, "thought jazz the ultimate form of existential expression, anything that might impede its progress was harmful. Arguably, Nazi politics would fall under that rubric by default, not by design, because jazz necessitated individuality. Therefore, swastikas and uniforms were antithetical to jazz praxis." Another curious thing about the Nazis' relationship with jazz musicians was that some high Nazi officials actually protected certain jazz musicians, like Fritz Schulz. Schulz appealed to an SS general that he knew to relieve him of SS service, so that he could focus on playing jazz. The general released him from his obligations, citing his past contributions to the SS, and Schulz was allowed to continue his life of playing in jazz clubs. The inconsistent enforcement of policies finally reached Goebbels himself. His wife Magda was taken by Goebbels' aide Karl Hanke to a jazz club several times. There were even storm troopers who were known to listen to jazz. General Secretary Hans Hinkel, the foremost jazz-hater of the Reich at times, was forced to accompany Fritz Brocksieper's band on a concert stop. "After announcing to the troops that Jewish and Anglo-American tunes were off limits, the men bombarded the General Secretary with apples."[33] The band then acknowledged the troops and played a popular, swinging tune called "*Bei Mir Bist Du Schoen*," a jazzy, rhythmic song that was a standard. (When I played in Burt Stratton's Jewish klezmer band during the 1980s, this song was still extremely popular with audiences.)

From the accounts of Werner Molders, a pilot who was one of Hermann Göring's greatest, we know that "Molders, and other Luftwaffe pilots, would soar toward the BBC in order to bomb it into the ground, but not without making contact with the airwaves beforehand. The fact was that having missed their targets, they could take in the British news as well as the music on their retreats home."[34] Molders eventually approached Goebbels and told him that the *Luftwaffe*'s pilots were listening to British jazz and news broadcasts on their missions, arguing that it was a threat to national security: it was, because Germans were being assailed with enemy propaganda as a consequence of their search for jazz. Goebbels took Molders' advice seriously, and he formed a German-type jazz orchestra with a budget of over one million marks per year. This new band, the DTU, had two purposes: it was supposed to keep the German military from listening to British stations, and it was supposed to satiate the civilians' hunger for jazz as well. The band was restricted, as far as what it could play. All American titles were banned; however, the *Luftwaffe* pilots requested *Rhapsody in Blue* by George Gershwin, a Jewish composer. Goebbels ignored the request, and they took to the skies, disappointed.

Brocksieper, who was admittedly one-quarter Jewish, was making 500 marks per week playing jazz for the Third Reich, while other German workers were making 200 marks per month. Brocksieper had a difficult choice; he had to either work for the Germans as a jazz musician, or work as an enlisted man on the battlefield. Had he picked up a rifle and started shooting, he would have most certainly killed Allies. In his situation, what would you do? Probably, anyone who was not there could not possibly answer that question. Jewish musicians risked their lives while playing jazz. Goebbels's attempts to suppress and destroy jazz were further impeded by SS member Dr. Johann Wolfgang Schottlander, a musicologist from the Berlin Conservatory whose research was funded by Heinrich Himmler. One of his duties was to develop the German film industry by using American films as a model. Germans who were at odds with the Nazi regime's measures aimed at banning jazz and jazz musicians found refuge in Dr. Schottlander's inner circle, which met to view American films. Schottlander's group had no designs on overthrowing the Nazi regime; "the group gathered there was not conspiratorial, but they were convinced of the genuine quality of American culture that shone through these films, and they all shared a great admiration for jazz." However, "in characteristically contemptuous fashion, Goebbels reiterated his long-held view that America possessed no indigenous culture."[35]

Another staunch defender of jazz during the Reich was trumpeter Carlo Bohlander. Bohlander was stationed near the site of Geissen, and he was trying to get out of military service in the early 1940s; "he was slipping out of the barracks on weekends and joined the Harlem combo, whose reputation in the Frankfurt subculture was growing by leaps and bounds." The Harlem club consisted of jazz musicians and teenagers who were jazz fanatics. This club was conspiratorial, rather than accommodating, towards the Nazi regime's policies. "Members did all the forbidden things, such as listening clandestinely to the BBC, for jazz and also news, and dodging Hitler Youth Service, for most were under eighteen. Whenever there were jazz like performances in Frankfurt for the soldiers, the sworn friends would attend." These activities brought even younger listeners into jazz; for example, sixteen-year-old clarinetist Emil Mangelsdorff would bring his 13-year-old brother Albert along on occasion. This, is turn, had quite an effect on the younger brother, who happened to be a violinist at the time. Albert became so inspired that he soon changed instruments so that he could play jazz using one of its prominent tools. These activities became increasingly dangerous, and many of the Harlem Club's teenage men were eventually forced to join the army. Therefore, it was the young women, like Jutta Hipp, who sustained jazz, in no small way, during this period, because they could not be forced to join the army. She studied harmony and sight reading with the orchestra of her church, and she idolized pianists Teddy Wilson, Fats Waller, and Art Tatum. Jutta listened to their music illegally over the BBC in her basement, and used a crude flashlight so that she could see as she transcribed the music for the jazz band that she helped to form. Young people in Hamburg, known as the Hamburg Swings, were behaving in the same way; many of these German youths from middle- and upper-class families were persecuted by the Gestapo for listening to, or dancing to, jazz. An untold number of them were thrown into concentration camps, though they really had no political agenda against the Nazi regime, per se. These were not political radicals, as they were portrayed by the Nazis: they were just young people exhibiting their penchant for "youthful exuberance, sexual adventure, jazz, and dancing. However, the Nazis misconstrued their actions: the Swings were politicized by a regime that loathed them because they had withheld their respect by dissociating themselves. It is true that such politicization became obvious to some only on the day they were put behind bars."[36] This is a stark example of how a repressive regime can become cannibalistic, feeding on the youth whose futures they are supposed to be protecting.

The German high command's resistance to jazz finally gave away in the middle of 1943, when it was clear that the end was near. They were faced with an increasing demand for jazz performances by their soldiers, and the decreasing availability of jazz musicians. The best musicians happened to be in the army, stationed at lonely outposts in many instances. Soldiers who were headed for the Eastern front, probably, were not going to be returning. "In 1943 Evelyn Kunneke was sent to entertain a suicide squad near Warsaw, before the men were dispatched to Russia. The general permitted her to vocalize American swing tunes, noting that they would be leaving tomorrow, and that when they reached their destination, there would not be any songs thereafter." Also in 1943, early one morning, there was a knock the door of pianist Martin Roman's rented room in Amsterdam. The Gestapo shot Roman's dog and took him to "the Dutch Westerbork concentration camp where he met other German-Jewish artists who had fled to the Netherlands." Roman had been playing with Coleman Hawkins, Lionel Hampton, and Django Reinhardt in Amsterdam. The SS commander of the camp happened to be a jazz fan, so Roman played for months with a band called the Westerbork Stage Group, the concentration camp's jazz band. Later, Roman was transferred to Auschwitz along with guitarist Coco Schumann and clarinetist Bedfrich Weiss.[37]

Weiss and his parents were killed at Auschwitz, while Coco Schumann and Martin Roman survived. "While in Auschwitz, musician inmates conversant with jazz styles met with a phenomenon that might seem strange but will not surprise anyone who has already encountered the entire spectrum of absurdities and contradictions in the Third Reich: an SS corporal who was bent on intoxicating himself with modern jazz." SS officer Pery Broad played accordion; his father was German and his mother was Brasilian. He was twenty-four years old, and he had learned several languages. However, Broad was known as a sadistic murderer among the inmates, even though he was never convicted of war crimes during the Frankfurt Auschwitz Trials of the 1960s. Jazz musicians Roman, Schumann, and Eric Vogel were liberated from Auschwitz by the allies at the end of World War II. German jazz musicians such as Hans Bluthner, Dietrich Schulz-Kohn, and Werner Daniels risked their lives during the Nazi occupation of Europe to promote American jazz musicians, and distribute news about what these musicians were doing. These newsletters were dropped in occupied France, sent to soldiers at the war fronts, and in the neutral countries, without any official authorization. This is quite remarkable, considering that Schulz-Kohn was a lieutenant in the *Luftwaffe*. The publications leaked sensitive stories that the Nazis would rather have suppressed. One article on Benny Carter, written by Gerd Peter Pick, included a clear drawing of a black man; it seems surreal to even imagine that such newsletters were being read at the Russian Front near the end of the war. Hans Bluthner later conceded that they all would have been hanged at least seven times, had they been caught. Both Schulz-Kohn and Bluthner contend that Schulz-Kohn, the *Luftwaffe* lieutenant, "provided the list of mostly military addresses and placed his own portrait, in full military regalia, on the cover of the first issue in late 1942, the latter intended as a protective shield, what ever good that may have done them. Schulz-Kohn was assuming a considerable risk for his own person." In that same year, the *Luftwaffe* lieutenant traveled to Paris to hear his favorite gypsy guitarist Django Reinhardt, and he even took a photograph with him. "In a memorable photograph, Schulz-Kohn is flanked by the Gypsy and four colonial black musicians; at the very far left stands Henri Battut, a French Jew, who was actually in hiding and whom Dietrich Schulz-Kohn was helping out with food stamps." Looking at the picture is somewhat astounding, because it illustrates that jazz was able to bring seemingly disparate cultures together, while politics was certainly separating them. It is an example of multi-culturalism taking place in Europe during the world's most violent conflict ever. Only now can this story be told, since it would have meant certain death for those involved, at the time.[38]

On May 8th, 1945, jazz musicians and jazz lovers alike thought that they would be able to gorge themselves. However, the new Russian administration in East Germany followed the Nazi policy of banning jazz, a product of the West.

The Third Reich did not achieve the Final Victory, rather, "it was jazz and not Third Reich that saw the Final Victory so often conjured up by the

Nazi leaders. This victory was possible because enough genuine musicians and true believers had managed to stay alive, quietly treasuring the music in their hearts."[39]

Notes

1. Michael Kater, *Different Drummers: Jazz in the Culture of Nazi Germany* (New York: Oxford University Press, 1992), 141.
2. Lewis Porter, Michael Ullman, and Ed Hazel, *Jazz from Its Origins to the Present* (Englewood Cliffs: Prentice-Hall, 1993), 47, 48.
3. Ibid., 48, 51.
4. Ibid. 53–55.
5. Leonard Feather, *The New Edition of the Encyclopedia of Jazz,* 3rd ed. (New York: Horizon Press, 1960), 211.
6. Jim Godbolt, *A History of Jazz in Britain 1919–1950* (New York: Quartet Books, 1984), 53.
7. Burton W. Peretti, *The Creation of Jazz: Music, Race, and Culture in Urban America* (Chicago: University of Illinois Press, 1992), 55–56.
8. Ibid., 56, 100.
9. Feather, 162–63.
10. Adolphus Doc Cheatham, Alyn Shipton, eds., *I Guess I'll Get the Papers and Go Home* (London: Cassell PLC with Bayou Press Ltd., 1995), 25, 27–31.
11. Ibid., 37, 39.
12. Ibid., 39, 41.
13. Ibid., 47–48.
14. Ibid., 81, 85.
15. Bill Moody, *The Jazz Exiles: American Musicians Abroad* (Las Vegas: University of Nevada Press, 1993), xvi, xvii, xxv.
16. Ibid., 32, 34.
17. Ibid., 35, 36.
18. Ibid.
19. Kater, 3.
20. Lothar Fischer, *Tanz zwischen Rausch und Tod: Anita Berber, 1918–1928 in Berlin* (Berlin, 1984), 60–90.
21. Kater, 18, 19.
22. Ibid., 20–22.
23. Ibid., 22–25.
24. Ibid., 25, 28.
25. Ibid., 29, 30.
26. Ibid., 33.
27. Ibid., 42, 44.
28. Ibid., 45, 47, 49.
29. Ibid., 49, 51–52.
30. Ibid., 56, 60, 64.
31. Ibid., 67.
32. Ibid., 70, 80.
33. Ibid., 81, 97, 101, 118.
34. Ibid., 126.
35. Ibid., 135, 141.

36. Ibid., 149, 152–53, 161–62.
37. Ibid., 162, 166, 167, 177.
38. Ibid., 179–80, 181, 199–200.
39. Ibid., 203.

Bibliography

Cheatham, Adolphus Doc, and Alyn Shipton, eds. *I Guess I'll Get My Papers and Go Home.* London: Cassell PLC with Bayou Press Ltd., 1995.

Feather, Leonard. *The New Edition of the Encyclopedia of Jazz.* 3rd edition. New York: Horizon Press, 1960.

Fisher, Lothan. *Tanz zwischen Rausch und Tod: Anita Berber, 1918–1928.* Berlin: Berlin Press, 1984.

Godbolt, Jim. *A History of Jazz in Britain 1919–1950.* New York: Quartet Books, 1984.

Kater, Michael. *Different Drummers: Jazz in the Culture of Nazi Germany.* New York: Oxford University Press, 1992.

Moody, Bill. *The Jazz Exiles.* Las Vegas: University of Nevada Press, 1993.

Peretti, Burton. *The Creation of Jazz: Music, Race, and Culture in Urban America.* Chicago: University of Illinois Press, 1992.

Porter, Lewis, Michael Ullman and Ed Hazel. *Jazz from Its Origin to the Present.* Englewood Cliffs, N.J.: Prentice-Hall, 1993.

II

BLACK POWER ANALYSIS

Essential to any discussion of the Black Power movement is an understanding of the artistic imperative and political impetus that drove social processes of self-determination. The effects of political education can reach much further than the simple exercise of voting. Politics in the context of Black Power can refer to the distribution of resources; the acquisition of information; the creation of alliances and coalitions; and participation in electoral politics on both local and national levels.

In chapters 3 and 4, Elice Rogers and Andrew Smallwood use nontraditional educational imperatives to examine Black social movements. Chapter 5 is Tanya Y. Price's penetrating discussion of the Congressional Black Caucus.

Rogers focuses on African American political participation in the Chicago community, and Smallwood looks at the communal political components of the Black Arts Movement. Both chapters emphasize the effect of education on public policy. Research on, and critical interpretation of, past and present social issues provides a theoretical and practical epistemological base for African American populations. Reflecting the period of protest in American history of the 1960s, the politics of assertion, which resulted from the Black Power movement, set in motion the processes intended to bring equity for African people throughout the diaspora, with respect to economics, housing, and finance. The information presented here by Rogers and Smallwood offers a basis for much-needed analysis within the disciplinary framework of Africana Studies.

Price's chapter on the CBC poses crucial questions: How effective has the caucus been in implementing its mission to be "Representative-at-Large for 20 million black people"? Has the Congressional Black Caucus earned legitimacy as the realization of Black Power? Price's conclusions offer an important perspective on the role of black members in the United States Congress.

3. Black Power, Chicago Politics, and Social Movements: What Have We Learned?

ELICE ROGERS

This paper presents an historical examination of African American politics in Chicago and addresses specifically African American involvement and participation as well as learning in social movements. The purpose of this article is threefold: 1) to examine the history of African American participation in Chicago politics, 2) to discuss African American political participation and education in social movements (i.e., civil rights) as a link to personal and social life, and to discuss how the education that African Americans adults received in social movements helped urban adults to look critically at, and to question, beliefs and behaviors as they occurred in the context of history in the lives of adult learners. The findings in this article demonstrate that African American adult participation in urban politics works to effectively empower those on the margins to cultivate and develop a political leadership that involves coming to the top in the name of community, humanity, service, and fighting injustice. Such attributes acquired through political participation, education, and learning operate to promote a Black political power with interests in improving the lives of African Americans and, hence the African American community (Akalimat and Gillis, 1989, p. 6).

Black Power as African American Participation in Chicago Politics

The evolution of African American participation in Chicago politics can be attributed initially to the migration of African Americans from the South to the North (Grossman, 1989, pp. 6, 262–263). One of the primary reasons African Americans migrated North was to have an opportunity to actively participate and engage in the political process. Because the importance of

political rights heavily outweighed the concern of integration, the segregation of African Americans in the Black Belt on the South Side of Chicago
permitted African Americans to obtain political offices such as alderperson,
state representative, and state senator, and to elect the first African American
Illinois Congressman, Oscar DePriest, in 1928 (Hawking, 1991).

The Chicago Republican Party welcomed and encouraged African American migrants to participate and to become actively involved in the political
process. Mayor William Hale Thompson, also known as Big Bill, encouraged
and cultivated African American participation as a potential source of votes.
Thompson's coalition, power base, and voting bloc was dependent upon the
African American vote. Thompson served as mayor of Chicago for three terms.
In return for their vote, Mayor Thompson provided African Americans with
employment opportunities, protection from police harassment, and political
representation. Mayor Thompson's opponents would have said that he provided African Americans protection from the enforcement of standing laws
(Drake and Cayton, 1962, pp. 348–351; Gosnell, 1969, pp. 49–55; Granger
and Granger, 1987, pp. 49, 52, 53; Hawking, 1991, p. 37; Kleppner, 1985, p.
29).

In contrast to the Republicans, the Democrats used Thompson's platform as a tool to promote race baiting tactics. For example, calliopes playing
"Bye-Bye Black Bird" were played in the streets and cartoons appeared which
depicted a train filled with African Americans piloted by Thompson with the
caption: "This train will start for Chicago, April 6, if Thompson is elected"
(Drake and Cayton, 1962, p. 347; Kleppner, 1985, p. 29; Hawking, 1991, p.
37).

Following "Big Bill" Thompson's election and rise to power African
Americans made some political gains as a result of the rewards received via
their political positions. African American Republicans such as Oscar DePriest
and Ed Wright achieved their political prominence through their relationship with Mayor Thompson. Oscar DePriest, in 1915, was the first African
American elected to the Chicago City Council and the first African American to serve as Congressman in the post-reconstruction era (Travis, 1987, pp.
54–55; Spear, 1967, p. 78; Rather, 1972, p. 57). Edward Wright became the
first African American ward committeeman in 1920. Wright, a recipient of
numerous appointments, served two terms on the Cook County Commission (Spear, 1967, p. 78; Drake and Cayton, 1962, p. 350). These early African
American politicians represented African American political leadership in
Chicago, and their concerns were focused primarily on personal ambition
and devotion to the African American community (Rakove, 1975, p. 257;
Akalimat and Gillis, 1989, p. 16).

After these early politicians came a second generation which replicated
characteristics of the Chicago machine. This second generation became

dissatisfied with the limited political power. A part of this dissatisfaction stemmed from conflicts between African Americans and European Americans, which resulted in days of rioting in the summer of 1919, and increased migration of African Americans from the South to Chicago. These African American migrants were not welcomed or accommodated in Chicago, as were European residents from foreign lands (Rivlin, 1992, p. 5).

In their effort to have more of an influential voice they transferred allegiance from the Republican Party to the Democratic Party and began to create a Black Chicago political machine. African American politics in Chicago witnessed the formation of a Black machine and the transition of African American support from the Republican Party to the Democratic Party (Akalimat and Gillis, 1989, pp. 16–17; Drake and Cayton, 1962, p. 352–353). A number of African Americans were offered positions and incentives to join the Democratic party. Mike Sneed began to lay the foundations of the Black machine following his election to the Third Ward Committee in 1932.

The transition of African Americans to the Democratic Party and the development of a Black machine was further enhanced with the election of Arthur Mitchell, an African American, to Congress in 1934. The Black machine gradually increased in political power and the transition of African Americans from the Republican Party to the Democratic Party was completed under the leadership of William L. Dawson (Akalimat and Gillis, 1989, pp. 16–17; Drake and Cayton, 1962, p. 352–353; and Rakove, 1975, p. 258).

Dawson was a Republican Alderman in the Second Ward who lost his bid for City Council in 1939. Following this failure, Mayor Ed Kelly offered Dawson a position as Democratic Committeeperson of the Second Ward in exchange for his political assistance and support. William Dawson accepted Kelly's offer as Second Ward Committeeman, joined the Democratic Party and emerged as a powerful African American leader in Chicago (Rakove, 1975, pp. 258–259).

Dawson's political power is evidenced by the far-reaching political tentacles he extended over the Black South Side. He "controlled massive patronage, dictated to half a dozen ward committeem[e]n and alderm[e]n, dominated a block of black votes in the Illinois General Assembly, was named secretary of the Democratic Cook County Central Committee, and had himself elected to Congress in 1922, holding the seat until his death in 1970" (Rakove, 1975, p. 259).

At the height of his political success William Dawson was instrumental in supporting Richard J. Daley for mayor in 1942. Later, Daley diluted Dawson's political power and strength by dealing and negotiating with other African American Democratic committeemen (Biles, 1995, p. 92; Hawking, 1991, p. 39). Although Dawson led the Black machine and made significant gains for African Americans throughout the '50s and '60s, African

Americans still did not hold parity with White Americans in the city of Chicago; in fact, they "held a clearly subordinate position to whites in the city. Mayor Daley reorganized and strengthened the machine, and he reaffirmed its maintenance of racial political hierarchy" (Penderhughs, 1987, pp. 238, 241). This hierarchy was crucial to the White majority who were uncomfortable with the rising African American population. Biles (1995, p. 102) commented that "for Daley and the shrinking white majority in Chicago, the unwillingness to share political power, living space, schools, and (ultimately) wealth emanated from self-interest, tribalism, racism, and fear."

Upon William L. Dawson's death in 1970, his followers included Claude Holman, Ralph Metcalf, the former Olympian, and Kenneth Campbell. Each had achieved a degree of political notoriety and influence. For example, Metcalph and Holman each served as president pro tem of the city council, and Metcalf was elected to Congress, became independent, and supported civil rights. None of Dawson's key lieutenants, however, managed to acquire the kind of political base and political power which Dawson had held (Rakove, 1975, p. 262).

Compared to many large urban cities, Chicago had more African American representation because the machine selected African American candidates. This representation was not always authentic because these African American office holders were largely controlled by Daley's machine and did not truly represent the majority of Chicago's African American population. There were six African American aldermen in Chicago during the 1960s; they were described as the "Silent Six" (Claude Holman, William Harvey, Robert Miller, Ben Lewis, Kenneth Campbell, and Ralph Metcalf) because they stood behind the policies of Richard J. Daley (Hawking, 1991, p. 40).

As the Civil Rights Movement came to Chicago, African American involvement in city politics moved beyond silence. The Civil Rights Movement was an era of demonstrations, massive protests, political struggle, and varying forms of social actions. In this period African American political leadership in Chicago became fragmented. African American political leadership was represented by African American machine politicians, independents, civil rights activists and Black Nationalists (Rakove, 1975, pp. 263–263; Hawking, 1991, p. 39).

The cadre of post–Dawson African American machine loyalist politicians included Cecil Partee, former state senator, Wilson Frost, former alderman and former president pro tem of the city council, former aldermen William Shannon and Eugene Sawyer, board commissioner John Stroger, and Joseph Bertrand of Chicago, an All-American basketball player at Notre Dame. This cadre of leadership cooperated with, and demonstrated their loyalty to, the machine.

Another faction of African American representation in Chicago was the

African American independents. Reform movements by the independents in Chicago consisted of those who earnestly had believed that the Democratic machine could be altered by their participation within the Democratic Party and those independents who believed that in order for tangible political change to occur they must remain outside of the Democratic Party (Joravsky and Camacho, 1987, p. 74; Rakove, 1975, pp. 191, 195, 262, 272; Rivlin, 1992, p. 59).

A primary goal of African American independents was to build a strong, independent organization which would penetrate throughout the wards. By achieving and maintaining an independent voice in each of the wards, independents believe that their power could be exerted in city council and ultimately on the Office of the Mayor. Another underlying goal of independents was to transform the machine in order that the interests and needs of Chicago's people were best served. Some of Chicago's African American independents include Richard Newhouse, who ran for mayor in 1975, former alderman Fred Hubbard, former alderman A.A. Sammy Rayner, newspaper publisher and former congressman, Gus Savage, attorney Roland Burris, and attorney Anna Langford. At one time, Anna Langford expressed interest in running for mayor while serving as alderwoman of the 16th ward. In 1971, Langford became Chicago's first African American woman to serve on the city council (Joravsky and Camacho, 1987, p. 47; Rakove, 1975, pp. 191, 195, 262, 272; Rivlin, 1992, p. 59).

While the independents continued to work with the establishment, civil rights activists more vehemently called to question injustices regarding many issues. Active organizations such as the Negro League of Voters attempted to slate and run African American candidates who represented the needs of the African American community. Protests were led by Al Raby and the Chicago Coordinating Council of Community Organizations. Raby also had a viable role when Dr. King and many of his followers came to the city of Chicago under the auspices of the Southern Christian Leadership Conference. The summit which took place between Daley and King was considered a failure by most African American activists, and many blamed Raby for this failure. The appearance of a settlement made it seem as though an understanding had been reached. This false sense of consensus, however, allegedly made the Democratic machine's control over African Americans even stronger (Hawking, 1991, p. 42).

Civil rights activist Dorothy Tillman was with Dr. King when he came to Chicago. Tillman eventually settled in Chicago and was appointed alderwoman of the Third Ward in 1984 and elected alderwoman in 1985. Another civil rights activist and eventual presidential candidate, Jesse Jackson also remained in Chicago and founded an organization known as Operation Breadbasket, which held as its underlying theme political education. Machine loyalists such as Eugene Sawyer were critical of Jackson's political efforts, citing that registration drives, for example, were the duties and responsibilities of Democratic committeemen (Hawking, 1991, p. 43; Fremon, 1988, pp. 37–38).

Although civil rights activists had a strong presence in Chicago, the more radically progressive Black nationalist organizations such as the Black Panthers and the Nation of Islam were also an important part of Chicago's political history. Black Nationalists have held a long relationship with Chicago, which is evidenced by Marcus Garvey's first visit to the city in 1919. Garvey focused on issues such as racial solidarity, self help, fighting racial, economic, and political oppression, a return to Africa, and advocating and fostering racial pride. Garveyism was present in Chicago for a number of years and was particularly popular among poor African American migrants who were searching for a different kind of hope to ease the new, difficult life they found in the city. Though the number of Garvey followers substantially declined by the 1920s, the spirit of Black pride was carried on by later organizations, the Black Panthers and the Nation of Islam (Spear, 1967, pp. 193–194, 195–197).

During the civil rights era the Black Panther Party for Self-Defense emphasized racial solidarity, self-help, and the eradication of racial, economic, and political oppression. The founders of the Illinois chapter of the Black Panther Party were Bobby Rush, Mark Clark, Fred Hampton, Jewell Cook, and Billy Brook. The Panther Party's call for revolution was illustrated in their ten point plan, which ranged from demands for freedom to an appeal for a United Nations meeting in a Black colony, whereby all Africans could gather and discuss the fate of their own futures.

People within the local community responded favorably to the goals of the Black Panther Party and warmly embraced the Panthers' social welfare efforts, such as the Panthers' breakfast program. In spite of their positive social efforts some politicians on both the local and national level responded with fear, outrage, and paranoia to the ideas, goals, and programs of the Black Panther Party. A heavy part of this response was centered around the Black vote. The Black Panther Party managed to receive support from the African American community and exposed a need that was not being dealt with by duly elected officials. Moreover, the Black Panther Party represented a threat to the status quo. The Chicago Police Department made numerous efforts to dismantle the Panther organization. The final destruction of the Black Panther organization occurred December 4, 1969, when Chicago police murdered Fred Hampton and Mark Clark. African Americans in the city responded to their death in a variety of ways. One serious response was that some African Americans really began to "think Black" for the first time (Travis, 1987, pp. 420, 423–424, 427, 436).

Many Black Panther themes were also emphasized by the Nation of

Islam, which sought to promote self-help, racial solidarity, and eradication of social, economic, and political oppression. Formerly led by Elijah Muhammad, the Nation of Islam is currently under the leadership of Louis Farrakhan, who receives national attention. The Nation of Islam holds strong roots in Chicago's South Side and is a political force which cannot be ignored by those in power. Although the city council has reluctantly recognized the Nation for its service to the community, its reform program, its emphasis on family, and its focus on education, politically the Nation of Islam is used by the establishment as a divisive tool to stir up conflict between African Americans and Jewish Americans within the city (Rivlin, 1992, pp. 304–305).

As a result of the Civil Rights Movement, political awareness increased in the African American community and serious attempts were made to elect an African American mayor. African American leaders and activists put their philosophical differences aside and began working together in their effort to find and elect an African American mayor. Such collaboration represented the origins of a populist movement, a movement for and by the people. The people chose Harold Washington. Harold Washington was unique because

> he carried the populist message to the black community. Washington's victory in the 1983 election was remarkable not only because he beat the machine and became the first African American mayor of Chicago, but his campaign motivated hundreds of African Americans to participate in local politics. With Washington's candidacy and election, blacks no longer accepted the old politics [Judd and Swanstrom, 1994, pp. 383–4].

Washington's emphasis as mayor was on people and coalition building. With Washington in the mayor's office African Americans had more genuine representation in city government. Grimshaw (1992, p. 221) describes Washington's leadership, movement toward change, and style of governance as that of "building a novel coalition with a promise of representation and empowerment to a host of 'have nots.'" Washington launched a reform government centering around redistribution of benefits, especially to the communities, broader representation, and greater access to significant decision-makers. Thus, the Black belt wards, once the Daley machine's electoral stronghold, became the "movement" wards under Washington.

By the end of Mayor Washington's first term, African American city council representation was highly evident. For example, in the Second Ward, Bobby Rush was elected in 1983, with Harold Washington's support. Dorothy Tillman was appointed, and then won an election in 1985, to maintain her seat in the Third Ward. Evans of the Fourth Ward, originally a machine politician, supported Harold Washington in the primary. In Ward Six, Eugene Sawyer, a machine holdover, endorsed Harold Washington. The Seventh Ward witnessed the election of Bill Beavers in 1983. Marian Humes of the

Eighth Ward was replaced by Keith Caldwell. Perry Hutchinson displaced Bob Shaw as representative at the Ninth Ward in 1983. Marlene Carter won the special election in the 15th ward with Harold Washington's help and was re-elected in 1987.

Anna Langford, Chicago's first African American alderwoman, came back to office with Harold Washington in 1983, and was re-elected to the city council in 1987. Allen Streeter was elected Seventeenth Ward alderman in a special election in 1982. In the Twentieth Ward, Cliff Kelley held the city council seat until 1987 and was replaced by Ernest "Lock-em-up" Jones. Niles Sherman, elected alderman of the Twenty-first Ward, maintained the position through Harold Washington's term as mayor.

Bill Henry represented the Twenty-Fourth Ward from 1983 and was re-elected in 1987. Due to a series of indictments, Wallace Davis made it possible for Sheneather Butler, a minister's daughter, to be elected Twenty-seventh Ward representative in 1987. In the Twenty-Eight Ward, Ed Smith was elected with Harold Washington's help in 1983.

Ward twenty-nine saw the election of Danny Davis in 1979. Davis held office until he became a county commissioner in 1990. Antoinette Bitoy was Thirty-fourth Ward alderwoman at the end of Mayor Washington's first term, having replaced Frost, who was elected to the Board of Tax Appeals. Lemuel Austin was elected in 1987 and was succeeded by his wife, Carrie Austin, after his death. Percy Giles was elected Thirty-seventh Ward alderman in the 1986 special election (Grimshaw, 1992, p. 182; Fremon, 1988; pp. 30–32, 37–39; Hawking, 1991).

Under Harold Washington's leadership more women were extended opportunities to engage in the political process and represented many areas of city government. Prior to Washington's bid for re-election about "forty percent of the city's commissioners and deputy commissioners were women. The city's two top financial officers were black women" (Rivlin, 1992, p. 246).

Unfortunately, Washington's populist movement and reform coalition fell apart with his death on the morning of November 25, 1987. Both machine politicians and Washington challengers were torn over who would become heir to the mayoral office: Tim Evans, Washington's city council floor leader, or Eugene Sawyer, part of the machine old guard, who had as good a claim as Evans to say that he supported Harold. This struggle for succession created internal conflict amongst African American politicians.

Any unity that had existed amongst African American politicians prior to Harold Washington's death was torn apart by political differences and culminated in an African American political divide (Rivlin, 1992, pp. 403–420). Grimshaw (1992, p. 222) described their damaging effects: "The new black divide opened the way for Richard M. Daley's entry into the mayor's office. Behind a facade of largely symbolic reforms, Daley is discreetly reconstituting what remains of the machine and putting it under his control. His machine politics, reform style of governance is rolling back gains made by blacks under Washington, for they now have no representation to speak of in either government or the party, while the affirmative action and set-aside programs have been substantially cut back" (Grimshaw, 1992, p. 222).

The erratic growth of African American political awareness in Chicago, African American participation in social movements (i.e., the Civil Rights Movement, the movement to elect Harold Washington) and Harold Washington's brief tenure created openings for African Americans to further advances causes important to the African American community and to assume unique and significant positions on the local, state, and national level (Rogers, 1997).

Black Power as Learning in Social Movements

The discussion of African American politics in Chicago demonstrates and supports political participation as a form of social action. It is the presence of social action which is the hallmark of social movements. In social movements adult education is alive and at work. Eduard Lindeman (Brookfield, 1987, p. 76) stressed the importance of adult education to society in 1937, by stating that

> adult education is not merely the education of adults; adult education is learning associated with social purposes. Wherever, adult education has been associated as an instrument of social change, as in Scandinavian countries for example, learning has invariably been accompanied by a redirection of social aims and values.

Lindeman's position regarding the role of adult education, learning, and social change raises the following question, as it relates to political participation and education in social movements: What kinds of learning occur in social movements? Adult education plays a vital role in social movements because it is influential in the learning experiences of adult learners. Schied (1993) discussed the relationship between the individual as intellectual, adult education, and social change in social movements:

> [S]ociety in its socialization process is inherently educational, and philosophy is an intrinsic activity in peoples' lives; all people are intellectuals in one form or another. The aim of education for those committed to social change is to develop ... a consciousness that rivals the hegemony of the dominant culture.

In social movements, adult learners are affected by their social contexts in which their formation occurs, and they are affected by historical forces. Hellyer (1988) supports the latter by commenting that we must come to the conscious realization that adult education activities cannot be understood in isolation from the particular historical junctures which spawned them. We must be constantly aware of the fact that the political, social and economic milieu cannot be separated from each other, and indeed, education must too be viewed as a permanent fixture within that totality, whether it be education of the traditional, schooling vintage or education in the non-traditional [sense].

In examining the kinds of learning which occur in social movements, the experiences and histories of adult learners are recognized and credibility is given to their experiences. This is important because participants in social movements tend to represent the voices of those who are left out of the conversation in dominant society.

Chicago African American political participation and education in social movements encouraged three main types of learning. African American adults encountered learning associated with the state of society and community, hegemony, and transformation. I will first discuss learning and the state of society.

Black Power as Learning About the State of Society and Community

Through their participation in social movements African Americans in the city of Chicago learned about the condition and status of society. As adult learners they learned about the constraints and difficulties associated with the everydayness of living life in society. In so doing, as adults they learned about the challenges that they faced within institutions and the problems associated with penetrating power structures within institutions (Melucci, 1989).

As participants in social movements African Americans also learned about crucial problems which faced them in the city of Chicago, and they began to question what options they had in society. Active participation in the Civil Rights Movement, for example, led African Americans to ask questions such as: What is the status of the current system in this society? Is change in this system necessary? What stance do I take in this system?

As a result of this inquiry, African Americans in the city of Chicago learned via their participation in social movements that there are certain problems in society that cannot be administratively controlled, monitored, and negotiated. Hence, as adult learners they were stimulated to new levels of consciousness about who they were and what their role should be in society as they know it (Melucci, 1989).

Learning about society also promoted learning in community for many African Americans in Chicago. In "Learning Within a Social Movement: The

Chicago African-American Experience," Cunningham and Curry (1997) described and analyzed the learning experiences of fifteen African Americans in social movements. Four themes were found instrumental in learning and community. First, the participants identified a defining moment in their lives which fostered a commitment and obligation to social change through collective participation. Second, participants created knowledge and self-reliance. Third, participants emphasized community and culture. Fourth, within the community, they learned from one another.

Black Power as Learning About Hegemony

African Americans in the city of Chicago employed their own parameters and constructs as a basis for interpreting the reality of the world they lived in, and they learned about the hegemonic box. Adult participants learned about hegemony and the use of power in society. In this hegemonic box African American through their political participation found the "good old boys," unshared power, control, status-quo, tradition, oppression, manipulation, marginality, gate-keeping, exploitation, coercion, inequities, and Eurocentrism (Rubenson, 1989, p. 56). Political participation also enabled African Americans in the city of Chicago to address the nature of the hegemonic box, whereby they also learned to identify characteristics associated with hegemonic consciousness. In "Political Consciousness and Collective Action," Aldon Morris (1992) describes features of hegemonic consciousness:

> A crucial feature of hegemonic consciousness is that it always presents itself as a set of values and beliefs that serve the general welfare. In this guise, it claims to be the best societal conception for all people and the most useful and legitimate guiding ideology for the society as a whole. Hegemonic consciousness is always sustained by public institutions that are meant to attend to the general welfare: the government, schools, the media, and a host of lesser institutions presenting themselves as representative of society as a whole and intent of benefiting the broadest range of people. In short, hegemonic consciousness is a ruling consciousness because it is rooted in and supported by the most dominant institutions in society. Its organizational expression enables it to wrap itself in institutional garments bearing labels proclaiming its universality.

Black Power as Learning and Transformation

Freire (1993) posits that once learners become conscious of the forces that control their lives, they become empowered, and empowerment leads to action. The emancipatory education that African Americans representing the city of Chicago received in social movements moved from awareness, to the awareness of the conditions of experiencing, and beyond, to awareness of the reasons why they experienced as they did and to action based on these insights. This emancipatory education helped African Americans to look critically at, and to question, beliefs and behaviors as they occurred in the context of history and in their lives (Mezirow, 1978, p. 101). This type of transformational learning fostered a political empowerment and a construction of "Black Power" which served to evoke a stronger sense of commitment to self and to materialize this commitment to self and community in the form of political action. Transformational learning involves the construction of meanings from adult learner experiences and using these meanings as an avenue for action (Mezirow, 1990).

Michael Welton (1993) provides insight regarding adult learner transformation and meaning in challenging institutional power structures. He states:

> Structures both create and constrain us simultaneously, and meaning is produced and challenged within the context of social life.

African American political participation in Chicago social movements, especially the Civil Rights Movement, led to a polity of democracy. A polity of democracy is constructed when personal and social transformation come together. Personal transformation and the development of a critical consciousness cannot occur independent from social transformation, which requires group participation. Cunningham (1992, p. 4) states:

> Developing a critical conscience should be linked to democratic participation in the group as well as society.

Transformative learning takes places when adult learners struggle with others against oppression, to act to change oppressive conditions. It is the struggle to make social change that confirms and validates adult learner biography and transformation (Cunningham, 1992; Freire, 1993).

Summary

What we have learned through examining the history of African American participation in Chicago politics is that historically African Americans have utilized political participation as a vehicle within which to fight for participation in the political system. Second, we have learned that an examination of Chicago's African American political history reveals an American story of political participation characterized by access and opportunity, triumph and tragedy, as well as conflict and compromise. This triumph of Black Power as embodied in the lives of Chicago African American participants raised the subplots of the African American story to challenge and compete with the American story.

Third, we have learned that African American political education and learning in social movements promoted three types of learning: 1) learning about the state of society and community; 2) learning about community; and 3) learning and transformation. Social movements reflect where adult learners are, and what is important to adult learners in society. The education of adults takes place in and around social movements. The education that African Americans in the city of Chicago received in social movements helped African American adults to look critically at, and to question, beliefs and behaviors as they occurred in the context of history and in the learner's lives.

Fourth, we have learned that African American participation in social movements has historically and traditionally empowered those on the margin to participate politically in non-formal ways in our society, and thus we witness that an education acquired "in the streets" must be included alongside formal learning.

Fifth, we have learned that early in Chicago's political history, African Americans exerted "Black Power" in assuming a more dominant role in Chicago by critiquing, defining, and determining what their relationship would be in relation to the Chicago White power structure. This relationship called for emancipation today and not tomorrow. This relationship called for a human existence outside of the hegemonic box. This relationship called for a dismissal of oppressive ideas about African American people and replacing these ideas with progressive thoughts of positive "Black Consciousness." This relationship called for a recognition of the self as subject and not object and to value all that is humane, dignified, and unoppressive.

Sixth, we have learned that all the prior conditions constitute "Black Power." "Black Power" is evidenced by freedom from hegemonic forces, the power to exert control over one's own destiny, the courage to affirm one's being, and the courage to question power for what it is, how it will be used, and for what purpose (Akalimat and Gillis, 1989, p. 6; Cone, 1969, p. 5–8).

Finally, we have learned from this discussion that African American participation in Chicago politics and social movements has, consistent with its past, present, and future, a commitment to an order which is about the recognition of African American people and an engagement in political action that will serve to improve the quality of life for African Americans in the city of Chicago (Cone, 1969, p. 134).

References

Akalimat, A., and Gillis, D. (1989). *Harold Washington and the Crisis of Black Power in Chicago*. Vol. I. Chicago: 21st Century Books and Publications.

Biles, R. (1995). *Richard J. Daley: Politics, Race, and the Governing of Chicago*. De Kalb: Northern Illinois University Press.

Brookfield, E. (1987). *Learning Democracy: Eduard Lindeman on Adult Education and Social Change*. Wolfeforo: Croom Helm Ltd.

Cone, J. (1969). *Black Theology and Black Power*. New York: The Seabury Press.

Cunningham, P. (1992). From Freire to Feminism: The North American Experience with Critical Pedagogy. *Adult Education Quarterly* 43 (3), 180–191.

Cunningham, P., and Curry, R. (1997). Learning Within a Social Movement: The Chicago African American Experience. In R. Nolan and H. Chelesvig (eds.), *Conference Proceedings of the 38th Annual Adult Education Research Conference, May 16–18, 1997*. Pp. 73–78. Stillwater: Oklahoma State University.

Drake, S., and Cayton, H. (1962). *Black Metropolis: A Study of Negro Life in a Northern City*. Vol. I. New York: Harper and Row.

Freire, P. (1993). *Pedagogy of the Oppressed*. New revised twentieth anniversary edition. New York: Continuum Publishing.

Fremon, D. (1988). *Chicago Politics Ward by Ward*. Bloomington: Indiana University Press.

Gosnell, H. (1969). *Negro Politicians: The Rise of Negro Politics in Chicago*. Chicago: Aldine Publishing.

Granger, B., and Granger, L. (1987). *Lords of the Last Machine: The Story of Politics in Chicago*. New York: Random House.

Grimshaw, W. (1992). *Black Politics and the Chicago Machine, 1931–1991*. Chicago: University of Chicago Press.

Grossman, J. (1989). *Land of Hope: Chicago Black Southerner and the Great Migration*. Chicago: University of Chicago Press.

Hawking, J. (1991). *Political Education in the Harold Washington Movement*. Unpublished doctoral dissertation, Northern Illinois University.

Hellyer, M. (1988). *The Politics of Adult Education Historiography in the United States: Implications of the Labor College Movement*. Unpublished doctoral dissertation, Northern Illinois University.

Joravsky, B. and Camacho, E. (1987). *Race and Politics in Chicago*. Chicago: Community Renewal Society.

Judd, D., and Swanstrom, T. (1994). *City Politics: Private and Public Power and Public Policy*. New York: HarperCollins College Publishers.

Kleppner, P. (1985). *Chicago Divided: The Making of a Black Mayor*. De Kalb: Northern Illinois University Press.

Mezirow, J. (1978). Perspective Transformation. *Adult Education* 28 (2), 100–110.

Mezirow, J. (1990). *Fostering Critical Reflection in Adulthood: A Guide to Transformative and Emancipatory Learning*. San Francisco: Jossey-Bass.

Melucci, A. (1989). *Nomads of the Present*. Philadelphia: Temple University Press.

Morris, A. (1992). Political Consciousness and Collective Action. In A. Morris and C. Mueller (eds.), *Frontiers in Social Movement Theory*. Pp. 351–373. New Haven: Yale University Press.

Penderhughs, D. (1987). *Race and Ethnicity in Chicago: A Re-Examination of Pluralist Theory*. Urbana: University of Illinois Press.

Rakove, M. (1975). *Don't Make No Waves ... Don't Back No Losers: An Insider's Analysis of the Daly Machine*. Bloomington: Indiana University Press.

Rather, E. (ed.) (1972). *Chicago Negro Almanac and Reference Book.* Chicago: Chicago Negro Almanac Publishing.

Rivlin, G. (1992). *Fire on the Prairie: Chicago's Harold Washington and the Politics of Race.* New York: Henry Holt.

Rogers, E. (1997). *An Ethnographic Case Study of African-American Female Political Leaders: Implications for Adult Continuing Education.* Unpublished doctoral dissertation, Northern Illinois University.

Rubenson, K. (1989). The Sociology of Adult Education. In S. Merriam and P. Cunningham (eds.), *Handbook of Adult and Continuing Education.* Pp. 56–57.

Schied, F. (1993). *Learning in Social Context: Workers and Adult Education in 19th Century Chicago.* De Kalb: LEPS Press.

Spear, A. (1967). *Black Chicago: The Making of a Negro Ghetto, 1890–1920.* Chicago: University of Chicago Press.

Travis, D. (1987). *An Autobiography of Black Politics.* Chicago: Urban Research Press.

Welton, M. (1993). Social Revolutionary Learning: The New Social Movements as Learning Sites. *Adult Education Quarterly* 43 (3), 152–164.

4. A Critical Assessment of the Educational Mission and Praxis of the Black Arts Movement

ANDREW P. SMALLWOOD

Introduction

The decade of the 1960s was one of great social transformation as people began to see a disparity between the ideal conditions that existed for very few and the reality of a social, economic and political system that limits access to groups of people based on a variety of factors: ethnicity, gender, class, and race, to name a few. Needless to say this decade witnessed the demand of many different groups of people to voice their concerns for equality of resources within existing institutions and particularly the construction of mechanisms within communities to address the various needs of local residents. As a by-product of the social unrest related to the Civil Rights, Black liberation, and Black Power movements, African Americans expressed a demand for educational institutions to provide access traditionally denied to them and asked for revisions of the curricula needed to reflect their contributions to local, national and world civilization. Specifically the Black Studies movement in the mid–1960s was the result of African American college students and local community residents requiring that institutions of higher education respond to the needs of people in their communities.

THESIS

This paper seeks to identify the function of non-formal education for residents of black communities during the period of the Black Arts Movement (of the 1960s and 1970s). More specifically I will examine seminal figures related to the Black Arts movement to uncover how these writers have identified the role of education for Black people in their communities.

RESEARCH DESIGN

This paper will employ Secondary Analysis with an emphasis on Content Analysis to assess the role of education during one of the seminal Black social movements of the 1960s.

THEORETICAL PERSPECTIVE

I will employ two variables from Kawaida Theory, an Afrocentric theoretical paradigm, to interpret the data collected related to Black community education: creative production and political organization. The goal of this interpretation will be to examine the function of art in the social context during the Black Arts Movement.

ORGANIZATION

In this paper I will discuss the function of education and art museums in a community context; the impetus, the evolution and function of community education for African Americans; and the role of Malcolm X for historical context. I will then examine the role of education as seen through the significant works about the Black Arts Movements, discuss the findings, and conclude by examining the role of education in the Black Arts Movement.

Historical Overview of Art Education and the Museum Movement

The field of adult education in the United States has a very rich and varied history dating back over 200 years. The history of the modern museum also dates back to the latter part of the 18th century, originating on the continent of Europe. As with most institutions there has been an evolution through education which has contributed to a change in the philosophy, ideology and praxis for how information is shared with museums' patrons. This paper will provide a historical discussion of the history of the museum, examine the role that education has played, and give some examples of how adult education currently is in practice at these institutions.

In the *Handbook of Adult Continuing Education* (1990), Mary C. Chobot offers a definition for the museum by stating: "A museum is a repository of artifacts of the past, preserved and interpreted for future generations."[1] Museums are generally divided into two categories, historical and scientific/ aesthetic. I believe that this information is important for the reader to understand how adult education functions in this context. In order to understand the present, we will begin with a discussion of past events that have both directly and indirectly affected the role of education in museums.

For the purpose of this paper I have divided the development of museums chronologically into four periods. It was in these periods that various significant events occurred that have both shaped and defined the role of education in museums today. The first period occurred during the latter half of the 18th and the entire 19th century. It was at this time that the first museum, the Louvre, opened in France in 1793. According to Rawlins (1978), the purpose of the museum was to display national treasures and to house artifacts stolen in conquest by Napoleon. Many of these treasures were previously not accessible to the general public as they were housed in palaces and cathedrals generally frequented by the French aristocracy. Discussion of the Louvre is significant because it, along with other European museums, set the tone for the definition of museum education, which has traditionally been only *exposing* patrons to works of art. Rawlins continues his discussion by stating that the museum movement did not come into vogue in the United States until the 1870s and 1880s, when most of the major museums were founded in many major cities. The major contributors to museums were the wealthy men of big business such as Andrew Carnegie, J.P. Morgan and the Fuller family of Boston. Their contributions came about over the concern of over increasing urban crime, poverty and the rising immigrant population in the United States. The philanthropists believed that exposing these groups to art, cultural refinement, moral education and vocational training would help address some of these urban problems. Museums were initially chartered as educational institutions but "education was defined by most museum administrators as 'the acquisition, preservation and exhibition of works of art.'"[2] This as stated earlier followed the European model, and thus any form of education in the formal sense was rather limited at best and at worst non-existent.

During the second period of museums in America (1900–1930), beginning in the early part of the twentieth century, there was the formation of the American Association of Museums. This organization engaged in the discussion of museum philosophy and procedures and openly addressed the topic of museum education. Here the seeds were sewn, though no serious implementation of any educational programs was to take place until the mid–1930s. The third period spanned the decades of the 1930s through 1960s. It was during the 1930s that the Great Depression severely cut back on the amount of private funding museums received. In order to obtain government money the museums had to prove that they were serving a public need; thus, educational programs were begun. In addition to the Depression's influencing museum education, there were two gentleman that were the visionaries and strong proponents of museums' developing educational programs. John Cotton Dana of the Newark museum in Newark, N.J., and Henry Watson Kent of the Metropolitan Museum in New York City, New York, believed strongly that education had an important role to play in museums. Dana was a strong advocate of museums' engaging with other institutions for the purpose of public instruction:

> To make itself alive the museum must do two things; it must teach and it must advertise. As soon as it begins to teach it will of necessity begin an alliance with present teaching agencies, the public schools, the college and universities and the art institutions of all kinds.[3]

Dana's contribution to museum education was in establishing the lecture series, art classes, and the apprenticeship program. Dana's colleague Henry Kent believed in "art for the people's sake." Kent's major contributions to museum education were establishing the gallery lecture system, publications, programs for schools, traveling exhibitions, films and broadcasts. Though these men strongly influenced the role of education in museums, it was not until the 1960s and 1970s that this issue came to receive major attention from museum directors and curators.

Period 4 covers the 1960s through 1980s. During the 1960s museums witnessed a large increase in patronage. In 1960 200 million visitors came to museums. In 1965 the number of visitors increased to 300 million, and by 1970 it increased yet again to 700 million. This led to one museum opening on the average of every 2.5 days during the decade of the 1960s.[4] Yet during this time a debate raged between museums and the public over the relevancy of museums and whether they should be inclusive of "the real world" or should provide an escape into another world in another place and time. Because there was such a demand for social relevance, museums responded by providing various educational opportunities for local community members to participate in. In addition, the National Endowment for the Arts offered grants for community education programs, increasing the pressure for museums to infuse education in to their day to day operations.

Types of Museum Adult Education Programs

Research shows that there are generally two types of museum education programs specifically geared to the needs of adults that seem to adopt some of the characteristics of a traditional adult education program: the community museum program, which focuses on issues specifically related to the surrounding community, and the teacher education program, which focuses on helping people understand the role of various exhibits so that they may attain some professional or personal goal.

For the history of the community museum we go back to France where in the city of Paris, the riots of 1968 influenced the French government to establish a series of museums to "preserve economic viability and included facilities to document the area's histories for community meeting."[5] At this same time the Smithsonian established the Anacostia neighborhood museum in Washington, D.C., and several other countries (Spain, Portugal and Brazil) followed this trend. In 1972 the International Council of Museums proclaimed that museums should be integrated with their surrounding community. One form of this museum is known as the eco-museum, which is a form of neighborhood museum which is organized around a community's relationship with its culture and physical environment. In this type of community museum, members of the community house artifacts in their homes, meet regularly to celebrate their culture and discuss issues related to community and empowerment. In Karp, Kreamer, and Lavine's *Museums and Communities* the author states:

> An eco-museum is an agent for managing change that links education, culture and power. [It is] also called a neighborhood or street museum.... [Its m]ethodology [is] based on concepts of life long learning and educational and psychological life stage development for the community [to] learn about their needs, themselves, and to act upon that knowledge in a democratic process.[6]

This philosophy seems to aligned with the adult education philosophy of Paulo Freire and Edward Lindemann. Also popular in museums are the teacher education programs that are helpful primarily but not exclusively to K–12 teachers wanting to relate their class curriculum to a museum tour. Participants of these programs are not always teachers but may attend for a professional reason or just for their personal enjoyment.[7] It appears that very little literature is available concerning these programs; however, Mayer and Berry state that their goal is to serve adults that have a particular goal in mind that they want to achieve by attending the program. This seems to address the characteristic of the self-directed learner often discussed in adult education literature and research.

Black Museums: A Brief Historical Overview

Given the state of race relations manifested in the institution of slavery and racial segregation, artistic expression was difficult at best, let alone the documenting of it. Betty Collier-Thomas (1981) points to the desire of African Americans in the 19th century to celebrate and document their achievements as the genesis of the Black museum movement in the United States:

> Prior to the development of specific black institutions such as museums, the church and the [black] church and the school performed museum defined functions. As early as 1800, free blacks in cities were sponsoring small, but significant exhibitions of black art and handi-work.[8]

Collier-Thomas further outlines the importance of Black benevolent societies, normal schools, colleges and independent political and social organizations for providing exhibitions in Black communities in the later 19th century.[9] In the early 20th century the development of Black research societies and the founding of the Association for the Study of Negro Life and History in 1915 and the *Journal of Negro History* offered "systematic and consistent study of black people." This would lay the foundation for the exploration of the African American experience in the 1920s and 1930s during the Harlem Renaissance through artistic expression. During this time African American museums experienced a shift in the function and structure from private collections to repositories housed in institutions, such as the donation of Arthur Schomburg's collection to the New York Public Library in May of 1925, eventually named the Schomburg Center for Research in Black Culture. Later the development of galleries and exhibitions by Black artists is noted by Collier-Thomas:

> Apart from university and college art galleries and library rooms designed as museums, black museums as separate and independent structures did not begin to develop until the 1960s. The civil rights Movement and the American Bi-Centennial celebration were major factors contributing to this development. In 1960, there were no more than three independent black museums or culture centers combining museum functions. As of October 1, 1980 the Bethune Historical Development Project has identified 96 such institutions, located in 26 states and the District of Columbia.[10]

Thus in the post–1960s era, we see the founding of Black museums such as the Du Sable Museum in Chicago, Illinois, and later the National Afro-American Museum and Cultural Center in Wilberforce, Ohio, both larger venues to house the artifacts documenting African life over various periods of history. Thus, with the advent of the Civil Rights, Black Arts and Black Power movements of the 1960s, an explosion in the number of museums has occurred, whose dual function is to serve as a repository and a pedagogical instrument to help educate patrons about the history and culture of African American people and their contributions to the larger society.

Community Education for African Americans

Community education in the broadest sense can be defined by Paul F. Delargy's citation of Weaver's 1969 research:

> [Community education] is based upon the premise that education can be made relevant to people's needs ... [and] assumes that education should have an impact upon the society it serves.[11]

This statement implies that community education is based on the needs of community residents and is an aspect of non-formal education. A historical examination of education in African American communities shows patterns of segregation in the public school system, resulting in separate and inferior learning experiences. During the late nineteenth century the growth of colleges and universities in the United States led to the creation of predominantly Black colleges in the South to provide training for Black teachers.[12]

During the 1800s, organizations educating Black adults consisted of beneficial societies and churches. These organizations were predominantly White and were interested in providing basic literacy skills to African Americans. Predominantly Black organizations (mostly churches) emphasized literacy but also focused on religious training for ministers and economic education for the development of Black businesses.[13] The main difference between Black and White organizations offering African Americans education was the extent of independence each program offered. Black community education was based on addressing pressing needs of economic empowerment and social protection from violence. White organizations most often were not interested in education emphasizing Black economic competition or social integration, but promoted basic skills for economic exploitation for the labor force needed for industrial jobs.[14] In the twentieth century Black community education was advocated by Black churches and government sponsored programs assisting with wide-ranging programs.

When we examine religion and African American community education, we see that Black churches provided a valuable service in offering education to community residents. The role of Black churches in assisting Black people in their adjustment throughout history has been well documented. Black churches have provided both secular and religious educational programs.

As discussed previously, a primary function of educational programs in many Black churches has been the training of ministers. Black ministers have served both as community leaders and teachers of the sacred text, and were important in providing non-formal education for Black people in their communities.

In examining community education for African Americans, political education promoted by Black organizations is crucial. The NAACP, Urban League, UNIA and others serve as instruments of informal political power in influencing social policies affecting Black communities. These organizations advocated social and political empowerment for African Americans attempting to overcome segregation. Franklin and Moss discussed the role of the NAACP in the early twentieth century in using the courts to overturn legal segregation in the South.[15] The importance of these organizations is significant, given the obstacles in place preventing Black participation in the formal political process, especially in the South between 1877 and 1965.

The Black Artists and the Role of Culture in the Early 20th Century

Kawaida Theory states that Creative Production "shows artistic and intellectual inventiveness and is inspired by and reflective of a people's life experiences and life aspirations. It includes art, music and literature."[16] The tradition of creative production in Black communities in the twentieth century is linked to the Harlem Renaissance of the 1920s and 1930s. As a mass movement toward the production of Black artistic expression, intellectual thought and cultural celebration, the Harlem Renaissance became a landmark period for Black art, music and literature.

To examine Black artistic expression during this period, we must understand the influence of Marcus Garvey. As an advocate of racial pride, Garvey and his organization helped to set the context for cultural celebration and self-expression that would later be expressed during the Harlem Renaissance and in Alain Locke's concept of the "New Negro." According to Karenga:

> Garvey advocated cultural nationalism, a bold redefinition of reality in Black images and interests. This thrust, he contended, should begin with a rescue and reconstruction of Black history, for little can be expected from Whites who "have tried to rob the Black man of his proud past." Blacks, he said, "have a beautiful history of their own and none of any other race can truly write it but themselves." Moreover, he urged encouragement of Black authors "who are loyal to the race" and exhibit race pride and severe criticism for those who prostitute their skills for White patrons and allies. Also, he urged an education that was socially relevant, i.e., applicable and inspirational in the struggle of Blacks to free themselves and rebuild the world in their own image and interests. To do this, Garvey called for a Black Vanguard, "men and women who are able to create, originate and improve, and thus make an independent racial contribution to the world and civilization."[17]

Garvey's UNIA was located in Harlem, in addition to the NAACP and Urban League, which were also located in New York. These organizations, along with Black migration from the South, provided the foundation for a cultural explosion that started in New York and spread to Black communities across the country. During this period there were two trends in Black artistic expression, the committed school and the detached school of art. The committed school represented artistic expression that would examine and address issues facing African Americans such as lynching, racism, segregation, and unemployment. Further, artists with this point of view were interested in celebrating Black culture and traditions ignored by society.[18]

The detached school of artistic expression was more interested in art for art's sake without identification with social issues. Thus, the African American artist identified himself as an artist first and foremost and did not primarily use artistic expression to alter the social reality of Black people. According to Karenga, the use of artistic expression in the African American experience must meet three qualifications if it is to address racism and suffering in Black communities. First, it must be *functional*, serving to address social issues affecting Black people; second, it must be *collective*, in that it represents the synthesis of the breadth and depth of the African American experience; and third, it must be *committing*, in that it urges African Americans in the struggle toward the realization of their potential beyond social limitations.[19]

Malcolm X: An Antecedent to the Black Arts Movement

An aim of community education for African Americans has been to address problems affecting individuals and families hurt by social forces in their communities.[20] At the end of his life, Malcolm X began to discuss new approaches to education and advocated both formal and non-formal adult education, making it socially relevant as an approach for African American community empowerment. In a speech he gave at the founding rally for the OAAU in June 1964, Malcolm X stated:

> We must establish all over the country schools of our own to teach our own children to become scientists, to become mathematicians. We must realize the need for adult education and job retraining programs that will emphasize a changing society in which [technology] automation will play a key role. We intend to use tools of education to help raise our people to an unprecedented level of excellence and self-respect through their own efforts.[21]

It is in this statement that Malcolm lays the charge for African Americans to educate themselves about their history and contributions to human civilization, based on the current and future needs facing Black people in the 1960s. Thus

Malcolm X laid a foundation of uncompromising Black cultural expression for Black people to follow. This became a significant influence on the Black Arts Movement of the late 1960s.[22] It is this charge that inspires a generation of Black artists to address Black life. Malcolm X also stated that:

> Our cultural revolution must be the means of bringing us closer to our African brothers and sisters. It must begin in the community and be based on community participation. Afro-Americans will be free to create only when they can depend on the Afro-American community for support, and Afro-American artists must realize that they depend on the Afro-American community for inspiration.[23]

Malcolm X's greater emphasis on culture in his final year taught Black people to be proud of African ancestors and their cultural heritage. Malcolm X's advocacy in cultural pride would lead to greater self-esteem and ultimately greater achievement for African Americans:

> This cultural revolution will be the journey to our rediscovery of ourselves. History is a people's memory, and without a memory man is demoted to the level of the lower animals. When you have no knowledge of your history, you're just another animal; in fact, you're a Negro; something that's nothing. The only black man on earth who is called a Negro is one who has no knowledge of his history. The only Black man on earth who is called Negro is one who doesn't know where he came from. That's the one in America. They don't call Africans Negroes.[24]

Karenga appropriately observes the importance of the African American community's need for a meaningful education at this time:

> It became important to break the White monopoly on knowledge and its manipulation and create a new context for the creation and dissemination of a new knowledge directed toward service to the community rather than toward its suppression.[25]

This would require the assertion of African American artists fusing their art with politics in order to address the totality of the Black experience. Kawaida Theory defines politics as the process of gaining and maintaining power. For African Americans this means examination of political organization in the "traditional African sense," meaning how this impacts the collective group.[26]

The Role of Education Addressed by Dudley Randall and Larry Neal

In this study I have chosen to explore the views of two significant figures regarding the role education played during the Black Arts Movement: Dudley

Randall and Larry Neal. In Julius Thompson's *Dudley Randall, Broadside Press and the Black Arts Movement in Detroit 1960–1995*, Thompson's biographical account of Randall uncovers a discussion of several kinds of education: first, the influence of the *Negro History Bulletin* on teachers and scholars;[27] second, the concerns of desegregation in Detroit in the 1960s and 1990s; third, the role of Black community organizations in conducting informal education; fourth, the discussion of the Black Studies and Black History movements; and finally, the role of the Black press (traditional and radical versions) in addressing issues pertinent to Black community residents. It is clear from Thompson's work that artists are attempting to use their craft to empower Black residents in their communities through knowledge and celebration of culture. The artists' connection to issues facing African Americans in their communities in the 1960s is a recurring theme reflected in various ways as art and politics collide during a time of great social upheaval. Kawaida Theory defines politics as the process of gaining and maintaining power. For African Americans this means examination of political empowerment in the "traditional African sense," meaning how does this impact the collective group.[28] It is the issue of African American empowerment in a community context via the arts that Larry Neal addresses.

In his article "The Social Background of the Black Arts Movement," Larry Neal vividly describes the emerging artists, their function and purpose in documenting the Black experience. Neal opens his article discussing the embracing of African philosophy and language by Leroi Jones (now Amiri Baraka) in the book MUNTU and his exploration of the blues in the book *Blues People*, making a broad statement about African American culture.[29] Neal calls for academic research about the great street orators in Harlem during the 1960s who "educated a lot of people politically" about their history and sociology in the urban areas of the northern United States. Neal sees this oral tradition in Harlem coming from Marcus Garvey, and continuing through Ed Davis and Malcolm X.[30] He also notes that the oral cadence of Dr. Martin Luther King Jr. and other ministers represents a tradition of the southern Black preacher and church rhythms of the Black Gospel tradition.[31]

Neal's discussion briefly addresses the growth of Black periodicals in the 1960s and the rise of nationalism through organizations like the Revolutionary Action Movement (RAM) and African American jazz musicians such as John Coltrane, Archie Shepp, and Albert Ayler. In discussing the "Loft Jazz" musicians who were interested in displaying Black culture in their music, Neal addresses the conversations between Black artists in various fields:

> Everybody came to these parties and at them you met all of the writers who were trying to get the thing together—the painters, the musicians coming to hear this new music. You could run into anybody in this context. And 27 Cooper Square was one of the places along the way where a

lot of ideas took shape, a lot of discussion, a lot of listening, a lot of com-
raderie. It wasn't like they were formal discussions. They were informal.
You're partying and you're talking. You know, listening to music. There
was something happening here. Something that was really consuming in
terms of your personality.[32]

Neal's discussion of informal education of Black artists further translates into
a call for political and cultural liberation of African American people. Through
style and substance of artistic expression, the development of the Black Arts
Theater and Repertory Company, Black poets, and literary figures raised the
question of the Black Aesthetic, which according to Neal served to communicate the further exploration and celebration of Africa and African American culture during the 1960s.

Conclusion

The debate has raged for many years over whether museums should promote the "high standards" of taste or offer educational services to the general public. It appears as if the role of education has increased substantially
over the past 40 years. In Cunningham and Merriam's *Handbook of Adult
Continuing Education* there are three basic issues facing museums currently:
one, the redefinition of the role of education that is taking place; two, the
need to be responsive to the users' need of museums, particularly involving
special groups like the adult learner; and three, the utilization of new tech-
nologies for effective education which is currently taking place. There are
several issues at stake here when addressing the role of education during the
Black Arts Movement, of which two stand out. First is the unique role of
African American artistic expression; second, the role of museums, especially
Black museums, and their function, and how both the artist and institution
attempt to use art to address social issues.

An issue concerning all educational programs serving African Americans
is whether professionals are able to successfully meet the needs of their population, utilizing theoretical perspectives and instructional methodology
appropriate for adult learners. In this instance it would be necessary for both
Africana Studies scholars and museum curators and educators to use an interdisciplinary approach to research and praxis related to presenting Black Art
that meaningfully explores the Black experience. The Black Arts Movement
represented the synthesis of various functions: community education of social
issues, artistic expression and appreciation, and involving African American
community residents. The degree of success is difficult to measure and would
prove fertile ground for a larger study. Yet, it is apparent that in the 1960s,
as during the Harlem Renaissance, issues of artistic expression and politics

were addressed in many African American communities by individuals and institutions attempting to realize the slogan of "Black Power!" in a pragmatic way at the dawn of the post–Civil Rights era in the United States.

Notes

1. M.C. Chobot, "Public Libraries and Museums," in *Handbook of Adult Continuing Education,* eds. S.B. Merriam and P.M. Cunningham (San Francisco: Jossey-Bass, 1990), 376.

2. K. Rawlins, "Educational Metamorphosis of the American Museum," *Studies in Art Education* 7 (1978).

3. Ibid.

4. Ibid., 9.

5. I. Karp, C.M. Kreamer, and S.D. Lavine, eds., *Museums and Communities: The Politics of Popular Culture* (Washington, D.C.: American Association of Museums and the Smithsonian Institution Press, 1992), 329.

6. Ibid.

7. S. Mayer and N. Berry, eds., *Museum Education: History, Theory and Practice* (Reston, Va.: The National Art Education Association, 1989), 196–197.

8. B. Collier-Thomas, "An Historical Overview of Black Museums and Institutions with Museums Functions: 1800–1980," *Negro History Bulletin* 44, 3 (1981): 56.

9. Ibid.

10. Ibid., 58.

11. P.F. Delargy, "Public Schools and Community Education," in *The Handbook of Adult and Continuing Education,* 289.

12. B.L. Lovett, "Black Adult Education during the Civil War," in *Education of the African American Adult* (Westport, Conn.: Greenwood), 40.

13. E.L. Ihle, "Education of the Free Blacks before the Civil War" in *Education of the African American Adult,* 11–13.

14. R.E. Butchart, "Schooling, for a Freed People: The Education of Adult Freedmen, 1861–1871" in ibid., 47–50.

15. J.H. Franklin and A. Moss, *From Slavery to Freedom* (New York: McGraw-Hill, 1994), 319–320.

16. M. Karenga, *Introduction to Black Studies* (Los Angeles: University of Sankore Press, 1994), 5.

17. Karenga, *Introduction to Black Studies,* 160.

18. Ibid., 394–395.

19. Ibid., 397.

20. L.S. Williams, "Black Communities and Adult Education: YMCA, YWCA, and Fraternal Organizations," in *Education of the African American Adult,* 136.

21. Malcolm X, *By Any Means Necessary* (New York: Pathfinder, 1992, 2nd edition), 45.

22. L. Neal, *Visions of a Liberated Future: Black Arts Movement Writings* (New York: Thunder's Mouth Press, 1989), ix.

23. Malcolm X, *By Any Means Necessary,* 55.

24. Ibid., 55–56.

25. Karenga, *Introduction to Black Studies,* 10.

26. M. Karenga, *Kawaida Theory* (Inglewood, Cal.: Kawaida Publications, 1980) 65.

27. J.E. Thompson, *Dudley Randall, Broadside Press, and the Black Arts Movement in Detroit, 1960–1995.* (Jefferson, N.C.: McFarland, 1999), 24.

28. Karenga, *Kawaida Theory*, 65.
29. L. Neal, "The Social Background of the Black Arts Movement," in *The Black Scholar* 18, 1 (1987): 12.
30. Ibid., 13.
31. Ibid., 13–14.
32. Ibid., 15–16.

References

Collier-Thomas, B. (1981). "An Historical Overview of Black Museums and Institutions with Museums Functions 1800–1980." *Negro History Bulletin* 44, 3: 56–58.
Delargy, P.F. (1990). "Public Schools and Community Education" in *The Handbook of Adult Education,* eds. S.B. Merriam and P.M. Cunningham. San Francisco: Jossey-Bass.
Fleming, John E. (1994). "Afro-American History, Museums and the American Ideal." *The Journal of American History* 81, 3: 1020–1026.
Franklin, J.H. and A. Moss (1994). *From Slavery to Freedom.* 7th ed. New York: McGraw-Hill.
Karenga, M. (1980). *Kawaida Theory: An Introductory Outline.* Inglewood, Calif.: Kawaida Publications.
_____ (1994). *Introduction to Black Studies.* 2nd ed. Los Angeles: University of Sankore Press.
Karp, I., C.M. Kreamer, and S.D. Lavine, eds. (1992). *Museums and Communities: The Politics of Popular Culture.* Washington, D.C.: American Association of Museums and the Smithsonian Institution Press.
Malcolm X. (1992) *By Any Means Necessary.* New York: Pathfinder.
Mayer, S., and N. Berry, eds. (1989). *Museum Education: History, Theory, and Practice.* Reston, Va.: National Art Education Association.
Merriam, S.B., and P.M. Cunningham, eds. (1990). *Handbook of Adult Continuing Education.* San Francisco: Jossey-Bass.
Miller, H.G. (1983). "Adult Education in Museums and Public Libraries." ERIC Document service no. ED 231 986.
Muhlberger, R. (1985). "After Art History, What? A Personal View of the Shaping of Art Museum Education." *Journal of Aesthetic Education* 19, 2: 92–103.
Neal, L. (1987) "The Social Background of the Black Arts Movement." *The Black Scholar.* 18, 1: 11–30.
Osborne, H. (1985). "Museums and Their Functions." *Journal of Aesthetic Education* 19, 2: 41–51.
Rawlins, K. (1978). "Educational Metamorphosis of the American Museum." *Studies in Art Education* 20, 1: 4–17.
Ruffins, F., and P. Ruffins (1997). "Recovering Yesterday." *Black Issues in Higher Education* 13, 25: 16–22.
Thompson, J.E. (1999). *Dudley Randall, Broadside Press, and the Black Arts Movement in Detroit, 1960–1995.* Jefferson, N.C.: McFarland.
Williams, P.B. (1985). "Educational Excellence in Art Museums: An Agenda for Reform." *Journal of Aesthetic Education* 19, 2: 105–123.

5. The Congressional Black Caucus: Black Power Realized?

Tanya Y. Price

Abstract

The Congressional Black Caucus, a political interest group composed of the African American members of the U.S. Congress, was officially formed in 1970. This was a pivotal moment of U.S. history following the Civil Rights Movement and immediately proceeding the 1972 National Black Convention in Gary, Indiana. The original 13 members of the caucus were William Clay (D–Mo.), John Conyers, Jr. (D–Mich.), Ronald Dellums (D–Cal.), Augustus Hawkins (D–Cal.), Charles B. Rangel (D–N.Y.), Louis Stokes (D–Ohio), Shirley Chisholm (D–N.Y.), George W. Collins (D–Ill.), Charles C. Diggs (D–Mich.), Ralph Metcalfe (D–Ill.), Parren J. Mitchell (D–Md.), Robert N.C. Nix (D–Pa.) and Walter E. Fauntroy (D–District of Columbia Delegate). The mission statement of the original 13 members was "to promote the public welfare through legislation designed to meet the needs of millions of neglected citizens." The CBC's original role was to act as "Representative-at-Large for 20 million Black People." The caucus has undergone numerous changes in personnel and strategy since its inception; however, its mission has remained the same. Based in part on field research conducted between 1990 and 91, this study attempts to assess the legitimacy and effectiveness of the caucus in the course of implementing its mission.

Introduction

Despite the Civil War, Reconstruction, the implementation of the Voting Rights Act of 1965 and massive demographic changes over the last forty years, upper-class, European-American males continue to hold congressional seats in proportions far exceeding their numbers in the general population. The most powerful house of Congress, the Senate, remains almost exclusively a rich White male's club, with the exception of four former African American members, Hiram R. Revels (R–Miss., 1870–71), Blanch K. Bruce (R–Miss., 1875–81), Edward Brooke (R–Mass., 1967–1979) and Carol Moseley Braun (D–Ill., 1992–98). The Congressional Black Caucus was founded in order to overcome the institutional barriers of poor representation within the 2 houses of Congress. If Congressional representation were proportionate to the actual numbers of African Americans, Latinos, and women in the American population, approximately 52, or 12 percent, of the 432 seats in the House would be assigned to African American members; 225, or 52 percent, of all seats would be occupied by women, and 39 members, or 9 percent, of all seats would be allocated to Latino members (U.S. Federal Census, 1990). In the absence of such proportional representation, in the 1993 House of Representatives only 13 Hispanic Caucus members represented over 22 million Hispanics, 39 CBC members attempted to represent the interests of nearly 30 million African Americans, and 24 Women's Caucus members represented nearly 130 million women. The 37 current members of the Black Caucus have come a long way since the original two African Americans took their Congressional seats in 1869. The question remains, however, if they have achieved much in the way of substantial representation or effected long-term change in the policy process that continues to reproduce biased policies undergirding an American culture and society that remains decidedly racist. Some African Americans continue to question the legitimacy of this group, which in 1970 pledged to represent the interests of "20 million neglected Black citizens." In the pages to follow, I will briefly analyze the changing strategies of the CBC and its members over the past thirty years, attempting to assess the Caucus legitimacy and its significance within the context of the Civil Rights and Black Power movements. Through an examination of these factors, this paper will determine the CBC's success or lack thereof in changing the overall racist institutional structure of social and political institutions in the U.S.

African Americans in the House of Representatives: A Brief History

The U.S. Congress was an entirely white male enclave until after the Civil War.

In 1869, Joseph H. Rainey of South Carolina and Jefferson F. Lone of Georgia, both former slaves, were elected the first Black members of Congress. The same movement towards true political representation brought Hiram R. Revels (R–Miss.) to the Senate. During the last two decades of the nineteenth century the implementation of the 13th–15th amendments to the constitution, along with the Civil Rights Act of 1875 facilitated the election of twenty additional African Americans. As Reconstruction failed around the turn of the century and Whites gradually re-established their dominance with the aid of various racist terrorist groups, however, Black political representation was once again shattered. Black disenfranchisement in the South was so complete that by 1901 only George White survived as the lone African American member of Congress. In 1899 he delivered a heartfelt speech before Congress expressing his frustration:

> Our representation is poor.... We have kept quiet while numerically and justly we are entitled to fifty-one members of this House; and I am the only one left. We kept quiet when numerically we are entitled to a member of the Supreme Court. We never had a member, and probably never will; but we have kept quiet. ... we should have the recognition of a place in the President's Cabinet. ... we are entitled to thirteen United States Senators, according to justice and our numerical strength, but we have not one and possibly will never get another; and yet we keep quiet [Swain 1993, 28].

Finally, amid growing hostility, Mr. White voluntarily vacated his seat. In a 1901 farewell speech he declared, "This, Mr. Chairman, is perhaps the Negro's temporary farewell to the American Congress; but let me say Phoenix-like he will rise up someday and come again. These parting words are on behalf of an outraged, heart-broken, bruised and bleeding, but God-fearing, people" (Swain 1993, 28). White's words were prophetic. Another African American would not be seated in Congress until 1929, the year Oscar De Priest, a Republican, was elected from Chicago, Illinois, one of the first Black population centers established in Northern cities during the Great Migration from the South. In 1934 he was defeated by Arthor Mitchell, a Black Democrat. Finally in 1943, William Dawson (Democrat) replaced the retiring Mitchell. According to Cross, African American legislators until recently "owed their elections to white political machines that used black elected officials to control the black vote." Accordingly, such members were timid and did little to advance African American interests. According to this "plantation overseer" model of political action, DePriest followed the Republican party line, failed to introduce a single piece of legislation, and refused to increase federal aid for the unemployed during the Depression years. Mitchell criticized DePriest for making too much fuss over race and Dawson was considered an "Uncle Tom" by many of his Southside constituents.

In 1945, Adam Clayton Powell of Harlem, New York, became the first Black member, owing his election entirely to African Americans. Unlike the "plantation overseers" illustrated above, Powell "[d]uring the 1960's ... made the powerful House Education and Labor Committee his private fiefdom" (Cross 1987). As the committee chair, much of the legislation he helped pass laid the groundwork for President Johnson's Great Society programs. According to Cross, Powell was instrumental in the passage of education and antipoverty initiatives; however, his civil rights agenda was limited to integrating the Congressional restaurant and swimming pool. Despite his somewhat limited agenda, Powell's bold behavior so angered his White colleagues that they removed him from Congress in 1967 on trumped-up charges of "contempt and misuse of public funds." Although Powell was reelected and reinstated by the Supreme Court, Congress stripped him of seniority and his committee seat. By 1970, Powell had lost political power and his congressional seat to Charles Rangel, who continues to represent Harlem at this writing (Cross 1987, 302–304).

The stories of African American representatives prior to 1970 thoroughly illustrate the intransigence and institutional racism characteristic of the U.S. Congress. Thoroughly outnumbered, unable to achieve substantive representation or to penetrate the power structure, Black members of Congress were ineffective and unable to use rules of Congress to their advantage (Swain 1993, 29). Prior to the institutionalization of the Black Caucus, African American organization within Congress was ad hoc, consisting of little more than a lose network of individuals with similar interests. The sudden enfranchisement of Blacks following the implementation of the Voting Rights Act of 1965, however, sent shock waves through American society, causing the number of Black elected officials to increase and enabling the Black Caucus to consolidate into a functioning organization. The origin of the Black Caucus is usually traced to Charles Diggs of Michigan, elected to Congress in 1954. At that time, Diggs took the lead in communicating with the other two African American members, Adam Clayton Powell, Jr. (N.Y.), and William Dawson (Ill.). As African American representation grew gradually, informal discussions on the formation of a political organization began. The election of three new Black members the year following Stokely Charamical's urgent demand for "Black Power" (1968) had substantial ideological impact. The election of Louis Stokes (D–Ohio), Shirley Chisholm (D-N.Y.) and William Clay (D–Mo.) increased Black representation to 9 members.

In 1969, Diggs called the nine members together and founded the Democratic Select Committee, or DSC, to "facilitate communication among black Representatives and between them and the House leadership." At this time the group was informal, decisions were made by group consensus, and there was no long-range planning, elected leaders, staff or budget. Although the group was politically active, many of its activities revolved around social gatherings. By 1970 the thirteen Black members of Congress had reached critical mass to consolidate into an institutionalized group calling itself the "Congressional Black Caucus" (Barnett 1981, 116–117). The mission statement of the original 13 members was "to promote the public welfare through

legislation designed to meet the needs of millions of neglected citizens."
Although Adam Clayton Powell and William Dawson helped create the caucus, both left office before its official inception.[1] Initially, CBC members
assumed the collective role of "Representative-at-large for 20 million black
people" and followed a largely activist strategy. To carry out this mandate,
CBC members used their office staffs to perform "casework services, gathering and dissemination of information, administrative oversight, articulation
of the interests of specialized groups within the black community, and development of legislative proposals." The CBC also held a series of hearings
around the country on health, education, black enterprise, the mass media,
Africa, and racism in the military. Members then incorporated the results into
the "CBC Black Agenda" (Gilliam 1975, 273–74).

Changing Political Strategies, 1970–2000

An incident taking place on May 5, 1971, illustrates the CBC's original
activist strategy: on this day Representative Ron Dellums of Berkeley, California, along with 4 other representatives, was addressing an anti–Vietnam
War demonstration on the east front of the Capitol steps. Suddenly Capitol
police blocked the area off, arresting over 1,000 demonstrators, striking Dellums in the abdomen with a baton and throwing his aide down the Capitol
stairs (Burger 1991, 18). Although Dellums and the aide won legal compensation years later, this case illustrates the inherent threat activism may pose
to the careers of elected officials.

In 1971, the caucus received its first national recognition. After their
1970 request for a meeting with then-president Richard M. Nixon was
ignored, CBC members boycotted his State of the Union Address. A meeting finally occurred the following March, some 13 months later. Predictably,
the meeting was a "fiasco and a disaster," with Nixon refusing to take the
CBC's 61 recommendations for foreign and domestic policy seriously, insisting instead that his policies were sufficient (Gilliam 1975, 273–274). Amid
the Watergate-era paranoia of the Nixon administration, the president signed
the entire caucus membership to his notorious "enemies list." The negative
outcome of this meeting strengthened caucus resolve to achieve better representation for Black America.

The 1972 National Black Political Convention in Gary, Indiana, marked
an important moment in caucus history, cementing its strategy to work within
the system for substantive change, rather than standing outside the system as
a group of political activists. Several CBC members were active in the convention, especially Charles Diggs, Jr., the president of the Convention Assembly. According to Walters, conflict between Black elected officials and "Black

Nationalists" over the character of a Black Independent Party was a major source of tension at the convention. The Black Nationalists prevailed, to the embarrassment of CBC members, who paid a heavy political price for their role in the gathering (Walters 1988, 143). Two controversial resolutions passed during the convention, one against busing to achieve integration in public schools and another opposing the state of Israel. These resolutions offended important elements in the CBC's coalition, including civil rights groups, White liberals, Jews and labor interests. Immediately following passage of the resolutions, the CBC issued joint press releases supporting both busing and the state of Israel. As a group, the CBC distanced themselves from the convention, despite the heavy stake some members had invested in the convention. The majority of CBC members believed the political price of participation in Nationalist pursuits too high, the benefits "uncertain, distant, and quite possibly, minimal." As a partial result of the inner conflicts and divisions brought out by the convention, by mid 1972 the CBC had replaced its orientation as a "united voice for Black America" with a more limited individualistic orientation, wherein members defined themselves primarily as "representatives of individual constituencies." During the period of time Barnett labels the "collective stage" (Barnett 1981), CBC members "struggled, often subconsciously, to seek an institutional means of collective political action." In the absence of a theoretical or practical exploration in this direction, however, the caucus "simply became ensnarled in debilitating conflict" (1981, 119). The retreat from activism into inward-facing evaluation, however, also allowed the CBC to lay institutional foundations for later activity, including the appointment of staff, the internal structure of chair, executive committee, and policy-oriented subcommittees and the establishment of the annual $100-a-plate fundraising dinner. Some CBC subcommittees, such as the Committee on Small Business, chaired by Parren Mitchell, became institutionalized features of CBC public activity.

Between 1972 and 1974, the CBC was partially successful in compelling Congress to extend Office of Economic Opportunity programs under the Economic Opportunity Act of 1964. The caucus also broadened its support by initiating relationships with national Black, liberal and labor organizations and increasing CBC visibility within Congress. The CBC also began to counter Nixon-era conservatism with its own "True State of the Union" address (Barnett 1981, 121). Amid congressional disillusionment following the Watergate scandal, the CBC took advantage of the early retirements of a substantial number of senior House members. In exchange for CBC votes for reform of House seniority rules, House leaders helped caucus members gain seats on previously "unassailable" committees (Cross 1987, 316–317). These shrewd political maneuvers made caucus members among the most "sophisticated political players in Congress." In the long term, this strategy would enable members to earn the seniority to become committee chairs and finally to take over leadership positions in Congress, further enhancing the Caucus' effectiveness (Barnett 1981, 121). According to Charles Rangel (D–N.Y.), "If and when the Democrats take over the House, the Black Caucus will enjoy four committee chairmanships and 19 subcommittees" (Burger 1999, 25). Dellums, Rangel and Conyers, for example, are three senior CBC members who have been chairs of prestigious House committees.

In 1997 Ron Dellums (Cal.) retired from the chairmanship of the prestigious House Armed Services Committee, after spending a number of years as a member. Considered somewhat of a radical and a maverick among his peers, Dellums led congressional efforts to end the apartheid regime in South Africa, starting in 1971. The bill passed 15 years later, overriding Reagan's veto and helped to bring down the regime. In 1991, he initiated a lawsuit against President Bush for declaring the Gulf War without congressional approval.

John Conyers (Mich.) was the chair of the House Operations Committee for years, and 69-year-old Charlie Rangel is poised to take over leadership of the House Ways and Means Committee if Democrats become the majority party. House Ways and Means, "arguably the most powerful in Congress," controls trade, taxes, health care and social security. According to House Minority Leader Dick Gephardt, "this is probably as close as any African American can come to being President of this country" (Burger 1999, 25).

Another important strategy, coined by former D.C. delegate Walter Faunteroy, involved the lobbying of southern members whose districts included a Black constituency of 25 percent or more to support home rule for the District of Columbia. To achieve this, he sent mailings to Black elected officials and influential individuals in these districts, asking them to contact their representatives to urge their support of the D.C. statehood bill. Faunteroy then followed up with personal visits to these representatives. Faunteroy's strategy was based on a Joint Center for Political Studies investigation concluding that in 58 Congressional districts, African Americans of voting age comprised more than double each member's margin of victory, indicating that African American turnout could be a decisive factor in defeat or victory for the targeted representative. Although some members and their staffs believed this approach violated congressional norms, the strategy was institutionalized into the "Action Alert Network" in 1975. The CBC still utilizes the network to target White representatives from districts where African Americans comprise over 15 percent of the voting age population. The CBC then mobilizes its African American constituency in these districts to retaliate if the Congressional representative votes against crucial caucus issues (Swain 1993, 38).

A third strategy, developed by Parren Mitchell, involved a gathering of

300 experts, or "brainstormers," to discuss policy issues. This "Mitchell model" has now been expanded to incorporate the entire caucus. Each member meets individually with his or her group on a regular basis, and these groups form the model for the "Braintrusts" and "Issue Forums" of the CBC Weekend (Barnett 1981).

As a result of the individual and organizational strategies developed during the '70s, "congressional leadership became far more responsive to black political influence than President Carter," despite the fact that his election was heavily predicated on Black support. By the end of the seventies, members of Congress had begun lobbying the caucus just as the caucus had lobbied other groups in Congress. On occasion, the caucus used bloc voting (voting as a unit) as a bargaining tool to obtain votes in favor of legislation deemed important to the caucus. For example, the caucus struck a deal with Southern members in 1973 to vote for renewed farm subsidies in exchange for Southern members' support of the minimum wage.

The Caucus Since 1980

Since their development and implementation during the 1980s the strategies examined above have proved effective tools to enhance CBC effectiveness. Bloc voting, for example, sometimes with a coalition including the Hispanic, Women's and Progressive caucuses, has given the caucus its reputation as a solid power within the left wing of the Democratic coalition. Cross cautions against exaggerating the importance of the bloc vote, since countervailing political pressures sometimes necessitates that the CBC's bloc contain less than half of its members (1987, 316–317). At specific times and places, however, the bloc vote is an effective tool. The CBC has used its bargaining power, for example, to help pass the Civil Rights Act of 1991[2] during the Bush administration, to launch South African sanctions, to oppose the Gulf War, to overhaul President Clinton's policy in Haiti, and to modify provisions of the Clinton Crime Bill (Price 1994). In addition, each year since 1981, the caucus has proposed an annual alternative budget emphasizing employment, health care and education over defense, crime and punishment (Amelia Parker, pamphlet, CBC, 101st Congress, 1988–89).

Impediments to CBC Political Power

Despite the success of the caucus on these measures, serious impediments to their influence remain. These include diligent opposition from Congressional conservatives and continuing court battles over Congressional redistricting, including the everyday discrimination and systematic harassment suffered by CBC members. In 1994, for example, the "Reagan Revolution" took hold within the House of Representatives as the Republicans, led by Newt Gingrich (Ga.) became the majority party for the first time in fifty years. Gingrich and the Congressional conservatives then set changes in motion designed to undermine the political power of liberals. Among these changes were the revocation of official status for the so-called "public interest caucuses," including the CBC, Hispanic and Women's caucuses. This ruling barred the CBC from using public funds from its members' staff budgets. Also, to the dismay of local D.C. residents, Republications dissolved the House District Committee, charging that it was a "haven of Democratic patronage." They revoked the voting privileges of the congressional delegates for D.C., Guam, Puerto Rico and the Virgin Islands, which president Clinton had granted only one year earlier, and finally, the power of the local District government was severely curtailed and a congressionally-appointed "control board" appointed. These measures, combined, had a serious effect on the political power of African Americans, as well as the ability of local District residents to control their own destiny. Washington, incidentally, is a 66 percent Black city, and all of the congressional delegates, who lack the power to vote on the floor of Congress, are people of African descent. Since all African Americans in congress are members except J.C. Watts (R–Okla.), senior CBC members in line for the chairmanship of prestigious committees were suddenly reduced to "minority" committee members, with limited power. Accompanying the sudden drop in power was the departure of Kweisi Mfume to become the executive director for the NAACP and the departure of three members due to political scandal or redistricting. As outspoken chair of the CBC, Representative Mfume had demonstrated negotiating skills and the ability to keep CBC directives in the national media. The result of these changes has been an astonishing drop in CBC visibility from the perspective of those who live "outside of the Beltway," despite the rise in CBC membership from 24 members in the 101st Congress (1991) to 37 members during the 106th Congress. This significant increase was a direct effect of the implementation of the 1991 Voting Rights Act. The act called for re-apportionment of congressional districts to form "majority minority" districts that would assure the election of a greater number of African American and Latino members of Congress. From 1994, new CBC members were elected from America's "Black Belt." Many of these states, including Louisiana, Florida, Georgia and Alabama, had not elected a single African American since Reconstruction. Political battles, however, have threatened the creation of new "majority minority" districts since their implementation. This conservative "Blacklash" has extended into the federal courts, where conservative Reagan nominees predominate. Rep. Cleo Fields of Louisiana lost his congressional seat when his new "majority minority" district was re-apportioned to include more Whites. Previously, Cynthia McKinney managed to retain her seat, despite the fact that into the judicial branch. In the case, "Shaw vs. Reno," some of the new Southern "majority minority" voting districts were struck down and redrawn. As a result, the CBC has lost three of its members to White Americans. True proportional representation, although a closer reality during the 105th Congress, is not yet here.

A third impediment to CBC Congressional empowerment is CBC members' vulnerability to harassment. CBC members, like all people of African descent, are subjected occasionally to subtle or blatant discrimination, including House employees who refuse to let Black members into House parking lots or elevators. A more serious form of discrimination is the fact that nearly all CBC members have at some time in their political careers been subjects of FBI surveillance, or legal investigation for dubious reasons. Underlining this perception of harassment, sensitive discussions were often held outside Congressional buildings for fear that CBC offices were being bugged, and government surveillance was a frequent subject of conversation in CBC offices. A frequent victim of harassment, Representative Mervyn Dymally (D–Cal.) held public hearings on the subject during my field research (Price 1994, 180). Most CBC members believe that frequent court cases and government investigations were part of a systematic pattern of harassment designed to discourage Black officials in order to make them less effective politically, thereby less threatening to the political "establishment" (Price 1994, 184). The government record on Black harassment, including COINTELPRO of the 1970s, and the observations of CBC members tend to support the systematic nature of harassment. For example, my 1991 research included an interview with Representative Floyd Flake (D–N.Y.), who was also pastor of an AME church in his Jamaica, Queens, district. At that time Flake was fighting government charges that he and his wife fraudulently used federal funds earmarked for a church-administered housing project. Representative Harold Ford (D–Tenn.) was also in the midst of court battles over bank fraud charges involving a political campaign. After several years and hundreds of thousands of dollars, both men were eventually cleared of the charges. Although their names were cleared, time and energy that could have been used representing their districts was spent fighting court battles. Flake said, "I think the government has a general disrespect for black leadership. Black politicians must do their work while carrying the burden of proof all the time" (Glasser 1991A, 3). According to Representative Mervyn Dymally (Cal.) "[Harassment] is a perception that demands the most serious attention because it calls into question the ability of African Americans to participate fully in the process of American self-government" (Duke 1990, 4). The systematic harassment of Black elected officials cited above is an indication that African American members of

Congress are subjected to greater scrutiny than their White American peers. In addition, the pitched political battles over "majority minority" Congressional districts indicate that in racist America, African American political gains are usually perceived as encroachments on White civil liberties, despite systematic gerrymandering and discrimination continually practiced on the behalf of White Americans for over 200 years. Institutionalized racism, then, is a serious deterrent to CBC political power.

An Appraisal of CBC Effectiveness

How do you know this is a Washington function? The only Black people in here, other than you, are serving drinks—Joke told to author during a congressional reception

Over the last 30 years, has the caucus been an effective representative of Black legislative interests? Political scientists, in particular, have explored this question through the examination of objective (voting behavior) and subjective (public opinion polls, legislative activities) factors. Cross, for example, writing in the late 1980s, believed that the CBC were largely ineffective agents for changing the legislative agenda, while Barnett supports the ideal that the CBC effectively influence the political behavior of others in Congress. Swain supports the ideal that Black interests may be just as effectively addressed by White progressive Democrats as they are supported by the CBC.

My own appraisal lies between the polarities of these arguments. It is my contention that CBC influence varies from extreme, under specific conditions, at certain historical moments, to minimal under normal conditions. Nevertheless, it is essential that sufficient African American representation exist at all times to present both ideological and material opposition to the normal social reproduction process within the Congressional institution.

What Are African American Interests?

In order to appraise CBC effectiveness, one must first determine which policy issues constitute African American interests. This is a complex issue that has always reflected African Americans' ambivalent relationship with government and United States society. As Swain points out (1993, 3), African Americans have historically experienced a deep sense of contradiction by virtue of their subordinate position in a society that promulgates the ideology of a relatively raceless and classless democracy with unlimited opportunity, despite structural evidence to the contrary. This position precipitates a deep mistrust of the U.S. government and the democratic ideal on the behalf of African Americans, despite the fact that African Americans have relied on the government as their foremost allies in the fight against poverty and discrimination. Polls indicate that most African Americans support an activist government agenda while simultaneously retaining a deep distrust of government. A 1990 *New York Times* poll, for example, found that 77 percent of Blacks, in contrast to 34 percent of Whites, "believe that it is true or most likely true that the government singles out black politicians for investigations to discredit them." Sixty percent of Blacks, in contrast to 16 percent of Whites, believe that the government makes drugs easily available in poor African American neighborhoods, and 29 percent of Blacks in contrast to 5 percent of Whites thought it was true, or possibly true, that the AIDS virus was deliberately created to kill Black people. African American opinion deviates significantly from that of White Americans on nearly every issue polled, reflecting the fundamental racial divide in American society. African Americans tend to disagree with Whites over whether the economic situation has improved for Blacks, whether adequate job opportunities exist, and whether racism in the U.S. has decreased. While African Americans tend to support government-driven redistributive programs for better health care, education and food programs for low-income families, White support for these programs is considerably less. While African Americans tend to uphold a liberal policy agenda in regard to economic issues including guaranteed employment and a government-ensured living standard, African Americans are also socially conservative. More Blacks than Whites, for example, disapprove of abortion on demand. These seemingly contradictory ideals set the stage for mistrust of the Black Caucus among African Americans (Swain 1993, 11), who frequently criticize caucus members for inaction or for "selling out." As long as morally conservative African Americans mistrust the government and conceive of it as all–White, the less faith they will have in politicians they must depend on to enact the liberal government agenda which most believe is in their interest (Swain 1993, 11).

Swain concludes that the positions of liberal political groups, accepted by over 50 percent of African Americans, are the closest available measures of a unified Black interest (1993, 13). Congressional ratings published by the National Association for the Advancement of Colored People (NAACP); the Leadership Council on Civil Rights (LCCR), an umbrella organization for almost 250 different groups representing women, workers disabled, religious groups, senior citizens and African Americans; and COPE (Committee on Political Education of AFL-CIO), an organization that monitors legislation on a broad range of issues in defense, foreign policy and domestic issues are objective measures to monitor votes cast by CBC members against the liberal standard. According to Swain, Democrats scored approximately two times higher on each scale than Republicans did and nearly all White Democrats were supportive of African American interests, no matter the percentage of African Americans in their districts. Republicans, in contrast, tended to rely on party platform rather than the number of Black constituents in their districts to guide their political behavior. Although most Southern White Democrats called themselves fiscal conservatives, they tended to vote like progressive Democrats on many issues important to African Americans (Swain 1993, 13–19). Although Congressional Black Caucus members rated consistently high on all measures, many achieving 100 percent on the COPE rating, Swain suggests that progressive White Democrats are nearly as effective as the CBC in advancing Black interests. According to a 1990–92 "NAACP Civil Rights Report Card," the CBC of the 102nd Congress voted for 90.87 percent of the ten issues that the NAACP targeted for that Congress.

Although voting participation is the easiest quantifier to identify, Barnett contents that the actual key to power in the House is the ability to shape the content of legislation in the process leading to the final vote. This power stems from several complex facts including party identification, relationship with outside lobbying groups, relationship with the White House, media access, respect among members of the House, committee assignments, seniority, and relationships with the state delegation (Barnett, 122–123). In a 1981 article in the NAACP journal, *The Crisis*, Barnett concluded that the CBC were, "almost without exception, strong liberals and party loyalists." In addition, all CBC members were "more loyal and show less opposition to the Democratic Party than the average Democrat." In 1979 none of the CBC even approached the 23 percent average of all Democratic House members for opposing the Democratic Party vote, nor the 20 percent average opposition in 1980 (Barnett, 124). From time to time, the caucus has been vilified for lack of unity, a criticism resulting from the "somewhat naive assumption that Black politicians are so bound by racial identity that they can readily put aside their political and ideological differences." This is not the case, as CBC members are as diverse in their opinions and judgments as their constituencies are diverse. Some CBC members represent districts where low-income people living in economically depressed areas predominate, others serve middle class African American constituents, and others represent districts with prominent interest groups or mixed racial composition. Members such as Charles Rangel represent the "pragmatic" school of congressional politics, while others are more militant in orientation (Cross 1987, 317–318), such as Representative Maxine Waters (Cal.).

Pinney and Serra contend that diversity has not compromised the cohesiveness of the caucus. To the contrary, they found the CBC to be one of the most cohesive political groups in Congress. Statistics from Americans for

Democratic Action (ADA) indicated that the CBC, on the whole, voted more cohesively than the member's regional or state party delegations, despite the diversity among CBC membership. Pinney and Serra found that districts with mixed racial composition and seniority were the factors that presented the greatest challenge to CBC cohesiveness. Committee leadership, for example, tends to act somewhat negatively on caucus cohesion. For example, CBC members vote most cohesively when a president of the opposite party is perceived as a threat to the interests of Black voters (Pinney and Serra 1999, 9).

In a 1987 assessment Cross concluded that "[t]he black delegation in the House now has a strong complement of educators and statesmen.... [Although] the group has acquired a deserved reputation for strong, purposeful, and energetic leadership ... by any realistic measure the black population, despite its political cohesion, does not have a position of significant legislative strength on Capitol Hill (1987, 309). Although the CBC had members sitting on all four of the most powerful committees in the House—Appropriations, Budget, Rules, and Ways and Means, the African American presence on these committees was "no more than a token representation." Cross also states that "the lineup of the House chairmanship suggests that blacks are not likely candidates for election to the powerful chairs that control taxation, military policy, foreign affairs, law enforcement, banking, and appropriations. In assigning high posts to the councils of legislative bodies, white legislators (both Democrats and Republicans) tend to be racial conservatives" (1987, 314). "No black Congressman has ever been in a position— by virtue of holding a committee chairmanship or other high post in the Congress—to influence, say, such critical matters as the impact of monetary controls on black unemployment, the effect of energy policy on the poor or the enforcement of affirmative-action employment rules in the over $300 billion defense industry" (1987, 312). In order for their Congressional influence to improve, Cross believes that caucus numbers and seniority must increase before African Americans can make important gains through the committee system (Cross 1987, 314). On the domestic scene, Cross believes the group "has not succeeded in becoming a moving force in influencing the behavior of presidents, other members of Congress, or the business establishment." Presidents either have ignored Black legislators or have paid mere lip service to their pleas to move the Black agenda. Department of Justice officials routinely table complaints of African American representatives about the failure of federal agencies to withdraw funding from organizations that discriminate against Blacks. Overall, "[i]n a society that continues to allocate power according to race, black congressmen usually stand by as observers of a lawmaking process in which the nation's programs are moved, shaped, and then either enacted or defeated by whites" (Cross 1987, 310).

How do CBC members assess their own effectiveness? In a series of interviews I conducted with 7 CBC members from 1990 to 1991, all of the members interviewed agreed that their role within Congress was to represent mainstream, Democratic values, thereby changing the emphasis of congressional debate. CBC members were widely divergent, however, on the effectiveness of the caucus. Most believed the CBC was effective in limited circumstances, such as changing the emphasis of the debate within the House. They also cited instances where CBC members determined whether or not a bill passed the House. A minority of the members believed the CBC was ineffective in changing either the system or the focus of debate. Mr. Dymally, in particular, seemed disheartened over the degree of impact he personally could make on the congressional system. After 12 years in Congress, he was ready to retire.

Although Cross is correct in his assessment that Black Caucus members have decidedly less impact on the legislative agenda than many of the White power brokers enjoy, I contend that the CBC has begun to meet many of the criteria for effective House leadership since the late 1980s, when Cross published his study (see chart). President Clinton now regards CBC members among his most powerful allies, and consults with them regularly. Caucus members are also poised to take over important leadership roles, unless Republican dominance, institutional racism and internal controls prevent this from happening. William Grey, for example, was able to achieve chairmanship on the House Budget Committee through skilled political maneuvering. He obtained the position of Minority Whip, the third most powerful leadership position in Congress, in a relatively short period of time and seemed poised to take over the House Majority Speaker post before leaving office suddenly to take over leadership of the United Negro College Fund in 1992. Observers believed that a congressional investigation that hounded Grey for years would have blocked his advancement to the House Speaker post. Since 1987, Dellums has also held the chairmanship of the House Armed Services Committee. From his position, Congressman Dellums was able to encourage the closing of military bases (and to discourage base closings in his own district) in order to free up more money for social concerns. In addition, Charlie Rangel is due to take leadership of the House Ways and Means Committee if and when Congress returns to Democratic hands. Although he died under questionable circumstances, Ron Brown served as an effective chairman of the Democratic Party and a powerful Commerce secretary under the Clinton administration until his death. Although the caucus plays a role in the shaping of bills, in my opinion they can not yet be considered a formidable force in the House (or the Senate). As a result of the increasing numbers and seniority of caucus members, however, this state of affairs is subject to change.

Conclusion: The Caucus Is Our Best Bet

This report has raised several questions regarding CBC effectiveness and ability to shape the content of the U.S. policy process. In the thirty years of its existence, has the caucus constituted a powerful political force that even the president must fear and respect, or is it a "largely ineffective school for inexperienced and uninfluential legislators?" (Cross 1987, 315). I believe that the truth lies between the two extremes.

Since the group's inception, the CBC members have considered themselves the "conscience of Congress," who, unlike most representatives, voted their consciences and supported mainstream Democratic values most of the time without the fear of a backlash from their constituencies. This position may be likened with the "outsider" role that anthropologist J. McElver Weatherford attributes to women within Congress. According to Weatherford, women, who have historically stood outside of the "good old boy" network, have been willing to face up to issues that other members ignored due to their entanglements within that network. This "outsider" status enabled women, as it enables CBC members, to stand alone on certain issues, making statements that are doomed to fail politically but make substantial ideological impact. Unanimous CBC opposition to the Gulf War of 1991 was a prime example of this tactic, used with great effect to express the overwhelming opposition of African Americans to the war with Iraq (Price 1994). The CBC regularly make such stands against the conservative momentum in the country. CBC members, for example, were among the few taking pride in the fact that GOP president Ronald Reagan refused to meet with them.

Having spent one year working for Congress and ten years researching it from a distance, I have reached the conclusion that the CBC have made a complete difference at certain historical moments, when certain political conditions are in place. Ironically, the caucus enjoyed many of its greatest success during the conservative Reagan and Bush administrations, when CBC cohesiveness reached its height and CBC members perfected opposition tactics. The passage of South African sanctions in 1986 over a Reagan veto and passage of the Civil Rights Bill of 1991 and the Voting Rights Act of 1992, as well as the Clinton foreign policy reversal that allowed Democratically-elected President Jean Claude Duvalier to resume the presidency of Haiti after his exile, were formidable victories that depended in large measure on CBC influence and lobbying activities.

Within the normative, day to day functioning of Congress, however, the impact of the caucus is limited. In these instances, the CBC performs a function similar to that expressed by Derrick Bell in his landmark work, *Faces at the Bottom of the Well*. The caucus, like Elisha of the Bible, plays the prophetic role of a voice in the wilderness, reminding America of its Democratic ideals and continuously warning it about the consequences of its failure. The CBC takes upon itself the mantle of the "Real Democrats," and "consciousness of Congress," calling from the wilderness for the fulfillment of the American ideal that America never lived up to. At its most effective moments, the caucus acts as the collection agency that bullies Congress to make good on Martin Luther King Jr.'s yet uncashed check for justice—the one that was returned from the government marked "insufficient funds." In his inaugural address incoming caucus chair James Clyburn (D–S.C.) identified three social justice issues as priorities during the present Congress: insuring that more federal courts reflect the racial composition of their jurisdictions, obtaining a full count of African Americans and Hispanics during the 2000 Federal Census, and "achieving environmental fairness based on scientific assessments rather than political decisions." According to Clyburn, this "is not a black or minority agenda, but an agenda for all Americans dedicated to the principle of fairness and equity for all citizens" (Williams, 16A). Clyburn also called for "the support and attention of those who share our common interests" (Clyburn 1998, 2).

In the last ten years, as the Black Caucus has capitalized on the Voting Rights Act and played the political game shrewdly, it has appeared poised to take over reins of real power from Congress. For the first time, an African American is poised to take over chairmanship on the most powerful committee in Congress, if the Democrats should regain the House, and CBC members are strategically placed on key committees in sufficient numbers that junior members will eventually gain leadership roles on some of them.

President Clinton, and most likely all future Democratic presidents, now realize they must gain the consent and counsel of CBC before making decisions that affect the members' constituencies. This scenario appears as close to optimal as possible in a racist American political system; however, for nearly every move the caucus makes, the GOP parries.

An important moment arrived during the 105th Congress, when Black members came within 12 members of true proportional representation, according to the 1990 Census. Conservative judges appointed by the Reagan and Bush administrations along with conservative legislators, however, changed the rules again, threatening the Congressional districts drawn under the renewed Voting Rights Act of 1991 that allowed several CBC members from the deep South to be elected for the first time since Reconstruction. This threatened the elections of some CBC members and caused Cleo Fields of Louisiana to loose his Congressional seat.

This development is a reminder that in the areas of voting, affirmative action, education and welfare, African Americans are at a continued disadvantage to their White American neighbors. The "Racial State" theorized by political scientists Omni and Wynant continues to adjust, realign itself, and change the "rules of the game," in a manner to assure White male dominance in all areas of American life. For example, as Rangel prepares to take over the Ways and Means committee, GOP party members fight all the harder to assure their status as majority party in Congress is maintained. The caucus has not succeeded in altering or realigning the fundamental structure of the policy process.

Similarly, as elite members of America's ruling class elected through "legitimate" channels, the CBC embody a profound contradiction: they are part of the very system they and other African Americans perceive as their oppressor. By remaining within the system in order to achieve concessions through power channels they risk being pacified by the same system they initially tried to change. In addition, they are "outsider" legislators who, by their very presence in the corridors of power, embody the contradiction of the American system. As more CBC members are absorbed into the power centers of American society, the more they are compelled to play by its rules, to become civil "committee Chairmen," and to resist playing racial politics over and above their functions as party leaders and committee chairmen. Co-optation of opposition indeed plays a role in the maintenance of the power structure (Piven and Cloward); however, it also introduces factors that White American elites are unable to control. As long as the CBC have been present in the U.S. Congress, for example, conservatives were compelled to fight harder in order to maintain their political dominance. As long as Senator Carol Mously-Braun was present at the Senate vote where the formidable Jessee Helms was forced to relinquish his plan to continue using the symbol of White dominance, the Confederate flag, to represent a prestigious voluntary association. Only Braun wielded the level of legitimacy and the audacity to openly oppose Helms. CBC members have been unable to reach anywhere near the level of influence of the aged Jesse Helms, an avowed segregationist known as "Senator no," or to wield the influence of an Orrin Hatch (R–Utah), the current chair of the House Foreign Policy Committee. Due to opposition and harassment caucus members may never take over the reigns of the House Speaker, or have more than a token representation of "one" within the more powerful Senate. As "outsider" legislators, CBC members are visual reminders of American ideals and the lack of their realization. Their speeches and their actions, as a result, have ideological impact that is greater than the sum of its parts. For these and other reasons, White members of Congress, whether Democratic or Republican, progressive or conservative, male or female, cannot take the place of the Black Caucus.

As long as the Black Caucus remains close to the centers of power, however, it does introduce the unknown factor that will eventually escape the control of elites and usher change into Congress, by definition one American institution most resistant to change. As American demographics continue to transform American society and White males struggle to hold reins of power as their actual proportions within the U.S. population declines, rancor within the House and Senate will increase with the rising political stakes. Whether the change that takes place is subtle (most likely), or great (less likely) (Giddens), change will and must occur, alliances must be forged and the CBC will be present to capitalize on them when these changes, however subtle, do occur. The survival of Black America, and the interests of Hispanics, the poor, and other groups who have been subordinated within American society, depends on their presence.

Notes

1. The Congressional Black Caucus is officially one of many legislative service organizations based within the House of Representatives of the U.S. Congress. A 1982 report of the House Ad Hoc Subcommittee on Legislative Service Organizations defines legislative service organizations (LSOs) as a "particular category of informal groups, or caucuses in the House of Representatives ... consisting in whole or in part of Members of the House, designed primarily to provide legislative services and assistance to members of such organizations, which has no official status under the Rules of the House or of the majority or minority caucuses, but receives, directly or indirectly, support from the House of Representatives" (Committee on House Organization 1982, 1). Legislative service organizations have proliferated in the House since the 1970s, reflecting various ideological, regional, industrial, economic and other specific issue concerns.

2. The Civil Rights Act of 1991 was passed in order to counteract several negative court actions against affirmative action.

Bibliography

Barnett, Marguerite Ross (1981). "The Congressional Black Caucus, Ten Years Later: An Analysis." *Crisis,* pp. 116–131.

Burger, Timothy (1999). "A Man of Means, Rangel Is Gavel Away from Heading Top House Panel." *L.P. Daily News,* Thursday, July 8, p. 25.

Clyburn, James (1998). "Remarks, Swearing-In Ceremony." www.house.gov/clyburn/cbc _chair.html.

Cross, Theodore (1987). *The Black Power Imperative: Racial Inequality and the Politics of Nonviolence.* New York: Faulkner Books.

Duke, Lynne (1990). "Black Caucus Takes Aim on Probes of Officials." *Washington Post,* Saturday, September 29, p. 4.

Giddens, Anthony (1979). *Central Problems in Social Theory: Action, Structure and Contradiction in Social Analysis.* Berkeley: University of California Press.

Gilliam, Reginald Earl (1975). *Black Political Development: Advocacy and Analysis.* Port Washington, New York: Dunellen Publishers.

Omni, Michael and Winant, Howard (1986). *Racial Formation in the United States.* New York: Routedege and Kegan Paul, Inc.

Piven, France Fox and Cloward, Richard A. (1971). *Regulating the Poor.* New York: Pantheon.

Price, Tanya Y. (1994). *The REAL DEMOCRATS: The CBC and the Struggle for Power on Capitol Hill.* Unpublished Ph.D. dissertation, Indiana University, Bloomington Dept. of Anthropology.

Swain, Carol M. (1993). *Black Faces, Black Interests: The Representation of African Americans in Congress.* Cambridge: Harvard University Press.

Walters, Ronald (1988). *Black Presidential Politics in America: A Strategic Approach.* New York: State University Press.

Weatherford, J. McIver (1981). *Tribes on the Hill.* New York: Rawson, Wase Publishers, Inc.

Williams, Eddie N. (1999). "Black Caucus As Relevant As When It Started in 1970." *USA Today,* September 17, final edition, p. 16A.

III

BLACK ARTS
MOVEMENT ANALYSIS

The emphasis on cultural reclamation stood at the center of the Black Arts Movement. This era marked the connection between community activists and the academy of higher education. As we saw in Part II, the Black Power and Black Arts movements were the transitional phases of student input to the national civil rights movement. In Part III, Maulana Karenga, Alonzo N. Smith, and Amir M. Abdurahman consider the cultural imperatives of the Black Arts movement. Focusing on political and cultural organizations within African American communities and icons such as Hoyt Fuller, the contributors assess the fundamental concepts of struggle and Black liberation.

As African Americans entered the political arena, their politics were infused with aesthetics; hence African Americans sought to redefine and interpret phenomena from their own sense of reality. As Karenga reveals, organizations such as Us, the Black Panther Party for Self Defense, and the Republic of New Africa, to name a few, attempted to offer alternative political and social mobilization strategies of self awareness. Smith shows how Amiri Baraka's imperative—"The role of the Black Artist in America is to aid in the destruction of America as he knows it"—translated into the actions of the Black Arts Movement in the far-flung locale of Omaha, Nebraska. Abdurahman shows how the respected writer, editor, and organizer Hoyt William Fuller influenced an entire generation of black writers, not only through his literary magazines but through the Organization of Black American Culture (OBAC), founded in Chicago in 1967. Hence Fuller used both political and cultural forces to advance the black cultural aesthetic in the United States.

Together, these essays demonstrate the crucial interplay between arts and politics that so influenced the rise of the black aesthetic in America.

6. Us, Kawaida and the Black Liberation Movement in the 1960s: Culture, Knowledge and Struggle

MAULANA KARENGA

Introduction

In its widespread and enduring impact on Black intellectual and political culture since its founding in the '60s, the Organization Us occupies a unique space in African American history. Through its organizing efforts and its philosophy, *Kawaida,* Us played a vanguard role in the major initiatives of the Black Liberation Movement in the '60s. This includes its important role in the Black Arts Movement, the Black Power Conference Movement, the Black Studies Movement, the Black Students Movement, the Black Independent Schools Movement, the Simba Wachanga Movement, and the development of a new Black theological and ethical discourse (Karenga 2002). This latter contribution culminates in the recovery and reconstruction of the ancient Egyptian Maatian tradition (Karenga 1994, 1984) and the initiation of an original discourse and practical engagement with the Ifa ethical tradition (Karenga 1999). Clearly, also important to the philosophical and practical impact of Us is its central role in the founding of the pan–African holiday, Kwanzaa, which is a celebration of family, community and culture and is practiced by over 28 million people throughout the African community on every continent in the world (Karenga 1998). Likewise, the Nguzo Saba, the Seven Principles of Kwanzaa and of Kawaida philosophy out of which both Kwanzaa and the Nguzo Saba are created, served then and continues to serve now as a fundamental framework and source of value orientation for a wide range of educational, cultural, economic and political institutions, organizations and projects both nationally and internationally (Karenga 1997, 1998). This is evidenced in a *Los*

Angeles Sentinel (Sept. 1995) newspaper announcement of the Nguzo Saba Conference, which drew groups from 37 cities who use the Nguzo Saba and aspects of Kawaida philosophy as a fundamental aspect of their various programs.

And yet, in spite of its past and continuing record of achievement and contribution, Us, more than any other organization which rose in the '60s, is routinely misunderstood and misrepresented in scholarly and popular literature (Karenga 1977). Although there are notable exceptions to this deficient and distorted treatment, the overall problem is pervasive and persistent (for some important exceptions to this, see Asante 1978; Smallwood 2001; and Gray 2001). There are several reasons for this deplorable state of the literature. First, there is the vicious and ongoing character-assassination of Us and its leader, Maulana Karenga, and the willful distortion of its philosophy, Kawaida, by former members of the Black Panther Party and its White and Black allies in and outside the academy. This hostility has its origin in the bitter rivalry and conflict between the BPP and the subsequent *rhetoric of vilification* the BPP developed and passed on in its efforts to deny, diminish and distort the substantive role of Us in the liberation struggle of the '60s (Ngozi-Brown 1997). Second, the problem is also caused by the intellectual dishonesty and laziness of scholars and writers, who, often for political or personal reasons, simply repeat the most available contentions without engaging in a critical interrogation of existing portrayals and the rigorous research which an alternative and more accurate understanding and presentation of the data would require.

An instructive example of such intellectual dishonesty can be found in the numerous books on the Counterintelligence Program (Cointelpro) established by the FBI to suppress the Black Liberation Movement, with special attention given to nationalist organizations (O'Reilly 1989; Churchill and Wall 1988). In these sources there is the usual tendency to give inadequate treatment to the FBI suppression of any Black group but the BPP and to suggest in the case of Us that it was not a victim but a collaborator. This is done in spite of the FBI's stated concern about Us' commitment to armed struggle and revolution, its continued surveillance and harassment of Us and its provocation of conflict and violence between Us and the BPP in order to "disrupt, discredit and destroy" both groups (FBI, 1978, Black Hate Group File 100–448006). In fact, those authors, who are often praised for rigorous research, could not plausibly have failed to note the various FBI memos and reports which state that "subject [Maulana Karenga] is a key figure on both the SI [Security Index] and AI [Agitators Index]," that he and Us are "armed and dangerous" and that the Bureau should "intensify" counterintelligence measures against him and his organization, including working to make other groups and even Karenga's own organization believe he was an agent (FBI File on Maulana Karenga 157–7244, memo dated 3/21/68).

Moreover, when the SI and AI programs were reorganized, Karenga and Us were moved to the KBE (Key Black Extremists) and ADEX (Administrative Index) Priority 1 lists. In an FBI memo dated 1/17/68, it says that Us (Karenga) "plans for a revolution, ... is currently training members in revolutionary tactics and is currently storing arms." Moreover, in a memo dated January 24, 1973, the FBI still classified Us as an "organization whose aims include the overthrow or destruction of the U.S. by unlawful means." And in a memo dated as late as January 23, 1975, the FBI claimed that it had "information which indicates Us is engaged in activities which could involve violation of Title 18, U.S. Code, Section 2383 [Rebellion or Insurrection], Section 2384 [Seditious Conspiracy], Section 2385 [Advocating Overthrow of the Government], Title 22, U.S. Code, Sections 401 and 1934 [Neutrality Matters] and/or Title 18, U.S. Code, Chapter 12, Section 231 [Anti-riot laws]."

Now, one could certainly argue that the FBI was overreacting concerning Us, as the Church Committee determined the FBI was overreacting about the BPP, finding that at no time were the Panthers a serious threat to the U.S. (U.S. Congress, Senate Select Committee 1976). But what is key here is that this classification of Us led to all kinds of brutal suppression and harassment of Us, imprisonment of its members on trumped up charges and the driving of many Us members underground and in exile in other countries (Halisi 1972). This classification and treatment came from local police and army intelligence agencies in proposals such as "Cable Splicer" and "Garden Plot," which also are clearly directed against the Organization Us (Ostrow, 1975). Thus, for some authors to character assassinate Us, claim an exclusive position for the BPP and leave out or diminish the impact Cointelpro had on Us, the Nation of Islam (NOI), the Student Non-Violent Coordinating Committee (SNCC), the Revolutionary Action Movement (RAM), the Congress of Racial Equality (CORE), the Southern Christian Leadership Conference (SCLC), and the Movement in general is not only intellectually dishonest but biased and deficient scholarship in one of its rankest forms. This data on Us, of course, is found in the same place as the data on the FBI's approach to the BPP and other groups like the NOI, RAM, CORE, and SNCC. So one cannot seriously claim lack of accessibility or insufficient data.

In the same practice of intellectual dishonesty or laziness, some writers routinely blame Us for the UCLA shootout between the BPP and the Simba Wachanga, the Young Lions of Us, in January 1969, even though evidence has long been available to the contrary. In fact, it was Elaine Brown who provoked the shootout and the Panthers who shot first (Karenga 1978;

Kitwana 1998; Olsen 2001). Geronimo Jijaga Pratt, former deputy minister of defense of the BPP in Los Angeles, reaffirmed these facts in an interview in *Source Magazine* (Kitwana 1998, 130–132) with Bakari Kitwana and also in his biography (Olsen 2001, 45). Moreover, in this interview and numerous speeches since his freedom, he also rejected as untrue and wrong the BPP's character assassination of Us and Maulana Karenga as collaborators with the established order. Yet in spite of the evidence and this corroborating testimony from such a credible and contemporary witness, many writers retain their prejudices and refuse to even cite Pratt or other evidence in their discussion of the shootout, its Cointelpro origin, and the character assassination which intensified after it (Karenga 1978).

Thirdly, the problem of the sustained denial, diminishing and distortion of Us' history is also due to the White, radical and liberal, political preference for the Panthers. In spite of the Panthers' claim to be nationalists, this was only one of their ideological hats, for they were integrationists and Marxists also. The BPP's use of the nomenclature of "nationalism" was compelled by the Movement; one simply had to be nationalist to be relevant or respected as a revolutionary in the '60s, especially during the Black Power period. Although the Panthers began as political nationalists, Eldridge Cleaver transformed the party into an integrationist and Marxist structure. Afterwards, the Panthers spent much of their time condemning nationalism while conveniently claiming to be nationalist, of a unique "revolutionary" kind. Actually, Us and all major nationalist groups considered themselves revolutionary, as did the FBI and other related government agencies as demonstrated by the documents cited above (Karenga 1966, 1969). It was like being nationalist, i.e., compulsory; one had to be revolutionary to be relevant and respected in the Black Power period of the '60s.

As Karenga (1969, 14) stated, "We see it as a mistake to make a distinction between cultural nationalism and revolutionary nationalism when nationalism today by its very nature has to be revolutionary if it's for liberation." To say cultural, political, religious or economic nationalism is to identify one's chief social focus. But to say revolutionary, radical, progressive or reactionary is to talk of quality of social motion. Any form of nationalism can be revolutionary or reactionary whether it is cultural, political, economic or religious. (For a detailed discussion of forms and motions of nationalism see Karenga's first dissertation, *Afro-American Nationalism: Social Strategy and Struggle for Community*, 1976.)

Furthermore, although the Panthers drew a theoretically clumsy distinction between cultural nationalism and "revolutionary" nationalism, they never produced a nationalist program nor were they prone toward quoting nationalist forerunners or citing them as models, although Malcolm received occasional reference. In fact, segments of the White left preferred this anti-nationalist "nationalism," for it was not rooted in nationalist thought or practice and thus, of necessity, was available for their Marxist and integrationist interventions and contributions (Foner 1970). One should note, however, that as Charles Jones (1998) argues, there were varied approaches to nationalism in the BPP. But whether we talk of a West Coast, East Coast or Midwest approach, there is scant building on nationalist tradition in either their thought or practice and no discussion of what nationalism as nationalism means or brings as a distinct approach to the liberation struggle. What we do have in early Panther documents and later self-exposures in autobiographies are unrestrained and irrational condemnations of nationalism with periodic claims of "revolutionary" nationalism appended.

Us early defined itself as both a cultural nationalist and revolutionary organization (Karenga 1966, 1967). But it is as the preeminent cultural nationalist organization and the source of the leading cultural nationalist philosophy, Kawaida, that it has received its main praise and its most vicious and ungrounded criticism. As noted above, often neither its achievements nor views are presented in depth or with intellectual integrity. Instead as in Van DeBurg (1992), whose treatment of the Black Power Movement is one of the most comprehensive and thoughtful, Us is mainly defined by the character assassination and name-calling of its critics. In Van DeBurg's parsimonious and prejudiced discussion of Us, he (1992, 171–173, 374) offers two pages, with no serious discussion of Kawaida or Us activities. But he follows this with virtually a page of direct criticism and one of general criticism of cultural nationalism from others, especially the Panthers, and a section in the index marking the pages of the direct criticism which is essentially *ad hominem*. For the Panthers, whom he privileges, he (1992, 155–166) has eight pages of praise, and of course, no criticism in the text or as a citation in the index. However, in spite of Van DeBurg's praise of the Panthers and distorted presentation and criticism of Us, he makes some observations which are important and merit revisiting. He (1992, 171) notes that "no group better conveyed the spirit of militant cultural nationalism than the Los Angeles–based Us organization." And after criticizing Us in particular and cultural nationalism in general, he suggests that beyond the pseudo-revolutionary rhetoric to the contrary, cultural nationalism was and is more valid, valuable, and widely accepted than he or the "so-called revolutionary nationalists" admitted. Moreover, he (1992, 176) states that perspective gained by the passage of time allows one to say, with some degree of confidence, that much of the cultural nationalist code was utilized and accepted as valid by remarkably broad cross section of Black activists. All that most required was that it be tinctured with their own essence. Inextricably involved in culture-creation, they found cultural expression valuable both in the conceptualization and in the promotion of Black Power.

He concludes by noting that "when viewed in this manner, the chief preoccupation of the cultural nationalists can be seen as a central concern of the movement as a whole." Indeed, he concedes, "often pigeonholed as one of the more esoteric, even aberrant expressions of the Black liberation ethic, *cultural nationalism actually provided much of its thrust and dynamic*" (italics mine). What Van DeBurg does not say is that Maulana Karenga, Kawaida and Us provided a core and vanguard element in the "thrust and dynamic" of "the Black liberation ethic and movement." A governing interest of this paper is to demonstrate this contention.

In 1996, the Department of African American Studies at Temple University devoted its annual Cheikh Anta Diop Conference to a scholarly evaluation of "The Impact and Significance of the Works of Dr. Maulana Ndabezitha Karenga." This intellectual engagement of the work and legacy of Maulana Karenga, Kawaida philosophy and the Organization Us represented a turning point in the critical study of the '60s. Notably, this thrust went beyond the privileging of Panther history and Panther hagiography which characterize so much of what passes as the history of the '60s. And in doing so, it invited a more critical, inclusive and fruitful discourse on the dynamic and complex process called the Black Liberation Movement of the '60s. What the scholars who presented at the '96 Diop Conference did was offer valuable evidence in various areas of inquiry of the profound and enduring impact that Karenga, Kawaida and Us have had on Black intellectual and political culture since the '60s. This paper seeks to continue and contribute to this ongoing critical discussion, relying heavily on primary sources of the organization and its advocates, and thus allowing them to speak for themselves, as distinct from being misinterpreted and miscast by others.

Self-Conception and Structure

Us and Kawaida philosophy evolved in the '60s and were conceived and constructed in the crucible of struggle—the Black Liberation Movement— both its Civil Rights and Black Power dimensions (Karenga 1980a). The '60s was a time of critical social struggle and sustained ideological discourse about the good and just society, the role of culture, the meaning of Black, the relevance of Africa and the road to revolution or broad and profound social change. And Us played a significant role in these ideological and social struggles. Maulana Karenga called together a cadre of men and women at his house to found the Organization Us, September 7, 1965, in the aftermath of the

Watts Revolt in August and the martyrdom of Malcolm X in February of that year. Us advocates (members) saw themselves as the ideological sons and daughters of Malcolm X and veterans and heirs of the Watts revolt. Maulana Karenga had met Malcolm X in the early '60s, talked with him regularly on his visits to Los Angeles and developed a profound admiration for him and his intellectual brilliance, dedication and discipline. Moreover, he embraced Malcolm's stress on self-determination, history, the right to self-defense and struggle for freedom by any means necessary (Malcolm X 1965a, 1965b, 1970; Karenga 1979, 1982).

Us was self-consciously structured to be a vanguard organization rather than one with a mass membership. What Us sought to do was to cultivate members who were uniquely grounded and committed to the masses and the struggle. To do this, they were to specialize in an area of professional practice and then use that expertise to engage and serve the masses. As Karenga noted in an interview in 1966, "We decided to form a cultural [vanguard] organization which was not a mass membership organization, because we did not believe it could function [as well] if it was a mass membership. We wanted technicians, people who specialized in a [certain] field" (Carson 1966, 12). However, these "technicians" and specialists would not be simply grounded in their own particular fields, but would also be grounded in Kawaida philosophy and be able to show a broad capacity for social engagement.

In this stress on active engagement in community and society, Us members are called "advocates." To be an advocate one is expected to be "conscious, capable and committed" at the highest level. Advocates are taught to constantly strive to be models of excellence at all times. Thus, Us privileged quality over quantity and taught its advocates that each one was and must be a *sigidi*, "one who is worth one thousand," a praise name of the Zulu emperor Shaka Senzagakhona. It is this vanguard self-conception that has led to some assessments of Us as elitist, even arrogant, in its self-assertion in the liberation movement.

However, in an article on the evolving new breed of leadership in the community in the '60s, Us was described, along with other militant groups, as representative of a new leadership which was "intimate with its community," rooted in an activist history, "making attempts to refashion the techniques of [the old civil rights movement] to the exigencies of the cities" and "intensely secular" as distinct from the historical expressions of religious leadership in the Black community (Sanders 1968, 34). Thus, Us sought constantly to balance its self-conception as a vanguard with its self-conception as a servant of the masses, deeply rooted among them and yet actively working to establish an alternative and more effective way of understanding and engaging the world. The essential strategy Us developed to do this was called *programmatic influence*. Through this process, Us would engage in educational, organizational and confrontational activities, for the people and against the established order, which provided a paradigm and concrete support for persons and organizations and thus would influence significantly how they understood and asserted themselves in society and the world. It would help build organizations and institutions in the community without leading them and cooperatively work together with them on organizational and joint projects of mutual interest. Thus, its work in Watts, Newark, Dayton and elsewhere was dedicated to helping build institutions like Ujima Village (Watts, California), the Committee for a United Newark (Newark, New Jersey) and the Pan-African Community Organization (PACO) (Dayton, Ohio) without seeking to lead or incorporate them into the central structure of Us.

In spite of its commitment to being a small vanguard revolutionary organization, Us was compelled to expand internally to create a paradigm and site of possibility which its philosophy Kawaida proposed. To teach, practice and promote the comprehensive doctrine of Kawaida, then, and to provide leadership in and for the Black community, it became necessary to build a comprehensive and expansive organization. Therefore, the advocates of Us sought to build a multidimensional structure which had seven main institutional forms and functions. In fact, an advocate joining Us in the '60s took the *Kiapo*, the organizational oath reaffirming this inclusive form and function saying, "For me Us shall be house and community, revolutionary school, *hekalu* and congregation, a revolutionary party and a nation becoming all in one" (Halisi 1971, 3). In the *Kitabu* or *Kitabu cha Mafundisho* (The Book of Teachings or Doctrine), these seven main institutional forms and functions of the organization are explained by Maulana Karenga in the following manner (Halisi 1971, 3–4). First, Us is the *House of Houses*, "the chief house in which all other houses dwell." The word "house" is used interchangeably with family, but has a larger cultural meaning. For it not only reflects an African orientation, but seeks to reaffirm the communal and institutional nature of the family. The concept of "house" in Kawaida philosophy is based on the African understanding that the family is more than a collective of individuals. It represents both a tradition and a lineage, a distinct set of practices and a network of relations, and it belongs to a community. Therefore, "houses must operate in accord with the values of the community. Furthermore, [the] House and the organization are complementary, and must be built simultaneously." Indeed, "the organization gives meaning to our family existence." For it provides larger identity, purpose and direction for the members of the House, as well as cultural grounding and a context of reciprocal support. But the House also gives ground to the community and becomes in a real and practical sense "the smallest example of how the nation works."

Secondly, Us is conceived as a *community*, "a place where we share common values based on and developed through the *Nguzo Saba*." Here Us makes a distinction between community and neighborhood. A neighborhood is a geographical concept, a place where people live without necessarily relating in a positive or meaningful way. But a community is a relational concept and context in which people self-consciously share a common vision and common values. The central source of this commonality of vision and values are for Us the Nguzo Saba (the Seven Principles) and Kawaida philosophy in which they are rooted.

Us also conceived itself as a *revolutionary school*, a context where advocates learn, "teach and develop theory and practice based on tradition and reason." Moreover, as a revolutionary school, Us was a site of mutual instruction "where each one teaches one and where we train Mwalimu (teacher in Swahili) to be both teachers and students." No organization in the '60s put more emphasis on knowledge than Us as central, even indispensable to the liberation project. For Us, the acquiring of knowledge was not only central to the overall process of liberation, but also the practice of seeking and acquiring knowledge was a form of practicing liberation. One began to free oneself by rejecting the views and values of the dominant society, breaking the monopoly it had on one's mind and discovering and pursuing possibilities of human freedom and flourishing in one's own culture, society and the world. Thus, it is an early and enduring contention of Kawaida, reaffirmed in the *Quotable*, that "[n]ationalism demands study. Show me a true nationalist and I'll show you someone who studies" (Karenga 1966, 10).

As a revolutionary school, Us sought to accomplish several aims. First, it sought to create, recreate and circulate African culture—continental and diasporan—historical and current, and to use it as a foundation and framework for life and struggle. Secondly, it sought to create a new language and logic for understanding and engaging the world. Thus, it put great emphasis on definition and redefinition of words, concept and reality itself. Third, Us sought to organize and train a body of students dedicated to ongoing rigorous research and study of ancient African and modern African paradigms of human excellence and human achievement to enrich and expand the African's sense of human possibility and responsibility for engaging and changing the world. These students would become and be "teachers of the good, the right and the possible."

In addition, Us defined itself as a *hekalu* (temple) and a *congregation*. As a hekalu, Us carries within its collective presence and in the places it occupies, sacred space where advocates "develop and practice the higher spiritual values which promote and preserve human life and development." It is the site for the conducting of ceremonies that the community and society consider religious or spiritual, i.e., life-cycle ceremonies such as *akika* (naming and integration into the community); *majando* (coming into adulthood or rights of passage); *arusi* (establishing a house or marriage) and *maziko* (passing into eternity). To perform these rituals and carry out practices which promote and protect human life and development and speak to the highest of human values, Us assumes the role of congregation.

As a congregation, Us is a spiritual and ethical community, committed to transcendent values, to truth, justice, harmony, mutuality and other good in the world. And because Us is a socially conscious congregation, it is also committed to two fundamental political projects: *revolution* and *nation building*. Thus, it defined itself in the '60s as a congregation which was "committed to revolution and to building and development a nation." To carry out the twin tasks of revolution and nation building, Us also conceived and constructed itself as a *revolutionary party*, "an organization dedicated to learning, teaching and participating in revolution, i.e., quick constructive change through the liberation of our people culturally and politically." The tasks Maulana Karenga posed and the advocates accepted for the revolutionary party were "the struggle to a) transfer power; b) transfer beliefs; and c) transfer technology to its people." At the center of the struggle to transfer power and technology to the people is the essential task of transferring belief. This belief transfer is another way of saying programmatically influencing the people so that they sense, believe deeply in and become profoundly committed to their own capacity and responsibility for their liberation.

This is reaffirmed in Maulana Karenga's 30th anniversary chairman's message, which says, "the essential tasks of the Organization Us is to provide a philosophy, a set of principles and a program which inspires a personal and social practice that not only satisfies human need, but transforms the people in the process, making them self-conscious agents of their own liberation" (Organization Us 1995, 4). Karenga (1966, 17) sums up Us' commitment to revolutionary change saying, "We are revolutionists. We believe in change. We believe in being realistic, but as for reality, we have come to change it."

Finally, Us defined itself as a *nation becoming*, the core and consciousness of a national community struggling to reconstruct itself in its own terms, image and interests. Us defines the nation-becoming as "a group of people who become a community of communities, ..., the chief context to which we owe our existence, our most meaningful reference for identity, purpose and direction." It saw itself as a vanguard organization in this process, laying an essentially cultural and institutional framework and foundation for an emerging self-conscious nation of people. It is within this context that Us embraced the nation-building initiative of the Republic of New Africa and Maulana

Karenga became its first Minister of Culture (Obadele 1975). Although Us did not embrace the RNA's or the NOI's stress on separation and statehood as an immediate viable strategy, it embraced with other nationalists the concept of African Americans as a nation within a nation. Therefore, it found common ground with efforts to develop and reinforce national consciousness and national institutions and above all a national culture which would provide foundation and framework for national thought and practice (Karenga 1976). In fact, Us argued that Africans in America were above all a cultural nation striving to come into consciousness of itself and to build institutions that housed and advanced its interests and aspirations. Here Us made a distinction between state and nation. The USA was, for them, a nation-state or more precisely a multinational state, but within it were many cultural nations. And African Americans were one of these cultural nations, indeed, a key and vanguard one.

Summing up Us' conception of nation and nation-building, Karenga (1978, 23) states:

> we want a body of committed people, men, women and children, capable not only of physical courage, but of mental and moral expansiveness, a revolutionary solidarity, capable of confronting and dealing successfully with problems on various levels in the struggle, a *nation*, conscious of and committed to its role and responsibility in terms of human history, actively and emotionally associated with the continuous evolution of mankind [Karenga 1978, 23].

Thus, a nation becoming is one which seeks to not simply free itself, but to expand the realm of human freedom and contribute to creation of the conditions for maximum human flourishing (ibid., 28).

Culture and Armed Struggle

For Us it was a central and urgent project to develop a model and practice of revolutionary struggle out of the life and culture of African people. Criticizing the various approaches of revolutionary rhetoric and projections, Karenga noted that "a lot of brothers *play* revolutionary; they read a little Fanon, a little Mao and some Marx. Although this information is necessary, it is not sufficient, for we must develop a new plan of revolution for Black people here in America." At the center of this overall revolutionary project was the cultural revolution, winning the hearts and minds of the people, recovering memories and ways of being African in the world and then creating a will to struggle to define, defend and develop the lives and interests of the people. Again and again, Us argued that "the revolution being fought now is a revolution to win the minds of our people.

[And] if we fail to win this we cannot wage the violent one" (Karenga 1966, 16).

This contention is repeated again in an article in the *L.A. Free Press* in which Karenga (1969, 14) criticizes the Panthers for using Mao Zedong's phrase "pick up the gun" without putting it within a framework of revolutionary ideology and an effective program for revolutionary practice. He reaffirms the priority of the battle to win the hearts and minds of the people. For Us, it was clear that revolution required theory and that this must rise out of one's own culture and socio-historical situation. As they maintained, "you can't have a revolution without direction and that direction can only come through an ideology developed for your own situation" (Karenga 1966, 17). Speaking to the stress the Panthers placed on Mao's call to "pick up the gun," Us argued that they had picked up the gun, but the question was how to get the masses to do likewise (Karenga 1969). It was Us' position that "as for guns, we can find them anywhere including on the bodies of the enemy. What is important is for the people to decide the struggle is necessary and they will determine and develop the method and the means."

Us called what it saw some groups engaged in little more than "adventurism" that grew out of "acting out a myth of revolution that they talk about bringing America to its knees and can't even wipe out one police station." Again, Us stressed the need for the political education and mobilization of the masses around their own interests and within the framework of the best cultural thought and practice. This, in turn, would lay the groundwork for their choosing to join the liberation struggle and becoming self-conscious agents of their own liberation.

Moreover, Us argued the importance of the Watts revolt and all other revolts going on in the country and their link to revolution. As Karenga (1967, 19) stated, "no revolt is isolated. When Blacks revolt in any section of the country, it is an expression of the entire nation of Afro-America." The revolts, Karenga, argued were necessary and important steps in the struggle to overturn the established order. He (1967, 16) stated that "a revolt is an attempt to overthrow the system while a revolution is the complete overthrow of that system." Furthermore, he said, "you can't fight a revolution on a local level. It has to be fought through a national struggle."

The need, then, was for a revolutionary organization, Us, and a revolutionary philosophy, Kawaida. In terms of an ideology or philosophy of revolution, Us argued that it could only come from the history and cultural practice of the people. As Kawaida argued, "Black people must understand history and from historical knowledge, we can evolve our own theory of revolution" (Karenga 1967, 19, 17). Furthermore, Us maintained, "You cannot have a revolution without direction, and that direction can only come through an ideology developed from your own situation." Combining this essential concern for the history and current situation or condition of Black people into a single concept, Kawaida's fundamental foundation and framework for engaging the world and informing revolutionary practice was and is *culture*. For Us and Kawaida, the key crisis and challenge in Black life is that of culture. In fact, the advocates of Us argued that "until the monopoly the oppressor has on the people's mind is broken, liberation is not only impossible, it's unthinkable. For what one can't conceive, one cannot achieve. In a word, if you can't imagine reform, you can't make revolution." Thus, Kawaida maintained "you can't have a revolution without culture because culture is the value system that will teach Blacks appreciation for revolution" (Karenga 1967, 22). Moreover, Us argued, "You must have a cultural revolution before the violent revolution. [For] The cultural revolution gives identity, purpose and direction" (1967, 19). Indeed, "culture provides the bases for *revolution* and *recovery*" (Karenga 1967, 14). Within this understanding, Us maintained that "the battle we are fighting now is the battle to win the hearts and minds of our people. And if we lose that one we can't hope to win the larger one" (Karenga 1969, 14), i.e., to change society in a broad and profound way and build a new world in a more human image and interests.

Reaffirming Us' self-conception as a revolutionary vanguard and the revolutionary potential of the people and groups of the Sixties, Maulana Karenga (1967, 19) stated, "We are the last revolutionaries in America. If we fail to leave a legacy of revolution for our children, we have failed our mission and should be dismissed as unimportant." Clearly, Us understood itself as engaged in the widest practice of revolution—a cultural one which required radical new practice in the seven basic areas of culture—religion, history, social organization, political organization, economic organization, creative production and ethos (i.e., collective psychology).

Initiatives and Issues

BLACK UNITED FRONTS

The Organization Us begins its political practice with building united fronts to organize the Los Angeles African American community in definition and pursuit of its interests. It was a founding member of the Temporary Alliance of Local Organizations (TALO), which included major organizations in the area. TALO's major project was the creation of the Community Alert Patrol (CAP) which sought to restrain and end police abuse in the wake of the Watts Revolt. CAP organized a pool of roving cars which drove through the community monitoring, reporting and intervening in police stops of Black people. It followed the police, photographing their stops of Black people and provided persons with cases with legal representation and persons with concerns with legal advice. It is this model provided by CAP that would inform the Black Panther Party later and similar efforts to deal with the problem of police abuse in the Black community of Oakland.

As a result of differing strategy and program, Us withdrew from TALO and began to organize another Black united front which resulted in the establishment of the Black Congress (Carson 1966, 12). This formation quickly became the center of social action in the community and included even a broader base of organizations. Among these, in addition to Us, were SNCC, CORE, the National Urban League, the United Parents' Council, a major educational advocacy group, the Opportunities Industrial Center (OIC), Westminster Neighborhood Association, SLANT, a youth organization, the BPP and several representatives from churches and community politicians. Although Maulana Karenga served as vice-chair of the Black Congress, with Walter Bremond as chair, Us held a distinct position as the group which took the initiative in the founding of the Congress, provided its philosophical framework of *operational unity* and was the strongest member organization in the Congress.

This central role and position of Us is made clear in its indispensable key support for a Free Huey Rally in support of the freedom of Huey Newton, the BPP leader, in February 1968 which the Panthers proposed as a Congress project (*Harambee*, November 1, 1967, 1–2, 8). As Carson (1981, 281) notes in his discussion of SNCC's role in helping to build this effort, "James Forman, SNCC representative, contacted Us. For he recognized that the disciplined Us members were a major force in the Black Congress, ... and that Karenga's backing was vital to the success of the Newton support rally planned for the city" (Forman 1972, 528). Also, Anthony (1970, 73) reports that "the motion to sponsor the Free Huey Birthday Celebration [Rally] was put on the floor by [Maulana] Karenga ... and in those days the direction in which Maulana Karenga swayed was the direction in which the Congress swayed." He reasons that "this was understandable, for Karenga's Us was the best organized and disciplined group in L.A. and the only organization with a uniform ideology and most important with an *army*," the Simba Wachanga, the Young Lions. This citation is important first because in spite of Anthony's obvious hostility and mischaracterization of Us in other places, he concedes the superior political and paramilitary strength of Us. Also, it suggests rightfully that at one time Us and the Panthers were not enemies and on the contrary, had worked together on numerous local projects when the Panthers had a different leadership. That, of course, changed under the leadership of Eldridge Cleaver.

BLACK POWER INITIATIVES

Us' assertion on the national level begins with an invitation by Congressman Adam Clayton Powell to Maulana Karenga and several other leaders to a Black Power Planning Conference on September 3, 1966, in Washington, D.C. (Stone 1968). The planning session included delegates from 37 cities, 18 states and 64 organizations. From these groups a Continuations Committee was chosen with the responsibility for planning the first National Black Power Conference. Among the five persons chosen for the committee, Nathan Wright of Newark was chosen chair, and Maulana Karenga of Los Angeles, vice-chair. The other members were Omar Ahmed of New York, Isaiah Robinson of New York, and Chuck Stone of Washington, D.C.

At the Newark Black Power Conference, Us and Karenga emerge as a major force in what Woodard (1999, 89) calls "the National Black Convention Movement." Woodard (1999, 86ff) rightly challenges Allen's (1969) mischaracterization of the Black Power Conference as a petty bourgeoisie project that diluted the militant thrust of the Movement. As Woodward (1999, 87–88) states, "the evidence suggests that rather than either ending or coopting the militant thrust of the Black Power experiment, the National Black Power Conference in 1967 coming on the heels of a wave of urban rebellions in Atlanta, Detroit and Newark marked the beginning of the National Modern Black Convention Movement" (see also Baraka 1972).

In discussing Us' understanding of Black Power, Karenga stated that he was aware of the importance of "Black power when Garvey said that we needed power in order to demand respect" (Carson 1966, 12). Describing Garvey as the father of modern Black nationalism, he goes on to suggest that power as a central nationalist concern is rooted in Garvey's (1967, 2) contention that "a [people] without authority and power are a people without respect." One of the central reasons for Black power is to command and insure respect. Malcolm X's (1965) concern with Black power also reaffirms these points of interest. Building on these insights, Karenga defined Black power as the collective struggle of Black people to achieve and sustain "three things: self-determination, self-respect and self-defense" (Karenga 1967, 25). In a word, it was to express and reaffirm the right to control their own destiny and daily lives, the right to assert themselves in dignity-affirming ways and the right to defend themselves against the violence of the state and its various institutions and practices of oppression.

The third annual Black Power Conference, held in Philadelphia on August 29 through September 1, 1968, provided an opportunity for Us to expand its leadership in the Movement. Woodard (1999, 197–108) notes this expanding leadership role and the increased national attention drawn to Maulana Karenga and Us. He states that "while Dr. Nathan Wright remained in the leadership of the National Black Power Conference Continuations Committee, by 1968, Karenga was recognized as its chief organizer and foremost theoretician." Among the resolutions passed were those to form a national Black party, demand U.S. withdrawal from Vietnam and encourage draft resistance among young Blacks to avoid their "being used as cannon fodder for [a] racist imperialistic war." The conference gave Karenga the charge to "convene a national constitutional convention for formation of the national Black party" (*Philadelphia Inquirer*, 9/2/68, p. 1). Karenga had told the convention that Black political self-determination must have two basic dimensions to its defense and development. He reaffirmed Black people's right to self-defense, but argued that without development the community would stagnate and eventually be unable to defend itself. Also, he raised his standard call for *operational unity*, unity in diversity and unity without uniformity, saying "We must learn to use every Black man in this struggle" (*Philadelphia Inquirer*, 8/31/68, p. 7).

In '68, pursuing the mandate of the Black Power conferences to develop a politics of Black Power, Karenga and Us delayed calling the national convention and decided to test the possibilities of political organization in a critical city. The city chosen was Newark, and Karenga returned to Newark with other Us advocates to help organize the campaign for expanding Black political power in the city, working closely with noted poet and playwright Amiri Baraka, who had become a Kawaida advocate. There Karenga "spent a great deal of time training Baraka and helping him organize the United Brothers," a key group in the 1968 campaign (Woodard 1999, 109). Furthermore, as Woodard notes, Karenga also taught political organizing, precinct work, self-presentation of candidates and the philosophy of Kawaida. Moreover, he raised funds for the campaign from local Black businesses and national churches for an extensive voter registration drive, pulled together a united front based on the principle of operational unity to wage the campaign, and suggested the name, the Committee for a Unified Newark (C-FUN).

Finally, Maulana Karenga proposed as the theme of the campaign, "Peace and Power," using the symbol of an ancient Egyptian ankh imposed on the Black Power fist to suggest in the aftermath and concern for revolt that peace comes through shared power and if there's no shared power for Black people, there could be no peace in the city. This campaign laid the foundation for the election of Kenneth Gibson as the first Black mayor of Newark and of a major eastern seaboard city. It also created an ongoing process that aided in increasing the number of Blacks elected to the Newark City Council. And in 1994, Maulana Karenga was invited to return to Newark by the city council to receive an award for his critical contribution to the politics of Black empowerment in the city and the country. It is Woodard's (1999, 92) contention that this political education, mobilization and organization process in the urban political areas between 1967 and 1972 expanded the political impact and practice of Black cultural nationalism. Moreover, he contends, "it crystallized in the modern Black Convention Movement under the leadership of Maulana Karenga and Amiri Baraka, who were engaged in forging the politics of nationality formation."

THE BLACK ARTS MOVEMENT

Clearly, one of the most visible and enduring initiatives of Us is its role in the Black Arts Movement. As part of its concern with winning the hearts and minds of the people, Us began to explore the terrain of art as a site of struggle and as an arm of the struggle. In an important piece, which was first published in 1967 in the *Negro Digest* under the editorial title "Black Cultural Nationalism" and republished later under its original title "Black Art: Mute Matter Given Force and Function," Karenga (1974a) lays out the Us position on art as a site and arm of the Black Liberation struggle. Gates and McKay (1997, p. 1973) note in their reprinting of the article in their anthology that "Maulana Karenga's statement of purpose for the Black Arts Movement, anthologized here, is judged by many as the clearest and most accessible statement of the Black aesthetic aims and was widely distributed during the 1960's and afterwards."

One of the fundamental contentions of Us concerning art and struggle was that "we must make warriors out of our poets and writers. For if all our writers would speak as warriors, our battle would be half won. Literature conditions the mind and the battle for the mind is the first half of the struggle" (Karenga 1967, 20). Thus, Us reached out to and programmatically influenced major figures in the Black Arts Movement including Amiri Baraka (1971, 1987), Haki Madhubuti (1973), Kalamu ya Salaam (1973), and Larry Neal (1968, 1997). In fact, Neal (1997, p. 1964) wrote in the '60s that "[i]n Watts, after the rebellion, Maulana Karenga welded the Black Arts Movement into a cohesive ideology which owed much to the work of Leroi Jones." And that ideology was, of course, Kawaida. Jones (Baraka) was greatly influenced by Karenga and Kawaida philosophy and was instrumental in introducing Kawaida to many writers. Val Gray Ward and Haki Madhubuti of OBASI in Chicago also used Kawaida as a framework for engaging art and doing their work and aided in the spread of Kawaida philosophy and the Kawaida aesthetic. But even in more recent times, one sees the continuing influence of Kawaida in the aesthetic discourse of the noted and accomplished playwright August Wilson. In his lucid and important article on the ground of African art and the African artists, Wilson reaffirmed the centrality of cultural rootedness and social commitment to artistic thought and practice. In fact, Wilson (1996, 15) situated himself in the cultural nationalist aesthetics tradition, citing the Kawaida definition of Black Power, saying, "the ideas of self-determination, self-respect and self-defense that governed my life in the 60's, I find just as valid and self-urging in 1996."

The Kawaida aesthetic was developed in the midst of the national discourse on the role and function of art in the struggle (Gayle 1971). Thus, it focused on criteria that would support the liberation struggle of the people. And Maulana Karenga (1974) begins his essay by saying, "Black art like everything else in the Black community, must respond positively to the reality of revolution." Thus, Black creative production or art must not only be technically sound but also socially purposeful and responsible. To achieve this, it must be, at its best, *functional, collective* and *committing* (Karenga 1974, 1997). To be *functional*, Us maintained, art must self-consciously have and urge social purpose, inform, instruct and inspire the people and be an aesthetic translation of the African will and struggle for liberation and ever-higher levels of life. Such an aesthetic also requires searching for and creating new forms and styles to speak African truth and possibilities. To be *collective*, Black art must be done for all, drawn and synthesized from all, and rooted in a life-based language and imagery rich in everyday relevance. "Language and imagery must come from the people and be returned to the people in a beautiful language everybody can easily understand" (Karenga 1966, 31). But it must be understandable without being vulgarly simplistic, i.e., so pedestrian and impoverished that it does damage to art as a discipline and to the social message it attempts to advance. And it must celebrate not only the transcendent and awesome, but also the ordinary, teaching the beauty and sacredness of everyday people and their struggles to live full, decent and meaningful lives. In fact, "the Black artists can find no better subject than Black people themselves, and the Black artist who does not choose or develop this subject will find himself unproductive."

Finally, Black art must be *committing*, i.e., not simply inform and inspire African people, but also commit them to the historical project of liberation and a higher level of human life. To do this, it must demand and urge willing and conscious involvement in struggle and building of a new world and new men, women and children to inhabit it. And it must move beyond protest and teach possibilities, beyond victimization and teach Blacks to dare victory. The best of the Black aesthetic teaches that art, then, must commit the people to what they can become and are becoming and inspire them to dare the positive in a world often defined and deformed by the negative.

SPIRITUALITY AND ETHICS

Another important area of Us initiative in the Black Liberation Movement is in the area of spirituality and ethics. Us develops its spirituality and ethics in two basic ways—by research and recovery of African tradition and by ongoing critical engagement and discourse with Christians and Muslims in the '60s concerning the nature, role and relevance of religion, especially its relation to the Black liberation struggle. Kawaida's contribution to theological, spiritual and ethical discourse in the '60s lies in several basic areas: (1) its insistence on and development of an African-centered spirituality and ethics with a God in the image and interest of Black people; (2) its insistence on the essentiality of religion as a social practice of service to the people; (3) its stress on ethics and values as the core of spirituality rather than stress on theology; and (4) its resultant influence on the thought and work of nationalist spiritual leaders and teachers as well as Christian theologians and preachers and to a lesser extent Black Muslim ministers who used or responded to Kawaida concepts in grounding, explaining and developing their own intellectual projects.

The point of departure for Kawaida spirituality is its rootedness in African reality—historical and current. In a word, Kawaida argues, the spirituality and its divine focus must be in the image and interest of African people. For Kawaida, "the fact that we are Black is our ultimate reality" (Karenga 1966, 10). And this governs Us' self-understanding and self-assertion in the world and thus its theological, spiritual and ethical project. Blackness here is not simply defined by oppression, but also by resistance and the internal creative capacity to establish and develop spaces and projects of freedom, meaning and beauty in one's life and the world. James Cone (1970, 32) in developing his *A Black Theology of Liberation* embraces this Kawaida contention, citing Karenga and arguing that "[t]his work further seeks to be revolutionary in that the fact that I am Black is my ultimate reality," and that "his identity with Blackness" controls his intellectual project. In his critique of the Eurocentric conception of the universal man without social grounding, Cone (1970, 158) again cites Maulana Karenga's (1966, 13) contention that "Man is only man in a philosophy class or biology lab. In the world he is African, Asian or South American." Thus, there is a need to root Black spirituality and ethics in the experience, interests and aspirations of the people to whom they are directed.

In this context, Kawaida insists also on a God in the image and inter-est of Black people, a people in oppression and in resistance. It establishes three basic criteria for a real and relevant God. Karenga (1967, 34) states that such "a God must be three things: historical, beneficial and like you." For Kawaida, to be historical means that this God is rooted and active in a people's history. Here Kawaida is insisting on the cultural authenticity and historical immanence of a people's God. That is to say, it is to insist that a people's God is in their own image and operates in their field of history from its beginning as distinct from that God being lifted out of another people's history. Karenga continues, saying, "we must carve out of our own being, (i.e., history and culture) things that speak to us" (ibid.). And nothing is more important than having a spirituality rooted in one's own historical experience and cultural self-understanding. A God who is real and relevant, Kawaida argued, must also be beneficial to the people, i.e., act in the interest of the people. Thus, "Blacks cannot accept the religion of another people or the mythology of another people and expect that religion's God to defend them" (ibid.). Likewise, a God "like you" meant for Kawaida a God in one's own image as Bishop Henry McNeal Turner (Turner 1971), Messenger Elijah Muhammad (1965) and Minister Malcolm X (1968) had argued.

Kawaida also insisted on the social rootedness and relevance of religion or spirituality through its focus on this world and its stress on ethics as a common ground as distinct from stress on theology, which tends to be different and divisive. In a lecture before the National Council of Negro Churchmen, Maulana Karenga outlined these points above, drawing a dis-tinction between a spirituality rooted in social practice and "a spookism" rooted in fear of the unseen and "believing you're going to fly away without the necessary means of transportation" (*Time*, 11/15/68, p. 78). In conclu-sion, Us sought to make spirituality, above all, a concrete social practice, and an ethical engagement in the project of liberation. At the core of its spiritual practice is the concept of *worship as service* rather than worship as ritual. Thus, Us creates a priesthood whose members are essentially moral teachers—*waal-imu wa maadili*, teachers of the good, the right and the possible, with focus on liberation. The *Mwalimu* is now called *Seba Maat*, using the ancient Egypt-ian term for moral teacher. But their expected practice and commitment then and now are summed up in their daily reaffirmation of commitment as *Seba*: "to be a good person in the world; to be a consistent servant of the people; to be a constant soldier in the struggle; to be a continuous student of the teachings (Kawaida) and to be a committed teacher of the good, the right and the possible."

Moreover, in the late '60s and early '70s, Us began to stress the ethical or moral dimension of the struggle in ways it had not done before, although value orientation and grounding were always a central part of its philosophy and practice. During this period of crisis and reorganization, Us began a profound reassessment of its fundamental tenets and practice. This is reflected in an article titled "Overturning Ourselves: From Mystification to Meaningful Struggle," first published in the *Black Scholar* in 1972 (Karenga 1978, 15–28). Stressing the need for "constant reassessment," the article sees it as indispensable to strengthening and developing both the culture and struggle of the people. Furthermore, it notes "culture must and does give a moral dimension to the struggle," providing a basis for rules, relations, resolving contradictions and acting in the interest of the people (Karenga 1978, 19). Thus, in order to move beyond the current crisis of both the organization and the Movement one must move to create and stress a moral vision of the struggle and the society the Movement seeks to bring into being. As it states, "In order to create a new faith, a new positive force for our people to support and promote, we must emphasize not the physical or pure political force, but rather the *moral and humanistic basis of our struggle*, authority and legitimacy (Karenga 1978, 19–20, 20). Indeed, "the worth of any act or idea must ultimately and always be determined by its moral and social benefit to the people as a whole, not to distinct and contending groups." Here Karenga builds on Amilcar Cabral's (1969, 110) contention that "if national liberation is essentially a political problem, the conditions for its development give it certain characteristics which belong to the sphere of morals." It is this stress on the moral character of the struggle that leads Us to emphasize ethics rather than theology and to begin to frame a common ethical discourse around the quest for a just and good society and world.

Continuing this dialog and discourse in Black spirituality and ethics, Us has continued to focus on the ethical and the need for spirituality or religion to be at its core a social practice to create and sustain good in the world. In this regard, it has compiled, translated and published a sacred text of ancient Egypt (Kemet) titled the *Husia* (Karenga 1984) and compiled and translated the ethical teachings of the *Odu Ifa*, of ancient Yorubaland. Also Maulana Karenga (1994) wrote his second dissertation on *Maat, the Moral Ideal in Ancient Egypt: A Study in Classical African Ethics*, an 800-page work which has become a standard reference in Kemetic ethics. And through these Us has continued to reaffirm the need and value of an African-centered spirituality in addressing the critical personal and social issues of our time.

PAN-AFRICANISM AND THIRD WORLD ALLIANCE

Building on the teachings of Malcolm X (1965) and of Garvey (1967), Us seeks to understand and place African Americans and their struggle in the context of the whole world, not simply in U.S. society. Their first thrust is to locate themselves and their internationalist focus in an active and meaningful Pan-Africanism and then to expand their activities to domestic and international alliances with other oppressed and progressive peoples. Us understands Pan-Africanism as a global project rather than simply a continental one. Its position is that "as Pan-Africanists we must build Pan-Africanism as a global project, not just a continental one (Karenga 1980, 72–73). Secondly, Us argues that Pan-Africanism is above all a practice, even though it has the emotional dimension of a common sense of belonging together, of a common origin of history, of common struggle and common projects to free African people—continental and diasporan—harness their human and material resources and enable them to push their lives forward and live full and meaningful lives.

In his public lecture at the Second World Black and African Festival of Arts and Culture (FESTAC) in Lagos Nigeria, Maulana Karenga (1977) summed up Us' position on Pan-Africanism. Serving as chair of the USA delegation to FESTAC, Maulana Karenga began his public lecture by asserting the world community dimension of Pan-Africanism as distinct from its continental dimensions. He (1977, 89) said, "We meet here as a world community of Africans, not just a continent." Delineating the basis for community and common interest, he stated that "the African world if it is anything, is a community which shares a common origin, a common experience at the hands of capitalism and racism and thus, a common need to free ourselves of various forms of rule and ruin." Furthermore, stressing Pan-Africanism as best expressed as practice, he noted that "although the African community is based on origin and experience, its more definitive basis must be the historical practice we pursue to reclaim and reconstruct our history and humanity self-consciously and in our own image." The achievement of this historical task "requires more than anything the mobilization and organization of the masses of African people to take their destiny and daily lives in their own hands, push their lives forward and create a new future."

For Us, Pan-Africanism is above all "a theory and practice of liberation" whose "ultimate objective is the freedom and liberation of African peoples wherever they are and ... crucial to our struggle is an independent socialist and unified Africa" (ibid., 90). But again, it is important to stress that pan–Africanism is a global project, not simply a continental one. For "Pan-Africanism is not limited to allegiance to the continent and it is not nor can it be a substitute for national struggles and the liberation of African peoples in the countries in which they find themselves."

Finally, Us put forth some practical suggestions to build Pan-Africanism. These include: (1) "permanent observer and ex-officio status for Diasporan

Africans on all OAU committees," (2) a global "All African People's Convention" as proposed by Nkrumah, (3) "a Pan-African university with students, faculty and staff from all over the world," (4) Diasporan African Studies in all major African universities, and (5) the adoption of Swahili as the pan–African language and its being taught throughout the African world community.

UJAMAA: AFRICAN SOCIALISM

Kawaida philosophy has from its inception severely criticized capitalism and upheld African socialism. The uninformed or willfully invidious criticism of Kawaida as pro-capitalist or anti-socialist misreads Kawaida's fierce commitment to cultural rootedness and self-determination. Thus, it roots itself in African tradition for a socialist initiative while remaining open to critical and humanist forms of socialism around the world. What Kawaida rejects is attempts by others to import and impose ideas and initiatives from other cultures in disregard for the unique and real conditions of a given society and people. Having read the early and later writings of Nyerere in both Swahili and English, Maulana Karenga incorporated Nyerere's concept of *ujamaa* in the Nguzo Saba and in Kawaida's concept of African socialism. In his discussion of his choice of the word *ujamaa* to represent an African approach to socialism, Nyerere (1968, 2) says that the choice was made first because "it is an African word and thus emphasizes the Africanness of the policies we intend to follow." And "second, its literal meaning is 'familyhood,' so that it brings to the mind of our people the idea of mutual involvement in the family as we know it." In a word, "[b]y the use of the word 'ujamaa' therefore, we state that for us, socialism involves building on the foundation of our past and building also to our own design."

Kawaida accepted these positions, sharing Nyerere's concern that an African concept of socialism must first grow out of African tradition and then develop in such a way that it "can embrace the possibilities of modern technology and meet the challenge of life in the [modern] world." Nyerere (1968, 1–32) goes on to discuss some of the defining aspects of African socialism including the centrality of the human person and issues of human dignity, development and equality, democracy, shared work and wealth, collective ownership of the means of production and the stress on cooperative values which culminate in a profound commitment to serve in the interest of the common good and mutual benefit of all. These essential concepts would be infused into the Kawaida understanding of *ujamaa* not only as a principle of the Nguzo Saba, but also as a fundamental part of Us' social thought and practice.

Within this broad framework of African socialist thought, Us linked political and economic freedom, arguing that "you cannot have political freedom without an economic base" (Karenga 1967, 25). In fact, "A man who is not economically free is still a slave" (ibid., 24). The question then evolves of what economic system will meet the needs of African people. Us chooses *ujamaa*, African socialism, and rejects capitalism as a "Eurocentric approach rooted in exploitation, competitiveness and vulgar individual[istic] concept," Karenga (1967, 25) argued. "Blacks can only reach a stage of economic force through a co-operative economic system." Moreover, "capitalism is based on the belief that competition is more valid than cooperation." However, "we believe man works better with maximum cooperation" and that "Black economics must benefit the maximum amount of the community."

Seeking to build institutions which house and advance the aspirations for cooperative efforts in the interest of common good, Us began to build cooperative projects within and outside the organization and inspired and assisted others in doing likewise. Its role in naming and collectively planning and brining to completing Ujima Village, a Los Angeles housing community, was pursued in this spirit. Likewise, Us' work with other community groups and persons to plan and build institutions such as the Kedren Community Mental Health Center; Mafundi Institute, a center for the arts; the Brotherhood Crusade, a community funding agency; and the Black Congress were conceived and carried out in the spirit of familyhood and community which Us interpreted as the core meaning of *ujamaa*.

THIRD WORLD ALLIANCE

From its earliest days, Us found common cause with the peoples of color of the world. This posture evolves first from Maulana Karenga's early appreciation of the culture and identification with the struggles of people of color. Also, it draws from reading the Messenger Elijah Muhammad's concept of the original people as all people of color, with Black people playing a special vanguard role in history and from Malcolm X's emphasis on the Bandung Conference of peoples of color who recognized commonalities in their situation vis-à-vis the European world and found common cause in their struggles against colonial, imperialist and racist domination (Muhammad 1965; Malcolm X 1965b, 5–6). But it also evolves from an ongoing dialog in the movement about the Third World, its common ground of oppression and resistance, and the shared understanding that the Third World, the peoples of color, the have-nots, and the oppressed represented the rising tide of history, the central source of revolution in the world. This consciousness and commitment is evident in an article in 1973 titled "Strategy for Struggle." In it, Karenga (1973, 49) says,

> We must learn to link issues and struggles and sees that the issue of wel-
> fare is linked to imperialist wars and with the struggle at Wounded Knee
> and that peace and freedom, Coachella Valley and Vietnam, Spanish
> Harlem and Johannesburg and all the struggles for liberation, independ-
> ence and revolution in Africa, Asia and Latin America (and North Amer-
> ica) are all interconnected and interrelated, all historical and heroic
> opposition to the same source of oppression and exploitation.

Thus, there is an ongoing need to build coalitions and alliances in the ongoing struggle for liberation and ever-higher levels of human life.

On the national level, this translated as building alliances with Latinos,
Native Americans and Asian activists and organizations, forming a Third
World Committee as a standing committee within Us as well as the Olmec
Committee, which studied Spanish and Latino culture; translated literature
from Spanish to English, and researched links between Blacks and Latinos.
Moreover, Karenga trained Black and Brown organizers at the Social Action
Training Center (SATC), teaching Kawaida methods of organizing the masses
around their own interests (Karenga 1977). Furthermore, Us built cooperative relations with the Brown Berets, led by David Sanchez; and La Cruzada
Para la Justicia (the Crusade for Justice), led by Rodolfo (Corky) Gonzales;
and supported and rallied with the United Farm Workers Union in its historic struggles to unionize farm workers. Us also built an alliance with the
Alliance Federal de Pueblos Libres (the Federal Alliance of Free Peoples), led
by Reies Tijerina. In fact, Us, SNCC, the Black Congress and the Black Panther Party of Southern California (not associated with the BPP of Oakland)
traveled to Albuquerque, New Mexico, in the summer of '67 to sign a historic Treaty of Peace, Harmony and Mutual Assistance with the Alianza who
initiated it, La Crusada and the Hopi Nation represented by Tomas Banya-
cya, its spiritual leader (Nabakov 1969, 222, 224). Maulana Karenga, speaking in Spanish, stressed themes of common ground, severely criticized White
racism and called for an ongoing operational unity in the midst of repeated
applause and *gritos* of approval. These were themes of commonalities of interest and struggle he would stress in later writings (Karenga 1995, 1996).

On the international levels, Us supported the liberation struggles of all
peoples of color. Among those of special importance to them were the liberation struggles of the Algerian, Palestinian and Vietnamese peoples. These
struggles became, along with the Cuban and Chinese revolutions, models for
study and emulation. Classes and study groups organized around these struggles were of great importance to Us' understanding of itself as revolutionary
organization and its role in social transformation.

Given the Vietnam War, Us focused on Vietnam in a special way. First,
Us members openly resisted the draft. As early as 1966, Us members refused
to report for induction in the military and filed petitions of habeas corpus in

federal court, arguing that they were colonial subjects and not really citizens, given the history of African enslavement and denial of civil and human rights to them (*Muhammad Speaks*, 6). This position of "non-citizenship," which was one of the main reasons for rejection of the draft, was reaffirmed by Us in a 1967 petition to the United Nations criticizing the lack of civil rights and the violation of human rights of Africans in the U.S. It represented a broad consensus in the movement and was signed by Maulana Karenga, representing Us, along with other activists such as James Boggs, Rap Brown, Stokely Carmichael (Kwame Ture), Florence Kennedy, Imari Obadele, Ella Collins, James Forman, Mae Mallory, John Henrik Clarke, Molefi Asante and Amiri Baraka.

Secondly, Us rejected going to war against the Vietnamese people based on two principles of the *Nguzo Saba—Kujichagulia* (Self-Determination) and *Kuumba* (Creativity). In its "Statement on the Vietnam War" (1967), Us argued that as African Americans struggling for self-determination themselves, morally it could not and would not fight to deny self-determination to the Vietnamese people. Secondly, the statement said that the principle of *Kuumba* required the preservation and protection of human life as opposed to the taking of it, especially in an unjust war. In his presentation of the Kawaida position at the first African Congress meeting in Atlanta, *Kasisi* (priest) Nakawa Sadikifu, the chair of Us' Anti-Draft Committee (1970, 393–397), reaffirmed the Kawaida moral obligation to resist the draft, placing it within the dual Us thrust of revolutionary struggle and nation-building cited above in the discussion of Us' self-conception.

In an interview, Maulana Karenga explained Us' resistance to the draft in an additional way. He rooted it in the principle of reciprocal obligation between state and citizen. He argued that Black people have no obligation to defend or fight for a state which does not defend them from the racist violence in U.S. society. He states that

> A man would be a fool to defend a government in Vietnam which refused to defend him in Georgia, Alabama, and Mississippi and in the streets of Los Angeles. I don't think the white man can expect us to be fighting in Japan and running in Georgia. I was under the impression that whatever the state asks me to do, it must do the same thing for me. Now, I ask for protection from the state and the state hasn't given me protection. So I don't feel I can protect the state [Carson 1966, 12].

Us also provided draft resistance and counseling to the larger community and began to counsel soldiers active in Vietnam. Us offered reinforcement for soldiers in Vietnam, and several chapter of Us were formed there. Us provided these soldiers with literature and integrated them in Us after their return. In a formation in Danang, members organized under the black, red and green flag of Us, based on the National Flag colors by Marcus Garvey, red, black and green. Taking the Simba self-understanding as spear to the oppressor and shield to the people, they used crossed spears and a shield at the center of the flag. They also wore the Us *talasimu* and saluted in the Zulu style of the Simba, crossing and hitting the chest with the fist. Moreover, they built tight brotherhoods based on Kawaida teachings and a sense of racial and cultural solidarity which evolved from this (Terry 1970, 13–14; Van DeBurg 1993, 104).

THE PAN-AFRICAN HOLIDAY, KWANZAA AND THE NGUZO SABA

Of all the contributions of Us, none is more well known or widespread than Kwanzaa and the Nguzo Saba. Kwanzaa, a pan–African holiday created by Maulana Karenga in 1966, is a celebration of family, community and culture (Karenga 1998). Carrying out a central goal of Us to create, recreate and circulate African culture, Karenga developed a seven-day holiday which would serve three basic functions. First, it would reaffirm African Americans' and other Africans' rootedness in African culture. Second, it would provide a time and occasion at which Africans throughout the world African community could come together to reinforce the bonds between them and celebrate the wonder and obligation of being African in the world. And thirdly, Kwanzaa was created to introduce and reaffirm the importance of African communitarian values, especially the Nguzo Saba.

Kwanzaa is organized around five basic activities: (1) the ingathering of the people to reinforce the bonds between them; (2) a special expression of reverence for the creator and creation in thanks for the good harvesting and recommitment to preserve the earth which produces it; (3) recommemoration of the past in the practice of honoring the ancestors, learning the lessons of history and raising models of human excellence and achievement for emulation; (4) recommitment to the highest of African ideals—the Nguzo Saba, truth, justice, loving-kindness, respect for the dignity and rights of the human person and the integrity of the environment; and (5) celebration of the good.

At the heart of the celebration are the Nguzo Saba around which the seven days of Kwanzaa (December 16–January 1) are organized. What Us seeks to do here is bring forth values and views which represent and reinforce the best of African community and culture. The Nguzo Saba were and are embraced not simply as the Seven Principles of Kwanzaa, but as a framework and foundation for cultural grounding and value orientation. Haki Madhubuti (1973, 79) stated that "[t]he Nguzo Saba in its righteous direction and pan–African scope has moved across this nation like honey giving energy to the brain." He goes on to say that "of all the concepts that Maulana Karenga has initiated, the Seven Principles is the most used! Most of the independent Black institutions and all the Black nationalist organizations have used the Nguzo Saba in one way or another." Stressing that the Nguzo Saba fits within a larger philosophical and political framework, he states that "it must be understood that the Seven Principles are only a part—a major part—of an entirely new revolutionary movement: Kawaida."

In September 2000, Us celebrated its 35th anniversary by holding a conference: "Nguzo Saba 2000: Bringing Good Into the World" (Organization Us 1995). It invited groups from around the country who do not belong to Us, but use Kawaida and the Nguzo Saba as cultural grounding and value orientation. Groups from thirty-five cities came, representing numerous kinds of programs and projects, i.e., independent schools, Black student unions, rites-of-passage programs, economic cooperatives, political organizations, religious formations, cultural centers, and various other kinds of community organizations and institutions. Moreover, it was a gathering of veteran activists who had not only helped build the world-wide presence of Kwanzaa, but also had integrated the Nguzo Saba in their local, national and international projects.

MALE-FEMALE RELATIONS

Another area of dishonest scholarship in the discourse on Us is in the area of male-female relations. This is expressed in several ways. First, these writers usually quote one or two chauvinist passages written in 1967 and refuse to engage literature as early as 1969 by the women of Us, the Malaika, and a 1975 essay by Maulana Karenga which marked a clear transition of the Organization Us from a position of male dominance to one of true complementarity based on equal dignity, worth and rights, mutual respect and shared responsibility in love and struggle among men and women (Malaika 1969; Karenga 1975). Nor do they cite or engage other essays which focus on male-female relations and clearly reflect a consistent position on the equal dignity and rights of women and men (Karenga 1975b, 1975c, 1978, 1979, 1992). Although she does not seriously engage Us' abundant literature on the subject and has an intellectually limited and limiting view of nationalism and complementarity, E. Frances White (1990) does admit the change in Us' position on the question of male-female relations. Moreover, she does not understand or engage the mutually beneficial dialog and exchange of women and men in the organization which led to this transformation.

Secondly, these writers failed to compare Us' male-focused discourse with organizations of the time, painting Us in the whitest terms and hiding or trying to reinterpret positively the Panther position and practice. In fact, virtually all groups in the '60s were male-focused and male-dominant—Christian, Jewish, Muslim, leftist, Marxist, nationalist, Panthers, Us, etc. Us' often-quoted early equation of "femininity and submission" and the advocacy of male rule was certainly wrong and eventually rejected as not representing the best of African morality and negative to the interest of the liberation struggle. Likewise, the BPP was also male dominant, saw the movement as a quest for masculinity, called their female members "Pantherettes," talked of women's power as "p-s-y power" and encouraged their women to engage in "socialistic f-ing" for the benefit of the brothers and the good of the Movement (Cleaver 1969; Foner 1970; Newton 1971; Seale 1991). But like Us, they also began to put forth a more egalitarian position based on response to internal and external factors which demanded change. (See also some comments on male-female relations from some Panther women who reaffirm the Black woman's role as essentially a supporter of Black men and her need to reject White concepts of equality which are frequently used as criticism of Us in Green 1968 and Bartholomew 1968.) Matthews (1998, 287–288) concedes that "their argument for complementary roles closely mirrored the positions taken by Karenga and other cultural nationalists," but refuses to acknowledges the same internal dialog and criticism and subsequent change in Us which she claims for the BPP in spite of the record.

Nevertheless, in spite of limitations imposed by male chauvinism, the women of Us carved out spaces of meaning and power within the organization even in the early years. Indeed, as in all Black organizations, the women of Us were indispensable to the organization's functioning, maintenance and development. They participated on all committees except the Simba committee, and that changed in the late '60s. A review of documents show that women headed such committees as education, legal affairs, archives, Third World, and public relations. Although these were clearly vital leadership roles, as in all groups, the women of Us' record of activity and achievement suffered also from the male-centered media image of the group—which was projected by the men and then cultivated and encouraged by the media, which itself is rooted in a male-dominated and male-privileged society.

Women of Us began in the late '70s to revisit and review their role and responsibilities in the organization, their conversations on male-female relations, the personal and social dimensions of organizational politics, and their contributions to Us and the Black Liberation Movement as a whole. The process of critical review was organized around ongoing conversations within the organization as well as within the Senut (the Sisterhood) Society and is yielding documents soon to be published. The text of this section is drawn especially from these conversations and documents.

The dialog on gender relations evolved in the context of an internal reassessment conditioned by four basic factors: (1) the increasing state suppression of the organization, especially its male members, who were increasingly put into captivity or went underground and into exile to escape the suppression; (2) the emergence of women in new and expanded administrative, security and public roles and the resultant reassessment of formerly defined roles and responsibilities; (3) the engaging of the overall movement discourse about male-female relations; and (4) the resultant need for Us to address these issues in terms of its self-conception as both a cultural nationalist and revolutionary organization within the framework of Kawaida in its expanding definition as "an ongoing synthesis of the best of African thought and practice in constant exchange with the world!"

Although the internal conversation about male-female relations was an ongoing process, the heightened suppression of the organization and its male leaders presented a crisis for the entire organization—women and men. And it thus required a joint effort to meet the crisis and overcome it toward the end of 1968 and even more so in early '69. After the UCLA shootout, the local, state and national police agencies increased their efforts to disrupt Us' relations with the community and eventually destroy Us itself through a policy of "alienate, isolate and then eliminate." The policy of fostering division and conflict between Us and the BPP leads to the shootout and the contradictory practice of the BPP calling the police "pigs" and Us members "agents" while cooperating themselves with the police to capture and imprison Us members. In fact, as the *Los Angeles Sentinel* reports, the Panthers provided names, photos, addresses and other information on Us members to assist the police effort to capture Us members and in the process to "disrupt, destroy and neutralize" the organization. It is indeed an irony of history that the group accusing others of collaborating with the police, actually engaged in it themselves in order to destroy their rivals.

To counter this suppression, members of Us began to go underground and in exile. Moreover, men and women began to take *noms de guerre* (war names) in order to hide their identities in the face of the police onslaught. To maintain the daily operation of the organization and its community work, women began to emerge as internal and public leaders and to assume new and expanded roles in administrative, security and public spheres. They also formed a new security structure parallel to the Simba called *Matamba*, a paramilitary formation, modeled on the women warriors of Queen Nzinga Mbande of Angola and those of Dahomey (Rogers 1972,

247–250). The Matamba were trained in the martial arts including *yangumi* (karate and other hand to hand combat), drill and formation, weaponry, security procedures for personnel and buildings, and intelligence gathering. This, in turn, led to partnering with men in these activities as well as taking over or being the lead persons in various assignments and tasks. Such a real and fundamental change in roles and responsibilities, of necessity, required and led to new and expanded understandings of and approaches to male-female relations.

Looking back at this transformation, the women of Us point out that it is important to note that it would not have been possible or as successful if the women had not already been knowledgeable in administrative, security and public activities and in fact were already participating in these spheres in less prominent or less recognized roles (Senut 1995). It was also noted that it would not have been as successful without the capacity of Kawaida philosophy to adapt, change and expand to meet ongoing challenges in ethnically grounded and progressive ways (Tembo 1996).

In the Malaika statement "View from the Woman's Side of the Circle," published in Us' paper *Harambee* (4/25/69, p. 4), one gets a sense of the dialog going on inside the organization as well as in exchange with conversations in the larger Movement. The point of departure for the Malaika is the Nguzo Saba, the Kawaida value system, especially the principle of *Ujima* (collective work and responsibility). They frame the change in terms of "the maximum practice" of the principle of *Ujima*, which means that during this period of transition, "The Saidi [brothers] and Malaika [sisters] have worked together in a oneness that verges on symbiosis." Now, this sense of "togetherness in love and struggle" speaks to the Malaika's understanding that they have moved from "minimum" and "medium" practice of shared work and responsibility to a "maximum practice" in which women and men share equal work, responsibility and recognition for it.

The move from minimum/medium to maximum involvement is one not of changing roles with the man, but of expanding them. Thus, they say, "We have done this, not by changing our role, but by broadening the scope of our role." Here, the Malaika are dealing with the problem of defining women and women's roles which maintains their distinctiveness as women while at the same time avoiding the disadvantages which could be attached to an exclusive woman's role. They assert that by practicing *Ujima* in its fullest form, i.e., its most moral and mutually respectful form, they have "proven that Black women do not have to wear overalls and combat boots in order to play an active role in the Black revolution." This is in response to external discourse which argues for or suggests "unisexism" as a way around rigid roles and the inequalities attached to them.

This is evident in their reaffirmation of the early Us position that "equality," which they translate here as "sameness," is a false concept, since men and women are not equal in the sense of being the same. Instead, they argue, "Our concept is complementary which means that you complete or make perfect that which is imperfect." As a fundamental principle of male-female relations, *complementarity* in Kawaida *is a completeness grounded in equal dignity, worth and rights, mutual respect and shared responsibility in love and struggle between men and women.* Women and men do not come to the relationship or struggle as duplicates of each other but as self-conscious agents striving to bring to the relationship and process what is lacking and needs to be made whole. This ideal was, of course, often put aside or diminished in daily practice, and instead concessions to the hegemonic norms of a male-dominated society and organization were introduced. Thus, the Malaika reaffirm the original ideal, rejecting the push for what is conceived as sameness and opting for a distinctiveness with equal status and rights and shared responsibility.

The Malaika note that within Us the role of the woman has been defined as "inspiration, education and social development." They now seek to redefine and expand that role. It will be redefined by stressing the practice of struggle as inspiration, i.e., "new ways to inspire" the men by "carrying on revolution in their absence" and inspiring them "even more by carry[ing] on the revolution in their presence." The stress was first placed on the absence of the Saidi, or men, in the organization and the need for women to assume new roles in their absence. But more important is the contention that the men "are inspired even more by Black women who can carry on revolution in their presence." For it affirms that this is not an "equality of convenience" which is born of necessity and will be reversed upon the return of the men. It is meant to be a rupture with the past and a projection of the future. This is reaffirmed in the statement that suggests revolutionary practice must prefigure the world it wants to bring into being. Thus, they state that this expanded revolutionary practice of inspiration through cooperative struggle "is conducted by Black women who do not have to wait for the future in order to make a contribution." In a word, they do not wait for freedom to be achieved by men but are engaged in changing reality "by working with the Saidi building brotherhood and sisterhood that is not only a preparation for the future, but also more fundamentally an example of complementarity of Black men and women."

Likewise, education is no longer exclusively or primarily education in the context of family, but above all to win the hearts and minds of the people. And they say "in order to win the minds of the people we must go to the people." This in turn requires that "not only must we be educated ourselves, but we must be able to educate the people by forming an unbroken circle between our education and the social development of our community." And this thrust for social development is the multidimensional struggle dedicated to liberating, constructing and reconstructing "a Black nation." At the heart of this effort, the Malaika state that the need to teach the people is to teach by example. "For the best lesson is a good example." And this means that the Malaika and Saidi set and maintain a public example of how men and women should treat each other and work and struggle together in mutual respect and shared responsibility to build the world they want and deserve to live in. Thus, they end the article projecting a "revolutionary woman" who values and asserts her voice, who is distinct and yet in harmony for the good and who with the man has in thought and practice "truly mastered the virtue of interdependence." The range and content of this internal dialog between the women and men of Us is reaffirmed and further developed in Maulana Karenga's essays in the early seventies, especially "In Love and Struggle." These conversations culminate in discussions and documents on Kawaida womanism reflected in a paper on womanism presented by Chimbuko Tembo, co-vice chair of the Organization Us and chair of the Senut Sisterhood (Us) at the 1995 Cheikh Anta Diop Conference, and a later paper on the historical origin of womanism by Tiamoyo Karenga (2000) at the African American Cultural Center (Us).

Building on the organizational conversations reflected in the Malaika's statement, Maulana Karenga (1973) speaks to Us' development of a new and expanded Kawaida position on male-female relations. The article which is part of an ongoing reassessment mentioned below is titled "A Strategy for Struggle: Turning Weakness into Strength." He addresses several fundamental questions raised in the ongoing dialog around issues of racism, capitalism and sexism. Specifically addressing sexism, he (1973, 44–45) notes that a central internal inadequacy of the Black struggle is the unethical treatment of Black women. In this regard, he asserts the need to (1) "especially ... stop denying our women their full and heroic role in the history and development of our struggle"; (2) "reject the twin myths of matriarchy and emasculation attributed to Black women" (3) and; accept the equality with men in all things relevant. He states that "[t]here can be no real argument against the human equality of man and woman, against the need for liberation and revolution to reach and raise to a higher level of life each and all of us, man, woman and child." Moreover, he says:

> We will never liberate ourselves as a people unless and until we liberate ourselves from reactionary and repressive attitudes and behavioral patterns of sexism, male chauvinism and parasitic and perverse pimpism in our relations with each other, and unless and until we build an expanding realm of freedom in our homes and in society in which man and women,

together in commitment, contribution and *creative complementarity* can realize themselves fully and stand and walk in a warmer sun.

However, it is in the 1975 article "In Love and Struggle: Toward a Greater Togetherness" that the fully developed Us position is put forth. In the article, Karenga (1978, 71) begins by insisting on the indivisibility of both human freedom of men and women and the joint effort to achieve it. "Revolution is rank and unreal if it is not a collective effort and experience, and if it does not reach and raise to a higher level each and all of us." He continues, saying, "Our freedom as a people is indivisible and to talk of liberation of less than all is sheer and shallow nonsense." Secondly, he argues that women's liberation is inextricably tied to the overall liberation of the people. In addition to the personal position on equality each must take, he (72) argues, "only the national liberation struggle can fully realize the full social liberation of both man and woman." For this process frees all from both psychological and social constraints. In a word, he (1978, 72) says, "it is in this context of national liberation *struggled for* and *achievement* that the Black woman can and will as [Sekou] Toure tells us become alive to the values and huge creative potentialities she represents."

Here one also finds a repeated call for constant reassessment and restructuring. "It is obvious," the article states, "that we must right now reassess, redefine and restructure our whole value system and view of ourselves and each other. We must alter the concern and content of our family, structures, review and redefine our concept of man and woman, marriage and family and make the *call for brotherhood* extend to include and complement the call for *sisterhood*" (73). Furthermore, the myths of the matriarch, mammy, Geraldine (emasculator), Julia (betrayer) and Jezebel (seductress) are criticized and rejected. The heroic, full and indispensable role of Black women in oppression and resistance is reaffirmed and praised. Likewise, Us' commitment of equality in the fullest sense is reaffirmed while it is distinguished from sameness. It means (1) "removal of inequalities that are social"; (2) an end to "submissive and subordinate" roles of women; (3) "equal rights, opportunities and treatment"; and (4) "full participation of the woman in any decision-making that affects or involves her, whether at home, in a relationship or in society" (73). Finally, Us argues for a genuine "partnership in love and struggle" based on roles of "shared tasks and collective action" and "shared responsibility in life and struggle." In a word, the Malaika point is reaffirmed that at the heart of the struggle to overcome internal contradiction and achieve is the full and active commitment to the principle of *Ujima*, collective work and shared responsibility in love, life and struggle.

Bibliography

Allen, Robert (1969). *Black Awakening in Capitalist America.* New York: Africa World Press.

Anthony, Earl (1970). *Picking Up the Gun.* N.p.: Dial Press.

Arnold, Martin (1967). "Newark Meeting on Black Power Attended by 400." Publication unknown. July 21, pp. 1, 344.

Asante, Molefi Kete (1978). *Afrocentricity: The Theory of Social Change.* Buffalo: Amulefi Publishing.

Baraka, Amiri, ed. (1972). *African Congress: A Documentary of the First Modern Pan-African Congress.* New York: William Morrow.

Baraka, Amiri (1971). *Raise, Race, Rays, Raze.* New York: Random House.

_____ (1987). "Black Art." *The Black Scholar,* January/February, 23–26.

Barbour, Floyd B., ed. (1968). *The Black Power Revolt.* Boston: Porter Sargent Publishers.

Black Panther (1968). "Warning to So-called 'Paper Panthers.'" September 14, p. 10.

Black Voice (1968). "Simba Mission Statement." October 24, p. 3.

Carson, Clayborne (1966). "A Talk with Ron Karenga, Watts Black Nationalist." *Los Angeles Free Press,* September 2, pp. 1, 12.

Carson, Clayborne (1981). *In Struggle: SNCC and the Black Awakening of the 1960's.* Cambridge: Harvard University Press.

Churchill, Ward and Jim Vander Wall (1988). *Agents of Repression: The Secret Wars Against the Black Panther Party and the American Indian Movement.* Boston: South End Press.

Cleaver, Eldridge (1969). *Eldridge Cleaver: Post-Prison Writings and Speeches.* Edited by Robert Scheer. New York: Random House.

Cone, James (1970). *A Black Theology of Liberation.* N.p.: J.B. Lippincott.

Fanon, Frantz (1959). "The Reciprocal Basis of National Cultures and the Struggles for Liberation." *Presence Africaine* 24–25: 89–97.

_____ (1967a). *A Dying Colonialism.* New York: Grove Press.

_____ (1967b). *Toward the African Revolution.* New York: Grove Press.

_____ (1968a). *Black Skin, White Masks.* New York: Grove Press.

_____ (1968b). *The Wretched of the Earth.* New York Grove Press.

Federal Bureau of Investigation (1978). *Black Nationalist Hate Groups,* File 100–448006. Sections 1–23 in COINTELPRO: The Counter Intelligence Program of the FBI (microfilm). Wilmington: Scholarly Resources.

Federal Bureau of Investigation (1967–1977). *Maulana Karenga,* File 157–7244 (3 parts).

Foner, Phillip (1970). *The Black Panthers Speak.* Philadelphia: Lippincott.

Forman, James (1972). *The Making of Black Revolutionaries.* New York: Macmillan.

Garvey, Marcus (1967). *Philosophy and Opinions of Marcus Garvey.* 2nd edition. London: Frank Cass and Company Limited.

Gates, Henry Louis, Jr., and Nellie Y. McKainy, eds. (1997). *The Norton Anthology of African American Literature.* New York: W.W. Norton and Company.

Gayle, Addison, Jr. (1972). *The Black Aesthetic.* Garden City, N.Y.: Anchor Books.

Gray, Cecil Contenn (2001). *Afrocentric Thought and Praxis: An Intellectual History.* Trenton, N.J.: Africa World Press, Inc.

Greene, Linda (1968). "The Black Revolutionary Woman." *The Black Panther* 28 (September).

Halisi, Clyde (1971). *The Kitabu.* Los Angeles: Saidi Publications.

Halisi, Clyde (1972). "Maulana Ron Karenga: Black Leader in Captivity." *Black Scholar* 3, 9 (May): 26–31.

Jones, Charles, ed. (1998). *The Black Panther Party (Reconsidered): Reflections and Scholarship.* Baltimore: Black Classic Press.

Karenga, Maulana (1967). *The Quotable Karenga.* Edited by Clyde Halisi and James Mtume. Los Angeles: Saidi Publications.

_____ (1969a). "Revolution Must Wait for the People." *Los Angeles Free Press*, May 16, p. 14.

_____ (1969b). "The Black Community and the University: A Community Organizer's Perspective." In *Black Studies in the University: A Symposium,* edited by Armstead Robinson, Craig Foster and Donald Ogilvie, 37–54. New Haven: Yale University Press.

_____ (1972). "Overturning Ourselves: From Mystification to Meaningful Struggle." *The Black Scholar* 4, 2 (October): 6–14.

_____ (1973). "A Strategy for Struggle: Turning Weakness into Strength." *The Black Scholar* 4, 2 (November): 8–21.

_____ (1974a). "Black Art: Mute Matter Given Force and Function." In *Black Poets and Prophets,* edited by W. King and E. Anthony, 174–179. New York: Mentor Press.

_____ (1974b). "Which Road to Revolution: Nationalism, Pan-Africanism or Socialism?" *The Black Scholar* 6, 2 (October): 21–31.

_____ (1975a). "Ideology and Struggle: Some Preliminary Notes." *The Black Scholar* 6, 5 (January/February): 23–30.

_____ (1975b). "In Defense of Sis. Joanne: For Ourselves and History." *The Black Scholar* 6, 10 (July/August): 37–42.

_____ (1975c). "In Love and Struggle: Toward A Greater Togetherness." *The Black Scholar* 6, 6 (March): 16–28.

_____ (1976a). *Afro-American Nationalism: Social Strategy and Struggle for Community.* Unpublished dissertation. United States International University, San Diego.

_____ (1976b). *The Roots of the Us/Panther Conflict: The Perverse and Deadly Games Police Play.* San Diego: Kawaida Publications.

_____ (1977). "Kawaida and Its Critics: A Socio-Historical Analysis." *Journal of Black Studies,* 8, 2 (December) 125–148.

_____ (1978a). *Beyond Connections: Liberation in Love and Struggle.* New Orleans: Ahidiana.

_____ (1978b). *Essays on Struggle: Position and Analysis.* Inglewood: Kawaida Publications.

_____ (1978c). "A Response to Muhammad Ahmad on the Us/Panther Conflict." *The Black Scholar* 9, 10 (July/August): 55–57.

_____ (1979a). "On Wallace's Myths: Wading Thru Troubled Waters." *The Black Scholar* 8, 9 (May/June): 36–39.

_____ (1979b). "The Socio-Political Philosophy of Malcolm X." *Western Journal of Black Studies* 3, 4 (winter): 251–262.

_____ (1980a). "From Civil Rights to Human Rights: Social Struggles in the Sixties." *The Black Collegian* 10, 4 (February/March): 10–16.

_____ (1980b). *Kawaida Theory: An Introductory Outline.* Inglewood: Kawaida Publications.

_____ (1982). "Malcolm and Muhammad: Beyond Psychological Assumptions to Political Analysis." *Western Journal of Black Studies* 6, 4 (winter): 193–210.

_____ (1983). "Society, Culture and the Problem of Self-Consciousness: A Kawaida Analysis." In *Philosophy Born of Struggle: Anthology of Afro-American Philosophy from 1918,* edited by Leonard Harris, 212–227. Dubuque, Iowa: Kendall/Hunt Publishing Co.

_____ (1984). *Selections from the Husia: Sacred Wisdom of Ancient Egypt.* Los Angeles: University of Sankore Press.

_____ (1988). "Black Studies and the Problematic of Paradigm: The Philosophical Dimension." *Journal of Black Studies* 18, 4 (June): 395–414.

_____ (1990). "The African Intellectual and the Problem of Class Suicide: Ideological and

Political Dimensions." In *African Culture: The Rhythms of Unity*, edited by. Molefi Kete Asante and Kariamu Welsh Asante, 91–106. Trenton, N.J.: African World Press.

_____ (1990*)*. *The Book of Coming Forth by Day: The Ethics of the Declarations of Innocence*. Los Angeles: University of Sankore Press.

_____ (1992). "Under the Camouflage of Color and Gender: The Dread and Drama of Thomas-Hill." In *Court of Appeal,* edited by Robert Chrisman and Robert Allen. New York: Ballantine Books.

_____ (1993). "The Oppositional Logic of Malcolm X: Differentiation, Engagement and Resistance." *Western Journal of Black Studies* 17, 1 (spring): 6–16.

_____ (1994). *Maat, the Moral Ideal in Ancient Egypt: A Study in Classical African Ethics*. Unpublished dissertation. Los Angeles: University of Southern California.

_____ (1995a). "Afrocentricity and Multicultural Education: Concept, Challenge, and Contribution." In *Toward the Multicultural University,* edited by Benjamin P. Bowser, Terry Jones, and Gale Auletta Young, 41–61. Westport, Conn.: Praeger Publishers.

_____ (1995b). *The Million Man March/Day of Absence Mission Statement*. Chicago, Los Angeles: Third World Press, University of Sankore Press.

_____ (1996a). "Black and Latino Relations: Critical Concerns and the Search for Common Ground." In *Multi-America: Essays on Cultural War and Cultural Peace,* edited by Ishmael Reed, 189–204. New York: Viking Penguin.

_____ (1996b). *The Million Man March/Day of Absence: A Commemorative Anthology*. Co-editor. Chicago, Los Angeles: Third World Press, University of Sankore Press.

_____ (1997a). "African Culture and the Ongoing Quest for Excellence: Dialog, Principles, Practice. *The Black Collegian*, February, pp. 160–163

_____ (1997b). "Black Art: Mute Matter Given Force and Function.*"* In *The Norton Anthology of African American Literature*, edited by Henry Louis Gates Jr. and Nellie Y. McKay, pp. 1972–1977. New York: W.W. Norton and Company.

_____ (1997c). "The Nguzo Saba (The Seven Principles): Their Meaning and Message." In *Modern Black Nationalism: From Marcus Garvey to Louis Farrakhan,* edited by William L. Van Deburg, 275–287. New York: New York University Press.

_____ (1998). *Kwanzaa: A Celebration of Family, Community and Culture*. Los Angeles: University of Sankore Press.

_____ (1999). *Odu Ifa: The Ethical Teachings*. Los Angeles: University of Sankore Press.

_____ (2002). *Introduction to Black Studies*. 3rd edition. Los Angeles: University of Sankore Press.

Karenga, Tiamoyo (2000). "A Brief History of Kawaida Womanism." Paper presented at the African American Cultural Center, March 5, pp. 1–11.

Kitwana, Bakara (1998). "A Soldier's Story." *The Source,* February, p. 132.

Madhubuti, Haki (1973). *From Plan to Planet Life Studies: The Need for Afrikan Minds and Institutes*. Chicago: Third World Press.

Malcolm X (1965a). *The Autobiography of Malcolm X*. New York: Grove Press.

_____ (1965b). *Malcolm X Speaks*. New York: Grove Press

_____ (1968). *The Speeches of Malcolm X at Harvard*. Edited by Archie Epps. New York: William Morrow and Company, Inc.

_____ (1970). *By Any Means Necessary*. New York: Pathfinder Press.

Matthews, Tracye (1978). "No One Ever Asks, What a Man's Role in the Revolution Is: Gender and Politics of the Black Panther Party, 1966–1971." In *The Black Panther Party Reconsidered,* edited by Charles E. Jones. Baltimore: Black Classic Press.

Muhammad, Elijah (1965). *Message to the Black Man in America*. Chicago: Muhammad's Temple of Islam No. 2.

Muhammad Speaks (1966). "L.A.—Two Who Refused to Go Say: Will Not Kill Asians for White Supremacy." July 1, p. 6.

Nabakov, Peter (1969). *Tijerina and the Courthouse Raid.* Albuquerque: University of New Mexico Press.

Neal, Larry (1968). "The Black Arts Movement." *The Drama Review* 12, 4 (summer): 29–39.

_____ (1997). "The Black Arts Movement." In *The Norton Anthology of African American Literature,* edited by Henry Louis Gates, Jr. and Nellie Y. McKainy, pp. 1959–1972. New York: W.W. Norton and Company.

Newton, Huey (1971). "Huey P. Newton Talks to the Movement." In *Black Protest Thought in the Twentieth Century,* edited by August Meier, Elliot Rudwick and Franci I. Broderick. New York: Bobbs-Merrill, Co.

Ngozi-Brown, Scot (1997). "The Us Organization, Maulana Karenga and Conflict with the Black Panther Party: A Critique of Sectarian Influences on Historical Discourse." *Journal of Black Studies* 28, 2 (November): 157–170.

Nyerere, Julius (1968a). *Freedom and Socialism, Uhuru na Ujamaa: A Selection from Writings and Speeches, 1965–1967.* Nairobi: Oxford University Press.

_____ (1968b). *Ujamaa: Essays on Socialism.* London: Oxford University Press.

Obadele, Imari (1975). *Foundations of the Black Nation.* Detroit: Songhay Press.

Olsen, Jack (2001). *Last Man Standing: The Tragedy and Triumph of Geronimo Pratt.* New York: Vintage Anchor Books.

O'Reilley, Kenneth (1989). *"Racial Matters," The FBI's Secret File on Black America, 1960–1972.* New York: The Free Press.

Organization Us (1967). "Statement on the Vietnam War." Us Archives.

_____ (1995). *The Organization Us: 30th Anniversary Celebration [Program].* Los Angeles: University of Sankore Press.

Ostrow, Ronald (1975). "Army Disclosing Its Role in Plans to Quell Urban Riots." *Los Angeles Times,* August 26, part 1, pp. 1, 14–15.

Pinkney, Alphonso (1976). *Red, Black and Green: Black Nationalism in the United States.* London: Cambridge University Press.

Robinson, Armstead, Craig Foster and Donald Ogilvie, eds. (1969). *Black Studies in the University: A Symposium.* New Haven: Yale University Press.

Rogers, J.A. (1972). *World's Great Men of Color, I.* New York: McMillan Publishing Co., Inc.

Sanders, Stanley (1968). "New Breed in the Ghetto." *Los Angeles Times West Magazine,* May 19, pp. 32, 34–38.

Seale, Bobby (1991). *Seize the Time: The Story of the Black Panther Party and Huey Newton.* Baltimore, Md.: Black Classic Press.

Senghor, Léopold Sédar (1964). *On African Socialism.* New York: Frederick A. Praeger Publishers.

Smallwood, Andrew P. (2001). *An Afrocentric Study of the Intellectual Development, Leadership Praxis and Pedagogy of Malcolm X.* Lewiston, N.Y.: The Edwin Mellen Press, Ltd.

Stone, Chuck (1968). "The National Conference on Black Power." In *The Black Power Revolt,* edited by Floyd Barbour, 189–198. Boston: Porter Sargent Publishers.

Tembo, Chimbuko (1995). "Kawaida Womanism: An Introduction to Its Theory and Practice." Paper presented at the Annual Cheikh Anta Diop Conference, Temple University, October 11–13, pp. 1–15.

Terry, Wallace II (1970). "Bringing the War Home." *The Black Scholar* 2, 3 (November): 6–18.

Time (1968). "Is God Black?" November 15, p. 78.

Toure, Sekou (1959). *Toward Full Re-Africanization.* Paris: Presence Africaine.

Turner, Henry McNeal (1971). *Respect Black: The Writings and Speeches of Henry McNeal Turner.* Edited by Edwin S. Redkey. New Haven: Yale University Press.

U.S. Congress, Senate Select Committee to Study Governmental Operations with Respect to Intelligence Activities (1970). *Final Report—Book II Intelligence Activities and the Right of Americans.* 94th Congress, 2nd session.

Van DeBurg, William L. (1992). *New Day in Babylon: The Black Power Movement and American Culture, 1965–1975.* Chicago: University of Chicago Press.

West, Cornel (1999). *The Cornel West Reader.* New York: Basic Civitas Books.

White, E. Frances (1990). "Africa on My Mind: Gender, Counter Discourse and African American Nationalism." *Journal of Women's History* 2, 1 (spring): 73–97.

Wilson, August (1996). "The Ground on Which I Stand: A Testimony, a Protest, an Emphatic Call for Change." *American Theatre,* pp. 14–16, 71–74.

Woodard, Komozi (1999). *A Nation Within a Nation: Amiri Baraka (Leroi Jones) and Black Power Politics.* Chapel Hill: The University of North Carolina Press.

Ya Salaam, Kalamu (1973). *Hofi ni Kwenu (My Fear Is for You).* New Orleans: Ahidiana.

7. The Black Arts Movement in Omaha, Nebraska

ALONZO N. SMITH

The Black Arts Movement

One of the forms which African American cultural nationalism took during the 1960s was the Black Arts Movement (BAM). With a few notable exceptions, the overwhelming majority of serious students of this period regard it as a major development in African American cultural history. BAM has often been referred to as "the artistic sister of the Black Power Movement." Younger activists produced thousands of creative works in the late 1960s and early 1970s, as BAM explicitly targeted a number of long-standing assumptions of literary critics and historians: in particular, the role of the text, the timelessness of art, the responsibility of artists to their communities, and the significance of oral forms in cultural struggles. But even though, or perhaps precisely because it was critical in orientation, BAM also produced works of great power and integrity. Elizabeth Catlett was one of major plastic artists of the period, and well-known writers included LeRoi Jones (Amiri Baraka), Ed Bullins, Nikki Giovanni, Harold Cruse, Ray Durem, Adrienne Kennedy, Larry Neal, and Sonia Sanchez. Two major publications of the movement were the *Negro Digest* and *Liberator* magazine.[1]

In the works of Amiri Baraka, "The role of the Black Artist in America is to aid in the destruction of America as he knows it."[2] In other words, the role of the Black artist was to eliminate existing canons of artistic expression, and replace them with ones that came from the grassroots of Black communities. In 1965, Baraka opened the Blacks Arts Repertory Theatre and School, in Harlem. The idea was to bring poetry and drama out into the streets of Harlem, and to involve local residents in dramatic cultural activities, thereby reducing the traditional distinction between playwright and audience. What was taking place on the streets of Harlem was part of a movement that was sweeping people of African ancestry across the United States, and it merits more extensive study at the local community level.

Background

Compared to some other Midwestern cities, Omaha is larger than Des Moines, but smaller than Kansas City. At approximately 10 percent of the city's population, the local African American community currently [as of 1986] numbers about 45,000 people.[3] More or less dispersed in the central business district near the Missouri River during the nineteenth century, the nucleus of a small Black community began to appear during the Great Migration, and by the 1920s, North 24th Street, north of the downtown area, had emerged as the main thoroughfare for Omaha's "North Side."

A growing African American middle class drew much of its support from domestic and other service occupations, as well as from employment as dining car cooks and waiters, and sleeping car porters on the Union Pacific Railroad. A major source of jobs for Omahans of African descent was the meat processing plants located in the southern part of the city, and it was this industry in particular that played a major role in the creation of a stable Black working class.

Despite the passage of state public accommodations legislation in the 1890s, there was widespread *de facto* Jim Crow in Omaha during the major part of the twentieth century. Employment and housing discrimination were the rule of the day. Although Omahans of African ancestry had contested White racism on many occasions, sustained activism did not really emerge until after World War II, with the formation of the De Porres Club in 1947. Named after St. Martin De Porres, a Black Latin American priest, the interracial group was composed of Creighton University students and mentored by Father John Markoe, a White Jesuit faculty member, and Mrs. Mildred Brown, editor and publisher of the *Omaha Star*, the local weekly African American newspaper. The group was successful in breaking the color bar in several places of public accommodation, as well as securing jobs for African Americans in North Side businesses. These gains were regularly publicized by the *Star*, but by 1957, the De Porres Club appeared to be in decline.[4]

By the early 1960s the effects of the Black freedom struggle in the South were beginning to be felt in northern cities like Omaha. In 1963 a new organization, the 4CL (Citizens Coordinating Committee for Civil Liberties), was formed by four African American ministers. The leadership and membership were African American, and in July of 1963 a pray-in was held at the city hall to press for a local equal opportunity employment ordinance.[5]

As the Black Revolution of the 1960s gained momentum, Black activism in Omaha intensified, and in 1968 the local chapter of the National Committee to Combat Fascism, which was similar in style and philosophy to the Black Panther Party, was organized. This group was usually referred to locally as "the Black Panthers." In 1966, 1968 and 1969, major outbreaks of community discontent erupted along North 24th Street. Each incident was preceded by the shooting, and in two instances the killing, of a Black youth by a White policeman. In 1969 after an African American teenager named Vivian Strong was shot in the back and killed by a White policeman, North 24th Street erupted in a major community uprising. Soon after this, the seat from North Omaha in the state legislature, which had been filled through-out the twentieth century by African American politicians with a more accommodationist style, was filled in 1970 with the election of Ernie Chambers, a charismatic, radical activist who has held the seat ever since.

Omaha's African American Cultural Life

Omaha, Nebraska, has always had a vibrant, if not well-known, African American cultural life. During the early years of the twentieth century, Florentine Pinkston was a vocalist who conducted a music school that catered to White as well as Black students. The bands of Dan Desdunes and the Omaha Night Owls performed throughout the Midwest. One of America's premier jazz saxophonists is Preston Love, a native son who played with Count Basie and the Motown Orchestra, and continues to reside in the city today.

By the late 1950s there were several popular entertainment places in North Omaha: the Dreamland Ballroom, the Carnation Ballroom, the Off Beat Lounge, and the Showcase Lounge. Black artists also performed down-town at the Orpheum Theater and the Paxton Hotel Ballroom, but often to segregated audiences. Names like Little Richard, Duke Ellington, Sarah Vaughn, Ray Charles, and Dinah Washington appeared frequently in the pages of the *Omaha Star*.[6]

Although several members of the Black community have distinguished themselves in dramatic productions, the first significant theater group specifically oriented to the expression of African American culture was the Afro Academy of Dramatic Arts, a result of the Black cultural awareness of the 1960s.

The Afro Academy of Dramatic Arts

Three of the principal founders of Omaha's first Black theater company were Dorothy Eure and her two sons, Darryl and Harry.[7] The Eure family had a history of creativity in the performing arts. The father, Albert Eure, who worked in Omaha's meat packing industry, was a native New Yorker whose mother had been a dancer at the Cotton Club. For family enter-tainment, when the TV set was not working, the little boys entertained the parents with song and dance routines, which received such strong parental encouragement that "Showtime," as it was called, became a regular family institution.[8]

In addition to the abovementioned factors which led them into the performing arts and social activism, it should be noted that the father was active in the packinghouse workers' union, and the boys' mother, Dorothy, was a native Omahan who had been a social activist in high school during World War II. She was a member of the De Porres Club during the 1950s and of the 4CL during the 1960s, and she helped organize and participated in several major demonstrations in the city. Mrs. Eure also encouraged her two sons to express themselves through dancing and singing at an early age, and around 1961, they took tap dancing lessons from a White woman, but they recall that it was an African American artist, Beverly Blackburn, who influenced them the most strongly. The two boys called themselves the Northside Review, and Reverend Darryl Eure recalls that "We were somewhat like the Nicholas Brothers." They performed with other children in shows throughout the city, and venues included social and fraternal organizations, as well as onstage in public theaters. In addition, they appeared in several Nebraska towns, including Nebraska City and Lincoln, as well as across the river in Council Bluffs, Iowa.

They began by just tap dancing, later singing. Both of the boys' parents worked together to help them compose some of the routines. The White instructor wrote up a contract, and wanted to take them to California and New York, but the parents, who had lived for a brief period in New York City, felt that that kind of life was not appropriate for children.[9] According to Reverend Darryl Eure, the parents also seemed to have some concern about whether admission was being charged and to whom the proceeds were going. By this time, in addition to performing in neighborhood theaters, they appeared in the ballroom of the Paxton Hotel, in downtown Omaha, as well as in some of the affluent neighborhoods of the city.

In 1962, while a student in junior high school, Harry appeared in an Omaha production of Lorraine Hansberry's play *A Raisin in the Sun*, which featured several local performers, one of whom, William J. Marshall, went on to play in off–Broadway productions. The play was well-received, and won an award.[10]

The Omaha Show Wagon was a mobile stage that was sponsored by the city's parks and recreation department, and that went from park to park in the summertime. Performers included Buddy Miles, Mark Lewis, and other local figures. The Eure brothers became a regular comedy routine, and performed tap-dancing and lip-synching. Some of the lip-synching included songs like "The Great Pretender," and routines from Stan Freburg. Reverend Eure recalls that the duo was quite popular: "We became recognized around the city as the Black act to see." They would perform at Peony Park and Elm-wood Park, which were major public gathering places in the city. Although they won several competitions, Black community leaders such as Rodney Wead and Charlie Washington were concerned that they were being discrim-inated against in some of the competitions.

Reverend Darryl Eure recalls vividly the segregated conditions of the performances, which were common for African Americans in show business. They were told to stay near the stage and not to mingle with the audience between numbers, and they usually had leave as soon as the performance was over. Mr. Harry Eure, on the other hand, remembers that they encountered little hostility, because in his words, "They liked what we were doing ... it was unique."[11] Mrs. Eure managed to combine her role as a home maker, an industrial manufacturing worker, a civil rights activist, and the manager of the Northside Review. The pair began perform-ing more in the Black community, at gatherings of the Links, the Elks, and other social clubs, as well as the Off Beat Lounge. They also performed for John Green, a White liberal legislator who supported civil rights legislation. By this time, there were numerous civil rights rallies in Omaha, where they performed.

This was during the mid–1960s, and boys' mother was extensively involved in the civil rights campaigns of the 4CL. Harry entered Central High School, which was the most prestigious public high school in the city, in 1963, and Darryl followed him year later. Although only separated by a year, Mr. Harry Eure recalls that "Darryl's class were even more demonstra-tive than we were."[12] Both young men became influenced by the intellectual and cultural ferment that was sweeping African Americans across the coun-try. He became aware of the Last Poets, and the works of Imamu Baraka, and Richard Wright. Reverend Darryl Eure recalls that he had been reading Mahatma Gandhi since he was in junior high school. The few African Amer-ican students at Central were eager to learn more about African American and African culture. Instead, they experienced White teachers who made them read Eugene O'Neil's *The Emperor Jones*, or Mark Twain's *Huckleberry Finn*, without explaining the racist attitudes that they conveyed. The use of the word "nigger" in American literature was not explained or discussed; the teachers just accepted it as part of the literature, or just brushed it off. Students felt that this kind of attitude implicitly sanctioned the use of the word, and the racist practices that it conveyed. The students also had the impression that some potentially sympathetic teachers failed to speak out because they were afraid of being fired.

Mr. Harry Eure recalls that, although African American students were encouraged to join athletic teams, they were virtually excluded from the school's cultural organizations. The drama club, the Thespians, was not congenial to Black students, and the only one who received any encouragement was a girl who was very light in complexion.[13]

Reverend Eure, along with other African American students at Central High School, formed BUSS (Black United Students of Soul) because they were "tired of the atmosphere," which included segregation in the school cafeteria, and hostile or indifferent attitudes from the teachers. The leaders of BUSS demanded the inclusion of more Black cultural materials in the curriculum, the elimination of literary works containing racially offensive language, and an end to what they felt were discriminatory attitudes from teachers.

Cultural politics were a very important part of the agenda of the Black activist students at Central. The only African Americans who appeared in the literature and history studies were Paul Lawrence Dunbar, Booker T. Washington, and George Washington Carver. The written list of demands that BUSS presented to the principal included the elimination of required readings that contained the word "nigger," and the inclusion of more coverage of Black people in the history courses. Mr. Harry Eure vividly recalls the feelings evoked in the Black students by reading *The Emperor Jones* in class: "This was almost like the New South.... Most white people had a sense of privilege.... It was like punching a hole in your dream."[14]

While a student at Central High School, Reverend Darryl Eure wrote his first play, entitled *Uncle Tom's Revolution.* The work included a series of vignettes in African American history, and was intended to reflect the new mood among Black people during the 1960s. When the principal refused to allow the play to be performed, a coalition of students and adult Black community leaders, including Mary Harvey, a counselor at the school, forced him to change his decision. Mr. Harry Eure recalls that at first, the principal, V.E. Mohler, "was totally opposed to any presented of Black culture," but the Black students were able to help educate him.

Harry graduated from Central in 1967 and enrolled at Omaha University, and the next year, he was followed by Darryl, who enrolled at the University of Nebraska at Lincoln. Both young men became Black student activists on their respective campuses, and both young men have memories of confrontations with White police officers who stopped and harassed them while driving in North Omaha. Reverend Darryl Eure recalls that among the several older community leaders to whom they turned for advice it was the barber Ernie Chambers, who was soon to be elected to the state legislature, who left the most memorable impression.

In October of 1968 several young community cultural activists, including the Eure brothers, got together to form the Afro Academy of Dramatic Arts. Although it was formally organized in that year, it did not present its first play until the following year. Mrs. Eure wrote the articles of incorporation and the new theater company began to perform at locations in the Black community, including Clair Memorial Church, at 25th and Evans, and the Off Beat Lounge. At the first performance, they did part of *A Raisin in the Sun*, by Lorraine Hansberry, and *Mojo*, by Ron O'Neal.[15]

The players noticed a building on the northwest corner of 24th and Ames, in the hub of the Black community, which was vacant. It was owned by an individual whom Mr. Harry Eure remembers only as "Glasses," who apparently had something of a reputation as a shady character. They were able to persuade him to refurbish it and put in a stage, and they salvaged seats from the old Beacon Theater, a few blocks away, where Darryl and Harry had performed as children. After *A Raisin in the Sun*, the company performed *The Obsolete Bird*, by Omahan Glen Butler. In addition, they did a series of one-act plays, including the works of Le Roi Jones, *Slaves* and *The Dutchman*. One of the main players was Margaret Pearson, who was shy and had no previous experience, but who with a little practice became an outstanding actress.

The theater was very small, and seated only 50–60 people. There were many Whites, mostly students from nearby Creighton University, in the audience. The theater company wanted more community participation, so they would go into the bar across the street and persuade the patrons to come over with the offer of free admission. Although most of them had never been to a live theater production before, they responded positively.[16]

Reverend Eure's play, *Uncle Tom's Revolution*, was performed at the Afro Academy's theater, again at Central High School, and at Creighton University. Harry wrote *Black Catharsis*, a poetry collage which was later incorporated into a piece called *Malcolm X, the Final Hour*. Harry also wrote grants, and secured support from the National Endowment for the Arts and the Nebraska Arts Council, but the players felt they didn't receive support at the same level as the White cultural organizations. Black community leaders Rodney Wead and Wilda Stephenson were helpful in pushing for funding, and they would attend the Arts Council meetings to advocate for the Afro Academy of Dramatic Arts.

In 1968 George Wallace came to Omaha in a bid to garner support for his presidential campaign. The BUSS went out to the campus of Omaha University, to join the 4CL, the Black Liberators for Action on Campus (BLAC), the Black Panthers, and progressive Whites, to protest his appearance. Later that evening the Alabama governor spoke again at the Civic Auditorium, in downtown Omaha. At one point, Wallace pointed to the vocal protestors, and exclaimed, "This is what I'm talking about; these are the kind of people I want to get rid of in this country." His provocative remark further inflamed the protestors. The police attacked them, and several people were arrested. Later that evening, disturbances erupted along Twenty-fourth Street, in which an African American youth was shot by policemen.

The civil disturbances and social tension increased African American attendance at the Afro Academy's productions, and Reverend Eure recalls that "for the first time, Black folks started attending Black theater." Their supporters in the community included the National Committee to Combat Fascism, and local underground newspapers such as *Buffalo Chips* and *Down on the Ground*. There was a lot of police harassment; when they performed, the police would circle the block, and they were stopped a lot. They often wore dashikis, which made them targets for surveillance.

In 1969, Black teenager Vivian Strong was shot in the back and killed by a White policeman after he allegedly told her to halt. But according to witnesses in the North Side's Logan Fontenelle housing project, the officer drew his gun and fired without warning. This incident was followed by Omaha's most violent civil disturbance of the 1960s, and the Afro Academy presented a play written by Reverend Eure comparing Vivian Strong to Emmett Till. The policeman was suspended, and the Afro Academy was among those groups that unsuccessfully pushed for his conviction for murder.

In 1972 the group moved from their small theater in the community to Our Savior Lutheran Church, at the invitation of the Reverend Vic Schoonover. Reverend Schoonover was the Omaha director of the Lutheran Metropolitan Ministries. The building had housed a Norwegian American congregation that had moved out as the neighborhood changed from Euro-American to African American. The church's stage was rebuilt, and it was able to accommodate about two hundred people. In the early 1970s, attendance was good and audiences were diverse, and many Creighton students, as well African Americans from different backgrounds attended. Reverend Eure's works were well attended, and "a lot of the Black bourgeoisie were coming." He continued to write plays for the company, and Sister Betty Shabazz, the widow of Malcolm X, attended one performance. The theater branched out, and a Children's Theater, organized by Mrs. Eure, was formed. Dramatic episodes were presented on the local Black radio station and there were even some exhibitions of Black community art. They performed at this venue until 1977, but funding was always a problem.

They left the church around 1978, purchased an old school bus, and took the company on the road, traveling to Dana, Seward, Hastings, and other Nebraska cities. Although the bus broke down sometimes, they reached a wide audience. Another of Darryl's plays was called *Who Got His Own*. Around this time it was through the theater company that he met his wife, Gretchen, who was a teacher at Technical High School in North Omaha.

The group continued to perform until the mid–1980s, when it finally disbanded. Several reasons can be cited for the fact that the Afro Academy of Dramatic Arts passed out of existence. One was the lack of funding from public arts groups, which often was insufficient or non-existent. Another was the decline in militancy and in a sense of urgency and crisis in the country at large. And finally, the members of the troupe were individuals who had other responsibilities and activities that claimed their attention. Today, there are other theater groups in Omaha that continue to interpret the African American cultural experience, and some of the local African American artists first performed with the Afro Academy. In Omaha, Nebraska, it was the Afro Academy of Dramatic Arts that took the first step as the organized expression of the Black Arts Movement in America's heartland.

Notes

1. A major Web site for the Black Arts Movement is located at http://www.umich.edu/~eng499/.

Literature includes Richard J. Powell, *Black Art and Culture in the 20th Century* (Thames and Hudson, Ltd., 1997); Addison Gayle (ed.), *The Black Aesthetic* (Garden City, N.Y.: Doubleday Publishers, 1971); Olaniya Tejumola, *Scars of Conquest/Masks of Resistance: The Invention of Cultural Identities in African, African American and Caribbean Literature* (New York: Oxford University Press, 1995); Mike Sell, "The Black Arts Movement: Performance, Neo-Orality, and the Destruction of the 'White Thing,'" in *African American Performance and Theatre History: A Critical Reader*, edited by Harry Elam, Jr., and David Krossnor (Oxford University Press, in preparation); Clovis E. Semmes (comp.), *Roots of Afrocentric Thought: A Reference Guide to Negro Digest/Black World, 1961–1976* (Westport, Conn.: Greenwood Press, 1998).

2. Roy Finkenbine, *Sources of the African American Past* (New York: Longman, 1997), p. 195.

3. "Blacks in Omaha; A Special Report," *Omaha World-Herald*, a seven-part series appearing September 14–20, 1986.

4. There are numerous articles in the *Omaha Star* during the 1950s which document the activities of the De Porres Club.

5. *Omaha World-Herald*, July 10, 1963.

6. *Omaha Star*, January 15, 1954; October 15, 1954; March 2, 1956; June 7, 1957.

7. The principal informants for this study were the Reverend Darryl Eure, who currently holds the position of director of the North Christ Child Center, in Omaha, in addition to being the pastor of Freestone Baptist Church; and his brother, Harry, who is an account manager with the Ford Motor Credit Association. The interviews with Darryl Eure were conducted on June 23 and June 27, 2000, and the interview with Harry Eure was conducted on June 25, 2000. Another helpful informant was the Reverend Victor Schoonover, a retired Lutheran minister who was prominent in social justice movements in Omaha. His interview was conducted on June 26, 2000.

8. Harry Eure, interview with author.

9. Ibid.

10. Ibid.

11. Ibid.

12. Ibid.

13. Ibid.

14. Ibid.

15. Ibid.

16. Ibid.

8. The Role of the Africana Writer in an Era of Struggle— The Case of Hoyt W. Fuller and the Black Arts Movement, 1961–1981: A Kawaida-Location Analysis

AMIR M. ABDURAHMAN

Hoyt Fuller was, for me, the breath and finer spirit of the cultural energies that I am trying to define. He was a man of the spirit—the mentor that so many of us had never known in the academy.—Houston A. Baker, Jr.[1]

Introduction

GENERAL OVERVIEW

This paper will explore the life and work of Hoyt William Fuller during the Black Arts Movement from 1961 to 1981, focusing on Fuller's life, views and role as a writer. While Fuller has been remembered for his achievements during his fifteen-year career as executive editor of *Black World* (formerly known as *Negro Digest*) from 1961–1976, there are few studies that systematically examine the contribution his life and work as an editor made to the Black Arts Movement. The literature reveals that under his editorship, the periodical was transformed from a small digest to an internationally recognized little magazine that served as the leading vehicle for the publication and promotion of the writers and thinkers of the Black Arts Movement.[2]

When *Black World* was discontinued in 1976, Fuller and other African American writers and intellectuals established a new organization and publication to fill the void left by the termination of *Black World*. As a result, the First World Foundation was organized in 1976 in Atlanta, Georgia, where Fuller assumed the position of executive editor of *First World: An International Journal of Black Thought*. Fuller served in this capacity while commuting from his home in Atlanta, Georgia, to Ithaca, New York, where he taught African American literature at the Africana Studies and Research Center at Cornell University from 1976 until he made his transition to the ancestral realm in 1981 at age 57.

While there have been minimal systematic studies of Fuller's work as an editor, his life, work, views, roles and contributions in the context of the struggle for liberation, preservation, empowerment and advancement of African people are generally neglected areas of research. While studies of Fuller are needed in his varied, yet interconnected roles as (1) editor, (2) literary critic, (3) creative writer, (4) news reporter, (5) Pan-African cultural advocate, (6) social activist, (7) educator and (8) organizer, this brief paper will focus on his life and views concerning the role of the Africana writer.[3]

In addition to being an editor, Hoyt W. Fuller was also a prolific writer. Through literary publications such as *Negro Digest* (1961–1970), *Black World* (1970–1976) and *First World* (1976–1981), and through the Organization of Black American Culture (OBAC) founded in 1967 in Chicago, Fuller influenced an entire generation of Black writers, many of whom first saw their works in print in *Negro Digest/Black World* and later *First World*. Fuller championed the Black Aesthetic and Africana women writers and defended the Black Arts Movement.[4]

An intellectual of immense proportions, Fuller, who was in his forties at the time of the advent of the Black Arts Movement, became a promoter and defender of the Black Arts Movement and premier advocate of the concept of the Black Aesthetic, although he had long argued in defense against the Euro-American literary establishment for the need for the creative production of Africana writers to be grounded in the cultural and historical experiences of the Africana people and that the creative production of the people should reflect and be interpreted from their cultural perspective, i.e., "a Black perspective."[5] Later, Fuller would coin the term "Black Aesthetic" in the form of a question to which critical debate, multiple answers, definitions and clarifications would be offered by Black Arts Movement writers and critics.

Through the Black Arts Movement, numerous writers, artists and intellectuals struggled to liberate and transform the consciousness of African people, and envision a new reality from "a Black perspective," seeing Africana people as agents of social change and subjects of their own cultural and historical experiences. The thrust of this study is to locate the life, views and work of Fuller in the context of his social ecology as well as the struggle for liberation during what John Oliver Killens terms "the smoking sixties."[6]

Research Methodology and Theory

RESEARCH DESIGN

The research design that will be employed in this qualitative study is Secondary Analysis, with emphasis on Content Analysis,[7] examining the life, views and selected Black Arts Movement writings of Hoyt W. Fuller from an Afrocentric perspective. In using this particular research design, the researcher will analyze secondary sources on the subject and selected primary sources.

PARADIGMATIC APPROACHES IN AFRICALOGY

In approaching the study of African phenomena, "[c]entrism, the groundedness of observation and behavior in one's own historical [and cultural] experiences, shapes the concepts, paradigms, theories and methods of Africalogy."[8] As such, the thrust of Afrocentric location theory is to locate the perspective and place of the African subject, viewing all African phenomena from the centrality of African historical and cultural experiences.[9]

In the discipline of Africalogy, there are three paradigmatic approaches to the study of African phenomena: (1) functional, (2) categorical, and (3) etymological.[10] As a biographical study that focuses on thematic concerns, this researcher's paradigmatic approach will be categorical. The Kawaida theoretical paradigm, an African value based framework for systematic analysis, with emphasis on location, will serve as the theoretical framework for analysis and interpretation of the subject.

THE KAWAIDA THEORETICAL PARADIGM

The theoretical paradigm that will be used to describe and evaluate the data collected for this study is the Kawaida theoretical paradigm. The Kawaida theoretical paradigm is an Afrocentric theoretical and analytical framework for cultural analysis. The Kawaida theoretical paradigm, based on Kawaida philosophy, served as the philosophical base of the cultural nationalist discourse on culture and cultural struggle during the 1960s, in general, and as the theoretical and practical base of the Black Arts Movement, in particular. Karenga defines Kawaida Theory as "a theory of cultural and social change, which has as one of its main propositions the contention that the solution to the problems of Black life demand[s] critiques and correctives in the seven basic areas of culture."[11] "Culture," as defined in the broadest sense, is "the totality of a people's thought and practice." There are at least seven basic areas of culture and these can be considered as "core variables of cultural analysis."[12] The Kawaida theoretical paradigm[13] has seven core variables of cultural analysis: (1) history (memory), (2) mythology (spirituality and ethics), (3) social organization, (4) political organization, (5) economic organization, (6) creative motif (creative production), and (7) ethos (cultural character and self-consciousness). These core variables are also informed by the seven principles of the Africana value system called the Nguzo Saba. The seven principles of the Africana value system of Kawaida philosophy are (1) *umoja*—unity, (2) *kujichagulia*—self-determination, (3) *ujima*—collective work and responsibility, (4) *ujamaa*—cooperative economics, (5) *nia*—purpose, (6) *kuumba*—creativity, and (7) *imani*—faith.

My interpretation of Fuller's views concerning the role of the Africana writer is informed by Kawaida and the Nguzo Saba—especially with regard to the three key Kawaida concepts of history, creative production and ethos. Kawaida defines history as "the struggle and record of humans in the process of humanizing the world, i.e., shaping it in their own image and interests."[14] Creative motifs are material cultural manifestations of the people that serve as indicators of cultural identity. They let the people know who they are in the most basic sense. Karenga refers to such cultural identity indicators as "creative production" or "cultural production."[15] Creative motifs as defined by Kawaida Theory are "cultural production informed by standards of creativity and beauty and inspired by and reflective of a people's life-experiences and life-aspirations."[16] As such, Black creative production, "as an expression of Black life experiences and aspirations, is the conscious and unconscious aesthetic contribution of Black people to their struggle to rescue and reconstruct their history and humanity in their own image and interest."[17] Kawaida defines *ethos* as "the sum characteristics and achievements of a people which define and distinguish it from others and gives it its collective self-consciousness and collective personality."[18] Ethos is what Wade Nobles calls "the cultural character of the people"[19] and is defined by itself under normal conditions conducive to the normal and healthy functioning of the people. "In Kawaida theory, self-realization has a double meaning, i.e., to know and produce oneself."[20] Kawaida also maintains that "the problem of ethos or self-consciousness is in essence a problem of culture and a task of cultural and social struggle."[21] Thus, according to Karenga,

> self-knowledge and self-production are at the heart of ethos and are clearly linked. For as a people struggles to overcome basic oppositions, then, it creates and defines itself and informs the world of its differences and distinctiveness, i.e., its ethos.[22]

All other areas of the Kawaida paradigm feed the concept of ethos since "a people's self-consciousness and self-definition is defined by their thought and practice in the other six fundamental areas of culture."[23] With these guiding principles in mind, Fuller's life and his views on the role of the Africana writer in relation to "the struggle and record" of Africans "shaping the world in their own image and interests" will be explored, using it as a framework with emphasis on the location of the perspective of the subject.[24]

Social Ecology of Hoyt W. Fuller[25]

Hoyt W. Fuller (1923–1981) was "an authentic struggler"[26] who dedicated almost his entire life to challenging the prevailing agents of the European hegemonic order. As an agent of the cultural struggle for liberation, Fuller fought against the imposition of the Eurocentric perspective of reality as the universal and ultimate standard of interpretation and evaluation by which the "cultural substance" and "cultural manifestations"[27] of African people should be measured. In his varied roles as editor, creative writer, literary critic, journalist, political activist, and Pan-African cultural advocate, Fuller struggled against racism—the systematic practice of "European dominance" and cultural violence that, Kershaw maintains are, "forces that negatively impacts on the life-experiences and life-chances of people of African descent."[28] Fuller's views concerning the importance of struggle and resistance and the need for Africana writers to create from the perspective of their own cultural base is rooted in the social and cultural experiences of Fuller in the context of the social climate of his birth and socialization in a historic Africana community in College Park, Georgia, during the Jim Crow period.

THE EARLY YEARS, 1923–1946[29]

Hoyt William Fuller was born on September 10, 1923, in Atlanta, Georgia, to Lillie Beatrice Ellafair Thomas and Thomas Fuller.[30] When he was very young, around four or five years old, his father died. Eventually, his mother became an invalid who suffered from seizures, a heart condition and walked with a limp that was caused by falling off of a buggy.[31] His mother, "Ms. Lillie," as she was affectionately called, took Hoyt and James, his older brother, to live with her mother and father, Mrs. Eugenia J. Brady Thomas and John Wesley Thomas[32] in College Park, Georgia. In the home of his grandparents and the many other relatives who also lived there, Fuller grew up and spent most of his youth. He spent much of his youth under the special guidance and direction of the women in the family, particularly his grandmother and his favorite aunt, Ms. Eva Louise Thomas, a school teacher and master educator who taught music in the public schools of Atlanta, Georgia.[33] Mrs. Eugenia, a devout supporter of the African Methodist Episcopal Church and Morris Brown College, founded by the A.M.E. Church,[34] planted the seeds in Fuller that bloomed into a desire to know the global history and culture of African people. Aunt Eva, after several unsuccessful attempts at teaching Hoyt to sing and play musical instruments, particularly the piano, finally tapped in Fuller's talent at drawing pictures. Although James was the better artist, Aunt Eva encouraged Fuller to write narratives about the pictures he drew. Thus, his Aunt Eva planted the seeds of what would become for Hoyt a successful, yet troublesome, literary vocation in later years due to the Euro-American racist practices of the literary establishment.[35]

Fuller attended the Princeton Avenue elementary school and, later, the Redwine Avenue school in College Park. Fuller was a bright and promising student but exhibited behavior problems in school. When he graduated, as "the smallest boy in his class," he went to the school where all the African American children went to school—East Point Junior High School,[36] where he often skipped school because his pride was hurt because he did not have enough money for lunch or clothes.[37] Again, this was the Jim Crow era when schools were segregated by custom and by law.[38] Fuller was aware as a youth that the system of racial domination was inherently wrong. Over the years, during his youth, a burning rage developed in Fuller that would be expressed in his critiques of Euro-hegemony in the defense and promotion of the liberation and empowerment of people of African descent.

In his junior year of high school at Booker T. Washington High School in Atlanta, Fuller moved to Detroit, Michigan, to live with his Aunt Mattie Wiggins and entered Northern High School in Detroit.[39] Fuller was forced to moved to Detroit because of a conflict that occurred between him and the police that resulted in a policeman getting beaten up by Fuller. When he went to trial, the judge dismissed the case. In fear for her son's life, Ms. Lillie, Aunt Eva and Ms. Eugenia made arrangements to send Fuller to Detroit to finish school. While Fuller hated Detroit, and College Park for that matter, because of the increasingly depressed state of the African American community, Fuller appreciated his experiences living in Detroit, especially the school that he attended. At Northern High School, Fuller became involved in activities such as producing the yearbook of the graduating class, for which he served as one of the editors. He also served as a staff reporter for the high school newspaper. Fuller probably thought of becoming a writer-journalist or editor during this period. Whether he did so or not, Aunt Eva still encouraged him to strive for excellence while at Northern High School. Upon graduation, Fuller, as expected by his strong willed grandmother, enrolled at Morris Brown College, which for Fuller was an unpleasant experience. He thought of college at MBC as advanced high school.[40]

When Fuller graduated from high school, he went to Morris Brown college for two years before enlisting in the army reserves in an effort to avoid serving in the second Great European Imperial War (World War II). Fuller was called to serve in the war and was sent to fight in Italy from 1943 to 1945.

When the war ended, he enrolled at the University of Florence, where he studied Italian language, art and literature. In 1946, he returned to Atlanta briefly, then he went back to Detroit and enrolled at Wayne State University, where he studied English literature and journalism.

THE INTERMEDIATE YEARS, 1946–1960

At Wayne State University, Fuller was a classmate with Dudley Randall, the great poet and editor who eventually founded the most successful of the independent African American publishing companies of the Black Arts Movement period.[41] While a student at Wayne State University, Fuller worked part time for the Detroit *Tribune*. In addition to working part time, Fuller studied African world history and culture under the tutelage of Mr. Fred Hart Williams, who also wrote for the Detroit *Tribune*. Fuller wrote for the *Tribune* from 1949 to 1951. In 1954, Fuller left Detroit for Chicago to work for *Ebony* magazine as associate editor. Fuller increasingly became disenchanted with *Ebony* and resigned in 1957 because he felt that it was not sufficiently relevant to the Black community and the struggle against European dominance.[42]

After almost involving himself in a confrontation with an unknown Euro-American man, in 1957, Fuller left the United States and went to Europe. While in Europe, he served as a West African correspondent for *Haagse Post*, a Dutch publication. While serving in this capacity, Fuller spent three months in Africa, during the independence explosion. His experiences in Africa during this time would eventually become the substance of his now classic work, *Journey to Africa*, published in 1971 by Third World Press. Later, Fuller would return to Africa and other parts of the world several times, particularly to Dakar, Senegal, where he forged ties with Alioune Diop, editor and publisher of one of the leading African scholarly magazines in the world during the 1960s, *Presence Africaine*. Upon his return to the United States, Fuller worked as an assistant editor for *Collier's Encyclopedia* in New York.

THE *NEGRO DIGEST/ BLACK WORLD* YEARS, 1961–1976

At the invitation of Johnson Publishing Company, Fuller returned to Chicago, where he served as an editor for *Ebony* and soon thereafter executive editor of *Negro Digest* in 1961. Fuller also published essays, poems and short fiction in other leading periodicals and anthologies around the country, sometimes under the pen name of William Barrow throughout the 1960s and 1970s.[43] Fuller also would later operate under other names that were variants of his birth name during his travels back and forth to Africa and Europe during the independence explosion in Africa, particularly Sekou

Toure's Independent Guinea, that would lead to his being investigated by the Central Intelligence Agency (CIA).

Under Fuller's editorship, *Negro Digest* became an internationally respected publication. While serving as the editor of *Negro Digest*, in 1967, Fuller co-founded the Organization of Black American Culture (OBAC) in Chicago. In the early period, OBAC sponsored writers and arts workshops for new and emergent writers. Fuller published new young writers as well as established writers in the pages of *Negro Digest*. Through these vehicles, Fuller cultivated a whole generation of young Black writers. In the spirit of the Black Arts Movement, Black Power Movement and other movements in the Pan-African struggle for African liberation, *Negro Digest* was renamed *Black World* in 1970. Under his editorship, *Black World* was widely recognized as the leading voice for Black writers and intellectuals during the Black Arts Movement and continued to publish the work of African writers from around the world.

THE FIRST WORLD YEARS, 1976–1981

In 1976, Black writers and intellectuals from around the world were devastated at the discontinuation of *Black World* by the Johnson Publishing Company. Although Fuller had for some time envisioned creating his own journal, it was due to this event that Fuller and other writers and intellectuals from around the country were catapulted into establishing the First World Foundation in Atlanta, Georgia. The First World Foundation was created to support the publication of *First World: An International Journal of Black Thought* as an effort to fill the void left by the termination of *Black World*. After its premiere issue was published in 1977, Fuller and the First World Foundation struggled to publish the magazine. During this time, Fuller commuted back and forth to Ithaca, New York, where he taught African American literature in the Africana Studies and Research Center at Cornell University, one of several colleges at which Fuller taught during his "great and mighty walk" as a writer, journalist, editor, publisher and organizer. From 1977 to 1981, after much struggle and personal expense, successfully published eight issues of *First World*. On May 11, 1981, on the same day of the death of revolutionary reggae singer Bob Marley, in the same year as the passing of Black Arts Movement theorist Larry Neal, Hoyt Fuller died in Atlanta, Georgia.[44]

HOYT W. FULLER'S VIEWS CONCERNING THE ROLE OF THE BLACK WRITER

From as early as 1954, Fuller heavily criticized the Euro-American literary establishment's control over African American literature and its imposition of its Eurocentric cultural values and standards as the yardstick of interpretation of that literature. Fuller's writings, as well as writings of those who would later become prominent figures in the Black Arts Movement and Black Aesthetic Movement, were often labeled "protest literature" by the establishment and rejected by publishers or forced to adopt the Western standard.

Black Arts Movement writers and critics, as it is well known, rejected the Euro-American literary establishment and their models of what constituted good and valuable literature. They sought the development of a Black aesthetic and did not separate politics from art nor art from life. Fuller, as a mentor to several of these writers, saw the role of the Black writer as one that can be described as writer-activist. Later, with the emergence of Black Studies, the role of the scholar is one of scholar-activist. In his mind's eye, this role is both a militant and a humanitarian role.

Fuller felt that in a time of struggle the Africana writer can not afford to be just a writer. Throughout Fuller's life, as a writer he led by example. As a writer activist, he launched an unrelenting assault on the literary establishment. Fuller felt that the struggle for freedom and human dignity must be waged in order to secure freedom and human dignity. The method for Fuller was to engage the enemy self-consciously, pro-actively as well as reactively. Fuller saw the struggle as both against the oppressor as well as among the people. He saw the role of the Africana writer as one in which the writer must, in the tradition of Kawaida, offer critiques and correctives to the conditions facing the people and the literature produced by the people. In several essays, Fuller offers critiques and correctives to manifestations of the cultural crisis as they pertain to identity, responsibility, unity, and agency. Through these writings Fuller saw the writer as one who writes literature that is an affirmation of the cultural heritage and history and humanity of the people rather than one who protests for small recognition from a dying culture. Thus, in short, in Fuller's view, the role of the writer in an era of struggle was to serve as agent for the liberation of African people, creating in the African's image and interest, while simultaneously criticizing the system in order to free African people and their creative production from alien hands so that they can create art and literature that will enable the people to envision a new world and new possibilities.

Notes

1. Houston A. Baker, Jr., "An Editor from Chicago: Reflections on the Work of Hoyt Fuller," in *Afro-American Poetics: Revisions of Harlem and the Black Aesthetic,* edited by Houston A. Baker, Jr. (Madison: The University of Wisconsin Press, 1988), p. 160.
2. Julius E. Thompson, "A Literary and Critical Analysis of the Role of Hoyt W.

Fuller (1927–1981), *Negro Digest* and *Black World* Magazine, during the Black Arts Movement, 1960–1976," in *African American Sociology: A Social Study of the Pan-African Diaspora,* edited by James L. Conyers, Jr., and Alva P. Barnett (Chicago: Nelson Hall Publishers,
1999), pp. 240–261.

   3. This researcher is currently engaged in a larger research project that will culminate in a dissertation-length, literary and cultural biography of Hoyt W. Fuller.

   4. Baker, "An Editor from Chicago," p. 163.

   5. See Fuller's correspondence to literary critics in the 1950s in the Hoyt W. Fuller
Papers.

   6. John Oliver Killens, "The Smoking Sixties," in *Black Short Story Anthology,* edited
by Woodie King, Jr. (New York: Columbia University Press, 1972), pp. xi–xviii.

   7. There are other biographical studies that utilize this method. In particular, see
the following works of James L. Conyers, Jr.: "Maulana Karenga, Kawaida, and Phenomenology: An Intellectual Study," in *Black Lives: Essays in African American Biography,*
edited by James L. Conyers, Jr. (Armonk: M.E. Sharpe, 1999), pp. 3–18; "Charles H.
Wesley, African American Historiography and Black Studies: An Historical Overview,"
in *African American Sociology,* edited by Conyers and Barnett (see note 2); and *Charles H.
Wesley: The Intellectual Tradition of a Black Historian* (New York: Garland Publishing,
Inc.), 1997.

   8. Molefi Kete Asante, *Kemet, Afrocentricity and Knowledge* (Trenton: Africa World
Press, Inc., 1990), pp. 12–13.

   9. This idea is promoted in all of Asante's works as well as the works of other scholars in the discipline.

   10. Asante, pp. 12–13.

   11. Maulana Karenga, *Introduction to Black Studies* (Los Angeles: University of
Sankore Press, 1993), p. 26.

   12. My understanding of this usage is informed by the view of Dr. James L. Cony-
ers, Jr., of the seven basic areas of culture in the Kawaida theoretical paradigm as core
variables for examining, describing and evaluating data. See James L. Conyers, Jr.,
"Maulana Karenga, Kawaida and Phenomenology: An Intellectual Study," in *Black Lives:
Essays in African American Biography,* edited by James L. Conyers, Jr. (Armonk: M.E.
Sharpe, 1999), pp. 3–18.

   13. The descriptions in parentheses of the seven core variables of cultural analysis
are structured and informed by the author's understanding of the concepts in the Kawaida
theoretical framework.

   14. Maulana Karenga, *Introduction to Black Studies* (Los Angeles: University of
Sankore Press, 1993), p. 70.

   15. Ibid., p. 393.

   16. Ibid.

   17. Ibid., p. 394.

   18. Ibid., p. 465.

   19. Wade Nobles, "African Psychology: The Attempt to Reclaim the African Character," Association of Black Psychologist's 1991 Convention, Keynote Lecture, August 15,
1991 (audio cassette).

   20. Karenga, *Introduction to Black Studies,* p. 466.

   21. Maulana Karenga, "Society, Culture, and the Problem of Self-Consciousness: A
Kawaida Analysis," in *Philosophy Born of Struggle: Anthology of Afro-American Philosophy
from 1917,* edited by Leonard Harris (DuBuque: Kendall/Hunt Publishing Company,
1983), p. 213.

   22. Ibid.

   23. Ibid., p. 465.

   24. The intention is to use Kawaida theory and Afrocentric location theory in a

flexible synthesized manner to examine the data, with the Kawaida paradigm serving as an African-centered value based paradigm in light of the critical analyses of James Stewart and Erskine Peters. Stewart advances the idea of synthesizing conceptual paradigms in the discipline. According to Asante, the Afrocentrist does not debate the idea of African cultural values being placed at the center of inquiry and analysis but rather what constitutes those values. Peters emphasizes the need to examine African phenomena from "African value based paradigms" in order for the study to be considered Afrocentric. See James B. Stewart, "Reaching for Higher Ground: Toward and Understanding of Black/Africana Studies," *The Afrocentric Scholar,* May 1992, pp. 1–63. A revised and more succinct version can be found in James L. Conyers, ed., *Africana Studies: A Disciplinary Quest for Both Theory and Method* (Jefferson, N.C.: McFarland, 1997), pp. 108–129. See also Erkine Peters, "Afrocentricity: Problems of Nomenclature," in *Leading Issues in African-American Studies,* edited by NiKongo BaKongo (Durham: Carolina Academic Press, 1997), pp. 57–77.

25. Much of this biographical account is based on Fuller's autobiographical statements from the Hoyt W. Fuller Papers. See this document and other corresponding biographical documents in the Hoyt W. Fuller Papers, Robert W. Woodruff Library, Clark Atlanta University, Atlanta, Georgia. See also Robert L. Harris' essay titled "Hoyt W. Fuller: The Man in Historical Perspective," in *Homage to Hoyt Fuller,* edited by Dudley Randall (Detroit: Broadside Press, 1984), pp. 11–18.

26. This concept of "the authentic struggler" is taken from Sutherland's conceptual model of orientations to struggle. The authentic struggler is viewed as the "ideal type" of five orientations presented while the other four are viewed as "non-ideal orientations— the non-struggler, the reactive struggler, the opportunistic individual, and the partially committed struggler." See Marcia E. Sutherland, "Individual Differences in Response to the Struggle for the Liberation of People of African Descent," *Journal of Black Studies* 20, 1 (September 1989): 40–49.

27. "Cultural substance," according to Wade Nobles' Africanity theory, "is a term used to connote the 'aspect' and are the overt expressions of a people's culture." In addition to behavior, values and attitudes, arts, literature, music, drama, science, etc., would be considered manifestations of the culture of the people who produced them and conceived the meanings (substance) that gives them their force, character, significance and power. Kawaida theory refers to these cultural manifestations as "creative production" or "creative motifs." Cultural manifestations or creative production are indicators of the identity of the people who produced them and their significance (meaning and power) depends on the cultural context and the cultural perspective from which they are viewed. See Noble, *Africanity Theory,* p. 102; Maulana Karenga, *Introduction to Black Studies* (Los Angeles: University of Sankore Press, 1993); Molefi Kete Asante, *The Afrocentric Idea* (Philadelphia: Temple University Press, 1987); and Linda James Myers, "The Deep Structure of Culture: Relevance of Traditional African Culture in Contemporary Life," *Journal of Black Studies* 18, 1 (September 1987): 72–85.

28. Terry Kershaw, "Afrocentrism and the Afrocentric Method," *The Western Journal of Black Studies* 16, 3 (1992): 160.

29. Hoyt W. Fuller Papers.

30. Several accounts of the date of birth of Fuller are incorrect. All recorded sources show that Fuller was 57 years of age when he died. However, some sources state that Fuller was born in 1927 while another states that he was born in 1925. It appears that various bibliographic sources simply copied the same incorrect information from incorrect sources. Fuller's correct birth is noted on the program brochure for his funerary/memorial service (Hoyt W. Fuller Papers).

31. The Hoyt W. Fuller Papers.

32. Mrs. Eugenia J. Brady Thomas was the eldest daughter of the14 children of

George and Eliza Brady. George and Eliza were formerly enslaved Africans in Savannah, Georgia, who, when they became free, settled in Millen, Georgia. During the great migrations of the late nineteenth and early twentieth centuries, they migrated and settled in College Park, formerly called Manchester, which was founded in 1894. Mrs. Eugenia had 12 children, the eldest daughter being Hoyt Fuller's mother, Lillie Beatrice Ellafair Thomas Fuller.

33. Eva Louise Thomas was such a celebrated teacher in Fulton County, Atlanta, Georgia, that a high school was named in her honor. The name of the school was changed to College Park Elementary School and is located in College Park, Georgia.

34. See *Morris Brown College: The First Hundred Years* (Atlanta: Morris Brown College, 1981).

35. Fuller, as a literary critic, cultural advocate and political activist, often criticized the Eurocentric literary establishment for its practices concerning the lack of representative publication of African American authors in anthologies that claimed to be authoritative on the subject of literature. He also strongly criticized writers of European descent who were declared authorities on the African American experience.

36. Princeton Ave. School and East Point Junior High School no longer exist. Redwine Avenue school was later named the J.F. Beavers school after one of the most powerful men in College Park and has been closed down for at least 20 years, according to several residents of the historic African American community of College Park.

37. The Hoyt Fuller Papers.

38. Lerone Bennett, Jr., *Before the Mayflower* (New York: Penguin Books, 1982); John Hope Franklin and Alfred A. Moss, Jr., *From Slavery to Freedom: A History of African Americans,* 7th ed. (New York: McGraw-Hill, 1994); and Karenga, *Introduction to Black Studies.*

39. Several sources, in reporting that when Fuller moved to Detroit "he was very young," give a misleading impression that Fuller moved to Detroit when he was in elementary school. However, Fuller did not move to Detroit to live with his aunt until his junior year of high school. He moved to Detroit when he was around sixteen years old to complete his final years of high school at Northern High School in Detroit. See Fuller's autobiographical sketch and other autobiographical essays in the Hoyt Fuller Papers.

40. The Hoyt Fuller Papers.

41. Julius E. Thompson, *Dudley Randall, Broadside Press, and the Black Arts Movement in Detroit, 1960–1995* (Jefferson, N.C.: McFarland, 1999). See also Don L. Lee, *Dynamite Voices* (Detroit: Broadside Press, 1971).

42. Robert L. Harris, Jr., "Hoyt W. Fuller: The Man in Historical Perspective," in *Homage to Hoyt Fuller,* p. 13.

43. See *Contemporary Authors,* 1975, vol. 53–56, p. 208; Carol A. Parks, *Nommo: A Literary Legacy of Black* (Chicago: OBAHouse, 1987).

44. Media reports indicate that Fuller died as the result of a massive heart attack. However, according to the family, the autopsy report indicates that Fuller died as a result of "choking to death." It is believed by some people that Fuller was murdered.

Bibliography

Baker, Houston A., Jr., (1987). "Moonlit Chambers and Sibylline Leaves, or, How the Black Aesthetic Changed My Life." In *Nommo: A Literary Legacy of Black Chicago (1967–1987),* edited by Carole A. Parks. Chicago: OBAHouse. 314–319.

_____ (1988a). *Afro-American Poetics: Reflections on Harlem and the Black Aesthetic.* Madison: University of Wisconsin Press.

_____ (1988b). "An Editor from Chicago: Reflections on the Work of Hoyt Fuller." In *Afro-American Poetics: Reflections on Harlem and the Black Aesthetic,* edited by Houston A. Baker, Jr. Madison: University of Wisconsin Press. 160–168.

Black Books Bulletin (1971). "Black Books Bulletin Interviews Hoyt W. Fuller." *Black Books Bulletin* 1 (fall): 19–23, 40–43.

Borders, James (1979). "What's Worth Reading: Black Editors Speak." *The Black Collegian* 10, 2 (Oct./Nov.): 114–123.

Brooks, Gwendolyn (1987). "Seeds for the Coming Hell and Health Together." In *Nommo: A Literary Legacy of Black Chicago (1967–1987),* edited by Carole A. Parks. Chicago: OBAHouse. 304–306.

Cash-Menzies, Pamela (1987). "Hoyt W. Fuller: A Capsule." In *Nommo: A Literary Legacy of Black Chicago (1967–1987),* edited by Carole A. Parks. Chicago: OBAhouse. 295–299.

Collier, Eugenia (1987). "Some Thoughts on the Black Aesthetic." In *Nommo: A Literary Legacy of Black Chicago (1967–1987),* edited by Carole A. Parks. Chicago: OBAhouse. 320–326.

Conyers, James L. and Alva P. Barnett, eds. (1999). *African American Sociology: A Social Study of the Pan-African Diaspora.* Chicago: Nelson-Hall Publishers.

Freeney, Charles, Dovie T. Patrick and Doris T. Shockley, eds. (1991). "The Hoyt William Fuller Collection: A Guide." Atlanta: Atlanta University Center/Robert Woodruff Library Division of Archives and Special Collections.

Gayle, Addison (1987). "Hoyt Fuller and the Black Aesthetic." In *Nommo: A Literary Legacy of Black Chicago (1967–1987),* edited by Carole A. Parks. Chicago: OBAHouse. 310–313.

Johnson, Arthur A. and Ronald Maberry Johnson (1979). "Black Aesthetic: Revolutionary Little Magazines, 1960–1976." In *Propaganda and Aesthetics: The Literary Politics of Afro-American Magazines in the Twentieth Century.* Amherst: University of Massachusetts Press. 161–200.

Harris, Robert L., Jr. (1984). "Hoyt Fuller: The Man in Historical Perspective." In *Homage to Hoyt Fuller,* edited by Dudley Randall. Detroit: Broadside Press. 11–18.

Henslin, James M. (1995). "How Sociologists Do Research." In *Down to Earth Sociology.* New York: The Free Press. 31–42.

Karenga, Maulana (1993). *Introduction to Black Studies.* Los Angeles: University of Sankore Press.

Karenga, Maulana Ron (1972). "Black Art: Mute Matter Given Force and Function." In *New Black Voices,* edited by Abraham Chapman. New York: Mentor Books. 477–482. Reprinted from *Negro Digest.*

Kent, George E. (1987). "Glimpses of Hoyt W. Fuller." In *Nommo: A Literary Legacy of Black Chicago (1967–1987),* edited by Carole A. Parks. Chicago: OBAHouse. 302–303.

Long, Richard A. (1987). "Watching Just the Same: Some Recollections of Hoyt W. Fuller." In *Nommo: A Literary Legacy of Black Chicago (1967–1987),* edited by Carole A. Parks. Chicago: OBAHouse. 326–331.

Madhubuti, Haki R. (1987). "Hoyt W. Fuller: No Easy Compromises." In *Killing Memory, Seeking Ancestors,* edited by Haki R. Madhubuti. Detroit: Lotus Press. 34–35.

Mayfield, Julian (1984). "Journey to Africa." In *Homage to Hoyt Fuller,* edited by Dudley Randall. Detroit: Broadside Press. 330–335. Republished from *Black World.*

Neal, Larry (1989). "The Black Arts Movement." In *Visions of a Liberated Future: Black Arts Movement Writings by Larry Neal,* edited by Scwartz, Michael. New York: Thunder's Mouth Press. Reprinted from *Tulane Drama Review.*

Parks, Carole A. (1987). "Consciously Hoyt: Colleague, Mentor, Friend." In *Nommo: A*

Literary Legacy of Black Chicago (1967–1987), edited by Carole A. Parks. Chicago: OBAHouse. 331–335.

Parks, Carole A., ed. (1987). *Nommo: A Literary Legacy of Black Chicago (1967–1987).* Chicago: OBAHouse.

Randall, Dudley, ed. (1984). *Homage to Hoyt Fuller.* Chicago: Broadside Press.

Thompson, Julius E. (1999). "A Literary and Critical Analysis of the Role of Hoyt W. Fuller (1927–1981), Negro Digest and Black World Magazine, during the Black Arts Movement, 1960–1976." In *African American Sociology: A Social Study of the Pan-African Diaspora,* edited by James L. Conyers, Jr., and Alva P. Barnett. Chicago: Nelson-Hall Publishers. 240–261.

Wilhite, Charlotte (1972). "Journey to Africa." *Black Books Bulletin* 1 (winter): 42–45.

ya Salaam, Kalamu (1987). "Making the Most of the Middle Passage." In *Nommo: A Literary Legacy of Black Chicago (1967–1987),* edited by Carole A. Parks. Chicago: OBA-House. 307–309.

IV

AFRICAN AMERICANS AND ISLAM

An exploration of the topic of African Americans and Islam can be perplexing, yet stimulating. In general, over the past few years, interest in Islam has increased in the United States. For African Americans seeking an alternative to Christianity, Islam has served in some ways as an instrument to reinterpret western theology; at the same time, it appears to offer a paradigm of self sufficiency, economic mobilization, and spiritual autonomy. Furthermore, the concept of religious autonomy lends support to Africana culture and kinship.

The essays in Part IV focus on the history of Islam in the United States. James L. Conyers considers how the Nation of Islam perpetuated Pan-Africanist thought and black intellectualism in America. Chapters by Malachi Crawford and Emerson Mungin offer perspective on two crucial figures: Elijah Muhammad and Noble Drew Ali, respectively. Saadi A. Simawe examines Islam's powerful influence on the American Civil Rights movement.

Often we find Black involvement in Islam has been labeled as derelict and polytheistic—despite Islam's unshakeable belief in one creator or life force. Through investigative studies of orthodox and unorthodox strains of Islam practiced by African Americans in the United States, the essays in this chapter aspire to set the record straight, and also to emphasize the rewards to be found in examining Black life and kinship through the lens of Islam. In summary, the study of African American participation in, support for, and sensitivity to the religion of Islam offers the potential for rich discoveries in examining ethos, motif, and history of Africana phenomena.

9. The Nation of Islam: An Historiography of Pan-Africanist Thought and Intellectualism

JAMES L. CONYERS, JR.

Introduction

One of the ongoing struggles of humanity is the search for meaning and substance in daily life. From the epoch of enslavement in America to the contemporary period, African Americans have exhibited a propensity for spiritual solemnity and pilgrimage, trying to unearth a voice of cultural autonomy (i.e., pan–Africanist, cultural nationalist, Black nationalism, and Afrocentric perspectives). In the 1940s, Charles H. Wesley offered a historical perspective on this topic:

> A consistent and continuous effort has been made during the history of the United States to present the American Negro as inferior beings and as a folk different from the normal American stock. Their biological inferiority and racial inequality have been readily accepted because they have been so treated by so many American thinkers. From the earliest colonial periods through the Civil War to the present time, one general belief has been dominant in the mind of the American people concerning the Negro. Conclusions have been drawn from differences in color, physique and other apparently inherited or acquired characteristics, which have been regarded as inescapable. Then, too, with variations in these physical evidences of race, the question remains unanswered as to what is a Negro. Even some of those who were the friends of the Negro people regarded them at times with the hopeful assurance, often reemphasized by religious convictions based upon revivalism, that they would ultimately improve and make progress during the advancing years.[1]

This article examines the Nation of Islam from a historiographic viewpoint, focusing on the organization's Pan-Africanist thought and intellectualism. When one attempts to discuss or examine Pan-Africanist thought and academics under the rubric of African American associations, the Nation of Islam can be considered one of the most meaningful Black organizations in the twentieth century. Aminah Beverly McCloud writes about this popularity: "The Nation of Islam, an indigenous African American Islamic expression founded by Wali Fard Muhammad and developed by Elijah Muhammad, became the American media prototype of Islam in the African American community. The core philosophy of the Nation was characterized by a combination of messianism and [a] form of chiliasm."[2]

The technical aspect of this essay draws attention to definitions, the theoretical paradigm engaged, and the methodology used to collect data and information. Likewise, the concept of Pan-Africanism centers thought and analysis on the retention and reflexivity of a continental African composite of culture sifting to Africans throughout the diaspora. Pedagogues have defined this cultural sifting as "the fomenting of unity among peoples of Africana descent going across barriers of land, history, and culture."[3] Staples refers to this concept as revolutionary Pan-Africanism, which operates on three levels: cultural, economic, and political.[4]

Historiography is the study of how and why history is written.[5] Again, maintaining the ideological view of Pan-Africanism, the prism provides a filter to interpret what variables are addressed and what data and information are omitted. To augment this point further, Evelyn Brooks Higginbotham offers a generative point on the social construction of race, noting its "powerful, all encompassing effect of the construction and representation of other social and power relations, namely, gender, class, and sexuality.... [W]e must recognize race as providing sites of dialogic exchange and contestation, since race has constituted a discursive tool for both oppression and liberation."[6] The NOI came into existence between two important periods in American historiography. The organization was founded in 1930 by Wallace Fard (sometimes referred to Farad Muhammad) in Detroit, Michigan. There was a period of protest prior to and after the initiation of the Nation of Islam. During the middle and latter parts of the 1920s, African Americans were engaged in the process of redefining and re-examining themselves, under the auspices of the concept "New Negro" and the socio-political movements of the Harlem Renaissance, the Great Migration and the Civil Rights Movement. The Civil Rights period in America actually dates to the period of the 1920s–1970s. During the early 1900s, the ideological schools of existentialism and phenomenology were earmarked as the leading schools of thought in the discipline of philosophy. Concurrently, the Muslim League was in formation by the early 1900s, which established the base for the formation of Pakistan.

Organization and Formation of Essay

This article addresses the following topics: (1) theoretical and methodological tools applied; (2) historical overview of the Pan-Africanist Movement; (3) impact on the formation of Islam practiced in the West; (4) historical overview of the Nation of Islam; and (5) conclusion with commentary and analysis. There have been a number of studies conducted on the Nation of Islam, however, few have addressed the role this organization played in the rehabilitation of African Americans ethos, memory, and logos. Instead, we consistently are able to locate studies that view this religious organization from a conflict perspective. It is not my goal to deify or deconstruct this organization. Rather, I seek to identify research tools of analysis—physical, mental, or spiritual—to augment the liberation of African Americans, attempting to address these questions: what it means to be African; what it means to love African people, and more so, what it means to be pro–African in a hostile, racist society.

Theory and Methodology

The conceptual paradigm used in this study is the Ujimaa model. Abstracted from a principle of Kwanzaa, this model addresses collective work and social responsibility within Africana phenomena. In this case, the emphasis is towards examining the historiography of the Nation of Islam. A meta-analysis is employed. This refers to the technique of examining the concept of culture through paradigms such as Kawaida and Systematic Africology (culture, location and agency). The methodology is qualitative, drawing upon secondary analysis as the primary design of collecting data and information, while simultaneously using tools from historical methods, content analysis, and ethnography. Therefore, triangulation is employed in this study, in order to examine as many variables as possible in the process of studying the historiography and intellectualism of the Nation of Islam.

Historical Overview of the Pan-Africanist Movement

The conceptual analysis of Pan-Africanism lends itself to addressing issues of self determination and cultural agency for people of Africana decent. Leaders such as Martin Delany, Sylvester Williams, W.E.B. Du Bois, Marcus M. Garvey and a number of others consistently agitated for these actions to be articulated to the masses of Africana people. Often there are discussions centered on the validity of the teachings of the Nation of Islam. Instead, we focus on the NOI as a Black Nationalist organization. Steven Tsoukalas provides hypothetical thoughts and mythology reviewing three theories of the development of the Nation of Islam, these being (1) Fard is a Moor; (2) Fard is Ford; and (3) Fard is a fraud.[7] I argue that the organization has its contextual base of ideological repertoire in a global Pan-Africanist perspective.[8] Equally important, some critics address the shortcomings of an orthodox practice of religion encouraged by Farad and Elijah Muhammad in African Americans in the West. Instead, when we engage in a process of discovery research, we see that Elijah Muhammad was part of a growing theological and spiritual movement in America in the late 1890s and early 1900s, and that the ideas and views of the Nation of Islam were grounded in a structural Pan-Africanist philosophy of liberation. Tsoukalas discusses this issue further by stating: "The Nation of Islam (NOI) is a product of the times. The movement, which began in 1930, did not appear within a vacuum. Several cultural, anthropological, and theological influences from the nineteenth and early twentieth centuries spawned it. Consequently, the movement cannot be understood without mention of slavery and the attitude it birthed among certain black people or without a study of a few key black leaders who promoted black nationalism and who preceded the rise of the NOI."[9] Richard Brent Turner addresses these points by identifying the role Edward Wilmont Blyden played in the intellectual and praxis development of Pan-Africanism and Al-Islam in the West.[10] To amplify this point, Malcolm X once offered comments to support the validity of global Pan-Africanism by stating: "Many of us fool ourselves into thinking of Afro-Americans as those only who are here in the United States. America is North America, Central America, and South America. Anybody of African ancestry in South America is an Afro-American. Anybody in Central America of African blood is an Afro-American. Anybody here in North America, including Canada, is an Afro-American is he has African ancestry—even down to the Caribbean, he's an Afro-American. So when I speak of the Afro-American, I'm not just speaking of the 22 million of us who are here in the United States. But the Afro-American is a large number of people in the Western Hemisphere."[11] (Few studies acknowledge the fact that Blyden was recognized by Muslim leaders in Africa and given two Islamic attributes.) Turner writes the following:

> It is impossible to understand fully the transition between the "old Islam" of the original African Muslim slaves and the "new American Islam" of the early twentieth century without giving some attention to nineteenth century Pan Africanism, which formed the ideological bridge between these phases of Islam in the United States. Moreover, the Pan Africanist ideas of Edward Wilmont Blyden (1832–1912) are key to understanding how and why the racial particularism and signification that was endemic to global Islam in the nineteenth century. Blyden, who is sometimes called

the "father of Pan Africanism," used the example of Islam in West Africa as the paradigm for racial separatism and signification in his Pan Africanist ideology and ultimately argued that as a global religion for blacks, Islam was preferable to Christianity. These ideals were destined to have a profound impact on black nationalist and Islamic movements in America in the twentieth century.[12]

Even more important, the movement of Pan-Africanism in the United States during the latter part of the 1800s and the early 1900s existed as a movement of self definition, autonomy, and acquisition of power. As such, a number of nationalist organizations embraced the idea of Africana cultural autonomy. The growth and development of the Nation of Islam sprouted from Blyden, the economic philosophy of Marcus Garvey, the Islamic foundations of the Moorish Science Temple, and the Temple of Islam.[13]

Adib Rashad also writes about the role of Garveyism and Black Nationalism in the foundation, context, and practice of Islam by African Americans. Equally important, Duse Muhammad Ali is often times referred to as a mentor to Marcus Gravey, in his development of the UNIA.[14] Still, it appears the concept of Pan-Africanism, which in many ways can be transmitted as Afrocentricity, is the cultural basis and context for the alternative interpretative analysis of the Africana experience, with emphasis on North America.[15] Historically, the Ahmadiyya movement in India during the late 1880s provided dialog and a base for engagement on Islam in the West. Turner points out that the World Fair of Religions held in Chicago in the 1890s provided the forum for Islam in the West, with advocates such as Mohammed Alexander Russell Webb.[16] Rashad expostulates this subject, writing: "His [Garvey's] objective was the redemption of Africa for Africans at home and abroad. He believed that if Africans in the United States were economically viable and independent they would be able to redeem the African continent and establish a world wide confraternity of African people. More importantly, he believed that Africans of the world once united by the consciousness of race and nationality, could become a great and powerful people once again. Even though Garveyites continued to use the term 'Negro' they passionately identified with their African origins. Garvey frequently used Ethiopian as a symbolic term for all of black Africa."[17]

Karl Evanzz comments on the naive nationalism and prophecy of the Nation of Islam under the leadership of the Honorable Master Wallace Farad Muhammad and Elijah Muhammad. This issue can be explained on the basis of two points: (1) the great migration of Blacks from the deep South to northern metropolises created participation in activist organizations espousing a rhetoric of Africana agency; and (2) the NOI was influenced by the social ecological attributes of Freemasons, the Jehovah's Witnesses, Baptist fundamentalism and the theological tenets of Reverend Frank Norris.[18] In a historical perspective, the teachings of Islam, adjoined with elements of religious nationalism, permeated the needs of the people at that place and time. Perhaps Evanzz' analysis misinterprets the short and long term goals of the late Honorable Elijah Muhammad and does not take into consideration the social, economic, and political condition of Blacks in America during the 1930s. Samuel Livingston cites Maualana Karenga's analysis on the issue of culture and its relatedness of the Nation of Islam:

> Karenga's Kawaida concept situates political thought as an essential area of cultural reconstruction, which is essential to any notion of liberation. He suggests that Americans of African descent are plagued by a form of "ideological deficiency," a general lack of culture specific perspectives, paradigms and ideologies. One particular aspect of this ideological deficiency is false consciousness, the tendency to assume the perspectives and ideological stances of dominating groups. Although the adoption of Eurocentric perspectives is the dominant form of false consciousness, Americans of African descent have adopted the point of view and, at times, the identity of other cultural-political entities.[21]

The structure of this probe focuses on the Black Muslim organization, examining variables of history, sociology, economics, criminal justice, and political theory. The terms African American, Islamic, and Black Muslims allude to the sacred evolution of African Americans' acquiescence to Allah as a divine being and their acceptance of the teaching and foundations of this religion. Ironically, most of the biographical or sociological studies conducted on this topic present African American Muslims as naïve nationalists who are anti–White and their movement as a polytheistic dogma of terrorism. Yet, many of these studies center too much attention on descriptive analysis and less on the memory of cultural norms, values, and mores of African Americans. Basically, the study of Black religion in America has been enigmatic, contentious, and cryptic.

In contemporary times, throughout the academic debate, it seems that, whenever one analyzes the conceptual typography of the African American Muslim movement in the United States, unconscious attention is given to the civil rights movement. Furthermore, with the exception of a few noted scholars who have studied and written on this topic, very few intellectuals, nonprofessionals, or independent researchers have studied the African American Islamic movement within the United States and abroad. Precisely, I am referring to issues such as examining the process of holy wars; examining the process of seasoning and enslavement; and the pivotal investigation concerning cultural connotations within Islam that identify the iniquity, neutralization, and progress of African people.

Lastly, we can identify patterns in African Americans' experiments with socialism and nationalism, along with religion, as implements of analysis for their sacred and secular tenacity of memory and belief.

Table 1.0 is a comparative historiographical charting of American and African American historical events from 1892 to 1914. The events illustrate the context and the places in which the United States was going through a period of transition. Even more important, the linkages in African Amer can historiography provide a framework to examine Black life in the United States from a macro perspective. It can be seen that the phenomena were related to events of protest and civil unrest in American culture and civilization.

TABLE 1.0 HISTORIOGRAPHIC TIME LINE OF AMERICAN AND AFRICANA HISTORY AND CULTURE[22]

Year	American	Year	Africana
1892	Populist party wants reform and picks James Weaver to run for president of the United States. Benjamin Harrison is elected as the 23rd president of the United States on the Republican Party ticket. In 1890 Wyoming is admitted as the 44th state on July 10, 1890.	1892	Southern Lynch Law; Ida Wells Barnett publishes her expose on "Southern Horrors: Lynch Law in All Its Phases."
1895	Austrian psychologist Sigmund founds the field of psychoanalysis.	1895	Booker T. Washington's Atlanta Compromise Speech
1896	Supreme Court makes the decision that segregation is not against the Constitution. Utah becomes the 45th state of the union.	1896	Mary Church Terrell becomes president of the National Association of Colored Women.
			Plessy v.s. Ferguson landmark decision of the Supreme Court: separate but equal public facilities.
			Ethiopian emperor Menelek II defeats the Italian army at the Battle of Aduwa in 1896. Ethiopia was the only African nation to maintain its independence from colonial domination.
1899–1902	South African Boer War; Dutch settlers fight to maintain domination of So. Africa.	1899	Composer Scott Joplin publishes the song "Maple Leaf Rag."
1899	First Peace Conference held in		

(Table 1.0, continued)

Year	American	Year	Africana
	Hague, Netherlands; twenty-six nations meet to discuss issues such as arms reductions and conditions of warfare.		
	United States' annexation of Hawaii.		
1900	Jazz appears in Europe. Existentialism and phenomenology are recognized as the two leading schools of thought in the discipline of philosophy in Europe.	1900	First Pan-African Congress meeting held in London, England.
1901–09	Theodore Roosevelt assumes presidency of the United States after the assassination of William McKinley. Roosevelt administration is aggressive in progressive reform and intervention in Panama, with the construction of the Panama Canal.	1901–09	Booker T. Washington dines with President Roosevelt. Many criticize this event based on segregation and Jim Crow laws.
1903	Orville and Wilbur Wright at Kitty Hawk, North Carolina, make the first successful flight of an airplane. Flight travels an estimated 37 miles.	1903	W.E.B. Du Bois publishes *The Souls of Black Folk*.
1905	The Niagara Movement organized and assembled in Niagara Falls, Ontario.	1905	Niagara Movement led by W.E.B. Du Bois and Monroe Trotter. W.E.B. Du Bois coins the term "The Talented Tenth"; college trained African Americans were to step into leadership positions to advance the cause and status of African Americans.
1906	President Theodore Roosevelt gives the order for 167 Black infantrymen to be given dishonorable discharges, with regard to	1906	Alpha Phi Alpha Fraternity is incorporated at Cornell University, the first African American student Greek lettered

Year	American	Year	Africana
	the conspiracy of a White citizen in Brownsville, Texas.		White fraternity. John Hope becomes the founding president of Atlanta Baptist College.
	Muslims in India from the Muslim League to represent them in negotiations against the British.		
1907	Gentlemen's Agreement is a process by which Japanese immigrants are discriminated against in America. Theodore Roosevelt ends segregation of Japanese school children and provides limited protection for Japanese immigrants.	1907	Black Primitive Baptist congregations formed by emancipated slaves, during the post–Civil War era, became the organization known as the National Primitive Baptist Convention, Inc.
1908	Ottoman military officers form CUP in 1899 (Committee of Union and Progress), also called the Young Turks. They called for a restoration of the Ottoman constitution, and advance the idea of a new national identity based on Turkish culture.	1908	Founding of the National Association for the Advancement of Colored People.
			Race Riot in Springfield, Ill.; several thousand Whites attack the Black community. Two elderly Blacks are lynched.
1909	William H. Taft is elected the 27th president of the United States on the Republican Party ticket.	1909	W.E.B. Du Bois begins research on the *Encyclopedia Africana.*
			NAACP is founded.
1911	Carl Jung founds the field of analytic psychology.	1911	Founding of the National Urban League in New York City.
1912	United States troops sent into Cuba.	1912	African National Congress originally referred to as the South African Native National Conference (NNC).
1914	Europe goes to war after the assassination of Austria's Archduke Franz Ferdinand and his wife.	1914–29	Great migration of African Americans out of the South to northern metropolises.
1914	World War I, which eventually involves 32 nations.	1914	Marcus Garvey founds the UNIA.

Nation of Islam

In reference to the central theme of this article, first, I will offer a work-ing analysis of Pan-Africanist intellectual thought. Second, I will provide a historical overview of the Nation of Islam.

It is important to note that the concept of Pan-Africanism has two aspects: 1) the unification of Africans on the continent of Africa, and 2) the unification of Africans in the diaspora. During the late 1800s and early part of the 1900s, the conceptual foundation of Pan-Africanism was taking shape. Specifically, in the 1900s, visionaries such as Edward Wilmont Blyden, Sylvester Williams, Anna Julia Cooper, and W.E.B. Du Bois were key lead-ership figures in the Pan-Africanist movement.[23] Furthermore, leading up to the 1920s, African Americans were engaged in redefining and reexamining themselves under the auspices of the "New Negro" movement, centered in the Harlem community. By the 1930s, the Negritude movement was an aug-mentation of Pan-Africanist thought being practiced in Paris.[24] Intriguingly, Moses points out, "From the mid–1930s to the mid 1960s, black intellectual leadership was overwhelmingly committed to intergrationism."[25] The con-ceptual foundation for Africana cultural autonomy was taking root in the Americas. Indeed, reclamation of culture would be identified as one of the key variables in the adjustment of memory and ethos of an African-centered perspective.

The Nation of Islam was founded in 1930, by Wali Fard (Farad) Muham-mad. It began with Muhammad's ministry to a few committed aspirants. E.U. Essien-Udom explains the development of the NOI in the following manner: "Historically, the Nation of Islam has much in common with the separate Negro church and associations, and more directly with the nationalist movements led by Noble Drew Ali and Marcus Garvey, but it differs from the earlier traditions in that its ideology is intensely chiliastic and buttressed by racial doctrines."[26] William Banks writes about the early foundations of this organization: "Wallace Fard's Teachings varied significantly from those of traditional Islam, which promotes brotherhood among people of all races. His religious movement, in fact, had more in common with Marcus Garvey's black nationalism and Noble Drew Ali's Moorish Science Temple of America. As a result, he attracted to the Nation of Islam many of the same people who had been drawn to Garvey and Ali. Fard's 'lost sheep' subsequently became known as Black Muslims."[27] Clifton Marsh adds the following information: "During the summer of 1930, Master Fard Muhammad, often referred to as Professor Fard, appeared in the Paradise Valley community of Detroit, Michigan, claiming to be Noble Drew Ali reincarnated. Master Fard's mission was to gain freedom, justice, and equality for people of African descent residing in the United

States. Master Fard proclaimed himself the leader of the Nation of Islam with remedies to cure problems in the African American community: 'social problems, lack of economic development, undisciplined family life and alcoholism.'"[28] One of the priorities of the organization was to locate the Lost Found Nation of Asiatics in the West. Often referred to as the Lost Tribe of Shabazz, African Americans represented the downtrodden masses of African Americans misplaced in the wilderness of North America.[29]

By 1933, because of internal and external strife in the Detroit community, as well as the departure of Fard and Ugan Ali—two of the early figures of leadership in the Allah Temple of Islam—the labor of instruction and management of this assembly was transmitted to the Honorable Elijah Muhammad.[30] From this period up until the 1940s, the organization went through ideological transition. By the end of the 1940s, Muhammad's strategic plan of operation was moving forward, and by the early 1950s, the Nation of Islam was identified as one of the largest Black businesses in America, while simultaneously being referred to as a threat to the internal security of the United States.[31] Interestingly, James Turner points out that the Honorable Elijah Muhammad is then referred to as a patriot saint in the history and structure of the organization.[32] Again, as was mentioned in the previous pages of this article, the context for describing and evaluating the Nation of Islam is registered from a Pan-Africanist perspective. Additionally, Minister Tynetta Muhammad describes the symbolism of the Nation of Islam, writing: "The Flag of Islam with the symbols of the Sun, Moon, and the Stars, represent the Universe and is also a Banner of Universal peace and harmony. Our Holy Temples of Islam were established in America as sanctuaries of peace and higher learning into the Knowledge of the Oneness of God."[33] Muhammad's analysis provides insight from her experience and work ethic within the NOI and observing growth and transition over the years, with reference to the historiography of this organization.

Prior to the founding of the NOI, there were at least four African American Islamic movements already established in the United States: 1) Moorish Science Temple (1913), Noble Drew Ali, Newark, New Jersey; 2) Ahmadiyya Movement (1921), Dr. Mufti Muhammad Sadiq, Chicago, Illinois; 3) The Universal Islamic Society (1926), Duse Muhammad Ali, Detroit, Michigan; and 4) the Islamic Propogation Center of America (1928), Shaykh al-haj Daoud Ahmed Faisal, Brooklyn, New York.[34] In addition, Clyde-Ahmad Winters notes that, as early as 1911, there were African Islamic movements in Brazil at Port Novo, led by a Yoruba trader named al–Haji-Mouterirou Soule: these movements' predecessors date back to the early 1880s with the activism of Jose Paraiso.[35]

Richard Brent Turner cites the Ahmadiyya Movement's method of recruitment of African Americans as relying on proselytes and evangelists: there is also documented information that notes Sadiq gave lectures period-ically at Garvey's UNIA meetings.[36] Recently, some of the biographies of African American Islamic leaders have tried to make correlations between the leadership of these movements, meaning that members left movements, and began to establish alternative interpretative analyses of Islamic doctrines and teachings.[37]

When the Nation of Islam was established, Blacks were at a stage of querying the validity of a Eurocentric hegemonic perspective. To obtain a historical perspective, one could begin by examining the writings, teaching, activism, and scholarship of Edward Wilmont Blyden, mentioned earlier in this essay. Turner notes how Blyden acknowledges that Islam would be the religion to provide liberation for African Americans. He writes: "Moreover, the Pan Africanist ideas of Edward W. Blyden (1832–1912) are the key to understanding how and why the racial particularism and signification of black American Islam became linked to racial separatism and signification that was endemic to global Islam in the nineteenth century. Blyden, who is sometimes called the 'father of Pan-Africanism,' used the example of Islam in West Africa as the paradigm for racial separatism and signification in his Pan Africanist ideology and ultimately argued that as a global religion for blacks, Islam was preferable to Christianity. These ideas were destined to have a profound impact on black nationalist and Islamic movements in the twentieth cen-tury."[38]

The social-ecological landscape of 1930 provided an impetus for the establishment and development of the Nation of Islam, which was called the Allah Temple of Islam from 1930 to 1933.[39] With emphasis on labor history, Joe Trotter writes that the African American population, as a result of the great migration, increased in urban areas in the northern metropolises from "forty-four percent in 1930 to nearly fifty percent during the depression years. The black population in northern cities increased by nearly twenty-five per-cent; the cities with black populations of over 100,000 increased from one in 1930 to eleven in 1935. Public social services played an increasing role in deci-sions to move.... The increasing migration of blacks to cities intensified the poverty of established residents."[40]

Table 1.1 is a social-ecological screen showing social movement events that led up to the foundation of the Allah Temple of Islam. During this period, and prior, the concept of Orientalism was associated with the teach-ings of Islam, African history, and metaphysics of spirituality. C. Eric Lin-coln writes about this topic with regard to Noble Drew Ali: "Drew never seems to have had formal education, but at some point he apparently had been exposed to Oriental philosophy. He was particularly impressed by the lack of race consciousness in Oriental religious thought and saw in it a possible answer to the Negro's plight in a color conscious America. If Negroes could somehow establish an identity with the Oriental peoples, whose religious philosophies either knew nothing of the curse of Canaan or else found it irrelevant, they might become less susceptible to the everyday hazards of being everyday–Negroes in America."[41] Unfortunately, because of the United States' internal security during both World Wars I and II, the concept of Orientalism, with accent on language, theology, history, and vernacular, were perceived in many cases as anti–American. With such allegations came surveillance and counter-intelligence ploys used as mechanisms to dismay and misdirect the foundation and purpose of African American Islamic organizations.

TABLE 1.1 SOCIAL ECOLOGY OF AFRICAN AMERICAN SOCIAL MOVEMENTS[42]

Year	*Social Movement*
1895	Booker T. Washington delivers his Atlanta Compromise speech.
1896	Plessy v. Ferguson decision by the United States Supreme Court on the "Separate but Equal" doctrine.
1900	First Pan-African Congress meeting held in London.
1903	W.E.B. Du Bois publishes the *Souls of Black Folk*.
1905	Niagara Movement of the NAACP.
1908	Race Riot in Springfield, Illinois.
1909	Founding of the NAACP.
1913	Founding of the Moorish Science Temple by Noble Drew Ali in Newark, New Jersey.
1911	Founding of the National Urban League.
1914	Great Migration of African Americans out of the deep South to northern metropolises.
1915	Carter G. Woodson organizes and founds the Association for the Study of Afro-American Life and History.
1916	Universal Negro Improvement Association founded.
1917	World War I.
1919	Red Summer of racial riots.
1920	Harlem Renaissance.
1926	Carter G. Woodson establishes Negro History Week.
1930	Founding of the Allah Temple of Islam.

Table 1.2 provides a limited listing of terms and definitions used throughout the literature by and about the Nation of Islam. The organizational thrust of this millenarian movement illustrates how African Americans were equipped to communicate and develop a system of etymological, cosmological, and axiological autonomy. This is related to the idea mentioned earlier

by Brooks-Higgonbotham with emphasis on metalanguage. The purpose of offering these terms is to allow the reader to have a general understanding of the Nation of Islam in a historical perspective. Equally important, these terms are an etymological cohort of African American vernacular theological terms, Kiswahili words, and Arabic terms. This list is a small sample of a comprehensive language used to provide context and synthesis for the divine messages and method of articulation of the Islamic conversion of African Americans.

TABLE 1.2 DEFINITION OF TERMS IN THE NATION OF ISLAM[43]

Term	Definition
As Salaam Alkaium	Arabic greeting of "Peace be unto you."
Asiatic	Name used to identify the international representation of people of Africana descent.
Bililian	Name given to identify the orthodox posture and representation of African Americans' belief in the religion of Islam. The name is taken after Bilal, the first Mu'adhdhin of Islam (caller of prayers for prophet of Muhammad).
Black Muslims	Term referring to African Americans who practiced an unorthodox form of Islam. This practice of religion combines elements of nationalism and Islamic lessons.
bori	Soul dominion among the Hausa.
El Hajj	Arabic identification for an individual who has made pilgrimage to the Holy city of Mecca.
Fruit of Islam	The semi-military unit of the Nation of Islam. Members are trained in hand to hand combat (i.e., martial arts).
Islam	The religion which identifies submission to the will of Allah.
Imam	The leader of Islamic prayers and within the community.
Polygyny	The belief in and practice of having more than one wife.
jama'a	Community, often used to refer to agrarian villages.
Lost-Found	A Black American who has visited Muhammad's mosque for the first time.
mganga	Swahili word for liturgy authority or healer.
Mwalimu or *walimu*	Swahili term for teacher of any kind.
Muslim Girls' Training	Alternate women's training for preparation of nutrition, family science, and healthcare of the family.
The "X"	Indicates membership in the Black Muslim program.
The "so called Negro"	The name members of the Nation of Islam give to African Americans who are perceived as assimilationists without a consciousness of being Black.
Registered Muslims	Financial and active members of the Nation of Islam.

Table 1.3 is a selected listing of events reflecting African Americans' participation in the Islamic faith from the period 1312 to 1889. This information shows how, through the process of voluntary and involuntary migration, African people retained a composite of spirituality, religion, and cultural norms from their ancestral homeland. The process of adaptive vitality enabled Africans to be somewhat reflexive and to envisage liberation and sovereignty through instruments accessible within the complicated system of politics and economics in America.

Table 1.4 is an illustrative analysis of African American Islamic movements in the United States. After the first movement began in 1913 with the Moorish Science Temple, under the leadership and direction of Noble Drew Ali (aka Timothy Drew), there were circumstances where African Americans changed the name of the Islamic movement or there were ideological transitions, moving from a nationalist to an orthodox practice of religion with residual elements of traditional West African culture. The movement of Islam among African Americans in the West is a relatively recent phenomena of the late 1890s to the early part of the 1900s. The study of religions outside the realm of conventional Eurocentric doctrine provided an avenue for African Americans to redefine themselves in a collective capacity. Indeed, as a result of African Americans being involuntary migrants, their quest for spiritual sobriety and cultural transmission exhibited itself in the practice of alternative religious doctrines, apart from White American Protestantism.

TABLE 1.3 AFRICAN AMERICAN AFFILIATION IN THE ISLAMIC FAITH[44]

Alliance	*Year*
African Muslims (Mandinga) arrive in the Gulf of Mexico for exploration of the American interior using the Mississippi River as their access route. These Muslims were from Mali and other parts of West Africa.	1312
African slaves arrive in America. During the slave trade, more than 10 million Africans are uprooted from their homes and brought to American shores. Many of these slaves are from the Fulas, Fula Jallon, Fula Toro, and Massina as well as other areas of West Africa. These areas are governed from their capital, Timbuktu. These slaves are sent to Mexico, Cuba, and South America. More than 30 percent of these 10 million slaves are Muslim. They become the backbone of the American economy.	1530
Ayyub ibn Sulaiman Jallon, a Muslim slave in Maryland, is set free by James Oglethorpe, founder of Georgia, and provided transportation to England. He arrived home (Boonda, Galumbo) from England in 1735.	1732
Yarrow Mamout, an African Muslim slave, is set free in Washington, D.C., and later becomes one of the first shareholders of the second chartered bank in America, the Columbia bank. Yarrow may have lived to be more than 128 years old, the oldest person in American history.	1807

(Table 1.3, continued)

Alliance	Year
Al Hajj Umar ibn Sayyid is enslaved in Charleston after running away.	1809
The Reverend Norman, a Methodist missionary, converts to Islam.	1870
Edward W. Blyden, noted scholar and social activist, travels throughout the eastern and southern parts of the United States proclaiming Islam. In a speech before the Colonization Society of Chicago, Blyden tells his audience that the reasons Africans choose Islam over Christianity is that "the Qur'an protected the black man from self-depreciation in the presence of Arabs or Europeans."	1889
The American Islamic Propaganda Movement is founded by Mohammed Alexander Russell Webb. He is regarded as one of the earliest White American converts. In that same year on Sept. 20 and 21, M.A. Webb appeared at the First World Congress of Religions and delivered two lectures: "The Spirit of Islam" and "The Influence of Islam on Social Conditions."	1893

Table 1.4 African American Islamic Movements

Name	Year	Location	Founder
American Muslim Brotherhood[45]	1892–1893	New York, N.Y.	Mohammed A. Webb
Moorish Science	1913	Newark, N.J.	Noble Drew Ali
Temple Ahmadiyyah Movement in Islam (Movement had central location in Chicago, Ill., within the African American community.)	1921	India	Mirza G. Ahmad
Universal Islamic Society	1926	Detroit, Mich.	Duse Muhammad Ali
First Muslim Mosque of Pitt	1928	Pittsburgh, Penn.	Walter Smith Bey (Master teacher in the movement)
Islamic Brotherhood	1929		
State Street Mosque	1929		
Islamic Mission Society (aka Islamic Mission of America, the name of this organization changed at least three times from the Islamic Brotherhood, to the State Street Mosque, and then to the Islamic Mission Society)	1939	New York, N.Y.	Sheikh D.A. Faisal (Sheikh Daoud Ahmed Faisal)

Name	Year	Location	Founder
Allah Temple of Islam (Originally named the Allah Temple of Islam from 1930–33; in 1933, the name of the organization changes under the leadership of the Honorable Elijah Muhammad)	1930	Detroit, Mich.	W. Fard Muhammad
Addeynu Allahe Universal Arabic Association	1930s		
Nation of Islam	1933	Detroit, Mich.	Elijah Muhammad

(The Honorable Elijah Muhammad takes over the leadership of the organization and then moves the national headquarters to Chicago, Ill., in 1934.)

Name	Year	Location	Founder
Fahamme Temple of Islam and Culture	1930s	St. Louis, Mo.	Paul N. Johnson

(Paul Nathaniel Johnson, aka the Ra-Rasool, the Culture Prophet, the Sheik Ahmad Din, the Prophet of Amun-Ra, the Ro-baitu-Ha, and the successor of Kem. The organization was also known as the Fahamme American Ethiopian Temple of Islam and Culture. Richard Brent Turner points out that Ahmad Din was a member of the Ahmadiyya Movement in 1922, primarily serving as a missionary to recruit members in St. Louis, Missouri. He speculates further that Din was believed to be a member of the Moorish Science Temple.)

Name	Year	Location	Founder
African American Mosque	1945	Pittsburgh, Penn.	African Americans purchased and established the first mosque in Pittsburgh, Penn.
Islamic Center of Washington, D.C.	1957	Washington, D.C.	
Hanafi Madh–Hab	1958	Washington, D.C.	Hammas Abdul Khaalis
Darul IslamCenter (Aka Abode of Islam)	1962	Brooklyn, N.Y.	Y. Abdul-Kareem
Muslim Mosque Incorporated	1964	New York, N.Y.	Malcolm X Shabazz
Five Percent Nation of Islam	1964	New York, N.Y.	Clarence 13X

(Group held that 5 percent of the population are prepared to save the population of African Americans; 85 percent are wandering through the hell of North America being death, dumb, and blind in the wilderness of America; and the remaining 10 percent of the population are blood sucking opportunists whose concern is selfishness and personal gain. Ironically, much of this same doctrine is supported by W.E.B. Du Bois in addressing the concept of the talented 10th.)

Name	Year	Location	Founder
Ansaaru Allah Community	1970	Brooklyn, N.Y.	A.M.A. Mahdi (Al Hajj Al Imam Isq Abd Allah Muhammad Al Mahdi)

(TABLE 1.4, CONTINUED)

Name	Year	Location	Founder
Islamic Party of North America	1971	Washington, D.C.	Yusuf M. Hamid
World Community of al–Islam in the West	1976–1981	Chicago, Ill.	W.D. Muhammad
Nation of Islam	1977	Highland Park, Mich.	John Muhammad
Nation of Islam	1977	Chicago, Ill.	Louis Farrakhan
Lost Found Nation of Islam	1977	Atlanta, Ga.	Silas Muhammad
American Muslim Mission	1981–1985	Chicago, Ill.	W.D. Muhammad
The Ministry of W.D. Mohammed	1981–1997		

(Second Resurrection of the Nation of Islam illustrates the organization moves to adopt the name of World Community of al–Islam in the West and then in 1978 to the American Muslim Mission. The focus of the organization then centered on an orthodox form of practicing Islam under the leadership of Chief Imam Warith Deen Mohammed. By the 1980s the national organization was terminated and the focus then addressed a council of Imams on state and regional areas.)

Name	Year	Location	Founder
The Islamic Society of North America (ISNA) is established in Plainfield, Ind. ISNA is now an umbrella organization for many active Islamic groups seeking to further the cause of Islam in the United States.	1982		
Naqshabandiyyah	1986	Key Urban Areas	Maulan Shaykh Nazim Adil Qubrusi
African American Shiite Muslim Community	1987	Los Angeles, Calif.	P.Q. Halifu
Muslim American Community	1990s	Chicago, Ill.	Warith D. Mohammed
Islamic Moorish Empire of the West Incorporated	1990s		
The Muslim American Society	1997–Present		

(See Martha Lee, *The Nation of Islam: An American Millerian Movement.*)

Though most of the discussion in this essay has focused on the founding years of the NOI, the point was to address the direct and indirect correlation of this organization to the intellectual history of Pan-Africanist thought in the United States. Surveying this topic further, by 1935, the Honorable Elijah Muhammad left the city of Chicago and began travel across the United States, as a result of the NOI experiencing internal strife and conflict with "rival factions."[46] This transitory life continued until 1942, when Muhammad was arrested for resisting the draft and sentenced to five years of incarceration in a federal correction institution in Michigan. It is not until 1946 that he resumed his role in a leadership capacity of the Nation of Islam.[47] In 1949, Malcolm X converted to Islam and accepted the teachings of the Honorable Elijah Muhammad while in confinement. This conversion led to him changing his last name from Little to X.[48] By the 1950s, the organization was gaining mass appeal. With Muhammad in the leadership position, many African Americans became attracted to the teachings of Islam and Black Nationalism. A number of leadership figures in the following years of the NOI were recruited from college campuses and local Black communities. The NOI was attracting the attention of the media, and a documentary titled *The Hate That Hate Produced*, aired nationally and produced by Louis Lomax, provided the American media and public a view of this African American Islamic organization.[49]

During the early part of the 1960s, the NOI was part of the national Civil Rights Movement in America. Though considered a separatist organization, the NOI ideology provided a way of studying the condition of African Americans from a Black perspective. Transition and advancement can best describe these years: Malcolm X established the weekly newspaper *Muhammad Speaks*; Malcolm X was appointed the National Spokesperson for the NOI; there was a decline in the physical health of the Honorable Elijah Muhammad; allegations of infidelity were spread defaming the character of the Honorable Elijah Muhammad; Malcolm X was suspended from public lectures and eventually left the organization; Malcolm X was assassinated; and there were a number of internal rival factions involved in shootings and murder.[50]

At the physical expiration of the Honorable Elijah Muhammad, his seventh child, Imam Warith Deen Muhammad, was named his father's successor in 1975. At this point, the movement took an orthodox shift. Interestingly, as illustrated in Table 1.4, by 1977, there were three factions of the NOI which emerged under the leadership of former members of the NOI. The 1980s and 1990s saw a great deal of media attention focused on the faction of the NOI headquartered in Chicago. Nyang expounds on this topic: "The history of the movement from 1975 to 1985 is thus a history of gradual but fundamental changes effected by Imam Muhammad in order to bring his followers to the mainstream of the Islamic umma."[51]

Paradoxically, the historiography of the organization appears somewhat complex during the mid–1960s. Some earlier detractors of the NOI saw the post-sixties as a time to attack the validity and effectiveness of the organization's religious, economic, and socio-political teachings. Again it was Imam Mohammed's method of transferring the organization to a form of Orthodox Islam, which became a palatable theme of research inquiry.

Still, many scholars and independent writers have apprehensions about writing on this topic. It was not until 1997 that Claude A. Clegg published the first biographical study of the Honorable Elijah Muhammad, titled *An Original Man: The Life and Times of Elijah Muhammad.*[52] Much of the speculation centered on the delay of this published topic can be attributed to the lack of accessibility to sources; difficulties in communication with former members of the NOI and members of the royal family; and the fear of physical harm from loyal members of the NOI, who believed in the reclamation of the Honorable Elijah Muhammad's name and were thought to be willing to avenge defamation of Muhammad's character.

The publication of Clegg's biography created a ground-swell of publications on the Honorable Elijah Muhammad and other leadership figures within the NOI. Ironically, a subject which was formerly met with intensity and fear has now become one of interest, a way to gain knowledge and information about African Americans inside the faith of Islam. Engaging a mixture of ideological views from integrationist and nationalists schools of thought, the issue still in many ways appears to evade the concept of Black cultural agency and autonomy.

Generally, the historiography of the NOI has undergone a number of transitions:

(1) It was labeled as a Voodoo cult in the 1930s; (2) It was identified as Black Nationalism; (3) There was a void of literature on this topic; (4) It became an American millenarian movement; and (5) It became an integrationist protest organization with the organization and advent of the Million Man March in 1995. Possibly with study of the array of information on this issue, scholars will attempt to examine as many variables as possible in describing and evaluating this organization its role in the social protest movements of African American historiography.

Conclusion

The purpose of this project was to address historiography, intellectual thought, and Pan-Africanism related to the Nation of Islam. Credited with being one of the most influential organizations in the intellectual tradition of African America, the NOI was able to attract those members of our society whom most institutions and individuals had given up on. C. Eric Lincoln's study raises the issue of the Muslim movement serving in the capacity of protest organization. However, the point centered on religious transition, transformation, and transcendence of the human spirit. Using metaphors and analogies of redemptive suffering of Africana people during physical bondage and institutional enslavement, the NOI was able to reinterpret this causation of suffering as a point of perseverance for collective memory and to use this memory and ethos for the liberation of Black people in the United States. Taking the moral high ground allowed the NOI to enable African Americans to see their own faults, and simultaneously to address the Eurocentric hegemonic perspective. Enslavement as an epoch involved the systematic subordination of Africana people on a global level. Still, although we are cognizant of the cruelties of this era, African Americans had not engaged this topic from a Black perspective. The Honorable Elijah Muhammad provided a lens for the fusion of the teachings of Islam, Africana historiography, and religious-economic nationalism. One of the primary advantages of historiography as previously mentioned in this essay has been its flexibility of interpretation. Indeed, the NOI used the concept of interpretation for examining religious, philosophical, historical, and political texts. This was one of the strong points of the organization. Yet, one of the shortcomings of research on this topic has been the dialectical way in which studies are organized and appear to unfold. The choice or selection of alternative religious practices by African Americans is one of realism. On the other hand, the desire to secure and practice these types of customs and rituals exhibits the quest for Black cultural autonomy. Saying this brings forth the repercussions of European hostility and the perception of a loss of privilege, gained by systematically subordinating people of Africana decent. Perhaps the role of future researchers and activist intellectuals is not to replicate the golden years of the NOI, but rather to examine what tools from this movement can be used in an info-tech society to aid in the cultural, political, economic, and social liberation of Africana people.

Notes

1. Charles H. Wesley, "The Concept of Negro Inferiority in American Thought," *Journal of Negro History*, pp. 540–541.

2. Aminah Beverly McCloud, *African American Islam* (New York: Routledge, 1995), p. 27.

3. *African American Desk Reference* (New York: A Stonesong Press Book—John Wiley and Sons, Inc., 1999), p. 63.

4. Robert Staples, *Introduction to Black Sociology* (New York: Oxford University Press, 1988), p.

5. See James L. Conyers, Jr. and Alva Barnett, editors, *African American Sociology*

(Chicago, Ill.: Nelson Hall Publishers, 1999), essay on Charles H. Wesley and historiography.

6. Evelyn Brooks Higginbotham, "African-American Women's History and the Metalanguage of Race," in *We Specialize in the Wholly Impossible: A Reader in Black Women's History*, edited by Darlene Clark Hine, Wilma King, and Linda Reed (Brooklyn, New York: Carlson Publishing, 1995), pp. 3–4.

7. Steven Tsoukalas, *The Nation of Islam: Understanding the Black Muslims* (Phillipsburg, New Jersey: P and R Publishing, 2001), pp. 21–22.

8. Karl Evanzz, *The Messenger: The Rise and Fall of Elijah Muhammad* (New York: Pantheon Books, 1999), p. 33.

9. Tsoukalas, *The Nation of Islam*, p. 1.

10. Richard Brent Turner, *Islam in the African American Experience* (Bloomington, Indiana: University of Indiana Press, 1997), pp. 47–48.

11. Bruce Perry, ed., *Malcolm X: The Last Speeches* (New York: Pathfinder Press, 1989), pp. 152–53.

12. Turner, *Islam in the African American Experience*, p. 47.

13. Clifton E. Marsh, *From Black Muslims to Muslims: The Resurrection, Transformation, and Change of the Lost–Found Nation of Islam in America, 1930–1995* (Lanham, Maryland: Scarecrow Press, 1996), p. 9.

14. Amir Nashid Ali Muhammad, *Muslims in America: Seven Centuries of History (1312–1998)* (Beltsville, Maryland: Amana Publications, 1998), p. 42.

15. Ronald W. Walters, *Pan Africanism in the African Diaspora: An Analysis of Modern Afrocentric Political Movements* (Detroit, Michigan: Wayne State University Press, 1993), p. 46.

16. Adib Rashad, *The History of Islam and Black Nationalism in the Americas* (Beltsville, Maryland: Writers' Incorporated, 1991), p. 61.

17. Adib Rashad, *Elijah Muhammad and the Ideological Foundation of the Nation of Islam* (Hampton, Virginia: U.B. and U.S. Communications Systems, June 1994), p. 121.

18. Tsoukalas, *The Nation of Islam*, p. 31.

19. Emory H. Tunison, "Mohammed Alexander Russell Webb: First American Muslim," *The Arab World*, Volume 1, No. 3, 1945, pp. 13–18, 15.

20. Tsoukalas, *The Nation of Islam*, p. 20, 46.

21. Samuel T. Livingston, "NOI: Divided We Stand," *The International Journal of Africana Studies* no. 5 (December 1999), pp. 50–51.

22. Encarta Encyclopedia CD-ROM; Britannica *Encyclopedia of Black Profiles*; *For the People, By the People* (Paterson, New Jersey: The People's Publishing Group Incorporated, 1998), pp. 283, 301, 356–357, 376; Robert Divine, T.H. Breen, George M. Fredrickson, and R. Hal Williams, *America Past and Present*, 2nd edition (Glenview, Illinois: Scott Foresman and Company), 1987 .

23. Wilson Jeremiah Moses, "From Booker T. to Malcolm X: Black Political Thought, 1895–1965," in *Upon These Shores: Themes in the African American Experience 1600–Present*, edited by William R. Scott and William G. Shade, p. 208 (New York: Routledge, 2000).

24. See the entry on Pan-Africanism in William L. Andrews, Frances Smith Foster, and Trudier Harris, *The Oxford Companion to African American Literature* (New York: Oxford University Press, 1997), pp. 558–559.

25. Moses, "From Booker T. to Malcolm X," p. 215.

26. E.U. Essien-Udom, *Black Nationalism: A Search for Identity in America* (Chicago: University of Chicago Press, 1971), p. 18.

27. William H. Banks, Jr., *The Black Muslims* (Philadelphia: Chelsea House Publishers, 1997), p. 35.

28. Marsh, *From Black Muslims to Muslims*, p. 37.

29. Minister Tynetta Muhammad, "A Brief History on the Origin of the Nation of Islam in America: A Nation of Peace and Beauty," <http:www.noi.org/history/html>.

30. Zafar Ishaq Ansari, "W.D. Mohammed: The Making of a Black Muslim Leader (1933–1961)," *The American Journal of Islamic Social Sciences* 2 (1985): 245–62, 248.

31. See Karl Evanzz, *The Messenger: The Rise and Fall of Elijah Muhammad* (New York: Pantheon Books, 1999). Evanzz posits an interesting journalist's analysis of the life and organizational structure of the Nation of Islam. Emphasis is given to Ugan Ali's role in the earlier formation and structure of the Nation of Islam.

32. Video tape from the biography series on African American Achievers, specific video on Elijah Muhammad.

33. Minister Tynetta Muhammad, "A Brief History on the Origin of the Nation of Islam in America: A Nation of Peace and Beauty," <http:www.noi.org/history/html>.

34. Amir Nashid Ali Muhammad, *Muslims in America: Seven Centuries of History (1312–1998): Collections and Stories of American Muslims* (Beltsville, Maryland: Amana Publications, 1998), pp. 47–48.

35. Clyde-Ahmad Winters, "Afro-American Muslims—From Slavery to Freedom," *Islamic Studies* 17, no. 4 (winter 1978): 187–203, 200.

36. Richard Brent Turner, "The Ahmadiyya Mission to Blacks in the United States in the 1920s," *The Journal of Religious Thought* 44, no. 2 (winter–spring 1988): 59–60.

37. For additional discussion on the merging of leadership see Marsh, *From Black Muslims to Muslims*; Evanzz, *The Messenger*; and Turner, *Islam in the African American Experience*.

38. Turner, *Islam in the African American Experience*, p. 47.

39. Evanzz, *The Messenger*, pp. 94–95. Evanzz discusses the strategic plan by which the organization of Islamic converts changed for ideological, political, and law enforcement reasons.

40. Robin D.G. Kelley and Earl Lewis, eds., *To Make Our World Anew* (New York: Oxford University Press, 2000), p. 410.

41. C. Eric Lincoln, *The Black Muslims in America* (Boston: Beacon Press, 1967), p. 51.

42. From the chronology in William R. Scott and William G. Shade, *Upon These Shores* (New York; Routledge, 2000), pp. xxv–xxvi.

43. Walter Dan Abilla, "A Study of Black Muslims: An Analysis of Commitment," Ph.D. Dissertation, Case Western Reserve University, January 1972, pp. 44–45; Aminah Beverly McCloud, *African American Islam* (New York: Routledge, 1995), pp. 193–97; Nehemia Levtzion and Randall L. Pouwels, eds., *The History of Islam in Africa* (Athens, Ohio: Ohio University Press, 2000), pp. 575–577.

44. McCloud, *African American Islam*, pp. 10, 69, 91; Richard Brent Turner, "Islam and Black Nationalism," in *Microsoft Encarta Africana 2000*, edited by Henry Louis Gates and Anthony Appiah, United States Trademark, 1993–1999; Marsh, *From Black Muslims to Muslims*, p. 81; Turner, *Islam and the African American Experience*, pp. 64, 120, 125–126, 225, 232–234; Lincoln, *The Black Muslims in America*, pp. 220–21; Dr. P. Chike Onwuachi, *Black Ideology in African Diaspora* (Chicago, Ill.: Third World Press, 1973), p. 58; Islamic Information Office of Hawaii, <http://www.iio.org/history/index.php>.

45. McCloud, *African American Islam*, pp. 10, 69, 91; Turner, "Islam and Black Nationalism"; Marsh, *From Black Muslims to Muslims*, p. 81; Turner, *Islam and the African American Experience*, pp. 64, 120, 125–126, 225, 232–234; Lincoln, *The Black Muslims in America*, pp. 220–21; Dr. P. Chike Onwuachi, *Black Ideology in African Diaspora* (Chicago, Ill.: Third World Press, 1973), p. 58; Islamic Information Office of Hawaii, <http://www.iio.org/history/index.php>.

46. William H. Banks, Jr., *The Black Muslims* (Philadelphia: Chelesea House Publishers, 1977), p. 121.

47. Banks, *The Black Muslims*, p. 121.

48. Banks, p. 121.

49. Banks, p. 122.

50. Banks, pp. 122–23.

51. Sulayman Nyang, "A New Beginning for the Black Muslims," *Arabia*, 1985, pp. 50–51.

52. Claude A. Clegg, *An Original Man: The Life and Times of Elijah Muhammad* (New York: St. Martins Press, 1997).

Bibliography

Abilla, Walter D. "A Study of Black Muslims: An Analysis of Commitment." Ph.D. Dissertation, Case Western Reserve University, January 1972.

Andrews, William L. Frances Smith Foster, and Trudier Harris. *The Oxford Companion to African American Literature*. New York: Oxford University Press, 1997. Pp. 558–559. (See entry on Pan-Africanism.)

Ansari, Zafar Ishaq. "W.D. Mohammed: The Making of a Black Muslim Leader (1933–1961)," *The American Journal of Islamic Social Sciences* 2 (1985): 245–62.

Banks, William H., Jr. *The Black Muslims*. Philadelphia: Chelsea House Publishers, 1997.

Conyers, James L., Jr., and Alva Barnett, eds. *African American Sociology*. Chicago, Ill.: Nelson Hall Publishers, 1999.

Divine, Robert, T.H. Breen, George M. Fredrickson, and R. Hal Williams. *America Past and Present*. 2nd edition. Glenview, Ill.: Scott Foresman and Company, 1987.

Encarta Encyclopedia CD-ROM. Britannica Encyclopedia of Black Profiles. *For the People, By the People*. Paterson, New Jersey: The People's Publishing Group Incorporated, 1998.

Essien-Udom, E.U. *Black Nationalism: A Search for Identity in America*. Chicago: University of Chicago Press, 1971.

Evanzz, Karl. *The Messenger: The Rise and Fall of Elijah Muhammad*. New York: Pantheon Books, 1999.

Higginbotham, Evelyn Brooks. "African-American Women's History and the Metalanguage of Race." In *We Specialize in the Wholly Impossible: A Reader in Black Women's History*, edited by Darlene Clark Hine, Wilma King, and Linda Reed, pp. 3–4. Brooklyn, New York: Carlson Publishing, 1995.

Islamic Information Office of Hawaii. <http://www.iio.org/history/index.php>.

Kelley, Robin D.G. and Earl Lewis, eds. *To Make Our World Anew*. New York: Oxford University Press, 2000.

Levtzion, Nehemia and Randall L. Pouwels, eds. *The History of Islam in Africa*. Athens, Ohio: Ohio University Press, 2000.

Lincoln, C. Eric. *The Black Muslims in America*. Boston: Beacon Press, 1967.

Livingston, Samuel T. "NOI: Divided We Stand." *The International Journal of Africana Studies* no. 5 (December 1999): 49–67.

Marsh, Clifton E. *From Black Muslims to Muslims: The Resurrection, Transformation, and Change of the Lost-Found Nation of Islam in America, 1930–1995*. Lanham, Maryland: Scarecrow Press, 1996.

McCloud, Aminah Beverly. *African American Islam*. New York: Routledge, 1995.

Moses, Wilson Jeremiah. "From Booker T. to Malcolm X: Black Political Thought, 1895–1965." In *Upon These Shores: Themes in the African American Experience 1600–Present*, edited by William R. Scott and William G. Shade, p. 208. New York: Routledge, 2000.

Muhammad, Amir Nashid Ali. *Muslims in America: Seven Centuries of History (1312–1998).* Beltsville, Maryland: Amana Publications, 1998.

Muhammad, Minister Tynetta. "A Brief History on the Origin of the Nation of Islam in America: A Nation of Peace and Beauty." <http:www.noi.org/history/html>.

Onwuachi, Dr. P. Chike. *Black Ideology in African Diaspora.* Chicago, Ill.: Third World Press, 1973.

Perry, Bruce, ed. *Malcolm X: The Last Speeches.* New York: Pathfinder Press, 1989.

Rashad, Adib. *Elijah Muhammad and the Ideological Foundation of the Nation of Islam.* Hampton, Virginia: U.B. and U.S. Communications Systems, June 1994.

_____. *The History of Islam and Black Nationalism in the Americas.* Beltsville, Maryland: Writers' Incorporated, 1991. *African American Desk Reference.* New York: A Stonesong Press Book—John Wiley and Sons, Inc., 1999.

Scott, William R. and William G. Shade. *Upon These Shores.* New York; Routledge, 2000.

Staples, Robert L. *Introduction to Black Sociology.* New York: Oxford University Press, 1988.

Tsoukalas, Steven. *The Nation of Islam: Understanding the Black Muslims.* Phillipsburg, New Jersey: P and R Publishing, 2001.

Tunison, Emory H. "Mohammed Alexander Russell Webb: First American Muslim." *The Arab World* 1, no. 3 (1945): 13–18.

Turner, Richard Brent. "Islam and Black Nationalism." In *Microsoft Encarta Africana 2000,* edited by Henry Louis Gates and Anthony Appiah. United States Trademark, 1993–1999.

Turner, Richard Brent. *Islam in the African American Experience.* Bloomington, Indiana: University of Indiana Press, 1997.

Turner, Richard Brent. "The Ahmadiyya Mission to Blacks in the United States in the 1920s." *The Journal of Religious Thought* 44, no. 2 (winter–spring 1988): 50–66.

Walters, Ronald W. *Pan Africanism in the African Diaspora: An Analysis of Modern Afrocentric Political Movements.* Detroit, Michigan: Wayne State University Press, 1993.

Wesley, Charles H. "The Concept of Negro Inferiority in American Thought." *Journal of Negro History* XXV (October, 1940): 540–560.

Winters, Clyde-Ahmad. "Afro-American Muslims—From Slavery to Freedom." *Islamic Studies* 17, no. 4 (winter 1978): 187–205.

10. Understanding Elijah Muhammad

MALACHI CRAWFORD

The objective of this paper is to delineate the political, social and economic ideologies of Elijah Muhammad. While acknowledging the importance of such factors as social ecology, this analysis is not primarily concerned with the beliefs of Muhammad's predecessors; it speaks to the productions of Muhammad instead of his producers.

This study makes use of a comprehensive and comparative framework from which to view and engage the research. In order that the depth and breadth of this analysis be better served, the historical and philosophical beliefs of Elijah Muhammad are placed next to current and past issues in Black America's fight for independence. This arrangement allows for a lucid understanding of today's Black leadership by observing the political, cultural, social, religious, and economic implications taken from the writings and interviews of Elijah Muhammad. Kawaida theory is used to understand and categorize the data under consideration.

Triangulation is the use of more than one research design in a study. Both historical analysis and ethnography are employed here, with the former being the lead design of the project. An historical analysis is a research design that systematically attempts to undertake the collection of primary source data in a way that discovers the true beliefs of the subject. There are both internal and external flaws with applying this design, one of which is the internal bias of the author. Through employing the method of historical analysis, this work attempts to answer two queries: What are the essential beliefs espoused by Muhammad; and, is there systematic refinement in the strategies employed by Black leaders to gain Black independence?

The strategic appeal of the Nation of Islam resulted from the circumstance surrounding Northern Black communities during the 1930s. Lawrence Levine notes a rising distinction between the sacred and secular aspects of Black life that began with the abolition of slavery (Levine 1977). Freedom for slaves led Blacks to partially accept White culture and marginalize Black

FIG. 1: THEORY AND METHODS

Theory: Kawaida   Method: Historical Analysis   Format: Intellectual Biography

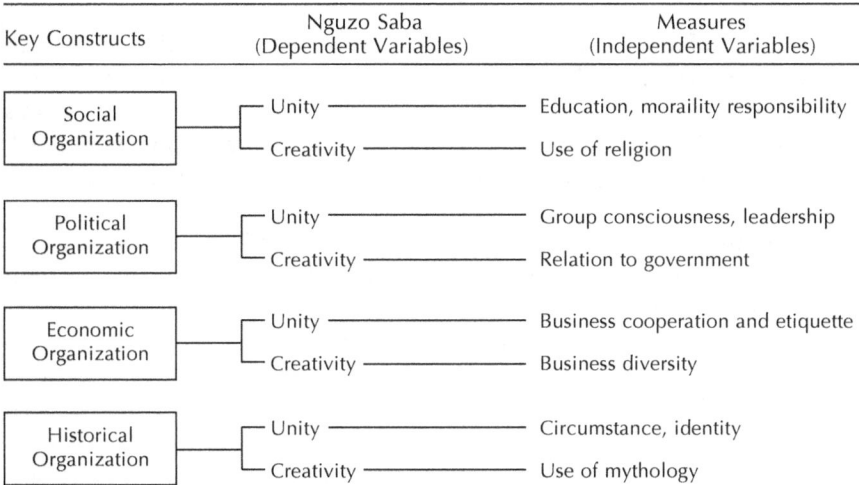

Key Constructs	Nguzo Saba (Dependent Variables)	Measures (Independent Variables)
Social Organization	Unity	Education, moraility responsibility
	Creativity	Use of religion
Political Organization	Unity	Group consciousness, leadership
	Creativity	Relation to government
Economic Organization	Unity	Business cooperation and etiquette
	Creativity	Business diversity
Historical Organization	Unity	Circumstance, identity
	Creativity	Use of mythology

culture. American education, for example, led to the decline of spirituals and those things associated with slave culture. Daniel A. Payne, a well known bishop in the African Methodist Episcopal Church during the mid-nineteenth century, went from one city to another decrying the need of Blacks to desist performing ring shouts (Levine 1977). Thus, freedmen were of the general opinion that no power existed in acting Black. Therefore, an apparent distinction in Black culture between sacred and secular led to changes in Black religious structure and song. This dichotomy formed the backbone of the disputes between Holiness and Spiritualist churches, the former accepting the ways of the past while the latter rejected them. Musically, with its focus on the afterlife, Gospel placed man in a position solely dependent on God. Blues, a highly personal musical genre, centered on depicting the day to day conflict in Black social interaction. Specific fields within Black culture failed to address the sacred and secular needs of the Black community together.

The Nation of Islam's (NOI) use of religion in combating the social, political, and economical powerlessness of Blacks in America was—at the time—culturally dissonant. Unsurprisingly, accusations against Black Christian preachers that Christianity failed to liberate Blacks resounds in this climate. Elijah Muhammad's focus on the enslavement of Blacks in America combined the sacred and secular components of the NOI's ideology. Muhammad's main contribution to the NOI, Black identity and nationalism, rests in the attention that he placed on slavery. After being released from prison in 1946, Elijah Muhammad's decision to call for Black separation within the

U.S. resulted from this change in ideology and had a dramatic influence on Black humanity (Evanzz 1999).

◆ ◆ ◆

On October 7, 1898, Elijah Muhammad was born Elijah Poole in Sandersville, Georgia (Marsh 1996). His life in Georgia as a sharecropper influenced his later thinking in life to an extraordinary degree. Muhammad's experience with sharecropping caused him to be a leading proponent of Black equity and economic independence among Black leaders of the twentieth century.

The American institution of sharecropping, and its predecessor, led to similarities in the platforms advocated by other Black leaders who have been directly affected by these institutions; for example, Booker T. Washington. Given the fact that Elijah Muhammad was born in Georgia, it is not too hard to find reasons why this man found moral discipline essential to the upliftment of the Black race. Similar to the Washingtonian School of Black social thought, which has its origins in the social conditions of the Deep South, Muhammad believed that Blacks must come to have good public behavior, at all times be good and honest, descent upstanding members within the community (E. Muhammad 1965). Moreover, the institution of sharecropping is one that pits Blacks without any land, money, or ownership of anything but themselves against a system of perpetual indebtedness. Muhammad made the same argument for Blacks working in industry.

"I have lived with you all my life. I was born in the South. I have looked upon the evil treatment of our people day and night. I have shed tears for you many times. No justice whatsoever. I have seen people kicked about who asked for a fair salary. I have heard it said to a brother, 'You take what I say, you don't figure behind me, Nigger'" (E. Muhammad 1965).

Another instrumental experience influencing the ideology of Elijah Muhammad is the fact that his father was a minister (Evanzz 1999). Muhammad came to see the hypocrisy in the treatment of Blacks in America and White America's professed adherence to the principles of Christianity. This inevitably leads to his disillusionment with Christianity and its ability to be a viable religion for the achievement of Black independence. Summarily, when Fard Muhammad introduced Elijah Muhammad to a modified form of Islam, Fard made his mark on a man with longstanding experiences of American institutionalized racism (R. Muhammad 1980).

As a sidebar, it would do a disservice to any understanding of Elijah Muhammad to ignore the extent to which such a person as Farad Muhammad, and doctrines as those of the Universal Negro Improvement Association and Moorish Science Temple, factor into the ideological formulations of Elijah Muhammad. The most obvious example of systematic strategical refinement within the fight for Black independence, as it relates to Elijah Muhammad, is seen in his connection with the teachings of Fard Muhammad and the Moorish Science Temple. As Clifton E. Marsh shows in table 1,

TABLE 1: ORGANIZATIONAL COMPARISONS BETWEEN MOORISH SCIENCE TEMPLE AND NATION OF ISLAM

	Moorish Science Temple	*Nation of Islam*
Nationality	Moorish Americans	Asiatic-Black
Prophet	Noble Drew Ali	Elijah Muhammad
Religion	Islam	Islam
Land	No desire for separate state; psychological separation through Moorish status	Separate
Sacred text	Koran created by Noble Drew Ali	Islamic Koran and Christian Bible
God	Allah	Allah in the form of Fard Muhammad
Race	Asiatics	Asiatic Blacks (Tribe of Shabazz)
Place of Worship	Temple	Mosque
Heaven	In the mind	On earth
Separation of Sexes	Yes	Yes
Names	Bey, El	X—Replace slave name because real name is unknown
Dress	Men—Fez worn during official functions, beards and mustaches allowed, suit and tie optional Women—Turbans optional, no make-up, pants, long dresses to shoe tops	Men—Suit and ties, clean shaven Women—Head covered, no make-up, long dresses to shoe tops
Citizenship	United States of America	Nation of Islam, Nation within a Nation

Muhammad's Nation of Islam is a hybrid of the Moorish Science Temple.

As a reaction to America's violence against Blacks, Noble Drew Ali figured that he could change the treatment of Blacks in America through changing their culture and identity. The Moorish Science Temple used religion to change the cultural identity of its members. Drew Ali sought an attached-appendage type of relationship within American culture and society. Likewise, citizenship was one of the pillars of membership within the Moorish Science Temple. The MST desired acceptance into the American political, economic, and social structure, and offered Blacks a rebirth in another culture—Islam. With this cultural rebirth, the integrationist philosophy of the MST willingly dismissed, that is, accepted, the enslavement of Blacks in America. Drew Ali noticed that even the darkest of Africans born outside of the U.S. received better treatment than Blacks in America.

Social Organization

Use of Religion

Elijah Muhammad's Nation of Islam used religious doctrine to create unity, invite economic prosperity, and incite social, moral, and psychological change among Black America. There are several important reasons for the effective influence of the Nation of Islam among Blacks, relative to religion. As previously stated, the NOI helped to halt the diffusion of the sacred and secular aspects of Black culture. Consistently, the NOI's popularity among Blacks rested on the organization's adherence to moral principles, also found within the Bible, that are not uncommon to any religion. Second, Elijah Muhammad examined Europeanized Christianity in such a way that forced Blacks to look at the inherent racism within that strain of the religion. One of the tenets of the Christian religion is that man is built in the image of God. Elijah Muhammad asked why the Bible does not show a savior in the image of Black people. Muhammad also related the suffering of Biblical peoples to that of Blacks in America. Invariably, this view toward Black suffering left Black humanity in the hands of Blacks to affirm.

The immediate value of Muhammad's work in religion can be seen when taking into account the role a shared experience plays in the future direction of a people. Muhammad's use of the Nation of Islam as a means for expressing the idea that Blacks in America have a common experience was intentional. The idea of shared experiences among American Blacks is indispensable, when considering the relation a common experience has to the level of trust amongst a people. For good reason, Muhammad exploited this relationship to the best of his ability. Trust is based on the shared historical experience of a people. The result of trust, fostered by knowledge of the historical experience of one's people, is love of that same people. In this systematic manner, Muhammad used religion to counteract a few of the primary methods of American slavery and White subjugation of the Black race, one of which is Black hate (see fig. 2).

Fig. 2: Elijah Muhammad's systematic attack on the psychological and societal effects of American slavery

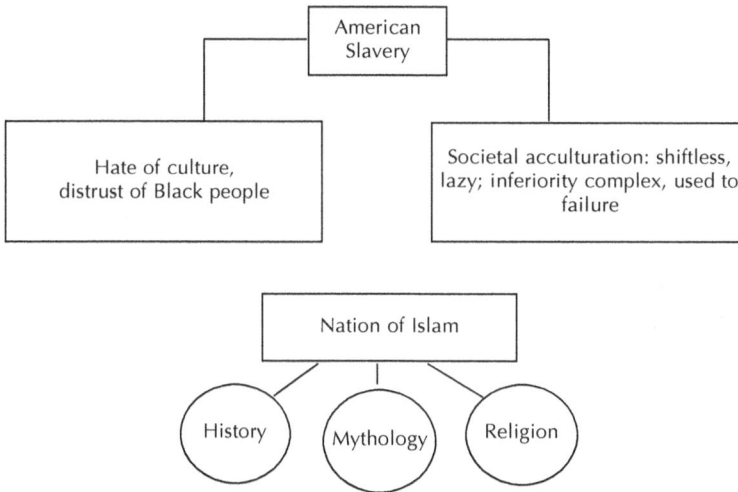

Muhammad's intentional use of a shared experience among Black people served yet another purpose. By relating the common experience of Blacks in America to an African past, Muhammad counters the stereotypical portrayals of Blacks as being an innately backward and lazy people. Consistently noting the African past of Blacks in America emphasizes the past successes of Blacks and fights the inferiority complex induced by oppression.

Morality

The concept of Blacks, especially Black men, being role models to other Blacks is a major vein of thought within the Nation of Islam. When one considers the appearance of the members of the Nation of Islam within Black communities today and the message of the Million Man March, one sees the historical manifestations of the ideological formulations of Black leaders out of the South. The difference between Booker T. Washington and the Nation of Islam under Elijah Muhammad on the issue of moral discipline resides in the rationals behind their policies.

For Washington, discipline was a prerequisite for the aversion of White aggression toward Black curiosity or noncompliance. The Nation of Islam, however, is often quoted as saying that morality runs counter to White philosophy because of his understanding of the moral paradox cast by White America. While Whites seek to question Blacks on their moral behavior, as if to desire it, the very idea of Black morality naturally opposes the American institution of chattel slavery. Any discussion on the morality of a people naturally requires an assumption of the inherent humanity of that people. The premise of American slavery works against this notion.

Historical Organization

MYTHOLOGY

The use of mythology within Black religion has always been of extreme importance. As a methodological technique, mythology establishes a foundation of common cultural beliefs within a group. Any thorough analysis of the introduction of Islam into Africa reveals that most Islamic contacts with Africa were conquests. The Nation of Islam made the Islamic tradition palatable to Blacks by infusing aspects of Islam into Black history. This was possible through the use of myths centering on the creation of people throughout the world.

The Yacub fable is just one component within the Nation of Islam's mythology designed to validate the social and philosophical views of the Nation of Islam and redefine the history of Blacks in relation to Islam. Essentially, the story is an allegory of the plight of Blacks and an elaborate collection of myths detailing the creation of the races. While depicting Whites as having come from evil circumstances, the story places Blacks at a point of control in world history.

The importance of redefining the history of Blacks so that Black history predates enslavement cannot be underestimated. Beginning with a technologically advanced African civilization (the Lost Tribe of Shabazz), the Yacub fable depicts the ancestors of Blacks as being intelligent creators of world history. In one sense, the purpose of the fable deliberately reshapes the images of Blacks used to failure. Still, in yet another sense, the fable questions the fall of Blacks from positions of power in the world and the rise of Europeans to the same. Aside from being just a factor for reshaping Black identity, the system of myths incorporated within the philosophy of the Nation of Islam challenged the political aspirations of Blacks on a global level. Paradoxically, however, the utilization of myths on the part of the Nation of Islam created undesirable aspects of Black history as well. As a consequence of using mythology to infuse and reshape the introduction of Islam into Africa alongside the historical experience of Blacks in America, the Nation of Islam necessarily identified the genealogical origins of Blacks with that of Asiatics. The identification of Black genealogy with Asiatics allowed the Nation of Islam to declare that Christianity is a religion for Whites.

According to the Nation of Islam, history had always shown Whites to be of an aggressive nature—inconsistent with those things pertaining to life and harmony. Therefore, White humanity was at its foundation evil. Consistently, the Nation of Islam allegorically employed this perception of White humanity within the Koranic principle of Jihad, the battle of good versus evil, to its advantage.

Quite different from the perspective of the Nation of Islam on the subject of White humanity was that of Martin L. King, Jr. King was of the opinion that the salvation of Blacks, or that of any other people, depended on the salvation of all other people in the world. Moreover, King insisted that for Blacks not to seek the humanity in other people questioned the humanity of Blacks themselves. There is probably no single factor more influential, in terms of affecting Black consciousness, than the dynamic of culture within the Black community.

Political Organization

Elijah Muhammad's successful rise to power primarily among Blacks with little or no education or labor skills is in keeping with a long line of ancestral precedent set by more than a few Black leaders before him, e.g., Nat Turner, Henry-Highland Garnett, and Marcus Garvey. One of the similar patterns of thought throughout the ideologies of these Black leaders is having Blacks confer upon themselves their own humanity. Elijah Muhammad talked about Blacks needing to be able to love themselves, the distinct, prideful and rich aspects of Black history, and the beauty of Black physical features (E. Muhammad 1965).

Besides being psychologically empowering, Muhammad's call for Blacks to realize their own humanity is politically strategic. Through his writings, speeches, and interviews one sees that Muhammad understood the real foundation of Black power as being Black people. It is within and from Black people that Muhammad sought to strengthen his Nation of Islam. Observing the behavior of this country through history toward people of color, Muhammad made obviously unrealistic intentions to petition a violently hostile government and people to make concessions of power.

Muhammad realized certain faults within the thinking of other Black social movements. For how could one petition an immoral and uncivil government or people for something it did not own and had not shown itself (E. Muhammad 1967)? Consequently, Muhammad's views on Black humanity gave many contributions to the Nation of Islam's dealings with the Black community.

As Muhammad (1965) aptly noted,

> You remain as a free slave to your slavemaster. You demand that he rec-
> ognize you as his equal. You are making yourself look small in the eyes of
> the world. If every so-called Negro were fired, what would you do? Would
> you unite and go to Washington and demand that the government give
> you a job? You would be foolish enough to do that! If they beat you by
> the thousands, what right have you to say that he should not lash you?
> You have made yourself his slave [63].

The Nation of Islam's views on Black morality in America shape and define the organization's political perspective. This becomes crucial when one seeks to link the political ideology of the Nation of Islam to other Black leaders. The Rev. Martin Luther King, Jr., addressed the issue of Black humanity through Black morality. It is germane to consider that engaging Black morality necessarily involves addressing the humanity of Black people. King insisted that as long as Blacks are not allowed political equality because of who Blacks are (which includes the system of beliefs held by Blacks), then it is impossible to begin discussion on the rights of Black Americans as Americans.

Although Rev. Martin Luther King, Jr., shared similar views with the Nation of Islam on America's necessary acceptance of Black morality for Black rights within America, King diverged with Muhammad on the possibility of engaging this strategy. In using King as a point of reference, one can, again, see the strategic refinement of political ideology within Black leadership.

Another point of digression between King's movement for civil rights and the ideology of the Nation of Islam centers on the humanity of Whites. Basing their beliefs on centuries of racial injustice and race oppression, the Nation of Islam viewed Whites as being an innately evil people.

ROLE OF BLACK WOMEN

Understanding the role of Black women in the NOI is essential in understanding the development and maintenance of the organization. While Black women may not control the avenues to status within the NOI and the Black community in general, they undeniably assign the values that people associate with status. Black women have power over priority and measure as they relate to status. Elijah Muhammad explained this phenomenon in terms of two principles: an administrative (male) principle and an organizational (female) principle. Given this analysis, one can conclude that Black women have enormous control over the timing of Black social movements. The periodization of Black social movements might swing on whether material possessions or moralistic principles are the highest measures of self-worth within the Black community.

Wallace D. Farad's approach to the members of the Paradise Valley

Community certainly reveals his knowledge of the importance of Black women in social struggle. Farad's initial entrance into the homes of Detroit's Blacks came via his peddling of cheap trinkets and goods to Black women. Could Farad have been as successful in approaching Black men?

Economic Organization

Elijah Muhammad worked several blue-collar jobs from 1923–1925 in Detroit, Michigan. Thus, Elijah Muhammad's introduction to the labor force was as a semiskilled worker (R. Muhammad 1980). Considering the fact that there were no labor unions for Blacks, and, given the caprice of White business owners toward Blacks (especially at the onset of the Great Depression), Muhammad, more likely than not, saw the need for Black economic independence as essential to the survival of Blacks within America. As Elijah Muhammad (1965, 173) notes, "The Black man in America faces a serious economic problem today and the white race's Christianity cannot solve it. You, the so-called American Negro, with the help of Allah can solve your own problem." Consequently, his speeches within the Nation of Islam stress the idea that Blacks must do for themselves (E. Muhammad 1967)

Apparent in the Nation of Islam's practice of Black economic autonomy is the purchasing of land, pooling of resources within the Black community, and the aggregation of Blacks with few skills and no skills at all. The nation of Islam owned grocery stores, factories, education centers and restaurants. Moreover, it is the practice of the Nation of Islam to give service contracts to Black entrepreneurs (E. Muhammad 1965). Consistently, a community of autonomous Black merchants parallels the ideas brought forth in the Washingtonian school of thought. Such is the influence and permeation of Elijah Muhammad's personal experience on the Nation of Islam. What does all this mean?

Analysis

An analysis of the extent to which the economic, political, and social ideologies of Elijah Muhammad's Nation of Islam and other Black leaders' movements are similar reveals a few subjects of future study. Noting the differences between Elijah Muhammad and other Black leaders, as they relate to White humanity, to what depth, historically, can the division among Black leaders seeking to dissolve Black plight be attributed to this single factor? On what grounds have past Black leaders with equivalent differences agreed to work cooperatively?

The Nation of Islam came to power during a time when Black identity was in a period of transition. Not surprisingly, Black culture became the foundation of the Nation of Islam's bid for membership from the Black community. The central components of the Nation of Islam's strategy for improving the condition of Blacks in America began through addressing cultural awareness among Blacks. Apparently, the Nation of Islam desperately wanted to change the xenophobic behavior that existed throughout Black communities. In attempting to address changes in the behavior of Blacks, a drastic modification of the negative self-images held by Blacks became necessary.

Black fear of Black culture had been deeply and systematically learned by Blacks since the time of enslavement in America. An undoing of this learned process required exposing Blacks to positive images of Black people throughout history. The Nation of Islam, therefore, sought to establish the history of Blacks in America prior to enslavement. This procedure was accomplished through the use of myths. The NOI made the Islamic tradition palatable to Blacks by incorporating aspects of the religion into Black history, partially through the use of these myths. Elijah Muhammad took the enslavement of Blacks in America and fused the history, mythology, and religion of the NOI. This gave Blacks a sense of nationhood. Clearly, analysis of American slavery and the NOI reveal that humanity is the minimum of all human comforts. For humanity gives any freedom life. In Muhammad's opinion, political assimilation and not theology (in and of itself) had been the opiate of Blacks in America. His life is a testament to the effects of slavery and an understanding of one crucial axiom: Black power resides in Black people.

Bibliography

Essien-Udom, Essien U. (1962). *Black Nationalism.* Chicago: University of Chicago Press.
Evanzz, Karl (1999). *The Messenger.* New York, N.Y.: Pantheon Books.
Levine, Lawrence (1977). *Black Culture and Black Consciousness.* New York, N.Y.: Oxford University Press.
Lincoln, Charles E. (1973). *The Black Muslims in America.* Boston: Beacon Press.
Marsh, Clifton E. (1996). *From Black Muslims to Muslims.* Lanham, Md.: Scarecrow Press, Inc.
Muhammad, Elijah (1965). *Message to the Black Man.* Chicago, Ill.: Muhammad's Temple No. 2.
_____ (1967). *An interview with Elijah Muhammad.* Sound recording. Los Angeles, Calif.: Pacifica Tape Library.
Muhammad, Rachelle (1980). *Black Muslim Movement after the Death of Elijah Muhammad.* Ann Arbor, Mich.: University Microfilms International.
Turner, Richard B. (1997). *Islam in the African-American Experience.* Bloomington: Indiana University Press.

11. Noble Drew Ali: An Historical Perspective

Emerson Mungin

This paper is a historical and philosophical analysis of the life and Islamic ideologies of Noble Drew Ali, founder of the Moorish Science Temple of America (MSTA). This research is based on his Islamic ideologies as they gave guidance to the Moorish Science Temple of America, during the 1920s. My objective is to see what parallels Noble Drew Ali's Islamic Moorish teachings and beliefs may have had with other theologies or Black nationalistic concepts.

Timothy Drew (Noble Drew Ali) was born January 8, 1886, in North Carolina. There are stories that were told, encompassing his identity and activities before 1913. One story has his followers claiming that Noble Drew Ali was a child of ex-slaves raised among the Cherokee Indians. Another story has him as a descendant of "Bilali Mohammet," the famous African Muslim slave who inhabited Supelo Island during the 19th century. Other stories tell of Noble Drew Ali traveling to and studying in Egypt, Morocco and Saudi at an early age (Turner, 91–92). Perhaps closer to the truth may be the Associated Negro Press report that said "He [Ali] was accompanying a Hindu Fakir in circus shows when he decided to start a little order of his own" (Turner, 92). Yet, there are some who believe that Noble Drew Ali was initially associated with Fard Muhammad, one of the original teachers of Islam, here in America. In 1913 Noble Drew Ali did start an order with help of Dr. Suliman, which was initially called the Canaanite Temple, located in Newark, New Jersey. This was the first "Moorish Community" ever to be established in the United States.

Exactly what motivated Noble Drew Ali in this direction? Was it one of the previously mentioned practitioners of an Islamic belief? His initial inspiration did come from Islam, as a global, religious, political and cultural phenomenon. Even though not sponsored by Indian (India) Muslims, Ali used their philosophy and central Quranic concepts in his early teachings. He developed the traditions of the Jihad, the struggle to be excellent in every endeavor a Muslim attempts (McCloud, 196); his Jihad was one of words, utilizing the written word to strive towards the path of God (Allah). Since Noble Drew Ali had once been associated with the Freemason movement, he was able to extract some ideologies from them that were also Islamic in nature. He saw the link between Islam and Freemasonry as rooted in global Islam (nationalistic and inter-nationalistic freedom). Additionally, he used some of the symbols of Freemasonry, such as the fez, turban, crescent and star, Circle Seven, all-seeing eye, clasped hands, sphinx of Giza and pyramids, for his movement. As Noble Drew Ali knew, Black Freemasonry was a cultural conduit for Eastern religious ideas and rituals. Along with Pan-Africanist ideologies, his Moorish concepts were packaged in a form that appealed to the Black masses (Turner, 94). The ancestors of these Moorish people were Blacks who had played a role in the ancient civilizations of Arabia, Nubia, the Sahara and the horn of Africa (Van Sertima, 146). Ali believed that the Moors had left a legacy of cultural, religious, scientific and even military contributions to Islam. This linkage of ethnicity through the beliefs and practices of the Moors would be critical to the concepts adapted by Noble Drew Ali in the creation of the Moorish Science Temple. While Noble Drew Ali was in the midst of his Islamic order, his association in political terms came from the Marcus Garvey Universal Negro Improvement Association (UNIA) (Turner, 72). Black nationalistic terms and concepts used by Garvey and the UNIA became prime examples for Ali's Moorish concepts. Garvey's emphasis on Black autonomy was but one concept adapted by movements of an Islamic nature. The ideologies shared between Garvey's UNIA and Noble Drew Ali's Moorish Science Temple of America would be one link that converted some of Garvey's followers into the Moorish Movement, especially during the aftermath of Marcus Garvey's deportation out of America.

Noble Drew Ali drew on nationalistic responses within the masses of the Black communities. His Moorish Divine and National Movement of North America, Inc., are umbrellas for the Islamic community, rejecting integration and asserted a distinctive nationality (McCloud, 11). Nobel Drew Ali's Divine Mission uplifted the spirits of fallen humanity and proclaimed the issues of nationality for self-autonomy, critical to the existence of ex-slaves (McCloud, 56). What he succeeded in with the Moorish Science Temple was viable worldview of Islam, emphasizing social justice and its ability to provide African Americans with historical identity, independent of slavery (McCloud, 167). Noble Drew Ali believed that African Americans were direct descendents of the Moabites of the Bible, whose homeland was said to be in and around Morocco. This is at the core of Moorish teachings, asserting that the primary need of African Americans, especially in the first decade of the 20th century, was a historically accurate nationality, giving a connection with a homeland (McCloud, 12).

Noble Drew Ali's earlier followers consisted of children and grandchildren of ex-slaves who had migrated from the South to the North (Turner, 71). Within the historical context, some of these earlier followers of Ali found it easy to associate with his teachings. Islamic practices existed among slaves as a direct result of those Africans having been brought to the Americas from the African regions dominated by Muslim beliefs and practices. This may have been key to these followers' relating to what Noble Drew Ali's concepts were emphasizing. Identifying these historic beliefs may also have created a nationalistic sense of hope for those who had just migrated to the North from the shackled concepts of the South. But by 1916, internal disagreements and jealously began to ruffle the Moorish-American community, causing an eventual division of the group into two. One group, the Holy Moabites Temple of the World, would remain in Newark, New Jersey. By 1925, Noble Drew Ali moved with his followers to Chicago, and formed the Moorish Holy Temple of Science. By 1928 the name was changed to the Moorish Science Temple of America (McCloud, 11). Animah Beverly McCloud's *African American Islam* emphasizes the important impact on a national level that the works of Noble Drew Ali and the Moorish Science Temple had. There were racial, social, cultural and religious assertions tied spiritually into the movements, which could and should uplift the humanity of African Americans.

Noble Drew Ali saw Marcus Garvey as a precursor to his organization. There are several links between Marcus Garvey, Noble Drew Ali and other men who were influenced in some fashion by Islam and nationalistic ideologies. W.D. Fard, founder of the Nation of Islam, was said to have originally been a member of the Moorish Science Temple (Smith, 327). We can also tie in the fact that the father of Malcolm X, Earl Little, was a Marcus Garvey follower. Noble Drew Ali wrote, "In these modern days there came a forerunner, who was divinely prepared by the great God-Allah and his name is Marcus Garvey, who did teach and warn the nation of the earth to prepare to meet the coming Prophet who was to bring true and divine Creed of Islam, and his name is Noble Drew Ali" (Turner, 90). This text, also called the "Circle of Seven," was designed to help members build knowledge of themselves as Moorish Muslims (McCloud, 13).

The teachings on nationality were a primary focus of the Moorish Science Temple, especially in Chicago. Upon becoming a full member, the initiate was given an identification card showing the symbol of Allah, Islam and Unity with the following inscriptions: "This is your Nationality and Identification Card for the Moorish Science Temple of America, and Birthrights for the Moorish American etc. We honor all Divine Prophets, Jesus, Mohammed, Buddha and Confucius. May the Blessings of the God of our Father Allah, be upon you that carry this card. I do hereby declare that you are a Moslem under the Divine Laws of the Holy Koran of Mecca, Love,

Truth, Peace, Freedom and Justice" (Low, 98–9). Noble Drew Ali's strongly believed that, as African Americans were misplaced from the region of Morocco, there was an individual responsibility to claim a nationality, separate from any concept of enslavement. This included the changing of one's last name by adding either "El" or "Bey," displacing the Eurocentric last name given African Americans by Whites. In addition to the nationality and identification cards, Noble Drew Ali wrote the "Divine Constitution and By-Laws," which gave the duties and responsibilities of members.

In addition, Noble Drew Ali developed another document, "Koran Questions for Moorish Children," which comprised 102 questions, giving a base foundation for his teachings. The first question and answer was "Who made you? ALLAH." Other questions consisted of: What is your nationality? Moorish-American." "For what purpose was the Moorish Science Temple of American Founded? For the uplifting of fallen humanity." "How many days are in the Circle? Seven days." "How many days are in a creation? Seven days." And question 102 is "According to Science, how many days are in a year? Seven days." (FBI Files BP62.B56F35).

Historical researchers have debated for years the validity of Noble Drew Ali's teachings of Islam within the constraints of the Moorish Science Temple. It has been suggested that, not unlike other teachers of Islam, Noble Drew Ali taught in such a manner, based on his interpretation of the religious, spiritual, political, social and economic virtues of the principles of Islam. History has shown us that there is no wrong way to practice, conform to or interpret the teachings of Islam through the presence of God, Allah. It has been unfortunate, as was the case with Noble Drew Ali, that some, who did not agree with his teachings, took a very negative approach to his contributions. From the division of his organization in Newark, New Jersey, to the problems he encountered in Chicago, Illinois, there always seem to be roadblocks to a peaceful existence, just trying to conform to the will of Allah.

Noble Drew Ali's work came to an abrupt end in 1929. A *Chicago Defender* newspaper reporter wrote about the strange circumstances surrounding the murder of Noble Drew Ali. According to the report, told July 20, 1929, it began with a reference to the murder of Claude D. Greene, Ali's business manager, by other members of the Moorish community. At the time of Greene's murder, the police moved in and arrested a number of Moorish community members, including Noble Drew Ali. Ali subsequently died, shortly after his release on bail, either from complications of police beatings, or from a beating administered by community rivals. It was a known fact during these times that Ali had been under Federal Bureau of Investigations surveillance for some time. These were ongoing attempts to discredit Nobel Drew Ali and any teachings of Islam, especially in the Black communities of the North. These attempts at control and surveillance were based on fear, contributed by the concepts of Black self-autonomy. Some reports say that the organization was under surveillance, more than Noble Drew Ali himself (Whitley, 2).

Noble Drew Ali's movement established temples in a number of urban centers, including Chicago, Detroit and Harlem, New York. According to one estimate, as many as thirty thousand African Americans may have passed through the ranks of the organization prior to the Great Depression. Unlike Ahmadiyyas, Ali and his followers offered Blacks a new "Moorish" or "Moroccan" identity outside of the constraints of their status as Negroes, and attempted to socialize them into a spiritual world in which a mythical "Asiatic" past was the central focus. In addition to constructing a nationality for Blacks, the Moorish-Americans tried to rid African Americans of those vices, such as alcohol consumption and extramarital relations, that undermined the moral fabric of their communities. Tailored to fit into ideological trends already present in Black America, such as Black Nationalism, the Moorish Science Temple of America was perhaps the preeminent Islamic group among African Americans during the decade following World War I. Consequently, while the group declined sharply in membership and appeal during the 1930s, the religious foundation it had laid—which was partially borrowed from the Ahmadiyys, the Garvey movement, and other sources—lasted long enough to be exploited by others (Clegg, 19–20).

In conclusion, Noble Drew Ali, the Moorish Science Temple and the Moorish-Americans are directly linked to historical patterns of Islamic practices. From the Muslim origins in Africa including Egypt and Morocco, Islam traveled through Western and Eastern Europe and Asia until reaching the Americas via the African slave trades. The self-proclaimed prophet Noble Drew Ali ignited a belief system and practice which has survived many attempts to discredit and eliminate them. He created a way of living that gave African Americans a sense of direction. He tied together the rich tradition of Islamic practices, the historical movements of the Moabites through Africa, Spain, Egypt, Europe and on through to the Americas, with a legacy of struggles by African Americans in this country during the 19th and onto the 20th centuries. In spite of ideological differences throughout the Islamic world, Muslims have demonstrated the common practices and beliefs in God-Allah. What is equally significant is the legacy, which was then carried on by such Islamic leaders as Fard Muhammad, Elijah Muhammad, Malcolm X and even present Islamic leaders like Louis Farrakhan and Wallace D. Muhammad. To have been an historical catalyst, with a Nationalistic-Islamic foundation, for Black self-autonomy, is an everlasting legacy of which Noble Drew Ali can rest assured, and it was a result of his concepts enveloped in the Moorish Science Temple of America and his beliefs in Moorish-Americans. The nation-building ideologies and self-identification concepts of Noble Drew Ali can be seen when you look at the Nation of Islam. The relationship of some Islamic practitioners throughout the world, in some small sense, can be credited to those who may have been a part of or associated with the Moorish Science Temple Movement of the 1920s. Noble Drew Ali was at the center of this, if only for a short period of time. It was time well spent, in the name of God–Allah.

Bibliography

Clegg III, Claude A. *An Original Man: The Life and Times of Elijah Muhammad.* New York: St. Martin's/Griffin, 1997.
FBI Files. *Moorish Science Temple of America.* BP62.B56F35, reels no. 1, 2 and 3, 1995.
Low, W. Augustus, and Virgil A. Clift, eds. *Encyclopedia of Black America.* Da Capo Press, 1981.
McCloud, Aminah B. *African American Islam.* New York: Routledge, 1995
Rashad, Adib. *The History of Islam and Black Nationalism in the Americas.* Beltsville: Writer's Inc., 1985, 1991.
Smith, Jessie C., ed. *Black Firsts.* Detroit: Visible Ink Press, 1994.
Turner, Richard B. *Islam in the African-American Experience.* Bloomington: Indiana University Press, 1997.
Van Sertima, Ivan. *Golden Age of the Moor.* New Brunswick: Transaction Publishers, 1992, 1999.

12. Islam in the Civil Rights Movement

SAADI A. SIMAWE

The role of the Nation of Islam in the Civil Rights Movement and the influence of Islam as a religion on the African American struggle for civil and human rights have never been fully explored. The fact that Islam functioned as a formative element in making Malcolm X a giant figure in the fifties and sixties cannot be overstated. However, when his historical role is discussed, scholars and historians usually seem unable to acknowledge the role of the Nation of Islam and later Orthodox Islam in shaping his political consciousness. There are many reasons for this politically remarkable omission of Islam from the cultural and political life of Malcolm X and from the official history of the Civil Rights Movement. One of the reasons is the deep-rooted hostility to Islam in the West, especially in the U.S. It has been politically incorrect to give Islam any credit in the discussion of civil rights and human rights, despite the historical role Islam played in the Algerian revolution and in the broader context of the Afro-Asian liberation movement of the twentieth century. In the West, Islam naturally evokes connotations of violence, terrorism, tyranny, and abuse of women. Historically Islam was the main enemy and threat that legitimized the launching of the crusades that ushered in the second millennium. More recently, Islam was the twin brother of Communism during the Cold War, and after the fall of the Soviet Union Islam was promoted to enemy number 1 of Western values such as democracy, human rights, freedom of speech, and the rights of women.

Other reasons for the omission of Islam and the Nation of Islam from the history of the Civil Rights Movement may be related to the general ignorance and unfamiliarity of the majority of American historians, including African American historians, with the basic tenets of Islam. Hence, even objective scholars who have no quarrel with Islam or who are sympathetic to Islam and Islamic people usually avoid discussing Islam primarily because they do not know what to do with it. Thus, between ignorance and deliberate omission, the role of Islam or the appropriation of Islam in the Civil Rights Movement is largely lost or rendered insignificant.

By contrast, the literature of the Nation of Islam and Malcolm X's writings and speeches reveal profound interest in Islam as an American religion as well as in Orthodox Islam. But the main thrust of this paper is not to explore Islam as an American religion; rather I would like to identify the elements of liberation that Islam, as interpreted by its black practitioners, has offered for the struggle for civil rights and human rights. Before I demonstrate the specific aspects of Islam that inspire what might be called an Islamic liberation theology, I would like to explore the politics of conversion to Islam in the context of African America. That politics becomes evident when we remember that both Islam and blackness have always been rejected by the dominant culture in the U.S. That rejection necessitates oppression and discrimination against both blackness and Islam and ultimately the construction of an ideology of anti-black and anti–Muslim racism. This context creates an affinity between Islam and blackness. Significantly, African Americans do not have to convert to Islam in order to be sympathetic or even to support Islam and Islamic people in their historical struggle against Western colonialism and neo-colonialism. Whether Christian or Jewish or Communist, African Americans' blackness naturally connects them with the blackness of Islam as a demonized religion.

Another factor that might account for the African American politics of conversion to Islam is the dialectical nature of the relationship between the master and slave. In 1840 Frederick Douglass's *Narrative* captured this existential struggle between slave and master, oppressed and oppressor, colonized and colonizer. When Mr. Auld finds his wife Sophia is teaching young Fredrick reading and writing, he is frightened by the sure danger of educating a slave. He orders his wife to stop immediately. Douglass at once realizes the master's perceived danger and vows to use it as a weapon:

> The very decided manner with which he [Mr. Auld] spoke, and strove to impress his wife with the evil consequences of giving me instruction, ... served to convince me that he was deeply sensible of the truths he was uttering. It gave me the best assurance that I might rely with the utmost confidence on the results which, he said, would flow from teaching me to read. What he most dreaded, that I most desired. What he most loved, that I most hated. That which to him was a great evil, to be carefully shunned, was to me a great good, to be diligently sought [37].

Because Islam has been perceived as evil and a threat and a political rival by the West, it appeals to those individuals who are treated like slaves and who do not have any stake in the dominant culture that view them as enemies. More than a century after Douglass articulated that deadly dichotomy between slave and master, Malcolm X in 1964 finds himself restating the same deadly situation:

No, I am not an American. I'm one of the twenty-two million black people who are the victims of Americanism. One of the twenty-two million
black people who are victims of democracy—nothing but disguised
hypocrisy. I'm speaking of this American system. And I see America
through the eyes of the victim. I don't see any American dream; I see an
American nightmare [*Malcolm X Speaks*, 26].

James Baldwin refers to this desperate political reality of black America in an
interview with an Arab journal in the sixties when asked to explain the attrac-
tion of Islam for African Americans. He said, "It is the white racist oppression that makes Islam possible in the USA" (*Hiwar*).

The cultural and political alliance between mainstream Christianity and
slavery and later capitalism has ensured the moral bankruptcy of Christianity in the West, especially in the eyes of the enlightened, or at least the politically conscious, African Americans. Again that moral bankruptcy is
powerfully articulated in Douglass's *Narrative*. It is true that African Americans rightly perceive themselves as the "last remaining 'Christians' in America," as Larry Neal observes in his "New Space/The Growth of Black
Consciousness in the Sixties." Yet, "one thing is certain," he writes; "the rise
of the Nation [of Islam] is a significant and a concrete denial of the viability
of contemporary Christianity. It especially denies to Christianity the ability
to liberate black people. In spite of its Eastern origins, Christianity is clearly
the religion of the oppressors. Its very symbology as projected in the West is
anti black" (*Black Seventies*, 19). In his powerful jeremiad *The Fire Next Time*,
which remained a best-seller for a long time after 1963, James Baldwin con-
demns Christianity. Though he cannot personally accept Islam, he is highly
impressed with the Nation of Islam's social activism among blacks:

Elijah Muhammad has been able to do what generations of welfare workers and committees and resolutions and reports and housing projects and
playgrounds have failed to do: to heal and redeem drunkards and junkies,
to convert people who have come out of prison and to keep them out, to
make men chaste and women virtuous, and to invest both the male and
the female with a pride and serenity that hang about them like unfailing
light. He has done all these things, which our Christian church has spec-
tacularly failed to do [51].

But by what power has Elijah Muhammad managed to do these miracles?
Baldwin, a secular thinker, does not attribute any divine powers to Elijah
Muhammad or to Islam. Yet he knows very well the power of myth in empowering the oppressed and in lending significance to their deprived lives. It is
very meaningful mythology, Baldwin argues, that Elijah Muhammad offers
to the rejected and the despised: his version of Islam has made God black,
the devil white, and black Muslims are loved by their black God. As a
powerful black preacher, Baldwin recognizes the spiritual power latent in

statements by Elijah Muhammad such as this: "Return to your true religion, throw off the chains of the slavemaster, the devil, and return to the fold. Stop drinking his alcohol, using his dope—protect your women—and forsake the filthy swine" (76). What both Baldwin and Elijah Muhammad are saying is that both Christianity and Islam are religions, but Islam is true to black spiritual needs. Unlike Elijah Muhammad, Baldwin suggests in *Fire* that both Christianity and Islam are myths, but Christianity has become a white myth and Islam, a black myth. On the relationship between myth, meaning and identity, Roland Barthes in *Mythologies* analyzes the power of myth as being located primarily in the particulars of a given discourse. Therefore the exact reverse of white mythology of blackness would naturally be most appealing to the most despised and rejected. The particular meanings of blackness the Nation of Islam was able to construct reflect the exact spiritual needs of black people, and they appeal to most blacks regardless of their religious affiliations. When Elijah Muhammad asked Baldwin, "And what are you now?" after he had left the church, Baldwin wrote,

> I had the stifling feeling that *they* [Black Muslims] knew I belonged to them but knew that I did not know it yet, that I remained unready, and that they were simply waiting, patiently, and with assurance, for me to discover the truth for myself. For where else, after all, could I go? I was black, and therefore a part of Islam, and would be saved from the holocaust awaiting the white world whether I would or not. My weak, deluded scruples could avail nothing against the iron word of the prophet [70–71].

The Nation of Islam's logic seems to draw its potency from the illogical realities of American racism. This racist ideology of whiteness also accounts for the black American version of Islam, which has been racialized and made racist to counter the unbearable white burden on the black soul. As one scholar put it, black Islam is typically made in America. There are so many sects of Islam all over the world, and it is only logical to make Islam black in America to fit black spiritual and political needs.

But again, why Islam, why not Judaism or Buddhism or any other religion? It seems to me that Islam has attracted a significant segment of black Americans and has played a major role in black politics in this country because of certain factors, some of them theological and other political. Unlike Christianity, Islam does not separate religion and politics. According to John L. Esposito's *Islam: The Straight Path*, "For Christianity, the appropriate question is, 'What do Christians believe?' In contrast, for Islam (as for Judaism), the correct question is, 'What do Muslims do?' Whereas in Christianity, theology was the 'queen of the sciences,' in Islam, as in Judaism, law enjoyed pride of place, for 'to accept or conform to the laws of God is *islam*, which means to surrender to God's law" (68). From both ideological and political points of view, Islam's imperative of practice of belief is as central as the concept of praxis is to Marxism. Karl Marx insists that what distinguishes his philosophy from previous philosophies is the fact that "all previous philosophers interpret the world, now it is time to change it." The Western divorce of religion from the state, which also meant the separation of politics from religion, has in effect emasculated Christianity and ultimately relegated it, in most cases, to the domain of the personal relation between the individual and God, a purely religious and spiritual relationship. Furthermore, this separation has ensured and legalized the monopoly of the Western secular state on political matters and the body politic. Thus for the urgent needs of the African Americans, Christianity not only never worked to liberate them from their Christian slavemasters, it actually legitimated their enslavement and later historical disfranchisement.

Another basic tenet in Islam that appealed to many African Americans who converted to Islam or who became at least sympathetic to it is the Islamic legitimacy of the use of violence in self-defense or in the struggle for equality and human and civil rights. Significantly, a recurrent theme in Malcolm X's speeches and interviews is the right of African Americans to use violence to defend their humanity, since their present situation is the product of centuries of systematic white violence. The phrase that became Malcolm X's ideological signature is "By any means necessary," which obviously means that black Muslims will fight for their legitimate human rights even by using violence. In his famous speech titled "The Ballot or the Bullet," Malcolm X defines his stand on violence:

> If you don't take uncompromising stand—I don't mean to go out and get violent; but at the same time you should never be nonviolent unless you run into some nonviolence. I'm nonviolent with those who are nonviolent with me. But you drop that violence on me, then you've made me go insane, and I'm not responsible for what I do. And that is the way every Negro should get. Any time you know you're within the law, within your legal rights, within your moral rights, in accord with justice, then die with what you believe in. But don't die alone. Let your dying be reciprocal. This is what is meant by equality. What is good for the goose is good for the gander [*Malcolm X Speaks*, 34].

This extremism in pursuit of rights and equality sounds to most American as un–American, foreign, Third Worldly, and typically Islamic, or terroristic and communistic. It coveys the vision of the Islamic jihad that has been distorted and demonized in Western culture, primarily because Western democracies have preserved the right to use violence against others and have denied their victims any right to use it. But from an objective point of view, the victims are naturally more legitimate in their use of violence. Yet, it is this jihad rhetoric, or jihad of the word, practiced by members of Nation of Islam that frightened most Americans and made them aware probably for the first time of what the white racist status quo has been breeding for centuries. Even Louis E. Lomax, who was critical of black Muslims, concedes in his *A Report on Elijah Muhammad, Malcolm X, and the Black Muslim World: When the World Is Given* (1963): "The Negro has always privately talked loud and bitterly about the American white man. The Black Muslims brought that talk into the open, on television and radio, and made it plain for all to see and hear. This was good for both the Negro and the white man: it shocked and frightened white people to hear what we have been thinking and saying about them for five hundred years; the Black Muslims were a catharsis for us, purging our innards of the bile brought on by slavery and segregation" (75–76). Even more than a catharsis, Islam functioned as a total rejection of the American democracy and of the possibility of redeeming the white man and his way of life. Psychologically, it is always empowering to reject and demoralizing to be rejected.

Bibliography

Baldwin, James. *The Fire Next Time.* New York: Vintage International Vintage Books, 1993.

Barbour, Floyd B. *The Black Seventies.* Boston: P. Sargent, 1970.

Barthes, Roland. *Mythologies.* Selected and traslated from the French by Annette Lavers. New York: Hill and Wang, 1972.

Douglass, Frederick. *Narrative of the Life of Frederick Douglass, An American Slave.* Cambridge: Belknap Press of Harvard University, 1960.

Esposito, John L. *Islam: The Straight Path.* New York: Oxford University Press, 1998.

Lomax, Louis E. *When the Word Is Given: A Report on Elijah Muhammad, Malcolm X, And the Black Muslim World.* Cleveland: World Pub. Co., 1963.

Neal, Larry. *Black Boogaloo: Notes on Black Liberation.* San Francisco: Journal of Black Poetry Press, 1969.

X, Malcolm. *Malcolm X Speaks: Selected Speeches and Statements.* Ed George Breitman. New York: Pathfinder, 1989.

V

CIVIL RIGHTS
AND REDEMPTION

When we consider American society today, the activism of the 1960s sometimes appears archaic. We find ourselves at a far remove, not in actual years, but in memory, dismissing a period in American history that saw mass action led by African Americans challenging the conventional wisdom and authoritarian personalities associated with white privilege in the United States. Many of the beneficiaries of this movement did not participate in the quest, for they had not yet been born. To them, the ideas of accountability and principle are anachronistic and even strange. However, as in most mass action struggles, the actions of the visionaries led to the greater good of the people, even if our memory of the visionaries has been sacrificed to the passing years.

The essays in this final group use specific topics as small windows that open onto a large vies—the broad landscape of civil rights in 21st century America. This perspective on civil rights necessarily raises the topic of *human* rights and erects a framework for the question of what it means to be human. In the tradition of black activist scholarship, African American scholars have considered how answers to this question have historically been influenced by a system of subordination and colonization. In the essays that follow, today's scholars offer their thoughts on how those influences can be put to rest for the betterment of American society.

13. Pathologies of Public Housing: An Antecedent to Crime and Delinquency

James Chambers

In keeping with this colloquium's important theme of civil rights, Black Arts and the Black Power movement, an analysis of housing appears to be apropos. Housing patterns or the lack thereof have been and continue to be instrumental in civil rights legislation. Housing patterns are critically important because they play a role in determining whether one's civil rights are being abrogated.

The ramifications of poor housing have been instrumental in black power movements and as the underlying theme for a large amount of black art. Giddings' *When and Where I Enter: The Impact of Black Women on Race and Sex in America* and Hunter's *The Slums: Challenges and Response* are but two texts that lucidly identify the nexus between poor housing and behavioral pathologies.

The failure of government to provide adequate means to all of its citizens to acquire affordable housing has been identified in the United States as being a form of inequality. Inequality in housing tends to be manifested in individuals in deviant behavior. The inequality creates a self-perpetuating phenomenon in that it manifests the conditions that are necessary for its continual existence.

It would be irrational to conduct an analysis of the differential structure of neighborhoods and communities without factoring in economic subordination and political disenfranchisement and the role each plays in residential segregation. It is also important to assess these spatial settings in regards to their composition, changes that take place within them, their internal organization, their expansion and contraction and the successes and failures they experience. It is also important to ascertain what their effects are upon the larger society and vice versa.

Even though the data reveals that in recent years significant strides have been made in the attempts to provide opportunity for all Americans to live in decent housing, there remain significant barriers to millions of households in their pursuit of decent, safe and affordable housing. This is due in large part to the failure of housing statutes to prevent the existence and proliferation of residential patterns that have been, many contend, absolutely essential to the consolidation of white power in urban areas.

The existence and extent of discrimination in housing and mortgage practices have generated considerable debate. Two seminal studies that focused on mortgage lending practices, the Boston Fed Study[1] and "The Color of Money"[2] (an examination of neighborhood lending practices in Atlanta), have demonstrated that there is discrimination in both private and public housing policies. Despite the fact that there has been considerable criticism of the Boston Fed Study the general conclusion remains that there is a large difference in loan denials to blacks that cannot be explained by data error, omitted variables, or misspecification of the model as some contend.

Even though there appears to be indisputable evidence that a factor in neighborhood and community composition is attributable to racial discrimination, this perspective must be juxtaposed to another reality, one that can be attributed in part to the desire by many individuals to retain their own unique insights, reflections, triumphs and tragedies. In essence, it is these values that can be, and often are, used to define and maintain the differential neighborhoods. These values persist because they are perceived to be strategies for survival. They are also strategies that are utilized as resistance to the attempts by the broader social structure to deny their cultural and social integrity as well as their neighborhood and community identities.

Despite these values, neighborhoods, like social organizations and networks, are the most transitory and diffused patterns of urban organization for most individuals. However, residential segregation by race precludes this mobility in the majority of U.S. cities. Despite its long existence, relatively little is known about residential segregation because analysis of the spatial ordering of households requires information that has not been of considerable importance to most social researchers.

It can be hypothesized that the single most significant feature of slums is the poverty of their inhabitants, but these sites involve considerably more than poverty and bad housing. Concomitant with poverty and bad housing are the social problems encountered by the residents that can be attributed to the slums. These pathologies are manifested in broken homes, personal and property crimes, drug addiction and other problems that are beyond the inhabitants' control. The intense spatial concentration of poor households, the massing together in dilapidated households and miserable living conditions, exacerbate these pathologies.

One can argue that it is more important to understand the social networks than the quality of housing units because the patterns of the inter-actions are more amorphous than neighborhoods. However, interactional patterns are necessarily tied to specific spatial locations. Even though the soci-ological understanding of these social networks remains somewhat more prim-itive, when it comes to stages of classification and explanation they are recognized as being extremely important.

Perhaps it would be more appropriate to refer to the interactional pat-terns that have emerged as collective behavior rather than pathologies. This is because collective behavior refers to the interactions that occur routinely in the public and semi-public places, e.g., parks, streets, sidewalks, malls, public buildings, theaters, meeting halls and other gathering places that are present in these enclaves. This collective behavior can be considered to be an appropriate response to the conditions and sometimes it takes on the char-acteristics of crowds, mobs, assemblies, audiences, spectators, or face-to-face encounters between strangers. Generally these topics are subsumed under social psychology; however, they are critically important units for analysis when we concern ourselves with crime, delinquency and other pathologies.

The assessment of crime, delinquency and other pathologies must also factor in the various interrelated factors, e.g., political, economic, social and organizational, and this can be accomplished through the use of a social struc-tural analysis. This type of analysis would provide evidence of the role that local neighborhoods tend to play in the development of social bonds, the varying arenas of social participation and either the meaning or order in urban life. Currently, the significance and meaning varies depending on the sociol-ogist. Despite this variance there is a persistent belief among sociologists that neighborhoods are an inherent part of the social fabric of modern urban com-munities. There is also a generally shared sense that one needs to fully under-stand the social processes operating on this level of urban social organization to completely understand the urban social structure.

These social processes are critical factors to operationalize when one makes an assessment of the nexus between housing patterns and the occur-rence, morphology and duration of crime and delinquency. That housing patterns are perceived to be a criminogenic factor suggests that there is a lin-ear relation between the distribution of these units and the type of people that inhabit them.

Historically, the majority of the nation's public housing has been con-centrated in the inner cities, but today its presence in these spots is attrib-uted to the dire need of housing for the poor, and urban renewal programs. More specifically, from an urban renewal perspective, urban public housing policies have attempted to be a response to the displacement of the many slum residents who were forced to seek access to public housing dwellings in the late forties.[3] Currently, there are in excess of 1.34 million public housing units, houses and apartments in 3,200 localities.[4] These enclaves shelter more than 1,360,000 million people.[5] The data reveals that families utilize approximately fifty-nine percent of these units and elderly individuals inhabit the remainder.[6] Leigh and Mitchell stated:

> The decade after the low-income public housing program was implemented (1937–1948) most of its tenants were predominantly white and working class, which came about because of vigorous screening and selection procedures employed by PHAs to net only the largely second and third generation European immigrants as tenants. Because of the great degree of local autonomy in tenant selection, PHAs were able to continue this patently racist process.[7]

This significant concentration of urban poor and ethnic minorities in the inner cities can also be attributed to federal policies, specifically, the 1949 Housing Act and subsequent government assistance programs, e.g., FHA and VA mortgage guarantees. These programs, coupled with the Federal Highway Act in 1956, made urban sprawl possible by expanding the boundaries outward and encouraging the development of the suburbs. These acts and programs were instrumental in the out-migration, from the urban areas, of moderate income groups by providing many affordable single family housing units that generally excluded blacks.[8]

This exclusion was premised on the perceived inability of these individuals to qualify for the preferential mortgages. However, studies revealed that in lending patterns, at least in Atlanta in the mid–1980s, there were wide disparities between white and black neighborhoods with similar income levels. For example, between 1982 and 1986, lenders made more than five times as many conventional home purchase loans in predominately white middle-income census tracts than in predominately black middle-income tracts.

Prior to the 1980s, housing disparities were even more acute due to the fact that blacks were systematically excluded by the federal and state governments' willingness to support the racist policies that were implemented by real estate enterprises whose primary aim was to establish and maintain racially segregated residential neighborhoods.

Therefore, the exponential increase in the percentage of non-white individuals occupying these concentrated substandard urban residential units is attributable to the policies of public housing and racist real estate enterprises. Ramifications of this high concentration of public housing in the inner city resulted in restricted socioeconomic mobility, under- and unemployment, family deterioration, physical decay and social pathologies that were and remain manifested in psychological maladies, delinquencies and crimes for a large segment of the population.

These problems should be expected when data reveals that the mean income is $6,571[9] for those who live in concentrated public housing. This is in contrast to $18,192 for those not similarly situated. The latter figure compares favorably with 1990 census data that shows a mean income of $21,846 for the country.[10]

Many tours have been taken by groups of politicians and civic leaders that were designed ostensibly to determine the causes of the wretched conditions in the worst slums in the United States. Invariably these tours are in communities that comprise primarily blacks and Puerto Ricans, teeming with abandoned, vacant and vandalized hulks known as apartment buildings. Predictably, these individuals promise to seek a no-holds barred answer to the question as to why such structures continue to exist and to take measures to alleviate these deplorable conditions. Surely politicians and civic leaders realize that these housing projects are one of the basic failures of American society. Perhaps it is the most important failure, because it is the failure to provide for a fundamental human need—the need for decent shelter for millions of citizens. This failure is ironic in a nation that thumps its chest at having achieved the greatest standard of living known to man.

Why do these places exist? To answer this, one must possess a fundamental understanding of urban renewal and the relationships between housing and race, housing and fiscal patterns, and housing and a dozen of other subjects.

Social Institutions

Social institutions are characterized by their ability to serve a specialized function or need. They also provide a set of guiding values that are instrumental in translating needs into specified objectives or goals. They also consist of a cluster of social roles and skills that translate ultimate goals into specific duties and responsibilities for individuals. Social institutions produce coordinated networks of social roles through the formation of social groups of one sort or another (primary groups, voluntary associations or bureaucracy).

They also are structured to involve the participation of the entire community in this network of values, roles and groups. Finally, they function in a manner that will ensure that the values and roles of dominant social institutions are internalized by a substantial portion of the population.

Social institutions are the largest and most abstract modes of social organization within the urban community, and, in the most general sense, they can be described as consisting of widely accepted patterns of behavior and expectations. These have evolved or were created to be long-term solutions to the recognized needs of a community or society. Urbanization may have radically altered the form and function of many social institutions. A number of more recent social institutions, e.g., mass communication, compulsory education, public welfare, commercialized leisure, and urban planning, have appeared in the attempt to help individuals manage the urban settings.

Many questions are raised in regards to the capacity of these varying social institutions to effectively respond to the changing demands and opportunities presented by urban living. As a result, there is some thought that their very survival is at risk.

It should be clear that social order contains a plurality of social institutions and that each possesses its own authority and function. It is important to note that each is also limited or constrained by the presence of the others. Nevertheless, despite these constraints, they become monolithic when it comes to the formation of the larger patterns of authority, functions and allegiances that identify a society. However, this pluralism is frequently the root cause of conflict and dislocation that is manifested in varying types of aberrant social behavior.

Crime, delinquency, mental illness, broken family life, poor housing, poverty, unemployment, under-employment, class conflict, racial and ethnic conflict, drug addiction, pollution and a host of other maladies are ramifications of this conflict and dislocation. Combined or singularly these are social pathologies that constitute the urban crisis. Despite the moniker used to describe these pathologies, it should also be clear that they are not the result of, nor are they caused by, the urban areas because, to one degree or another, they are also present in the rural areas.

Pathologies Manifested

An analysis of Wichita, Kansas, a perceived upscale city, illustrates the presence and manifestation of urban pathologies. In Wichita the housing was so segregated it provided the impetus for a local magazine to dub itself *ZIP code—67214*. This was because the narrow northeast band of the city identified by the zip code contained more than ninety percent of the black community. Adjacent to this site is the Latino community, and not surprisingly both neighborhoods are close to a decaying downtown area that has been slated for revitalization for approximately twenty-five years.

In the late seventies, and continuing today, public substandard housing in northeast Wichita, Kansas, shared a dominance with private substandard housing in this area, and this environment appeared to be far removed from the seamy underbelly that characterized too many cities. Even though these units were isolated environmentally, this did not negate the omnipresent negative elements; at least one felt in Wichita that these individuals and the problems that they presented needed to be controlled.

Internally, blacks and Latinos who could afford to move away from the dreaded "northeast" found Wichita to be less despicable. However, their exodus has been instrumental in ensuring that the northeast area has suffered more due to the closing of more businesses and further development of a malignant apathy. Since the seventies, this area has become an area known for its crack houses, drive-by shootings and people that are afraid to leave their homes at night or to let their children go anywhere unsupervised. Crack houses did not create these conditions; rather they could be attributed to the legacy of public housing policies that permit segregated housing, suffocating poverty, expanding drug markets, violence, death and the prevalent oppressive fear.

Initially, in Wichita, the violence, death and drugs were attributed to gangs like the Bloods and Crips. This ignored the growing Asian gang that had been involved in extortion activities for years. Eventually, the criminal justice system was forced to acknowledge the Junior Boys, home grown hoods that were formed to provide competition for the drug market. In response, a local Latino gang quickly formed in order to grab a share of the action. To further exacerbate the problem, white youths also banded together to engage in dope dealing and gang banging.

Naively, despite these problems, Wichita, a perceived landlocked Midwestern safe harbor, had come to believe that these conditions were something you would expect in Detroit, Los Angeles, Chicago, New York, Miami or Philadelphia but not there, at least not city-wide. It was this naiveté that permitted the schools, police and the local government to believe that these conditions were merely aberrations or transitory because they were supposed to occur only in the parts of town and to the types of people that no one cared about.

In Chicago's Cabrini Green, as in many other large urban public housing units, there is a code of survival that all young people must learn, *duck the bullet*. To the inhabitants, this means considerably more than merely hitting the ground when snipers start shooting and gunfire crackles. To the inhabitants the code also means the avoidance of gangs, drugs and other demons that conspires to destroy so many lives and cause so many deaths in the public and segregated housing projects.

In these negative surroundings a young person is susceptible to being grabbed up, swallowed whole, spit out and made to run wild until a bullet hits them. However, despite this awareness, it is difficult to duck the bullets in Cabrini and other similar sites. For example, Dantrell Davis was a mere child who meant much to his family and certainly was worth more than he received. He is a statistic because he did not have a chance to duck.

Dantrell Davis was a fatality because a sniper aimed an AR-15 semiautomatic rifle equipped with a scope from a tenth floor window and murdered this seven-year-old baby. This child had not committed a single malevolent act to warrant this fate. It happened because he was poor and therefore basically inconsequential to those who do not live in Cabrini Green and similar war zones. This young boy was slain as he walked with his mother from their home to his school—a one-hundred-foot, one-minute journey that proved too perilous even with the police parked nearby. This despicable event might be less tragic if it had been the only one to occur; however, Dantrell was the third pupil from his school to be murdered in a seven-month period. Sadly but predictably none of these incidents commanded the public's attention as did the Columbine High School shooting and other horrific sites where students were also killed in this nation.

In fairness, the death of this child did shock a part of the city, grabbed some headlines and even spurred the mayor, police and public housing officials to state that "the killing must stop, this must never happen again and something must be done." But individuals who were either born or raised in Cabrini Green wonder when and if the killing of children will ever end and what these luminaries will do to ensure it. They know that although there is continual talk about the deaths, ranting and raving, and news coverage, the murders do not cease. To them it is heart breaking, but to the wider public it is generally an unknown phenomenon. The majority of the individuals who live in these environments want to hold the police more accountable; however, they realize that the police are not committing these crimes nor are they responsible for the pathological social conditions that give rise to them. These inhabitants realize that the conditions are the result of an apathetic public that includes aunts and uncles in addition to parents.

However, in public housing facilities like Cabrini, being accountable is a difficult thing to do; it may not be impossible, but it is difficult to achieve. It is easy to talk profoundly about what these parents should do and engage in psychobabble. This is because it is more important for mothers to teach their children survival skills than manners. It is also important for these parents to teach their children how to steer clear of windows in case of shootings, how to avoid the clutch of gangs and how to stay alive. These are survival skills and in this environment they are more crucial than manners, formal education, arts and other values.

Realistically, what is the probability of any of these children achieving future success when more than half of Cabrini's 7,000 residents are under the age of twenty and many are being raised by single mothers in surroundings where hope sometimes is as scarce as gainful employment? What sense does it make to hope when you live in a place where only nine percent of the residents have paying jobs? Perhaps, rather than condemning these individuals' failures there should be a celebration when anyone who lived in these types of places succeeds.

Despite the odds against them, there are people that lived in these horrid places who are extraordinary. For example, it was a badge of courage for one mother to send her twenty-year-old son away when gangs started pressuring him, shooting and burning his car because he refused to succumb to the pressure to join their gang. His mother had lived in Cabrini Green all of her life, and she states that current conditions are nothing like her childhood days when kids were able to play outside freely. To the inhabitants of this environment this, by all measures, is a success story because her child is still alive.

Despite the tendency to place blame on the victims, many factors have contrived to make the conditions impossible for parents who want to control their children, and not all of these can be attributed to some personal failing. This does not negate the fact that there are parents who are not able to take care of themselves for one reason or another and that, as a result, there is no hope that they can take care of their children.

The individuals that I am referring to are those that trade food stamps for crack or get high in front of their babies. These are the types of people the media and politicians routinely exhibit as being emblematic of the people that live in these deprived environments. The portrayal is an injustice because there are many, many more people living there who are law abiding and struggle daily to stay alive. They also hope that some one will care but they know better. Nevertheless, these individuals believe that there is a lot of good in the projects and that some of the people just need a chance, something they have never experienced. They will be denied these opportunities because in places like Cabrini Green people come and go, violence flares up and dies down and, as long as this occurs, there is no real urgency for politicians to address the dreadful conditions.

While hope is transitory, there has been one constant, the gangs. When you drive through Cabrini's seventy acres, a mile from the city's elegant Gold Coast, you will note the graffiti-scarred high rises. You will also be able to identify which gang the graffiti belongs to. It could be the Disciples, Vice Lords or Cobra Stones. Once you make the identification, you will know who controls the building and the streets surrounding them. This is their turf and they will defend it with their lives. Even though they may be impotent in many other social ways, a large measure of the power that a gang enjoys is derived from their ability to control this space.

Another major source of power they possess is the selling of drugs, but this economic enterprise can only be conducted if the turf is protected from potential threats. In addition to protecting the area, there is the need to constantly recruit new members. These groups can and do place a lot of pressure on those they arbitrarily select to become part of their gang. If you are a child, it sometimes seems easier to live by their rules than the code that you have been taught, because you either join the gangs or get beat up. What choice does a child really have? How long can anyone rationally endure the constant threat of being beaten up every day for refusing to join?

To those of us who do not live in this type of environment, the death of a child is sad and scary. However, to the children who are forced to live in them, death is not shocking. Rather than shock it raises the terrible question, "Will I be next?" Sadly, there is no rush of counselors to help these youths cope with the heavy emotional losses and traumas as there is when these occur in the more affluent urban and suburban areas. These children are left to their own emotional and psychological devices as they harbor and confront these horrible thoughts and experiences. Sadly, no one seems to gives a damn except the people that live here.

These children are tired of the violence and continual threat to their well being. Many would like to move away from the projects, but where could they go? In total exasperation and resignation, one twelve-year-old child wrote a note regarding the shootings, "They should do it some other time, not while kids go to school." It is unbelievable that a nation that professes to value our children and education would tolerate conditions that would permit any child to be afraid to go to school. Yet this is what happens daily, and we lament the fact that the children do not score well on standardized tests. We condemn the teachers for not teaching the rudiments of subjects like math, reading and arithmetic that are meaningless to children who are constantly afraid. How are teachers supposed to surmount this condition alone and in isolation when they are unable to be ensconced in a classroom that is conducive to learning and no one will work to ensure that this becomes a reality?

These children start out with a value for learning and practical knowledge. However, they are forced to constantly seek knowledge on how to protect themselves from the omnipresent threats that are their constant companions. While the majority of these children plead for protection from gang violence and drug sellers, the others are more fatalistic. One nine-year-old, for example, wrote: "When a boy goten shot I ... tell God to help him, to let him be in your hands, let him be with you, just like they say the odds be with you and you be with the odds."

The Death of Little Man

The dearth of decent public housing and surroundings provides the impetus for decadence that too often plagues individuals despite their best intentions. The legacy is uninterrupted because there are many individuals that deny the existence of these places. Policymakers and researchers also engage in studies that tend to blur the distinctions between discrimination of the individual and discrimination against the neighborhood or community. For example, the Boston Fed Study (which used the best data available) concluded that neither it nor any other study has been able to demonstrate whether the presence or absence of disparate treatment discrimination or disparate impact discrimination in loan approvals for a sample of lenders exists.

The decadence of public housing can be seen in the life and death story of Preston "Little Man" Simmons. It is the tale of too many minority urban youths. This child was a fourteen-year-old black marijuana peddler, and his death illustrates this nation's inhumanity and indifference to all poor children regardless of race. This child was shot and killed or, more accurately, executed, in the courtyard of his housing project in the Bronx. He became one of one hundred forty homicide victims, aged eighteen or younger, that had occurred that year up to that date in New York City. For the past few years ten percent of the total number of homicide victims have been in this age group, and many of these children have been killed in drug related incidents.

The Preston Simmons case illustrates the correlation between public housing and youth violence. Despite this correlation, the legacy of despair he left behind provides little hope of a better life for the next generation. His underclass existence at the Castle Hill Houses, a sprawling public housing complex in the East Bronx, continues to be typical of environments that stifle hope.

Preston was killed at about 8:15 p.m. while walking from his girlfriend's apartment to his family's apartment a block away. Because Preston Simmons was a broad shouldered and self-reliant youth, he had been called Little Man since childhood. He was friendly and outgoing and he often played the role of the family clown. He was also susceptible to peer pressure. He was, like so many minority children, diagnosed as hyperactive, an assessment that resulted in his enrollment in a special education class at Intermediate School 174. However, one of his teachers described him as an average student who did his homework, rarely skipped school and showed respect for authority. From all indicators he seemed to possess a good self-image. Despite learning some elementary karate moves from a friend, his mother and other friends said that his life was devoid of positive role models or heroes.

According to friends and family, Preston began selling marijuana after meeting his supplier the summer prior to his execution. Along with several other boys he would station himself in a playground (near the spot where he was killed) to deal. Preston's friends said he sensed the danger in the drug trade although he thought the threat came more from the police than from his counterparts in the commerce. Despite the dangers, it was a risk he thought worth taking and, besides, what real option did he really have? On a good day he would sell at least twenty to thirty bags for $5 each. From each bag, he was permitted to keep $1.50 and he spent the money on pricey clothing and shoes for himself and on food and gifts for his girlfriend. Although he occasionally kept some of the marijuana to smoke, his sister and friends said that he preferred a Heineken beer to a joint. His mother claims that she was unaware of her son's drug dealing despite his unaccounted-for sudden wealth.

Reports state that he was murdered shortly after encountering his drug supplier. As Little Man talked to him, a group of at least four men approached, and one of them pulled a 9-millimeter automatic pistol from his waist and shot him twice, once in the head and once in the body, and then they shot him nine more times. This kid lay dying full of holes on the street. Despite the barbarity of this act, there are those who find it difficult to have compassion for this child or any one else that chooses to deal drugs. However, these individuals conveniently forget that he was involved in the trade for the same reasons that the other young dudes are: he was too young and too black to get a legitimate job, and this was the only activity that could place some quick change in his pocket.

Although residents of Castle Hill are accustomed to bloodshed, they were stunned by Preston's death because of the coldness of the killing, particularly given the victim's age and his low position in the drug hierarchy. Prior to his killing there had been four homicides that year. One of these occurred when seventeen-year-old Jamal Graham was shot twice with a .32-caliber automatic. Police labeled the killing a territorial drug dispute and charged a twenty-year-old man from another housing project in the shooting. Although police officials were reluctant to declare Preston's killing a drug hit, his family and friends believe that he was killed because he threatened to break with his marijuana supplier and set up a competing operation.

Preston's girlfriend was a teenage mother when she delivered his child. This was the same condition his grandmother and mother experienced. Given this, the girlfriend doubts that her child's life will be much different from that of his father, whom she described as a personable individual who made spending money by selling bags of marijuana for $5. Wise beyond her years and knowledgeable of history, she reasons that if she is still living in the same environment, her child will also be either forced to sell drugs, use drugs or have a lot of other bad habits.

The Preston murder made children and elderly people afraid to leave their apartments. On the positive side, it encouraged some of community leaders to philosophize about the spiraling cycle of poverty and drugs that seems to pull each generation's youth farther away from hope. They realize that the drug cancer is metastasizing and is profoundly impacting both their and the young children's lives, and that its impact prevents their family units from being functional. However, in Preston's case, it is difficult to determine whether drugs were the cause or the effect of a dysfunctional family.

Preston was the fourth of seven children ranging in ages from eighteen years to fifteen months. An eighth child died as an infant. His mother, when she first got pregnant, dropped out of high school in the 11th grade. Preston's father, reputed to have been an abusive drug user, wandered in and out of her life. When he did enter, it was often through a smashed window or door. During the two years they lived together, he regularly beat her and the children. Preston's mother eventually grew tired of the abuse and got a protective court order that prohibited him from seeing his children. Then, basically on her own, she and her children spent a number of years crowded into her mother's two-bedroom apartment. Later, she made two moves that did not elevate her or her children's life chances appreciably. The first was into a shelter in Queens, and the second was into a four-bedroom apartment at Castle Hill.

She attempted to work but was unemployed the last six years of Preston's life, and therefore, she was forced to receive welfare checks. This was a condition she had experienced since 1969 when she first became pregnant. She received a $235.55 check from that department every two weeks, and a $371 monthly check for one of her sons' mental disability supplemented this. From this total, she paid $266 a month in rent for her apartment at Castle Hill. Her condition was not the norm at Castle Hill; data from the New York City Housing Authority reveals that approximately only one-fourth of the 2,025 families that lived there were recipients of full welfare payments.

However, this statistic does not fully explain the sense of hopelessness reigning in this type of environment. For example, $11,022 was the average family income at the complex of crowded fourteen-apartment, twelve-story buildings clustered around playgrounds and courtyards. While most of the apartments are spacious, the elevators smell of urine and are often extremely dangerous to use. The tiled hallways are marred with graffiti. There is little wonder that the residents report the project is overrun with crack dealers. Perhaps this would be bearable if it were not so common to have gun fire reports from roofs and windows. These are the conditions for the 7,000 people living there, where almost half are younger than twenty-one.

In these public facilities, people die over jackets, drugs, money and even the way you look at people. It is common knowledge that for $5 there is someone willing to shoot you in the head, and some of these are children. Why are these children so willing to kill? Because they want the same items, clothing, fast food, etc., that you and other youths desire. Because their parents lack the ability to help provide these amenities, they feel that they are forced to take matters into their own hands.

Despite all of these problems and before the emergence of crack, Castle Hill was a relatively quiet place. Some of the residents fondly remember their mothers placing beach chairs on the grass in the late afternoon in order to spend much of the evening there. It was a time and place like many other urban places when there were capable and alert guardians to protect both the children and the neighborhood.

Now, many of the residents are forced to spend most of their time locked in their apartments, watching music videos, preparing meals and peering through grime-stained windows at a view of the Empire State Building framed between two Castle Hill high rises. Although they can see the citadels that are artifices of progress, wealth, justice and freedom, they are light years removed from them, and American's consciousness and concern.

Americans need to come to the realization that gang formation, drug dealing and violence happens in areas that are deserted by former residents who sense that they have lost their voice, will, courage and knowledge of how to address problems. They also need to understand, in brief, that these conditions exist because those with powers to change things do not care about these people's education, job opportunities, recreational facilities or general well being. They also do not care because they are poor whites, blacks, Puerto Ricans, Mexicans and other surplus people.

The different gangs situated in the public housing facilities do care. Even if America feigns that it does not understand why these youths join gangs, the individuals in these gangs know why they do so. It is because they appeal to America's throwaway people who refuse to be thrown away. They also know that they offer viable alternatives to this condition because the gang provides a sense of belonging, education on how to commit crimes, prospects of a high paying job and a version of how to have fun.

A 1998 Congressional study by the House Select Committee on Children revealed that 45.1 percent of black children live in families with incomes below the poverty line and 68.3 percent of these children live in households headed by women living below the line. Hispanics, the study showed, tend to do somewhat better overall, but the percentage of Hispanic children living below the poverty line in homes headed by women slightly exceeded that of blacks. The study also indicated that among children living in two-parent families, income distributions look much more similar across all races.

The report outlined statistics on race and poverty among children and concluded that the nation's birth rate remained well below the peak baby boom years. However, non-whites continued to have a higher birth rate. This means that there is a steadily growing number of children that are disadvantaged and that by the year 2010, one of every three children in the United States will be from a minority group.

The Congressional study also showed that for America's youngest and most vulnerable children and their families, the 1980s and '90s were disasters. This trend was consistent with the findings of two earlier studies conducted in 1983 and 1987. Sadly, this nation is not motivated enough to act swiftly to reverse these alarming trends and to prevent the condition from existing in the 2000s. The evidence suggests that we will enter the 21st century besieged by the worst effects of our failure.

There are politicians who disagree with this assessment. They continue to believe that the problem is the breakdown of the family, and they argue that this cannot be resolved by the federal government. This is a specious argument if one considers the following facts:

- There is a demonstrated need for government intervention when we consider precisely the pressure points, e.g., that a large number of families are no longer capable of or doing the jobs for themselves.
- Politicians continually insist on welfare reforms as these broken families fail to receive child support from fathers who are absent.
- The government has failed to provide affordable child care.
- The government has failed to develop a rational and effective program to reduce the use of drugs in this society.
- The government is ineffective in helping its citizens to learn that illicit sexual activity carries a high risk of undesired consequences.

Intervention into these family matters may demand a Solomonic judgment, and this is rarely found in the Federal Register. More importantly, the government does not have to possess the wisdom of Solomon to help these individuals if it wanted to. It merely needs to be cognizant and caring enough to provide help to the growing number of children who arrive at school ill fed, in poor health, often homeless and frightened. It could also ensure that the children have access to quality education in school buildings that do not resemble bombed out World War II buildings.

There is a contention that the requirements for getting out of poverty in this country are so minimal that it takes a mutually reinforced cluster of behaviors to remain in poverty even if you are a black male or a female of any color. It is felt that if you follow a set of modest requirements, you are almost surely going to avoid poverty. These requirements for a male, whether black, brown or white, are to go to a free public school and complete high school. Get into the labor market and get a job, any job, and stick with the labor market.

Historically, the facts suggest otherwise. The transition from urban areas in response to the growing fear of minorities, the shrinkage of employment opportunities in the abandoned areas, the use of public resources to subsidize non-urban life styles and a rigidification of racism all show how difficult this simple proposed remedy would be to accomplish.

Notes

1. A.H. Munnell, G.M.N. Tootell, L.E. Browne and J. McEneaney, "Mortgage Lending in Boston: Interpreting HMDA (Home Mortgage Disclosure Act) Data." *American Economic Review* 86 (March 1996): 25–53. This study is often referred to as the "Boston Fed Study." The article was initially circulated as a working paper in 1992.

2. In 1988, the Atlanta *Journal-Constitution* published "The Color of Money," a series of articles based on research by Stan Fitterman that examined differences in mortgage lending patterns in Atlanta neighborhoods. The study relied on HMDA data for 1982 through 1986 to document wide disparities in lending by depository institutions between white and black neighborhoods with similar income levels.

3. Council of Large Public Housing Authorities, Boston, *Public Housing Today*, 1986.

4. According to a 1989 HUD report there was 4,070,000 HUD assisted rental units. This represented twelve percent of the renter households in the United States. The total number of rental units in the country was 31,808,000. This represented forty-one percent of the total available rental units.

5. Among All Income Eligible Assisted and Assisted Units:

Race/ Ethnicity	Public Housing	Certificate/ Voucher	Private Proj. Based	Total Eligible
White	40%	57%	66%	67%
Black	53	40	30	28
Hispanic	12	12	9	14
Other	3	3	4	5

6. The actual number of private dwellings in these areas is difficult to ascertain because there has been a lack of reliable surveying.

7. W.A. Leigh and M.O. Mitchell, "Public Housing and the Black Community," *The Review of Black Political Economy* 17, 2: 107–129.

8. R.J. Vaughan, "The Urban Impacts of Federal Policies," in *Recent Contributions to the Urban Policy Debate,* edited by P. Morrison et al. (Santa Monica, Calif.: Rand Corporation, 1979).

9. Ibid.

10. Two-thirds of the public households contained no workers. See J.C. Weicher, "Urban Housing Policy," in *Current Issues in Urban Economics,* edited by Miezkowski and M. Staszheim (Baltimore, Md.: John Hopkins University Press, 1979), and P. Kivisto, "A Historical Review of Changes in Public Housing Policies and Their Impact on Minorities," in *Race, Ethnicity and Housing in the United States,* edited by J.A. Momeni (New York, N.Y.: Greenwood Publishing Co., 1986). Also see *The National Data Book, Statistical Abstracts of the U.S. 1995,* table 706, p. 456.

14. Constitutionalism Within the Political Ideologies of Malcolm X and Martin Luther King, Jr.

Otis B. Grant

The political ideologies of Malcolm and King were a reflection of their socialization. King perceived the United States Constitution as the moral substructure of justice. Malcolm believed that the Constitution merely reflected the rules and policies of the white majority. Malcolm was correct to disagree with King and assert that African Americans were suffering from "oppression," not "discrimination"—a condition that made integration inappropriate. King and Malcolm could never have affiliated, not because of their distinctive religions, but because of their different assumptions about the Constitution.

Introduction

During the middle of the twentieth century, Malcolm X and Martin Luther King, Jr., espoused divergent political ideologies which attempted to repair the moral and socioeconomic detriments of slavery. Whereas many were cognizant that Malcolm advocated Black Nationalism (hereafter, "nationalism") and King was an integrationist, there does not seem to be any significant scholarly research which examines their respective renditions of the United States Constitution ("Constitution") as it applied to civil rights.

In this article, the author argues that King became a staunch integrationist because he interpreted the Constitution as a moral charter, and Malcolm embraced nationalism partly because he construed the Constitution to be merely a set of rules and regulations that reflected the law and policies of the white majority. In addition, this article contends that King believed in the virtue of integration because he was nurtured in a racially segregated environment, whereas Malcolm, who was reared in a racially integrated environment, considered the integration postulation to be overly simplistic.

Socialization of Malcolm and Martin

Because the socialization[1] experiences of Martin Luther King, Jr., and Malcolm X were disparate (Cone 1992), comparing their early childhood experiences provides a clue to their radically different perspectives on American law in their later lives.

An Early Life of Violence, Poverty and Domestic Upheaval

Malcolm was born in Omaha, Nebraska, on May 19, 1925, the seventh child of J. Earl Little,[2] and the fourth of M. Louise Norton, a West Indian mulatto from Grenada. Malcolm's parents were actively involved in the nationalist movement. Earl Little was the president of the Omaha chapter of Marcus Garvey's Universal Negro Improvement Association and Louise served as the reporter. The family was constantly exposed to violence because of their commitment to Garveyism. According to Malcolm:

> When my mother was pregnant with me ... Ku Klux Klan riders ... Surrounded the house.... [They] shouted threats and warnings that we had better get out of town because "the good Christian white people" were not going to stand for my father's "spreading trouble" among the "good" Negroes of Omaha with the "back to Africa" preaching of Marcus Garvey [Haley 1965, 3].

By most accounts, Malcolm's early childhood was harsh (Goldman 1979). When he was four years old, the Black Legionnaires, a white hate group, burned his house down. Witnessing the racist actions of the Black Legionnaires was so traumatic that Malcolm often referred to it as his "earliest vivid memory" (Haley 1965).

> I remember being suddenly snatched awake into a frightening confusion of pistol shots and shouting and smoke and flames [3].

While growing up, in addition to witnessing violence by whites, Malcolm also observed the tumultuous relationship between his mother and father and their violence against his brothers, sisters and himself.

> My father was belligerent toward all of the children.... [T]he older ones he would beat almost savagely if they broke any of his rules—and he had so many rules it was hard to know them all [Haley 1965, 4].

In 1931, Malcolm's father died under suspicious circumstances, possibly at the hands of white supremacists.[3] After his death, the Little family became destitute and Malcolm's mother was forced to accept public relief. At about that time, she began to exhibit signs of serious mental illness. According to Malcolm, because of the impoverishment of his family and the psychological deterioration of his mother, the social welfare workers began to exert authority over the family. Eventually, the welfare workers broke up the family. Louise Little suffered a mental breakdown and was placed in the state hospital at Kalamazoo. Malcolm and his siblings became wards of the state and were placed in several different homes.

Some have argued that Louise's mental health was the catalyst for the family breakup (Perry 1991), however, Malcolm contended that it was white officials functioning under official state authority that undermined the family's mutual natural support and unity (Haley 1965). Malcolm's belief that the welfare workers operated under the authority of law helps explains his unwillingness to perceive whites as allies in the struggle for black progress and his intense belief that whites create and enforce laws for their own benefit, much to the detriment of the blacks.

After reaching early adulthood in Lansing, Michigan, Malcolm later moved to New York City and Boston, Massachusetts, where he worked various odd jobs until he was arrested and subsequently incarcerated.[4]

AN EARLY LIFE OF PRIVILEGE

Martin Luther King, Jr., was born in Atlanta, Georgia, on January 15, 1929, to an upper-middle-class family.[5] He was the second child and first son of Alberta Christine Williams and Martin Luther King, Sr. When the children were young, Martin Sr. taught them the values of self-help because he believed that African Americans should make something of themselves, regardless of the disadvantages of living in a white, racist society (Riley 1980). Notwithstanding, Martin Sr.'s ideology of self-help is not necessarily congruent with the Black Nationalistic postulation of self-help. Like most integrationists, Martin Sr.'s concept of self-help was an embracement of American capitalism, a manifestation of the person who pulls himself or herself up by their own boot straps, embodying the merits of thrift, service, responsibility and sacrifice. Despite the fact that more than half of the African Americans in Atlanta were on some form of public relief, the King family owned their own home and never collected public assistance.

Martin's parents had a loving relationship and provided for his educational and religious needs during childhood (King 1958). Nevertheless, despite his family affluence, Martin was exposed to racism at a very early age. However, unlike the young Malcolm X, Martin's family consistently assured him of his self-worth and his exposure to white racism never affected his self-esteem.

THE EFFECTS OF POSITIVE AND NEGATIVE INFLUENCES

In contrast to the King family, Malcolm's parents could not protect their children from racism or the violence of white hate groups. Malcolm was six years old when his father was killed and at the age of twelve he became a ward of the state when his mother was committed to a mental institution. Without demonstrative parental support to instill self-confidence, Malcolm did not have the vivacity to cope with a white society that refused to acknowledge his humanity.

Both Malcolm and King spoke in metaphors (Flick and Powell 1988). In attempting to ascertain their interpretation of the Constitution, it is important to contrast not only their family environment but also their religious and educational experiences. When they were born, and throughout their life, the black Christian church was the dominant institution in the social life of African Americans. In addition to providing a protective shelter against racism, the church also served as the source of leadership development (Cone 1992).

From a young age until early adulthood, King attended segregated churches and schools and rarely came in contact with whites, thereby enabling him to develop a sense of himself as an African American before he entered the mainstream of a racist America.

Unlike the racial homogeneity of King's socialization environment, Malcolm lived a thoroughly integrated life, including attending schools that were predominantly white. His developmental and educational experiences were circumscribed by whites, and in later life, he often articulated that he did not have any pleasant memories about the whites he encountered in his youth or young adulthood (Breitman 1965). Whereas Martin was influenced by his father's optimistic ideology of integration, Malcolm was affected by the pessimistic nationalist worldview[6] of Earl Little. These disparate worldviews were further shaped by their respective religions. Martin's religion of Christianity stressed love, and Malcolm's religion of Islam[7] stressed brotherhood (Cone 1992; Lincoln 1973).

Integration, Nationalism and Christian Moral Law

As with many social movements, the civil rights crusade had disparate viewpoints. At the crux of the debate was the delineation of equality (Brooks 1974), the consequences of racial difference (Franklin 1988), and the most efficient remedy for racial disparity (Williams 1987).

INTEGRATION

Integrationists maintained that the solution to racial disparity was equal treatment on an individual level and integration on an institutional level. They argued that equal opportunity would lead to integrated institutions. As the races got to know each other, they would come to appreciate each other as individuals who would be judged on character rather than skin color. This, in turn, would replace the ignorance of racism with the knowledge that actual contact provides. This "contact hypothesis" helps explain their focus on public education. According to integrationists, if children attended integrated schools, they would learn the truth about each other's individuality before they came to believe negative racial stereotypes.

The contact hypothesis made integration indispensable to eradicating racial stereotypes. Integrationists asserted that only with daily interaction with blacks would whites learn that blacks are not less intelligent, less honest, or less human than whites. They contended that being exposed to an integrated environment was the best way to end racial disparity.

BLACK NATIONALISM

Often portrayed as antithetical to integrationism, Black Nationalism is actually an accommodating response to white segregation. Rooted in seventeenth century slave conspiracies when Africans rebelled against slavery, nationalism is also characterized by mutual-aid societies, black-led churches, and black-led emigration programs. Pride in African heritage (Garvey 1923), unity as a people (Burkett 1978), the creation of autonomous institutions (Blake 1969), and the search for a territory to build a nation (Hall 1978), were the constituents which shaped nationalist consciousness. In addition to self-help, nationalism employs a theme of self-dependence which mandates that blacks control their own political futures. Malcolm argued that:

> The political philosophy of black nationalism means: we must control the politics and the politicians of our community [Breitman 1965, 21].

During the Civil Rights Movement, Black Nationalists were portrayed as "militant," "radical," "anti-white bigots." Notwithstanding the radical label and widespread reports to the contrary, all Black Nationalists were pro-black, but only a few were anti-white. Despite their willingness to associate with whites, two important things happened to repress nationalist ideology: (1) whites' acceptance of Martin Luther King, Jr., and his theory of nonviolence, and (2) *Brown v. The Board of Education.*

After white America accepted King, integration exemplified intergroup relations. Proponents claimed that integration was evident when blacks were conspicuously represented, broadly disseminated, and shared power and equality. King and his followers maintained that integration was optimal when there was equal status between blacks and whites to pursue common, mutually supportive goals and when there were official sanctions and support for the process of achieving those goals. In contrast, nationalists embraced self-dependence while asserting that they did not have to acquiesce to a white power structure in order to control their own economic and political destiny. Unlike integrationists, nationalists were race conscious and constantly distinguished blacks from whites, noting that the latter

> Come from different communities, neighborhoods, churches families and histories and ... [are] in various different ways foreigners to each other [Overton 1994, 478].

Christian Moral Law

In contrast to Malcolm's fiery nationalistic persona, the leadership tradition personified by Martin Luther King, Jr., epitomized the black middle class, the ruling black elite of the Civil Rights Movement. King and his followers were strongly influenced by the spiritual values of love, justice and obedience, and most believed that if members of the black community practiced those values, they would gain the political and economic benefits of equality.

King's leadership also reflected his religion, which was primarily Christian in the African American Baptist tradition. However, unlike most black Baptist ministers, King's exposure to white Protestant liberals reshaped his interpretation of the Christian tenets. King believed that America was a Christian nation which had failed to live out the true meaning of its destiny, a destiny defined by the nation's moral vision of freedom and justice. America's religious identity was the Kingdom of God, the "beloved community" that he constantly referred to in his numerous speeches.

Under King's leadership, political protest during the African American civil rights movement of the 1950s and 1960s was associated with the Old Testament theme of justice, a theme that is found in the prophets and that is dominant in songs and sermons of the black church. Accommodation for integration was closely related to the New Testament idea of love, particularly emphasized in the Sermon on the Mount, and like justice, a major theme in black religion (Cone 1992). It is through this prism that King molded his moralist interpretation of the Constitution.

Romanticizing the Past for a "Dream"

Both Malcolm (1964) and King (1963) proposed using the Constitution to alleviate racial disparity. Whereas they concluded that racial prejudice was inconsistent with the fundamental tenets of American ideology, it was their disparate assumptions of the Framers' intentions that differentiated their perspective interpretations of the Constitution. King believed that the Framers were guided by moral righteousness, and Malcolm believed that the Framers were merely trying to free themselves from English sovereignty. Malcolm (1963a) noted:

> The Revolutionary War was never fought to provide freedom and democracy in this white country for the black man. Our people remained slaves here in America even after the Declaration of Independence was signed.

In contrast to Malcolm's description of the Founding Fathers, King spoke of Americanism within the metaphor of the "dream," a phrase that he began to use in the 1960s. During the Civil Rights Movement, the dream conceptualized the integration hypothesis. King derived his "dream" from two sources: (1) the American liberal democratic tradition delineated by the Declaration of Independence and the United States Constitution, and (2) the Biblical tradition of the Old and New Testaments explicated by Protestant liberalism and the black Christian church (Cone 1992). According to King, the Founding Fathers purposely adopted a colorblind, universalist approach when drafting the Declaration of Independence by using language articulating that "all men," rather than "all white men," are created equal.

> [T]hat all men are created equal; that they are endowed by their Creator with certain inalienable rights; that among these are life, liberty, and the pursuit of happiness [Declaration of Independence 1776, para. 1].

In keeping within the Baptist tradition, King (1968) also espoused a natural law premise contending that

> [E]ach individual has certain basic rights that are neither conferred by nor derived from the state ... they are God given [10–15].

King and Malcolm believed that the Constitution conferred equality. When Martin beseeched white Americans to support equal rights, he was referring to the moral supposition of the Framers' intent. When Malcolm rebuked whites for failing to comply with the Constitution, he repudiated King's assertion that whites would heed a natural law premise that blacks and whites have equal rights. Notwithstanding, throughout the Civil Rights Movement King's moralist interpretation of the Constitution was inspiring, but nonetheless flawed. Historians readily acknowledge that the Founding Fathers intended to create a nation of whites for whites, and purposely incorporated blacks into the Constitution as slaves in order that they remain separate from whites, the true "Americans." As Malcolm (1963a) astutely pointed out:

> Most of the white Founding Fathers who signed the Declaration of Independence were slave owners themselves.

Although Americans often espouse the benevolence of the Founding Fathers, the true intentions of the Framers can be found in the deliberations that took place at the birth of the Republic.

Compromise for Slavery

Like many eighteenth century American thinkers, the Founding Fathers accepted Locke's notion that the state of nature is the original, pre-political condition of mankind (Farber and Sherry 1990). In the absence of an established political society, all men are free and equal, and possessed of certain inalienable rights. According to Locke, government was formed by the consent of the governed, primarily to provide protection of these inalienable rights. In order to be legitimate, any government established out of this state of nature must respect both equality and natural rights.[8] Madison, however, believed that in a pure democracy the majority may overwhelm the minority (Macpherson 1980). To quell Madison's apprehensions, the Constitution prescribes that both the national and state governments be republican.[9] A republican form of government allows for delegating the task of governing to a relatively small number of citizens. This, in turn, would

> refine and enlarge the public views, by passing them through the medium of a chosen body of citizens, whose wisdom may best discern the true interest of their country [Macpherson 1980, 65].

Nevertheless, almost immediately after the ratification of the Constitution, dissension emerged between northern "free states" and southern "slaveholding states." To appease the southern states, the Framers conceded the republican premise of the Constitution and rejected the *moral* idealism of the Declaration of Independence by sanctioning slavery.[10] This capitulation, which Madison called the "compromising expedient" of the Constitutional Convention, allowed for the creation of the Union and the exoneration of white supremacy (Glennon 1994).

White Supremacy as the Law

The American courts sustained white supremacy by affirming slavery. In *Dred Scott v. Sandford*,[11] the petitioner, a slave, sued for his freedom after having been taken to a free state and returned to a slave state. The Supreme Court held that individuals of the Negro race are not considered "citizens" in the constitutional sense. "Citizens," for constitutional purposes, referred to the sovereign people of the United States as they were understood to be at the time of the Constitution's adoption. At that time, blacks were considered to be an inferior class, one having no inherent liberty or property rights.

Whereas some have argued that *Dred Scott* was a rationalization for white supremacy *per se*, this article maintains that the decision was fairly consistent with the ideals of "strict constructionism." Under strict constructionism, the Court looks to the intent of the Framers and attempts to be consistent with them.

PLESSY FURTHERS THE NOTION OF SUPREMACY

The white supremacy doctrine in *Dred Scott* was confirmed by the Supreme Court in *Plessy v. Ferguson.*[12] Plessy was arrested for trying to sit in a railroad car which was designated "for whites only." At issue was a Louisiana statute that segregated black and whites in "separate but equal" facilities or accommodations. In arguing against the statute, proponents of integration asserted that the law stigmatized blacks and stamped them with the badge of inferiority, thereby violating the Thirteenth and Fourteenth amendments. In deciding *Plessy*, the Court created a new standard of review which analyzed the "established usages, customs and traditions of the people." The Court held that black "inferiority" could not be overcome by legislation, claiming

> Legislation is powerless to eradicate racial instincts or to abolish distinctions based upon physical differences, and the attempt to do so can only result in accentuating the difficulties of the present situation. If the civil and political rights of both races be equal, one cannot be inferior to the other civilly or politically. If one race be inferior to the other socially, the Constitution of the United States cannot put them upon the same plane.[13]

The "separate but equal" ruling in *Plessy v. Ferguson* was overturned sixty years later by the Supreme Court's decision in *Brown v. The Board of Education.*[14] In *Brown*, the Court ruled that segregated schools generated a feeling of inferiority in black students who were deprived of the opportunity to attend schools with white students. Moreover, as articulated in *Brown*, the Thirteenth and Fourteenth amendments of the Constitution created a national citizenry, which defined the rights of citizenship, allowing for the national government to protect the rights of those who wanted to implement school integration.

With *Brown* as the catalyst, King reaffirmed his belief that the Constitution guaranteed individual rights against an oppressive majority that was exercising the powers of government. He believed that the Court asserted an excellent solution to discrimination, which he saw as the main problem facing black-white relations. When whites resisted *Brown*-mandated integration, King implored the federal government to safeguard the "constitutional rights" of black Americans.

In contrast, Malcolm (1963b) argued that American society was oppressive, not just because of the aversion white Americans had to enforcing equal rights, but also because the American government, through the politics of the white majority, did not want blacks to return to Africa and would do anything to keep them in America as second class citizens:

> The government is deceiving our people with false promises so that we won't want to return to our own land and people.

Oppression Not Discrimination

Malcolm contended that blacks, like the white colonials, were being exploited and oppressed. Although he was often depicted as un–American, Malcolm actually promoted the same axiom as did white colonial Americans. Whereas Malcolm's assertion of "oppression" rather than "discrimination" was analogous, it was also controversial. Nevertheless, in retrospect, there is support for his position.

Young (1989) argues that a group is oppressed when it or a significant number of its members suffer (1) *exploitation* of their work or energy without reciprocity; (2) *marginalization and exclusion*, particularly from the workplace; (3) *powerlessness,* in the sense of living under the authority of others with little autonomy or authority over others; (4) *cultural imperialism,* in the sense that they are stereotyped even while "their experience and situation are invisible in the society in general, and they have little opportunity and little audiences for the expression of their experience and perspective on social events"; and (5) *random violence and harassment* that are motivated by group hatred or fear (261).

Oppression often leads to caste. According to Goldenberg (1978), the two basic structures through which oppression is manifested, both institutionally and socially, are *containment* and *expendability.* Physical or psychological containment restricts and narrows a person's sense of the possible, and as a daily reality, removes positive meaning from individual and group distinctiveness.

> Oppression ... is a condition of being in which one's past and future meet in the present—and go no further. To be oppressed is to be rendered obsolete almost from the moment of birth, so that one's experience of oneself is always contingent on an awareness of just how poorly one approximates the images that currently dominate a society [Goldenberg 1978, 3].

During the Civil Rights Movement, as they have throughout their history, Black Nationalists contended that the five prongs of oppression had been met and blackness was indeed a caste. Blacks were used as slave labor to build America, and when no longer enslaved, never received comparable compensation. Blacks faced constant marginalization in the workplace, and had to depend on a non-sympathetic government to enforce their constitutional rights. In an effort to accommodate, integrationists sacrificed black culture, to no avail. Blacks were considered the epitome of crime, and those who embraced the American tradition of self-defense rather than passivity were considered violent, ill-informed and unpatriotic. Malcolm believed that many whites thought that blacks were less than human and would never consider the notion that the Constitution protected blacks as well as whites. Rather than hope that whites would acquiesce when legally compelled to associate with blacks, Malcolm and the nationalists correctly asserted that integration could not remedy oppression.

Constitutionalism to the United Nations

Though some argued that Malcolm was a militant who advocated repudiating the Constitution, upon closer examination it is apparent that he espoused the same strict constructionist constitutionalism that has been embraced throughout American history, and is currently *en vogue* within the Rehnquist court. Rather than embrace the universalist postulation of King in analyzing race relations, Malcolm (1963a), like the Framers, insisted on separating justice from notions of equality:

> It is not wrong to expect justice. It is not wrong to expect freedom. It's not wrong to expect equality. If Patrick Henry and all of the Founding Fathers of the country were willing to lay down their lives to get what you are enjoying today, then it's time for you to realize that a large, ever-increasing number of Black people in this country are willing to die for what we know is due us by birth.

Malcolm believed that all Americans possess constitutional rights by virtue of being born in America. Therefore, in issues of racial disparity, blacks need not substantiate their claims for equal rights, but rather, whites must expiate their historic persistence against equality. Malcolm asserted that this was something that whites would not do. Subsequently, he argued that equal rights for blacks could only be achieved by transforming the black civil rights movement to a human rights movement. Malcolm (1965) thought that by framing civil rights issues as human rights violations, it would be possible to remove cases involving racial issues from the United States courts to within the jurisdiction of the United Nations:

> As long as the Black man in America calls his struggle a struggle of civil rights—it's domestic, and it remains within the jurisdiction of the United

States ... but when you call it "human rights" it becomes international. And then you can take your troubles to the World Court.

After Malcolm's death, King was given credit for turning the Civil Rights Movement into a human rights movement. King refused to renounce his belief that the Framers intentionally designed the Constitution to be color-blind. Never a proponent of Black Nationalism, it is not ironic that his words are now being used by those who wish to rescind the gains of the Civil Rights Movement for the sake of a morally colorblind society.

Conclusion

The political ideologies of Malcolm and King reflected their socialization. For Malcolm, the issue had always been oppression. During the Civil Rights Movement, he focused on the racial factor in human exploitation. King argued that equality existed as long as there was a universal set of rules which evenly applied to everyone, without regard to race. Malcolm, however, defined "equality" by reference to the conditions and experiences of blacks as a group.

The disparate ideologies of Malcolm and King cannot be reconciled because of their respective presumptions of the Constitution. Both asserted that the Declaration of Independence is binding on the states, and therefore sustains black citizens. However, as Malcolm astutely pointed out, the Founding Fathers intentionally disconnected the ideology of the Revolution from the axiom that all men are created equal. Thus, despite King's assertions to the contrary, the Constitution is not a moral decree, but rather, an instrument that promotes formal rules and statutes.

Whereas King could be as critical of whites as Malcolm, he maintained that in order to achieve racial parity, blacks and whites must interact on a daily basis. Like most integrationists, King believed that whites discriminated against blacks due to ignorance. In contrast to the discriminatory hypothesis posed by King, Malcolm correctly surmised that blacks were suffering from "oppression," not "discrimination," and this oppression was a manifestation of white supremacy, a situation that integration could not overcome.

Notes

1. *Socialization* is the process through which people learn to participate in group life through the acquisition of culture, and refers to the continuing process of learning in a social setting in which an individual's personality is formed, maintained or changed.
2. Malcolm's father had three children by a previous marriage: Ella, Earl, and Mary.

3. But see Bruce Perry (1991, 12–13), according to whom Earl Little was struck by a street car. The insurance company insisted it was suicide. According to the state police and the coroner, his death was accidental. However, Malcolm believed his mother's theory that Earl Little had been killed by white supremacists.

4. Malcolm was sentenced to the Charleston State Prison on February 27, 1946.

5. Martin's family included prominent Baptist ministers. His maternal grandfather, Alfred Daniel Williams, and Martin King, Sr., were both prominent Baptist preachers in Atlanta, Georgia.

6. For the purpose of this essay, "worldview" refers to a person's conceptual framework. In its simplest terms, worldview refers to how one thinks the world works. See, e.g., Allen E. Ivey, *Counseling and Psychotherapy* (Englewood Cliffs, New Jersey: Prentice Hall, 1986), pp. 4–5.

7. This author has often argued that the Nation of Islam does not practice the orthodox Islamic religion. Accordingly, when Islam is referred to in this essay, it is the religion that Malcolm practiced after he left the Nation of Islam.

8. Further rights, however, were civil in origin and could be rescinded.

9. The U.S. Constitution. art. 4, sec. 4 provides that "The United States shall guarantee to every State in this Union a Republican Form of Government, and shall protect each of them against Invasion...." See *Baker v. Carr*, 369 U.S. 186, 223 (1962): "Guaranty Clause is not a repository of judicially manageable standards which a court could utilize independently in order to identify a State's lawful government"; *Pacific States Tel. & Tell. Co. v. Oregon*, 233 U.S. 118 (1912) (claim that state initiative and referendum violates the Guaranty Clause is nonjustifiable); *Luther v. Borden*, 48 U.S. (7 How.) 1, 42 (1849) (Congress is the proper body to determine if a state's form of government meets Article 4's republican guarantee).

10. Ten sections of the United States Constitution allowed slavery.
Article 1, sec. 2 (amended by U.S. Constitution, amend. 14, sec. 2) provides:

> Representatives and direct Taxes shall be apportioned among the several States which may be included within the Union according to their respective Numbers, which shall be determined by adding to the whole Number of free Persons, including those bound to Service for a Term of Years and excluding Indians not taxed, three fifths of all other Persons.

Article 1, sec. 9, clause 1, provides:

> The Migration or Importation of such Person as any of the States now existing shall think proper to admit, shall not be prohibited by Congress prior to the Year one thousand eight hundred and eight, but a tax or duty may be imposed on such Importation, not exceeding ten dollars for each Person.

Article 1, sec. 9, clause 4, provides:

> No capitation, or other direct, Tax shall be laid, unless in Proportion to the Census of Enumeration herein before directed to be taken.

Article 4, sec. 2 (superseded by Amendment 13), provides:

> No Person held to Service or Labour in one State, under the Laws thereof, escaping to another, shall, in Consequence of any Law or Regulation therein, be discharged from such Service or Labour, but shall be delivered up on Claim of the Party to whom such Service or Labour may be due.

Article 5 provides:

> [N]o Amendment which may be made prior to the Year One thousand eight hundred and eight shall in any Manner affect the first and fourth Clauses in the Ninth Section of first Article.

Other provisions also helped to secure chattel slavery. See Article 1, sec. 8, cl. 15 (to suppress slave uprising); Art. 1, sec. 9, cl. 5 (prohibiting federal or state taxes on the products of slave labor); Art. 4, sec. 1 (full faith and credit required free states to respect the laws of slave states); Art. 4, sec. 4 (requiring federal help to quell "domestic violence").

    11. *Dred Scott v. Sandford,* 60 U.S. (19 How.) 393 (1857).

    12. *Plessy v. Ferguson,* 163 U.S. 537 (1896).

    13. *Plessy v. Ferguson,* 163 U.S. 537 (1896), p. 542.

    14. *Brown v. Board of Education,* 347 U.S. 483 (1954).

Bibliography

Bennett, Lerone, Jr. (1964). *What Manner of Man.* Chicago: Johnson Publishing Co., Book Division.

Blake, Herman (1969). "Black Nationalism." *Annals of the American Academy of Political and Social Science,* no. 382: 15–25.

Booker, Simeon (1964). *Black Man's America.* New York: Prentice Hall.

Breitman, George (ed.) (1965). *Malcolm X Speaks.* New York: Grove Press.

Brooks, Thomas R. (1974). *Walls Come Tumbling Down: A History of the Civil Rights Movement, 1940–1970.* New York: Prentice Hall.

Burkett, Robert (1978). *Garveyism as a Religious Movement: The Institutionalization of a Black Civil Religion.* Metuchen, N.J: Scarecrow Press.

Cone, James H. (1992). *Martin and Malcolm and America.* Maryknoll, N.Y.: Orbis Books.

Draper, Theodore (1969). *The Rediscovery of Black Nationalism.* New York: Viking Press.

Farber, Daniel, and Suzanna Sherry (1990). *A History of the American Constitution.* St. Paul, Minn.: West.

Flick, Hank, and Larry Powell (1988). "Animal Imagery in the Rhetoric of Malcolm X." *Journal of Black Studies* 18 (4): 435–451.

Franklin, John H. (1988). *From Slavery to Freedom: A History of Negro Americans.* 6th ed. New York: McGraw Hill.

Garvey, Amy Jacques (ed.) (1923). *Philosophy and Opinions of Marcus Garvey.* New York: Universal Publishing House.

Glennon, Robert (1994). "The Jurisdictional Legacy of the Civil Rights Movement." *Tennessee Law Review* 61: 873.

Goldenberg, Ira (1978). *Oppression and Social Intervention.* New York: McGraw Hill.

Goldman, Peter (1979). *The Death and Life of Malcolm X.* New York: Harper Row.

Haley, Alex (1965). *The Autobiography of Malcolm X.* New York: Ballantine Books.

Hall, Raymond (1978). *Black Separatism in the United States.* Hanover, N.H.: New Hampshire Press.

King, Jr., Martin Luther (1958). *Stride Toward Freedom: The Montgomery Story.* New York: Harper and Row.

_____ (1963). *Why We Can't Wait.* New York: Harper and Row.

_____ (1968). "The American Dream." *The Negro History Bulletin* 31 (May): 10–15.

Lincoln, Eric C. (1973). *The Black Muslims in America.* Trenton, N.J.: Eerdmans Publishing Co.

Macpherson, C.B. (1980). *John Locke: Second Treatise of Government.* Indianapolis, Ind.: Hackett Publishing.

Malcolm X (1963a). "Twenty Million Black People in Prison." Address. Michigan State University. January 23.

_____ (1963b). *America's Greatest Crisis Since the Civil War.* Address. University of California. October 11.

_____ (1964). "The Ballot or the Bullet." Cory Methodist Church. Address. April 3.

_____ (1965). "Not Just an American Problem but a World Problem." Address. February 16.

Overton, Spencer (1994). "The Threat Diversity Poses to African Americans: A Black Nationalist Critique of Outsider Ideology." *Howard Law Review* 37: 465.

Perry, Bruce (1991). *Malcolm.* Barrytown, N.Y.: Station Hill Press.

Riley, Clayton (1980). *Daddy King: An Autobiography.* New York: William Morrow.

Williams, Juan (1987). *Eyes on the Prize: America's Civil Rights Years, 1954–1965.* New York: Viking Penguin.

Young, Iris M. (1989). "Polity and Group Difference: A Critique of the Ideal of Universal Citizenship." *Ethics* 99: 250–271.

15. Revising the Best Western View: Civil Rights, Wilderness, and Racial Relocation[1]

STEVE ANDREWS

The Vista Before Us

Late night television ad: a nice new sedan pulls up and the driver helps the passenger out. The passenger seems blind, as suggested by the close-up of eyes that don't appear to return the camera's gaze; and, too, the camera lingers on the cane hanging from the door. Casually dressed, clothes not too baggy, the two men carefully make their way to a railing, the one giving the other the bodily and visual assistance necessary to front the vista that opens before them, before us. We television viewers see them, then, from behind, and they too, become part of our view. As they gaze off into the distance, a caption scrolls onto the screen: *because everyone should experience it at least once.* And what is this primal experience? It's the Grand Canyon; and Best Western, the corporation behind the ad, wants us to know that they respond affirmatively to the Americans with Disabilities Act of 1990, as well as to Title II of the Civil Rights Act of 1964, which prohibits "discrimination or segregation on the ground of race, color, religion, or national origin" in places of public accommodation.[2] The two black men in the ad are visible proof of this affirmation.

But given all the movies and ads that use Monument Valley and otherwise cite the American Southwestern landscape, can we imagine for a moment that an ad with two white subjects lingering in front of the Grand Canyon would need anything by way of a rationalizing "because?" Take, as an example, another recent ad, this time for Chrysler: a man and woman (they appear to be white) drive up to the edge of what appears to be the Grand Canyon. No one gets out. The woman passenger snaps a picture, the car squeals away, and the tag-line informs us, "It's not the destination; it's the ride."[3] While the purported smoothness of "the ride" might very well be the selling point for Chrysler, the capturing of the photographic image, no matter how shallow and perfunctory, seems to underscore the symbolic value of the once in a lifetime experience that the blind man in the Best Western ad cannot *quite* achieve.

Nevertheless, Best Western is insisting that visual disability ought not to hinder one's experience of the Grand Canyon. Hence the extraordinary *experience* proffered for consumption is not visual so much as performative, not a sight so much as a citation.[4] For the blind man, seeing must be replaced by saying, as if to underscore our ordinary tendency of asking not whether one has ever *seen,* but rather if one has ever *been to* the Grand Canyon. Indeed, the blind man can now answer that question in the affirmative, provided he can trust the driver. Sighting and saying are merged, then, as subsets of a larger citational gesture—*being there*. This is the vanishing point at which the blind man and the Chrysler couple converge, only to go their separate ways.

While the couple can always point to the photograph and confirm that they've "been there and done that," to what, or to whom, must the blind man turn to corroborate his once in a lifetime experience? Turning to someone for assistance or corroboration (the issue of trust I raised above) is structurally integral to the Best Western ad. Given the trope of blindness and the sublimity of a subject position poised—posed—on the edge of the great American abyss, who would deny that trust is everything? Or that nothing can be taken for granted, this moment least of all? Such heightened sensation, aided and abetted by the sentimental tug of blindness and race, seems to index a history in which a black man's place in the American landscape has, until very recently, required another sort of corroboration, that of white validation. The "destination" of black Americans, to borrow a word from the Chrysler ad, has always mattered a bit too much in the United States, where, as in its nineteenth century version, the trope of destination seems so much a manifestation of destiny. In the binary relationship between free and slave, and then later, white and black, where you are allowed to go in the U.S. is a function of who you are, the promissory notices of The Declaration and The Constitution notwithstanding. Within that context, exclusion is as much a manifestation of identity as sanctioned movement.[5] Best Western wants to remedy that history of failed promise. That's the affective burden of the convergence between blindness, race and the ad's caption: *"because* everyone *should experience it at least once."*

The ambivalence between civil rights and wilderness as white privilege is not, however, a registered trademark of Best Western. The deep division between provisions marked out in the Fourteenth Amendment and the ongoing rhetoric of Manifest Destiny was played out to dramatic effect in the Senate hearings leading up to the passage of the Civil Rights and Wilderness acts on July 2 and August 20 of 1964. These acts have each received a fair amount of attention in and of themselves, but not enough attention has been focused on the interrelationship between them. Each issues from the same legislative body, but, as subsequent racializations of these two acts make clear, where blacks and whites were concerned, that legislative body reacted to the same exigent circumstances—urban unrest—in profoundly different, but nonetheless connected ways. In the forty-two years since the passage of these affirmative legislative actions, the Wilderness Act seems increasingly a manifestation of flight into the *preserve* of white privilege, while the Civil Rights Act, viewed from the ultra-conservative wing of that preserve, has been construed as "black" and inherently undemocratic.[6] While we too often imagine these legislative actions as segregated, and while the "events" interpreted in this paper are represented in sections, each with a particular story to tell, I cannot stress enough the ways in which the legislative overlap between passage of these two acts exposes the constitutive relationship that we Americans have historically imagined between civil rights and wilderness.

In the three sections that follow, I analyze some key aspects of the cultural and political exchanges that occur on "The New Frontier." In section II, I discuss interconnections between white masculine privilege and the "place" of blacks in America, as revealed in the Senate debate over the Civil Rights Act of 1964. Specifically, I read Georgia Senator Richard Russell's sponsorship of an amendment to relocate black folk from places where they are demographically dense to places where they would represent less than 10.5 percent of the population as an extension of the logic of slavery. On the surface, Russell's project seems motivated by racial revulsion, but beneath such contempt, there is, I argue, a submerged erotic element of white masculine anxiety. In section III, I link the rhetoric of the Kennedy-Johnson administration's "New Frontier" legislative agenda, of which the Civil Rights and Wilderness acts of 1964 would be lasting legacies, with the erotically charged "continuous touch" of savagery and civilization that the historian Frederick Jackson Turner imagined created American democracy. This nexus of gender, violence and race is then linked back to the Civil Rights Act, in section IV, in two ways: first, the way in which Russell imagines Indians as exemplary models of racial decorum in an exchange with Senate colleagues in which Zora Neale Hurston's written comments about *Brown v. Board of Education,* and her attitudes about Indians, play a surprisingly pivotal role; and then in terms of passage of Title II of the Civil Rights Act which (as previously noted) prohibits discrimination in places of public accommodation and enables black folk to begin to imagine access to the cultural project outlined in the Wilderness Act. Whether we—the "we" of black folk, or the larger Constitutional "we" of the Fourteenth Amendment—wish to do so within the cultural logic I am concerned to expose, remains to be seen. For we, at any rate, should remember: since 1517, when Bartholomew de Las Casas advocated successfully on behalf of Indians, and Charles V, Holy Roman Emperor, allowed the transport of African slaves in their place, the destinies of Native and African Americans have been intertwined.[7] The potential of "the wilderness" to transform lowly European immigrants into ostensibly self-possessed Americans has always been a function of the denial of personhood, the denial of what we now call civil rights.

Filibuster (Circumlocution)

I begin with a filibuster and a subsequent attempt to tack on a Racial Relocation Amendment to the eleven titles of the Civil Rights Act, the better to find out where "we" are, *circa* 1964, and where "we" are "supposed" to be. In the next few pages, racial "location," as a function of geographic placement and socio-political status, is intimately connected to a type of "locution," the power to speak on behalf of others that we call political representation.

Immediately prior to the Senate debates on the Civil Rights Act of 1964, Senator John Stennis of Mississippi made it clear that those in opposition to the bill before them intended to filibuster. He asked for, and received, permission to have read into the record of March 16 an article written by Senator Richard Russell published by *The New York Times Magazine* on Sunday, March 15. In that article, Russell defends the "right of extended debate—popularly known as the filibuster—to oppose some measure that was counter to deeply held convictions." Tracing the tradition of filibustering back to 1841, Russell implies that should a "gag rule" be instituted, the "loss of freedom of debate in the Senate would be followed by an attempt to abolish the Senate's time-honored right of amendment."[8]

Invoking the language of the Constitution, Russell raises the "right" to filibuster to the exalted status of a Constitutional guarantee: "The right of free speech in the Senate is particularly important because the Senate is the only institution of the Federal system in which smaller states exercise an equal influence over the conduct of the affairs of the Nation." This "principle of equality of representation," he continues, is "greatly weakened" when a "majority" is allowed to "gag freedom of debate." Thus gagged, the Senate would, in Russell's estimation, be "reduce[d]" to "little more than an ineffective appendage to the House of Representatives." Rhetorically opposing "equality of representation," "free speech" and "the right of amendment," with a "gag rule" and a "dangerous" disruption of the "entire system of checks and balances," Russell implies that the minority filibuster is the last best hope for a flagging democracy: "Freedom of debate in the Senate, so long as it is preserved, serves as a protection of the fundamental rights and liberties for which men for thousands of years have fought, sacrificed, and died" (CR, 5324, *passim*).

What some of these rights are, and what particular war he might have had in mind, is made clear when Russell, during the subsequent Senate debate, engages in the following exchange with Senator Paul Douglas of Illinois:

> MR. DOUGLAS. ... In 1954, by unanimous decision, the Supreme Court reversed Plessy against Ferguson. If the civil rights decision of 1883 is quoted, we can say the Supreme Court acted ultimately with wisdom. Incidentally, all the southern judges on the Supreme Court voted in the Topeka case to reverse Plessy against Ferguson.
> MR. RUSSELL. There are southerners and there are southerners.
> MR. DOUGLAS. The Senator draws a distinction, does he?
> MR. RUSSELL. I do. I draw a distinction. There has never been a greater distinction drawn between people than that drawn between those who came home barefooted from fighting in the Civil War, misguided though they might have been, but who thought they were fighting for the right, and the scalawags who preyed upon the women and children while they were gone [CR, 5342].

Still fighting the allegorical battles of the "barefooted" battalions of the Lost Cause, Russell's return to antebellum origins purifies the parliamentary tactics he will deploy in opposing the Civil Rights Bill before the Senate in two ways. It legitimizes the technique in its appeal to *democratic* tradition, and its appeal to *tradition* legitimizes a desire to perpetuate a segregated way of life for which the well-shod but nonetheless misguided Russell is willing to filibuster.

What Russell's historical elaboration of the tradition and necessity of filibustering doesn't explain, however, is the origin of the word itself. In March of 1856, in an article on William Walker (a Southerner who filibustered Nicaragua and overturned a constitution that had outlawed slavery), *Blackwood's Magazine*, a British publication, defines "filibuster" in the following way:

> a French and Spanish corruption of the English word freebooter, an appellation which, in former days, from its being frequently assumed by a certain class of men, who disliked the harsher name of pirate, became familiar to the inhabitants of the West Indies Islands and Central America: but as filibusterism is now used, it expresses the action of the American people, or a portion of the people, in the acquisition of territory which does not belong to them, unrestrained by the responsibilities of the American Government.[9]

While the *Blackwood's* article is critical of American redefinitions of words and treaties, an excerpt from the American *Harper's Weekly* (Jan. 10, 1857) is just as clearly irritated by the imputation of piracy.[10] Acknowledging that "filibuster came to signify robber on the high seas," the editor for *Harper's* goes on to "protest" "this notorious corruption of the mother tongue." Calling on the August "shade of Noah Webster," he seeks to "restore to the polyglot freebooter-flibustier-filibuster—its only true and original meaning—namely a man who, fairly and honestly, in the light of day, desires to roam the world by sea and land, breaking no quiet man's head, paying for what he wants, but setting his wits and strength to the work of spreading commerce, and industry, and civilization, and freedom throughout the habitable globe.[11] What *Blackwood's* slyly defined as piracy and naked aggression, *Harper's* idealizes as assertive, but nonetheless fair-minded, liberal manhood.

What liberal manhood might mean for an upper-class male Southerner in the antebellum United States is made clear by William Walker in chapter eight of his *The War in Nicaragua*, written in 1860 while he awaited execution by firing squad:

> Africa is permitted to lie idle until America is discovered, in order that she may conduce to the formation of a new society in the New World. A strong, haughty race, bred to liberty in its northern island home, is sent forth with the mission to place America under the rule of free laws; but whence are these men, imbued with love of liberty and equality, to derive the counterpoise which shall prevent their liberty from degenerating into license, and their equality into anarchy or despotism? How are they, when transplanted from the rugged climate where freedom thrives to retain their precious birthright in the soft, tropical air which woos to luxury and repose? Is it not for this that the African was reserved? And is it not thus that one race secures for itself liberty with order, while it bestows on the other comfort and Christianity.[12]

More than a hundred years later, Russell likewise imagines himself to be just such a purveyor of "liberty with order," a staunch last guard against the civil extravagance of the Northern horde. But, in a recent study of the role that Russell played in the legislative battle over civil rights, Robert Mann moves Russell rhetorically closer to the definition proposed by *Blackwood's*. "Nothing had made Russell's southern troops more imposing on the Senate floor than their ability to pirate a debate, preventing any civil rights measure from coming to a vote.[13] What curious repressions this vexed issue of civil rights returns! For in 1820, some twenty years before the first Senate filibuster, Congress had defined the slave trade itself as "piracy."[14] In 1964, having already "pirated" the civil rights debate, Russell would further supplement his filibuster, and extend the social consequences of slavery, with his proposal to "establish a commission to be known as the voluntary relocation commission" (CR, 5338).

Forwarding proposals that he had made previously in 1949 and 1958, Russell wanted the Federal Government to "provide ... financial and technical assistance to effectuate a more equal distribution of the races" (CR, 5340).[15] In "areas predominantly or almost solidly white," white persons would likewise be "eligible" for assistance to "relocate" to the South. The "overall objective," according to Russell, was to "bring about" a distribution of African Americans more "in line" with the overall national percentage of about 10.5 percent (CR, 5340). If civil equality for African Americans were to be the law of the land, Russell insisted that the ensuing social problems (as he saw them) be shared by those from Northern and Western states in which the population of African Americans was less than 10 percent. "I favor," he said, "inflicting on New York City, the city of Chicago, and other cities the same condition proposed to be inflicted by this bill on the people of the community of Winder, Georgia, where I live" (CR, 5342).[16]

In partnership with Senator John Stennis of Mississippi, Russell offered his amendment (which would have been Title XII) as a solution to the "long series of mass demonstrations, marches, boycotts, picketing, sit-ins, sit-downs, lie-ins, lie-downs, and other acts of civil disobedience designed to protest existing conditions" (CR, 5338). From Russell's perspective, as his rhetoric suggests, such "protest" had dubious foundation in existing social conditions: "These convulsions are generally considered as being aimed at procuring certain rights, it is *claimed,* are being denied to some of our Negro citizens" (5338, emphasis added). Implicitly blaming those same "Negro citizens," Russell insists that "the demonstrations reach their greatest magnitude and violence, generally speaking, in areas in which the percentage of the Negro population is greatest" (5339). "[T]he vast majority of people," Russell noted, "have held firmly to the conviction that a social order based upon separation of the races is best and wisest for the welfare and progress of both races" (5344). He then pointed to a map in the back of the chamber on which "the pattern of the racial composition" of the United States was mapped out in terms of "percentages of Negro population." Russell went on to insist that "it is neither fair nor right, when dealing equally with the civil rights of all the American people, for the sections of the country having the smallest percentages of Negroes to undertake to dictate the social relationships for the sections of the country having the preponderant concentration of Negroes" (5347).[17] Russell's amendment would thus offer a countersolution that would be acceptable to whites from states such as Georgia and Mississippi, where the percentage of African American population was indeed greatest.[18]

Two days later, on March 18, Senator Jacob Javits of New York voiced what he termed the "unspoken premise" behind Russell's relocation amendment. "Whites in some areas in the South," he said, "deny the Negro the right to vote because Negroes are in the majority in those areas and the white minority fears that it will lose political control if the majority votes" (CR, 5578). Looked at from that angle, even though Russell invoked the filibuster as a function of free speech, the tacit effect of its contents (as Javits astutely exposed) was precisely designed to silence black political power. Indeed, the relocation amendment would, in Javits' view, "make sure that Negroes are permanently—and throughout the Nation—a minority" (5578). Masquerading as an attempt to maintain the Constitutional provisions for "equality of representation," Russell's "pirating" of the civil rights debate by way of filibuster had now, in effect, been unmasked as outright exportation of blacks, an exportation designed to bolster, if not extend, the waning power of the white population and thus maintain the political and social status quo.

Such exportation had earlier been imagined by William Walker as an integral component of the calculations of providential history. As did most other Southerners of the antebellum period, Walker imagined Africa and the African as an embodied "reserve" upon which the (white) "intellect of society" could draw its economic sustenance as it "push[ed] boldly forward in the pursuit of new forms of civilization" (259). Indeed, between 1517 and 1865, "some 15 million slaves" had been relocated from Africa to America for that express purpose.[19] Operating within the context of the new form of citizenship ushered in by the Fourteenth Amendment, however, and recently re-established in the landmark *Brown v. Board of Education* decision, Russell imagined "order" to be a function not of something new, but rather of maintaining precisely the old antebellum civilization in which the William Walkers of the world reigned supreme. But since the Fourteenth Amendment extended to black folk the abstract, disembodied quality of citizenship, and since the legal mandate in *Brown* and the Civil Rights Bill before the Senate compelled de-segregation, then the most politic thing to do would be to transport black folk once again in order to enhance white political and economic power.[20] Thus Russell's amendment, while not technically slavery, certainly relied for its rhetorical effects on what slavery left behind in its wake—a deep reserve of revulsion from whence too many Americans tendered their images of race.

What Russell's amendment and its correlative revulsion disavows, however, is the use of black bodies in the original affirmative action imbedded in Article I of the Constitution. This affirmative action is canonically known as the three-fifths clause, a clause designed to ensure something approaching equal representation between the North and the South in the House of Representatives.[21] Obviously, the appropriation of black bodies for purposes of

white masculine representation can, and should, be read as one more extension of the master-slave relationship, in this case a political manifestation of
the "reserve" status to which Walker designates the black body. This point
is not lost on James Madison who, in Federalist 54, insists that slaves "par-
take of both" the "qualities" of "persons" and of "property." In light of this,
the notion, popular among some conservative American commentators, that
slaves were not degraded or dehumanized in the imaginations of many of the
Founding Fathers, must confront Madison's statement that the "compromising expedient" within the Constitution "regards the *slave* as divested of two
fifths of the *man*."[22]

In his successful plea on behalf of the fugitives on board the *Amistad*,
John Quincy Adams exposes a rather startling connection between Madison's
stress on "man" and "slave" in conjunction with the verb "divest." According to Adams, "the words slave and slavery are studiously excluded from the
Constitution. Circumlocutions are the fig-leaves under which these parts of
the body politic are decently concealed.[23] Before proceeding, we should note
that *divest* and *invest*, representing the convenient split between person and
property, respectively, are both derived from the Latin *vestis*, or "garment."[24]
In the scandalous relation of "these parts of the body politic" and the "fig-
leaves" of "circumlocution," Adams exposes the three-fifths clause, to which
he is surely referring, as a fall from grace. He also invests the word "slave"
with a phallic power that the political whole of "circumlocution" ought not,
in all decency, to represent or divest. In Adams' configuration, the "man"
ought to be divested of the "slave." Thus the anxious masculine authority that
circumlocution betrays and the erotic component "concealed" (but implied
nonetheless) in the adverb "decently," are two strands of the complicated
message which Russell's filibuster twists into one more form of divestiture
nearly 125 years later.

Linked to the Constitution by their respective speakers, *circumlocution*
and *filibuster* both embody forms of verbal evasion. For Adams, circumlocution finds us lacking in our commitment to the promise of America; for Russell, the filibuster against civil rights is figured as a problem of "equal
representation." But the burden of representation, as Russell views it, fundamentally rests on the House, and the House is degraded in two significant
ways. There, members are not allowed to filibuster, and the number of congressmen (and hence the legislative power of each state) is, as per the provisions in Article I of the Constitution, dependent on population. Since Russell
knows full well that each state was guaranteed equal representation in the Senate without the affirmative action of such egregious demographic manipula-
tions as the three-fifths clause, it stands to reason that he imagines the Senate
as a "purer" site of republican value, as the following denigration of the House
indicates: "Under gag rule, Senators would serve little other purpose than to

act, in effect, as additional Members of their State's delegation to the House of Representatives. For once the Senate yields the right of its Members to express themselves fully, it undoubtedly would be only a matter of time before Senators would find themselves begging for the privilege of speaking for 5 minutes—as can and does happen under the rules of the House" (5324).

Desiring to preserve the privilege of the pure, disembodied voice of the filibuster, Russell finds the House to be unruly in its distribution between voice and body.[25] In his value system, the opposition between "full expression" and "begging" to speak for a paltry five minutes enacts a drama of presence and degradation that parallels American racialized attitudes toward labor. To be more embodied, in the American scheme of labor value, means you have less power, and to have less power (or less voice) means you are "blacker."[26] Furthermore, within the logic of racial relocation, to be demographically blacker means more civil unrest, more of those domestic "convulsions" to which Russell earlier referred. Thus, the thought of senators becoming "additional Members of their State's delegation to the House of Representatives" is one more domestic convulsion, the root of which is Russell's revulsion for the idea of sharing social space and political power with blacks.

It should really come as no surprise, then, that the House was so degraded in Russell's hierarchy of value. After all, propped up as it had always been by substantially more than a single drop of black blood, the House, in terms of the Southern imaginary, was always already *black*. God forbid that the Senate should follow suit—for that august body, according to Russell, is "the last bastion within our Federal system wherein the rights of the States and the rights of the minorities are protected. Without freedom of debate in the Senate, the United States eventually will go the way of the unlimited democracies; we will reach the stage where a misguided majority can destroy the liberties and rights of individual citizens in the name of some currently popular cause" (CR, 5324). Here, domestic concerns converge with foreign policy (those "unlimited democracies") as the Senate stands guard against the new-old threat to the Republic: the equitable distribution of civil rights to all Americans. Imagining themselves as "minorities" in need of "protect[ion]," fiercely unreconstructed Southerners, such as Russell and Stennis, must rely on the ironic prestige of "equality of representation" to justify a filibuster designed to purify them of the "popular" affliction—the acute hipness—of equality of representation as outlined in the provisions of the Fourteenth Amendment:

> All persons born or naturalized in the United States, and subject to the jurisdiction thereof, are citizens of the United States and of the State wherein they reside. No State shall make or enforce any law which shall abridge the privileges and immunities of citizens of the United States; nor

shall any State deprive any person of life, liberty, or property, without due
process of law; nor deny to any person within its jurisdiction the equal
protection of the laws.

Russell's racial relocation amendment, when all was said and done, was a
defense, not just of a permanent white majority, but of a democracy imagined to be, as W.E.B. Du Bois had lamented some sixty years before, "*For
White People Only.*"[27]

The conflation of voice with both political and phallic power suggests
we ought to consider anxieties more latent than Russell's stated concern about
America becoming an "unlimited democracy." Such considerations would
also warrant a re-vision of the Best Western ad with which we began, a revi-
sion that would bring the civil liberty implied in Title II in close proximity
to the sanctions that motivate racial relocation. We can place them both
under the rather startling rubric of lynching and castration by taking a closer
look at what we imagine happens to us and to America when we sight-see.

Viewed from the doubly conscious angle of symbolic reclamation and
historical intervention, the two African American men need to have their
presence rationalized because, according to Walter Benn Michaels, "[m]aking
itself available for aesthetic contemplation turns out to be America's way of
making more Americans."[28] The rhetoric of sight-seeing, as Michaels implies,
and the rhetoric of wilderness, as we shall come to understand, is very often
a generative performance. And lest we imagine that America will make herself available to one and all, we should recall the words of Toni Morrison,
who reminds us that to be "American" is to be "white," a whiteness that is,
in turn, mediated through a "choked representation of Africanist presence,"
for "buried deep within the word 'American' is its associations with race."[29]
By utilizing the blind man as a doubled sign of race neutralization—of color-
blindness *and* emasculation—the Best Western script, like Russell's racial
relocation amendment, becomes a paradigmatic reflection of Morrison's
"choked representation" from whence whiteness emerges. If, in the United
States, miscegenation has the symbolic power of incest, as Werner Sollors has
suggested, and aesthetic contemplation produces more Americans, then the
ad can be read as a primal scene of white sexual privilege, whereby the phallic power of vision is proscribed, thereby depriving the ostensive subject of
the once in a lifetime experience.[30] The ad thus neatly expresses the ambivalence with which early twenty-first century corporate America, and the markets to which it sells, cuts people of color and people with disabilities just
enough slack to be self-righteous about the corporations' concern for civil
rights while pulling just hard enough to constrict their participation.

Scopic limitation in the Best Western ad takes the form, in Russell's rhetoric, of a desire to negate the potential effect of full citizenship for black folk

through the amplification of voice. Russell cannot abide the thought of sharing his "America" with those citizens who had once been the abject property of the Lost Cause. That he rhetoricizes the problem as a problem of phallic proportion suggests the return of history as a reserve in which disavowal and nostalgia prop up a past that can only be repeated by displacing the disruptive presence of black power into a fantasy of absence. Given the political context, it is a fantasy of black dismemberment from what is conceived to be a white body politic.

The historical fact of lynching and castration as expressions of white power in the aftermath of Reconstruction provides a way of reading ourselves out of Russell's fantasy of dismemberment. In an important "anatomy" of lynching, Robin Weigman discusses the interrelationship between personhood and embodiment in connection with citizenship, especially the citizenship as defined by the Fourteenth Amendment.[31] Within that racialized nexus, the "threat of ritualized death provide[s]" the "means," according to Weigman, for consolidation of "white supremacy" within a larger social space perceived by many whites as flawed by the ratification of the 13th, 14th, and 15th amendments. Lynching thus reinscribes onto black bodies the corporeality that the Fourteenth Amendment ostensibly removes. "In the disciplinary fusion of castration with lynching," moreover, "the mob severs the black male from the masculine, interrupting the privilege of the phallus, and thereby reclaiming, through the perversity of dismemberment, his (masculine) potential for citizenship" (445–6). While Weigman's is an important and instructive consideration, part of my point is also to show that the rhetoric of representational and phallic power, from Madison to Adams and then to Russell, is very much vested in bodies that have to be counted every ten years, and some of these bodies, as we have seen in the three-fifths clause, were always already dismembered. Looked at from that perspective, it should come as no surprise that the anxiety around which Russell's defense of the Lost Cause is to rally, the anxiety that racial relocation cannot "decently conceal," is the very thought that the United States Senate (and, by synecdochic reduction, Senator Richard Russell), that "last bastion" of white masculine supremacy and republican virtue, just might become an "ineffective appendage."

On March 26, 1964, Dr. Martin Luther King, Jr., in Washington to "attend a climactic session of the Senate debate," imbued the proceedings with more than a touch of cosmic irony as he "looked down from the visitor's gallery on Senator's Russell's racial relocation map.[32]

That "Continuous Touch"

The Civil Rights Act was passed on July 2, 1964, with only eleven titles. On August 20 of that same year, Congress passed the Wilderness Act, an act

designed to preserve some portions of the American landscape "in their natural condition" for the express purpose of "secur[ing] for the American people of present and future generations the benefits of an enduring resource of
wilderness" (*Laws*, 1013). While the wording of the act provides for "present"
and "future generations," the rhetoric of those who had been instrumental
in getting the bill before Congress was clearly grounded in a nostalgia for an
"exceptional" American past—a past that had terminated Indians, and used,
abused, and then excluded African Americans.[33] On December 6, 1963, Phillip
S. Hughes, assistant director for legislative reference, invoked the rhetoric of
American exceptionalism in response to a letter received (November 22, 1963)
from Congressman Wayne Aspinall. Hughes reminded the powerful chairman of the Committee on Internal and Insular Affairs that President John F.
Kennedy (recently assassinated and deeply mourned) had "belie[ved] that a
nation such as ours, which had conquered vast wilderness areas on its way to
preeminence in the world, had a peculiar and unique responsibility to preserve portions of our country in a state approaching that in which our forefathers found it."[34] Stewart M. Udall, Kennedy's Secretary of the Interior,
had likewise underscored the administration's commitment to "New Frontier" rhetoric in a 1962 article for *The Living Wilderness* when he stated that
"the public has demanded assurance that the wilderness remnant will be protected for the recreation and re-creation of the American people."[35] Once
again, we encounter the idea of sight-seeing as generative. In this section, however, I shall be concerned to analyze the fantasy of generating American identity out of wilderness experience and how that experience is imagined to relate
to civil rights, especially to Title II, which Best Western ostensibly affirms.

Both Assistant Director Hughes and Secretary Udall were affirmatively
responding to the dominant mytheme propounded by Kennedy in his nomina-
tion acceptance speech delivered in Los Angeles before the Democratic National
Convention on July 15, 1960. Seizing on the geographic and temporal apposi-
tion between the extreme westerliness and hyper-modernity of Los Angeles,
Kennedy made the declaration that was to become a clarion call for a generation of Americans to renew their commitment to the exceptional promise of the
American enterprise: "we stand today on the edge of a New Frontier."[36] The
speech was a resoundingly successful rhetorical performance, for in making the
"frontier" *new* he had used the frontier in precisely the way that Frederick Jackson Turner had imagined Americans were using the frontier right up to 1890,
when the Superintendent of the Census declared that it "can not ... any longer
have a place in the census reports."[37] "American social development," Turner
insisted, "has been continually beginning over again on the frontier. This peren-
nial rebirth, this fluidity of American life, this expansion westward with its new
opportunities, its continuous touch with the simplicity of primitive society, fur-
nish the forces dominating American character" (SF, 28).

Kennedy's addition of the quintessentially American modifier "new," even as it acknowledges the limits and "perils" of geographic expansion, seeks to open up a rhetorical space of social rebirth, of "unknown opportunities" (JFK, 100). The idea of renewing the world by powers imagined to be invested in the word, however, was not in itself a new idea. One might point out that the trope of the "New World" as the scene of providential promise is precisely a manifestation of that idea at the level of ideology, vestiges of which can be traced in the rhetoric of Adams, Walker, Russell, and Kennedy. In its quest for formal and semantic newness, American modernism, for instance, is a more recent manifestation at the level of poetic language. Indeed, Tim Dean usefully relates these two when he states that "the modernist dictum 'Make it new' constitutes not only a methodological imperative for poetic technique but also an ideological imperative upon which American culture is founded."[38] Modified by its own "imperative," we can read the *New* Frontier as a meta-frontier where Turner's "history" is revised by Kennedy as performativity, *where saying can make it so.*[39] Thus the Kennedy administration's "renewal" rhetorically re-opened the closure that Turner had so famously bemoaned in 1893, while reminding its constituents of the enduring power of the frontier as myth.

Richard Slotkin, arguably our greatest critic of the mythic status of the frontier, defines myth as "the primary language of historical memory."[40] As the quintessential American story whereby myth is translated into "history," and vice-versa, the frontier thesis is "primary language" writ large. Turner begins that American story by imagining the frontier as being in "continuous touch with the simplicity of primitive society." Such a "touch," which signals a "return to primitive conditions," can be read as the subject-predicate relation in the syntax of the primary language of frontier myth. But if touching denotes the verb, who, or what, is the subject? By way of answer, Turner provides the following: "The true point of view in the history of this nation is not the Atlantic coast, it is the great West" (SF, 28). And then, a few pages later Turner writes, "[t]he United States lies like a huge page in the history of society. Line by line as we read this continental page from west to east we find the record of social evolution" (34). Given "point of view" and "line," we can deduce the subject of Turner's "page" by parsing the definition of frontier offered in the census reports: "it is treated as the margin of that settlement that has a density of two or more to the square mile" (28). Since this definition is immediately preceded by the declaration that the frontier "lies at the hither edge of free land" and that the "true" point of view is always west of our settlements, then it stands to reason that the subject of Turner's frontier is located on "free land" beyond the "settled" density of two or more per square mile (28–9). Since point of view pre-supposes *some* density, the subject to whom the "true point of view" belongs must be first person singular.

For Turner, "the most significant thing about the frontier is, that it lies at the hither edge of free land" (SF, 28). While we should always keep an eye on the semantics of the "huge page" of American history in order to focus on the manner in which that "free land" is acquired, the syntax of Turner's history ought not to be ignored. A closer look at syntax will expose Turner's most "significant thing" as a primary manifestation of the trope of generation implied in my earlier citation of Michaels, who claimed that "making itself available for aesthetic contemplation turns out to be America's way of making more Americans." This generative trope, we recall, is further elaborated by Udall when he claims the wilderness as a site in which to "re-create" Americans. How is this re-creation possible?

As we have seen, the primary language of the frontier myth reveals a syntactic relation of a first person in "continuous touch" with predicating "primitive conditions." And implied in that continuous touch is a generative copula—"the most significant thing about the frontier *is*." Both Sigmund Freud and Jacques Lacan, arguably the twentieth century's two most important practitioners of psychoanalysis, have made useful connections, for purposes of my argument, between copula, logic, and erotic energy. Freud himself imagines the ego, beset by the demands of "service" from "three masters" (the "external world," the "libido of the id," and "the severity of the super-ego"), as "a frontier creature" that "tries to mediate between the world and the id, to make the id pliable to the world and, by means of its muscular activity, to make the world fall in with the wishes of the id." The Freudian world "falls in" as a function of two instinctual drives, *eros* and *thanatos,* creative and destructive energies, respectively. Accordingly, "the main purpose of Eros" is "that of uniting and binding." Much of this binding energy is displaced or "sublimated" into other activities, of which Freud includes "thought processes in general."[41] Lacan, making a similar link in a different way, imagines the phallus as a metonym for the "effects of the signified"—that "mark in which the role of the logos is joined with the advent of desire." In the symbolic order of language, the phallus, he says, is "equivalent to the (logical) copula."[42] Turner's "history," then, read as desire—personal, national, and textual— reflects the logos of the America it lacks ("*in the beginning, all the world was America," said John Locke*[43]; *now it's closed*); and within this problematic "space" of closure, the desiring "I" of history enacts a fantasy of freedom enabled by the very potency, as Manfred Frank suggests, of its identifying copula.[44]

Since potency can be read as both creative and destructive (and within the context of American history it is imagined to be both), the muscular mediations of the Freudian "frontier ego" articulate, in America, a narrative schema that Richard Slotkin identifies as separation, regression, and regeneration through violence.[45] But the violence against Native Americans that is constitutive of American identity in Slotkin's analysis, is finessed by Turner as a "*meeting point* between savagery and civilization," a point that extends out to become the "line of most effective Americanization" (SF, 37). Recognizing and resisting Turner's disavowal of violence, Tim Dean likewise points out that the frontier thus "becomes ... the space of 'versus' in the binary logic which structures the account," a "reified and hypostasized punctum" which "produces 'America' as the effect of its movement."[46] But if "America" is a metonym for, among other things, a conglomeration of selves whose effects are cast as history, then what kind of political selves does a spatial punctum produce?

Tracing the trajectory of what he calls the disengaged or objectified subject from Descartes to Locke, Charles Taylor suggests that what is "reified and hypostasized" in American space is precisely a "punctual self."[47] According to Taylor, it is Locke who "develops ... to its full form" this "punctual self" (160). One of the consequences of the capacity to objectify one's own self is that it "generates and also reflects an ideal of independence and self-responsibility, a notion of reason as free from established custom and locally dominant authority" (167). For Taylor, this "punctual agent seems to be nothing else but a 'self,' an 'I'" (175). "Disengagement," he goes on to say, "requires a first-person stance" (176), and it is this disengaged stance that "hold[s]" the "package" of "freedom," "independence," and "procedural reason" together (174). In the political space defined by Turner, this "I," trailing clouds of Lockean liberalism's most cherished values, is projected out and made concrete, or "proper," in the legal frame of the first-person bounded by his square mile. Looked at in this way, we could say that the interrelationship between free land and the muscular mediation of the European settler generates a sovereign "I" that is imagined to be omnipotent over the space of 640 acres, per Locke's definition of property.[48] Hence the squared space, the census report's "unsettled" mile, is emblematic not just of the potential transformation of the state of nature into civil government, but more specifically of the potential for disengaged, punctual selves consenting to become an *unum*. This political potential was not lost on Thomas Jefferson, who platted unsettled space, and plotted the shape of "America," in the form of a democratizing grid.[49] But in order to have the grid become a narrative frame for an allegory of selfhood and consent, the epistemology of the punctual self, the rational capacity to imagine better selves, must answer to a psychology that manifested its "self" in a history of wilderness violence and that maintains its "self" through the soft violence of political procedures of denial.

Articulating the "page" of history in this way helps explain why the semantic of redemption that resides in Kennedy's "unknown opportunities and perils" and "unfulfilled hopes and threats" (JFK, 100) is reliant on an oppositional syntax where threats conjoin with opportunities in order to be transformed into an assumption of new, that is to say improved, civilization. Such assumptions are prefigured by Turner as "interpenetrat[ion]" of "wilderness" by "lines of civilization growing ever more numerous" (SF, 37). Rather more violent, now, than his aforementioned "touch," the result of such interpenetration is a "democracy born of free land" (52). In Turner's democracy, however, the historically violent process of its own begetting is minimized. And this disavowal is not relegated to Native Americans only. Indeed, the primal language of the frontier myth has no place for women. As demographic purveyors of the two or more persons per square mile implied by "settlement," women are structurally an afterthought in the logic of frontier.[50] Such exclusion implies that they cannot really embody the self that is born of it. But this is not to say that the *feminine* is excluded. We need look no further than the title of Henry Nash Smith's *Virgin Land* to understand the place of the feminine as the "untrammeled" ground of possibility—to borrow the language of the Wilderness Act—in the generation of America.[51] Thus, as the space where the historical fact of Indian genocide converges with the trope of virginity, "free land" is both the site of murderous masculine rage and of promiscuous feminine receptivity, a receptivity that, for all its promiscuity, is nonetheless the exclusive domain of the "interpenetrating" white masculine subject.

The historical presence and agency of real women is not the only exclusion that constitutes the mythic frontier. "[W]hen American history comes to be rightly viewed," Turner says, "it will be seen that the slavery question is an incident" (SF, 46). It can only be incidental if we disregard the very premise of Jeffersonian settlement. As was noted earlier, Jefferson imagined "America" as a function of individual squares being settled by yeoman farmers whom he calls "the chosen ... of the world."[52] The "chosen" of Jefferson's world, however, viewed their prospects through the prism of the disproportionate amount of wealth and power that the planter class enjoyed, a cultural power-base that was anchored in the liquidity of slaves.[53] For as Philip Fisher points out, the "hard fact within the Jeffersonian setting was slavery,"[54] and the hard fact of the slave's life, as Frederick Douglass's *Narrative* and Harriet Jacobs's *Incidents in the Life of a Slave Girl* attest, is systematic, often sexualized, terror. Written in the narrative lives and on the historical bodies of slave men and women, our national myths are constructed of such incidentals. Indeed, by 1893, when Turner was delivering his thesis to the American Historical Association at the Chicago World's Columbian Exposition,[55] the "line of most effective Americanization" had gradually, perhaps even imperceptibly, become a reified color-line, a line that would, as Du Bois's famous declaration in *The Souls of Black Folk* made clear, become the "problem of the twentieth century."[56] The binary opposition of *that* problematic line would no longer be "savage vs. civilized" but "black vs. white."

However repressed it might be in Turner's thesis, the issue of slavery and race returns to haunt Kennedy's New Frontier. There, the fundamental assumption of civilization over savagery, figured now as the historical "turning point" of democracy vs. communism, is posed as a probative challenge that, like Russell's defense of the filibuster against Civil Rights, invokes the ghosts of the Civil War:

> For the harsh facts of the matter are that we stand on this frontier at a turning point in history. We must prove all over again whether this nation—or any nation so conceived—can long endure; whether our society—with its freedom of choice, its breadth of opportunity, its range of alternatives—can compete with the single-minded advance of the Communist system [JFK, 101].

The "harsh facts of the matter" in Kennedy's speech seem to point to the proving ground of the "single-minded advance of the Communist system" with which he ends the paragraph. But we ought not lose sight of the fact that for Kennedy's audience, the threat from alien outsiders is mediated by the clearly recognizable citation of what is arguably the most famous speech in American history.[57] Here is Kennedy's citation:

> whether this nation—or any nation so conceived—can long endure.

And here is how Lincoln phrased it in the first two sentences of his Gettysburg Address:

> Four score and seven years ago our fathers brought forth on this continent, a new nation, conceived in Liberty, and dedicated to the proposition that all men are created equal.
>   Now we are engaged in a great civil war, testing *whether that nation, or any nation so conceived* and so dedicated, *can long endure.*[58]

The strategic thrust of Kennedy's "New Frontier" citation is to compel his audience to make a series of comparative inferences: not Lincoln's "civil war," but a battle nonetheless for civil rights; not a revolutionary new beginning, but a Cold War that America cannot afford to lose. Given these inferences, the New Frontier, in its newness (and in its belatedness, too), is empty of value unless the singular proposition of Lincoln's "new nation" can prevail. Hence we cannot get to the meeting point between democracy and communism in Kennedy's syntax, that space where we must "prove" ourselves, without implicitly dedicating ourselves to the defining "proposition" of that democracy, "that all men are created equal." It would be a mistake, however, to understand this consolidation of American democracy as void of aggression, for, as Slotkin reminds us, Kennedy's ideological finesse of the frontier myth was used to "legitimatize" "counterinsurgency 'missions' in the Caribbean and Southeast Asia."[59]

By way of gaining rhetorical momentum for such consolidation, Kennedy concludes with a turn to the biblical Book of Isaiah (ch. 40, v. 31), the better to recall to his audience a sense of the providential nature of America. "They that wait upon the Lord shall renew their strength," he says, "they shall mount up with wings as eagles; they shall run, and not be weary" (JFK, 102). The Democratic nominee then merges national destiny with personal quest by underscoring his own westward migration to what he hopes will be his country's highest elective office: "it has been a long road from that first snowy day in New Hampshire to this crowded convention city" (102). Translating the too distant "they" of Isaiah into the more intimate first-person plurality of "we" the people, Kennedy then assures his fellow Democrats that "[a]s we face the coming challenge, we, too, shall wait upon the Lord, and ask that He renew our strength. Then shall we be equal to the test. Then we shall not be weary. And then we shall prevail" (102). These lines trace a trajectory from complex supplication ("we, too, shall wait upon the Lord, and ask that He renew our strength"), to hopeful consequence wavering anxiously between proposition and imbedded question ("then shall we be equal to the test"), and then ultimately to simple declaration ("And then we shall prevail"). The rhythmic repetition of the adverbial "then," which prefaces each of the last three sentences, marks the site—the syntactic frontier—upon which time, space and word converge. The unsettling affect of those earlier harsh reminders of civil unrest and global threat is thus rhetorically balanced by Kennedy's affirmation of the American mission. Its citational gesture toward civil rights notwithstanding, what ultimately prevails, then, in Kennedy's acceptance speech, is the democracy born of free land that Turner had extolled, with providential history as its messenger. In so doing, "the frontier" becomes a renewable rhetorical resource for fueling America's resolve against the continuous touch ("the single-minded advance") of a primitive other, those "enemies" that "threaten," says Kennedy, "from without and within."

To better regulate that resource, the Kennedy-Johnson administration, as Hughes reminds Aspinall, sought to ground its own prevailing myth by preserving portions of exemplary American wilderness. We need look no further than the opening paragraph of the Wilderness Act to understand what is preserved when "wild" spaces—be they cognitive or geographic—are marked for preservation:

> In order to ensure that an increasing population, accompanied by expanding settlement and growing mechanization, does not occupy and modify all areas within the United States and its possessions, leaving no lands designated for preservation and protection in their natural condition, it is hereby declared to be the policy of Congress to secure for the American people of present and future generations the benefits of an enduring resource of wilderness. For this purpose there is hereby established a

> National Wilderness Preservation System to be composed of federally
> owned areas designated by Congress as "wilderness areas," and these shall
> be administered for the use and enjoyment of the American people in such
> manner as will leave them unimpaired for future use and enjoyment as
> wilderness, and so to provide for the protection of these areas, the pres-
> ervation of their wilderness character, and for the gathering and dissemi-
> nation of information regarding their use and enjoyment as wilderness;
> and no Federal lands shall be designated as "wilderness areas" except as
> provided for in this act or by a subsequent Act [*Laws*, 1013].

In protecting the "wilderness" from "increasing population," "expanding settlement," and "growing mechanization" (all the things that Turner had
bemoaned some seventy years before), Congress fences in and underscores its
own performative agency by designating all other desiring agents as, in effect,
trespassers.

After a short paragraph that reassures legislators and relevant agencies
that jurisdictions "shall continue" as before the wilderness "inclusions," and
that no additional "appropriations" (read: tax dollars) for the administering
of the new system "shall be available,"[60] the act then goes on to define wilderness in the following manner:

> A wilderness, in contrast with those areas where man and his own works
> dominate the landscape, is hereby recognized as an area where the earth
> and its community of life are untrammeled by man, where man himself
> is a visitor who does not remain. An area of wilderness is further defined
> to mean in this Act an area of undeveloped Federal land retaining its
> primeval character and influence, without permanent improvements or
> human habitation, which is protected and managed so as to preserve its
> natural conditions and which (1) generally appears to have been affected
> primarily by the forces of nature, with the imprint of man's work sub-
> stantially unnoticeable; (2) has outstanding opportunities for solitude or
> a primitive and unconfined type of recreation; (3) has at least five thou-
> sand acres of land or is of sufficient size as to make practicable its preser-
> vation and use in an unimpaired condition; and (4) may also contain
> ecological, geological, or other features of scientific, educational, scenic,
> or historical value [*Laws*, 1014].

Out of the "wilderness" of semi-colons that link the four defining qualities
of its performative utterance, Congress "hereby" solidifies a national narrative that clearly recapitulates Slotkin's structure of separation, regression, and
regeneration (I have linked the phrases that follow with their corresponding
numbered clause in the Wilderness Act): "untrammeled" space (1) is separated off (3), and then penetrated by white males in a "primitive and
unconfined type of recreation" or regression (2), that then demarcates the limits of what is "sufficient" and "practicable" (3), for the further discovery, elaboration, or regeneration (2, 4) of the liberal project in the New World.

Wilderness, as articulated by Congressional fiat, is New World fantasy writ large. Freud, in fact, described the "establishment of 'reservations' and 'nature-parks' *in places where the inroads of agriculture, traffic, or industry threaten to change the original face of the earth rapidly into something unrecognizable,*" as something akin to "the mental realm of phantasy." Both fantasy and reservation, he says, are designed "to maintain the old condition of things which has been sacrificed to necessity elsewhere else; there everything may grow and spread as it pleases, including what is useless and even harmful."[61] In its desire to counteract the consequences of "expanding settlement" and "growing mechanization," Congress engages in a fantasy whereby a primitive and recreative *past* is troped as a primitive and recreative *space.* Engaging that space is then imagined to be keeping that past alive. Unfortunately, the power of the myth is so strong that we often disavow what might be "useless" or "even harmful" about that past, just as we disavow some of the historical implications imbedded in the phrase "to ensure that an increasing population ... does not occupy and modify all areas within the United States." It has been one of the points of this paper to show that the desire to keep some American space unpopulated, and the desire to keep some populations out of American space, are inextricably related. Consider, for instance, that for geographer Denis Cosgrove, concepts such as national parks and wilderness reserves seek to preserve, "in Turnerian terms" the kind of environment in which "earlier—and racially purer—immigrants were believed to have forged American national identity."[62] Indeed, as we have seen, Turner's own terms, even though cloaked in the authoritative guise of thesis, can nonetheless be troped as a sort of nostalgic reserve that seeks to maintain the fantastic contours of the very past it articulates as history.

Given the convergence between Freud's symbolic and Cosgrove's historical renderings of our national fantasy of *identity out of wilderness,* where do we situate the Kennedy administration's desire to preserve wilderness "in a state approaching that in which our forefathers found it?" When Stewart Udall, in his official capacity as the secretary of the interior, urges the "protect[ion]" of "the wilderness remnant" for the "recreation and re-creation of the American people," how is he defining "American?" Answers to such questions ought to take into account the pleasure that Americans take *in* the wilderness (American recreation) and the pleasure of *taking or appropriating the wilderness* (re-creating Americans). For these pleasures, as we have seen, are a function of the logic of whiteness whereby American identity construction transforms *versus*—as in savage *vs.* civilized; black *vs.* white; woman *vs.* man— into copula; and copula, as we have seen, engenders the pathos of potency at the heart of the civilized white man.[63] In order to show how debilitating such potency can be in a democratic context, I want now to turn to the debate on civil rights, where the Kennedy administration's Turnerian reading of wilderness as a permanent resource for the re-creation of Americans con-verges with Senator Russell's threat to inflict *blackness* within the domain of those very spaces imagined to be *pure, pristine,* and hence worth preserving.

The Contours of Our Fantasy

One of the more ironic moments to emerge out of the exchanges in which Russell engages his Senate colleagues is his use of Native Americans as exemplary models of racial decorum. The genesis of this exemplum is a bit of a surprise. At one point in the debate, Russell cites "a brilliant article by a Negro authoress in Florida" who "expressed her resentment at [the *Brown*] decision, and against the feeling that the Negro children were not capable of learning in school unless they were sitting by the side of white children" (CR, 5351). The author to whom he refers is none other than Zora Neale Hurston, who, in a letter to the editor of the Orlando *Sentinel* (August 11, 1955) did, indeed, "regard the ruling of the U.S. Supreme Court as insulting rather than honoring [her] race."[64] Linking the Court's unanimous decision to "the evils of Communist penetration," Hurston refuses to participate in the fetishizing of whiteness that she calls the "doctrine of the white mare," wherein "mules will automatically follow a white mare," thereby allowing "[d]ishonest" mule-traders to profit by this tendency (956–7). Post-*Brown* "antics" over segre-gation are figured by Hurston as a white mare "calculated to keep us busy" while the misdirecting mule-trader—"government by fiat"—will bring "more ominous things ... to pass" (957).

Hurston's arch-conservatism—one might even call it nativism—is pre-figured by a fierce identification of, and with, an abstract "Indian" position from whence her editorial emerges. Refusing to fetishize whiteness, Hurston instead will fight an imagined communist threat with her own "red" fetish:

> The whole matter revolves around the self-respect of my people. How much satisfaction can I get from a court order for somebody to associate with me who does not wish me near them? The American Indian has never been spoken of as a minority and chiefly because there is no whine in the Indian. Certainly he fought, and valiantly for his lands, and rightfully so, but it is inconceivable of an Indian to seek forcible association with any-one. His well-known pride and self-respect would save him from that. I take the Indian position [956].

Hurston articulates a narrative in which the valiant but nonetheless defeated Indian reserves, for himself, the right to seek association. While the values of self-respect and cultural autonomy (stop whining! she says) are laudable, tak-ing the "Indian position" has its dangers, especially in the hands of someone like Senator Russell.

What is essentially *Indian* about Indians for Hurston (no forcible association) is precisely the attitude that Russell would like more black folk to
adopt. Hurston no doubt imagines that she is articulating a patriotic point
of view in which "government by fiat" ought to be scrapped in favor of
upholding the laws already in place and strengthening the existing educational
system (958). But from Russell's perspective, Hurston's nativist appropriation of the "Indian position" is *exactly* appropriate, since it merges the concept of the "good Indian" (defeated, but too proud to mix, hence a vanishing
race) with the "good Negro" (disenfranchised, but too proud to mix, hence
an invisible race). Such a position gives people like Russell (defeated, but too
proud to admit it) the impression that they just might be right after all:

> It might surprise some Senators to know that the Department of the Inte-
> rior currently operates a relocation program for Indians precisely along the
> lines I am proposing. I am advised by the staff of the Committee on Insu-
> lar and Interior Affairs that since 1952, more than 45,000 Indians have
> been moved from reservations under the Indian relocation program. The
> Bureau of Indian Affairs maintains relocation field offices in various cities
> of the country to assist in relocating Indians to become established in their
> new homes and new jobs, just as I propose in my amendment that both
> whites and Negroes may be relocated in new homes under this plan [CR,
> 5348].

The Committee on Insular and Interior Affairs was chaired by Congressman
Wayne Aspinall, to whom Philip S. Hughes wrote his reminder of Kennedy's
investment in wilderness. The Indian relocation program to which Russell
refers is, according to Francis Paul Prucha, a "corollary" of the Federal policy of tribal "termination."[65] And termination meant what it sounds like—
the trustee relationship between Indian tribes and the federal government
was terminated or liquidated by individuals cashing out their tribal status in
favor of cultural and economic assimilation into mainstream American culture. The primary advocate for the termination policy, Senator Arthur
Watkins, of Utah, also conflated Indian termination with civil rights: "Following in the footsteps of the Emancipation Proclamation," he said, "I see
the following words emblazoned in letters of fire above the heads of Indians—these people shall be free."[66] Under the guise of what Watkins was calling freedom, the federal government, for all intents and purposes, was
institutionalizing the age-old racist axiom that the only good Indian (assim-
ilated) is a dead Indian (terminated). From the perspective of most Indians
and their supporters, the program was an unmitigated disaster. Not surprisingly, the termination program back-fired almost immediately and, according to Prucha, quickly became a rhetorical "rallying-point" for "unified Indian
voices" (350–1).[67]

But, as Russell points out, some Indians did terminate their tribal status, and these, for him, are exemplary because they are willing to measure themselves by his standards. Thus, Indians become "Americans" by virtue of giving up their tribal status, and "Negroes" become acceptable, but not quite ever "American," by virtue of being relocated. While both of these transitions are imagined to be voluntary, we ought not to be misled by the rhetoric of relocation. We need to remember that the salient point for Russell is revulsion—the hope that revulsion at the mere mention of "inflicting" black folk on places like Montana, Idaho, Minnesota, Oregon, and Washington would be enough to stop passage of the Civil Rights Act. Keeping that in mind, the crucial similarity between Indian and black relocation is that each is being imagined by Russell as divested of a special relationship between a protected group and the federal government. And both of these groups are mentioned in the infamous three-fifths clause: *Indians not taxed and three-fifths of all other persons.* Losing tribal status, Indians disappear, "never having been spoken of as a minority," as Hurston reminds us; while blacks, relocating to areas in which white folk would vastly outnumber them, become politically less viable, as Javits reminds Russell—a permanent minority on the uncivil map of America.

By way of conclusion, I'd like to make a final connection between civil rights and wilderness, a connection that is central to this project. During the hearings before the Senate on the Civil Rights Act, anecdotal evidence was brought to bear by Roy Wilkins (among others) concerning the impact of passing Title II for a vacationing black family. In what follows, Wilkins's rhetoric about vacations neatly merges with the syntax of exclusion and violence that I have all along been articulating:

> For millions of Americans this is vacation time. Swarms of families load their automobiles and trek across country. I invite the members of this committee to imagine themselves darker in color and to plan an auto trip from Norfolk, Va., to the gulf coast of Mississippi, say, to Biloxi. Or one from Terre Haute, Ind., to Charleston, S.C., or from Jacksonville, Fla., to Tyler, Tex.

As Wilkins implies, the pleasure we get from vacations, and the liberty of movement necessitated by them, are an entitlement: this is vacation time. But he quickly goes on to show that entitlements do not always openly declare themselves when the rubber hits the proverbial pavement. Shifting from first to second-person, the better to provoke empathy, Wilkins poses a series of rhetorical questions.

> How far do you drive each day? Where and under what conditions can you and your family eat? Where can they use a rest room? Can you stop driving after a reasonable day behind the wheel or must you drive until you reach a city where relatives or friends will accommodate you and yours

for the night? Will your children be denied a soft drink or an ice cream cone because they are not white?

By way of answer, Wilkins continues, shifting again, this time from second to third-person, as if to reinstate the distance between ostensive equality (personhood, humanity, citizenship) and ultimately unimaginable racial difference:

> You just live uncomfortably, from day to day. *It must be remembered that the players in this drama of frustration and indignity are not commas or semi-colons in a legislative thesis*; they are people, human beings, citizens of the United States of America. This is their country. They were born here, as were their fathers and grandfathers before them, and their great-grandfathers. They have done everything for their country that has been asked of them, even to standing back and waiting patiently, under pressure and persecution, for that which they should have had at the very beginning of their citizenship [LH, 2370, emphasis added].

Apprising us of the gap between the syntax (commas and semi-colons) of Constitution as "thesis" and a praxis that elaborates "indignity," Wilkins would replace the "drama of frustration" with a genealogical narrative, an embodied history of citizenship as defined by the Fourteenth Amendment. There, the geography of invisibility and denial (all those questions in which one's citizenship is constantly under assault) is supplanted by an account—a counting of bodies—in which patience "under pressure and persecution" becomes both the source and limit of good citizenship. As Wilkins knows full well, if we follow the map of the Fourteenth Amendment, geography and genealogy converge at the site where we are born. *All persons born or naturalized in the United States, and subject to the jurisdiction thereof, are citizens of the United States and of the State in which they reside.*

Real citizens, as Wilkins reminds us, are not commas or semi-colons. But as anecdotal evidence, they can be useful pawns. If passage of Title II repatriates the black family within the nexus of values and ideals that emanate from the cultural artifact of vacations and wilderness, it is also imagined by others to shore up America's reputation abroad. "Our Nation," wrote several congressmen in advocacy of the provisions of Title II, "is engaged today in cold war combat with an alien ideology. On every front—military, economic, political, and social—we must demonstrate the worth of our system" (LH 2493).[68] Thus wilderness, cold war, and civil rights all converge as rationale for Title II, passage of which would "demonstrate" the ostensibly superior value of this "democracy born of free land."

These same concerns (minus the cold-war rhetoric) also converge in the following sentiment expressed, in 1963, by a white male Southerner when confronted with the possibility of sharing the democratic franchise with blacks:

"We killed two-month-old Indian babies to take this country," he said, the intonation rising, no doubt, into incredulity, "and now they want us to give it away to the niggers."[69] Killing two-month-old Indian babies (that continuous touch) is precisely how American forebears founded this country, and our anonymous but easily recognizable speaker finds civil equality with African Americans more repugnant than the history of genocide in which he willingly implicates himself. In fact, it is genocide that underwrites the value from which the African American is excluded. Fetishizing America's violent relationship with Indians, he, like Hurston, takes the "Indian position." Hurston's Indian, we recall, "fought valiantly" and "properly," but, as our speaker reminds us, to what avail? And, like Russell, the speaker desires "to maintain the old condition of things," where "everything may grow and spread" around the contours of his fantasy, "including what is useless and even harmful." The disavowal of black bodies that cleared the land stolen from two-month-old Native American babies, bodies that, tabulated at ⅗ of whole free persons, supplemented the representational power of the white male in 1787, exposes the rhetoric of the Wilderness Act as an erotics of commas, semicolons, and copulas motivated by liberalism's first-person perspective of "free land" as an extension of white selves. Denying that personhood to African Americans *circa* 1964 implies that the arena of civil rights is itself imagined to be the pure, unsullied scene of a violent, sexualized affliction we call whiteness. That is the reservation, the deep national fantasy, from whence we—all of us—must relocate ourselves.

Notes

1. An earlier version of this paper was presented at the Fourth Annual Colloquium of The Black Studies Department, University of Nebraska–Omaha (May 7–9, 2000), on "Civil Rights, Black Arts, and the Black Power Movements." Portions of this paper appear, in radically different form and context, in my unpublished dissertation, "Salvaging Virginia: Transitivity, Race and the Problem of Consent." For their critical engagement with the connections between civil rights and wilderness that formed the conceptual framework for this paper, I wish to thank the students in English 498: "Troping Turner: Confession, Thesis, Diary" (University of Washington, spring 1999), as well as students in English 328: "Beat, Black, and (Sometimes) Blue: Poetry of the 50s and 60s from San Francisco to Black Mountain to the Black Arts Movement" (Grinnell College, spring 2000). I would also like to thank my colleagues Saadi Simawe, Christopher Parker, and Ralph Savarese, who read and commented on drafts of this paper.
2. *United States Code. Congressional and Administrative News, 88th Congress, Second Session, 1964, Volume 1: Laws,* p. 289. Subsequent references to this volume will be cited parenthetically as *Laws.*
3. I'd like to thank Galen Andrews for bringing this ad to my attention.
4. See J.L. Austin, *How To Do Things with Words, Second Edition,* eds. J.O. Urmson and Marina Sbisa (Cambridge: Harvard University Press, 1975), p. 7. For Austin,

"performative" is a term that "indicates that the issuing of the utterance is the perform-ing of an action—it is not normally thought of as just saying something" (6–7). The per-formative I am most concerned with throughout this essay is the category of "promising."

5. I refer readers to three canonical examples of such validation: the prefatory remarks by Wendell Phillips and William Lloyd Garrison for Frederick Douglass's *Narrative*; David Walker's reminder to the colored citizens of the world as to the limits of "freedom" without white validation in the Preamble of his *Appeal to the Coloured Citizens of the World*; and W.E.B. Du Bois's critique of Southern Black Codes in "Of the Quest of the Golden Fleece" in *The Souls of Black Folk*. The use of racial profiling to warrant detention of drivers guilty of nothing more than "driving while black" is, I think, a man-ifestation of this logic.

6. The radical white-supremacist factions provide evidence of the *whitening* of wil-derness in their desire for a racial homeland in the heart of the Western wilderness spread out over Washington, Oregon, Idaho, Montana and Wyoming (see Robert Miles, "Five States Is All We Ask," *From the Mountain*, March–April 1985, p. 7). As for the Civil Rights Act being imagined as black and undemocratic, see Andrew Macdonald, *The Turner Diaries* (New York: Barricade Books, 1980). This infamous and virulent 1978 novel, cast as nar-rative retrospective from the year 1999, depicts a racial dystopia, which, from the perspec-tive of Macdonald (aka William L. Pierce), is a direct result of such affirmative judicial and legislative actions as *Brown v. Board of Education*, "which took our schools away from us and turned them into racially mixed jungles," and the 1964 Civil Rights Act in which "the 'equal opportunity boys' have really done a wonderful wrecking job on the FBI and other investigative agencies" (pp. 33, 7).

7. See Eric Sundquist, *To Wake the Nations: Race in the Making of American Lit-erature* (Cambridge: The Belknap Press of Harvard University Press, 1993), p. 136.

8. *Congressional Record,* March 16, 1964, p. 5324. Further reference to this volume will be cited parenthetically as CR.

9. "Nicaragua and the Filibusters," author not named, *Blackwood's Magazine* LXXIX (March 1856): 314.

10. The treaty in question is the Clayton-Bulwer Treaty of July 4, 1850, preventing both Britain and the United States from "assum[ing] or exercis[ing] dominion" in Cen-tral America. See Albert Z. Carr's *The World and William Walker* (New York: Harper and Row, 1963), pp. 42–55, on the treaty negotiations.

11. *Harper's Weekly* 1 (1857): 24.

12. William Walker, *The War in Nicaragua*, with a foreword by Robert Huston (Tucson: University of Arizona Press, 1985 [rpt. of first edition published by S.H. Goet-zel and Co., Mobile, Alabama, 1860]), pp. 272–3.

13. Mann, *The Walls of Jericho: Lyndon Johnson, Hubert Humphrey, Richard Russell, and the Struggle for Civil Rights* (New York: Harcourt Brace and Company, 1996), p.78, emphasis added.

14. David Brion Davis, *The Problem of Slavery in the Age of Revolution, 1770–1823* (Ithaca: Cornell University Press, 1975), p. 34.

15. Mann, p. 230. Nothing if not dogged in his desire to maintain segregation, by 1964, racial relocation had become almost a reflex action for Russell whenever the issue of civil rights came before Congress.

16. See also Taylor Branch, who cites these words in his *Pillar of Fire: America in the King Years 1963–65* (New York: Simon and Schuster, 1998), p. 258.

17. On King's presence in the balcony, see Branch, p. 258.

18. According to the *Congressional Report,* Black population densities "rang[ed] from a high of 42 percent in Mississippi, to a low of one-tenth of 1 percent in both Vermont and North Dakota" (5347).

19. See Sundquist, p. 136.

20. It should be remembered that what we now call the Great Migration of black folk from rural, agricultural contexts in the South, to urban, industrial contexts in the North, was a function of black folk being squeezed out when repeated crop failures and lack of industrial opportunities made finding jobs difficult for both blacks and whites.

21. The exact location within the framework of the text is Article 1, section 2, paragraph 3, sentence one: "Representatives and direct taxes shall be apportioned among the several States which may be included within this Union, according to their respective numbers, which shall be determined by adding to the whole number of free persons, including those bound to service for a term of years, and excluding Indians not taxed, *three fifths of* all *other persons.*" I rely on the text provided in *Summaries of Leading Cases on the Constitution,* 12th ed., eds. Paul C. Bartholomew and Joseph F. Merz (Totowa, New Jersey: Rowman and Allenheld, 1983), p. 396, emphasis in original. As to whether this compromise action is affirmative for the South or the North is arguable; what is not arguable is that black bodies are counted in ways that boost white representative power while still denying the abstract person within the body any rights of citizenship at all.

22. James Madison, Alexander Hamilton, John Jay, *The Federalist,* ed. Benjamin Fletcher Wright (Cambridge: The Belknap Press of Harvard University Press, 1961), p. 370, 372, emphasis in original. In a recent article for NPR entitled "Myths About the Founding," (www.dineshdsouza.com/founding.html), Dinesh D'Souza takes no little pleasure in reminding his readers on "Planet America" that the Founding Fathers were saying "nothing" about the "intrinsic worth of any individual or group" in the "three-fifths clause." Madison's comments suggest otherwise.

23. John Quincy Adams, *Argument of John Quincy Adams Before the Supreme Court of the United States in the Case of The United States, Appellants, vs. Cinque, and Others, Africans* (New York: S.W. Benedict, 1841), p. 39, cited in A. Leon Higginbotham Jr.'s *Shades of Freedom: Racial Politics and Presumptions of the American Legal Process* (New York: Oxford University Press, 1996), p. 69. I have omitted Judge Higginbotham's emphases.

24. *The Random House College Dictionary,* revised edition, 1975.

25. My brief mention of embodiment and voice is indebted to Elaine Scarry's *The Body in Pain: The Making and Unmaking of the World* (New York: Oxford University Press, 1985), especially chapter one, "The Structure of Torture: The Conversion of Real Pain into the Fiction of Power."

26. For a classic articulation of the degradation of the white laborer as a result of his proximate status with slaves see Frederick Douglass, *Narrative of the Life of an American Slave* (New York: Penguin Classics, 1986), chapter X, especially pages 130–33. Having gone to work alongside nominally free, white laborers in Gardner's shipyard, Frederick Bailey astutely recognizes that his "fellow-apprentices very soon began to feel it degrading to them to work with [him]" but not before he was scape-goated and subsequently brutalized by a sudden burst of whiteness.

27. Du Bois, "Of the Faith of the Fathers," in *The Souls of Black Folk* (New York: Penguin, 1989), p. 168.

28. Walter Benn Michaels, "The Souls of White Folk," in *Literature and the Body: Essays on Populations and Persons,* ed. Elaine Scarry (Baltimore: Johns Hopkins University Press, 1988), pp. 185–209.

29. Morrison, *Playing in the Dark: Whiteness and the Literary Imagination* (New York: Vintage, 1993), pp. 47, 17, 47.

30. See Werner Sollors, "'Never was Born': The Mulatto, An American Tragedy?" in *The Massachusetts Review* 27, no. 2: 293–316. Articulating American tragedy by way of the "melodrama of race and family," Sollors writes that "the fear of miscegenation is established with the emotional power of the incest taboo" (302). It is with this "emotional" or symbolic "power" in mind that I address the issue of blindness. I do not intend to imply

that blindness as positive disability is an emasculation. Clearly, as I have indicated, Best Western wants us to know that they accommodate the disabled. But given the scopophilic context, though, the man's blindness, as a *black* man's blindness, can be taken up as part and parcel of the nexus of overdetermined sexuality and underrepresented personhood (the melodrama of race and family that Sollors invokes) with which black men and women are so often imbued.

31. Weigman, "The Anatomy of Lynching," *Journal of the History of Sexuality* 3, no. 3 (1993): 455. Subsequent reference to this text will be cited parenthetically.

32. Branch, p. 269. Within moments, King met Malcolm X in an adjoining conference room. As King readied to go, Malcolm very strategically, according to Branch, "placed himself directly in King's path." They shook hands, an image that was then carried by the news bureaus. The map of racial relocation, which Malcolm must also have seen, becomes the third side of a socio-political triangulation in which King's non-violent advocacy of full citizenship, Malcolm's Black Nationalism, and Russell's segregationism were all acutely joined.

33. I rely on a broader definition of "American exceptionalism" than that propounded by twentieth century scholars of American history in response to Werner Sombart's question, "why is there no socialism in the United States?" As Larry G. Gerber states, "commentators have applied the concept of American uniqueness to various aspects of the American experience ever since the Puritans first envisioned their colony as a 'city on a hill.'" (See Gerber, "Shifting Perspectives on American Exceptionalism," *Journal of American Studies* 31, no. 2: 254.) While the fact of slaves and the convenient illusion of "free land" helped mitigate labor pressures (at least from the perspective of employers), the concept of the "city on a hill" became "naturalized" in the form of providential history, a history which viewed America and Americans as a divinely sanctioned, manifestly destined, cultural project whose representative embodiment, at least for Thomas Jefferson, was the yeoman farmer, the "chosen ... of the world." (See his *Notes on the State of Virginia*, Query XIX.)

34. *United States Code. Congressional and Administrative News, 88th Congress, 1964, Volume 2: Legislative History* (Washington, D.C.), p. 3622. Subsequent references to this text will be cited parenthetically as LH. Here, Aspinall is reminded of the date of his letter in the first sentence (constituting the first paragraph) of Hughes's response, and the reference to Kennedy is made immediately after, in a separate paragraph of two sentences. The rest of the letter (three additional paragraphs) is dedicated to emphasizing wilderness goals, resolving issues concerning those goals, and recommendation of "favorable committee action" toward implementing those goals.

35. Cited in T.H. Watkins' "Untrammeled by Man," *Audubon Magazine* 91, no. 6 (Nov. 1989): 89.

36. John F. Kennedy, *"Let the Word Go Forth": The Speeches, Statements, and Writings of John F. Kennedy,* selected and with an introduction by Theodore C. Sorensen (New York: Delacorte Press, 1988), p. 100. References to this text will be cited parenthetically as JFK.

37. Frederick Jackson Turner, *The Significance of the Frontier in American History,* ed. Harold Simonson (New York: Frederick Ungar Publishing Co., 1963), p. 27. Subsequent references will be cited parenthetically as SF.

38. Tim Dean, *Gary Snyder and the American Unconscious: Inhabiting the Ground* (London: Macmillan, 1991), p. 83.

39. Austin, *How to Do Things with Words*, p. 7. Austin uses the question "can saying make it so?" as a sub-heading in his initial delineation of performatives. For him, yes, some utterances, such as promising, betting, marrying, and so forth, are actions made so precisely by way of saying in the first person singular present indicative active form embodied in, for example, "I promise to help you." Failure to abide by the terms implicit in the

utterance of a performative is never a matter, for Austin, of truth or falsity, but rather of happiness or unhappiness, since, as he reminds us, "our word is our bond" (10). In the trajectory of American history, where all are ostensibly promised the "pursuit of happiness," the performance of promises given, to Native Americans and African Americans especially, has all too often been "unhappy."

40. Richard Slotkin, "Myth and the Production of History," in *Ideology and Classic American Literature,* eds. Sacvan Bercovitch and Myra Jehlen (Cambridge: Cambridge University Press, 1986), p. 70.

41. Freud, *The Ego and the Id and Other Works,* v. XIX, standard edition, trans. James Strachey (London: The Hogarth Press), pp. 56, 45.

42. Lacan, "The Signification of the Phallus," in *Ecrits, A Selection,* trans. Alan Sheridan (New York: Norton, 1977), p. 287.

43. John Locke, *The Second Treatise of Government,* ed. Thomas P. Peardon (Indianapolis: BobbsMerrill, 1952), ch. 5, "Of Property," p. 29. Locke, in this incomplete citation, is referring to the relationship between money, possessions, and perishability. But it is, I think, an enduring legacy of the myth of the frontier that so many critics (as C.B. Macpherson reminds us) take this citation out of context, as I have done, to mean something of primal significance about America's role in the liberal project. See, for instance, Michael Rogin in "Liberal Society and the Indian Question," where he writes, "the intimate historical encounter with the Indians still further undermined liberal identity. 'In the beginning,' John Locke had written, 'all the world was America.' Then men relinquished the state of nature, freely contracted together, and entered civil society." *(Ronald Reagan, The Movie, and Other Lessons in Political Demonology* [Berkeley: University of California Press, 1987], p. 135.) Rogin's conceptualization of liberal society is grounded in a Kleinian analysis that graphically narrates the murderous rage of white settlers enacted against Indians as a "scapegoat[ing]" that "projects" both the "bliss" of infant plenitude and the guilt of "primitive rage" directed toward the body of the mother onto the figure of the Indian (145).

44. Frank, "Identity and Subjectivity," in *Deconstructing Subjectivities,* eds. Simon Critchley and Peter Dews (Albany: State University of New York Press, 1996), p. 139. Frank, in an analysis of Shelling's absolute identity, suggests that the relation of identity between two differences (A and B) is a function of the "potency" of each to each.

45. Slotkin, *Gunfighter Nation: The Myth of the Frontier in Twentieth-Century America* (New York: Athenum, 1992), pp. 11–12. It should be noted that Slotkin, to whose work I am very much indebted, begins with an analysis of Kennedy's speech, and then proceeds, necessarily, to an analysis of Turner's Frontier Thesis.

46. Dean, p. 43.

47. See Charles Taylor, "Locke's Punctual Self," in *Sources of the Self: The Making of the Modern Identity* (Cambridge: Harvard University Press), p. 159. Subsequent references to this text will be cited parenthetically.

48. I refer the reader to Locke's canonical definition as elaborated in *The Second Treatise of Government,* chapter 5, paragraph 27: "Though the earth and all inferior creatures be common to all men, yet every man has a property in his own person; this nobody has any right to but himself. The labor of his body and the work of his hands, we may say, are properly his. Whatsoever then he removes out of the state that nature has provided and left it in, he has mixed his labor with, and joined to it something that is his own, and thereby makes it his property. ... it has by this labor something annexed to it that excludes the common right of other men." (I am citing from the edition edited by Thomas P. Peardon [Indianapolis: Bobbs-Merrill Educational Publishing, 1952], p. 17.

49. On the Jeffersonian grid, see Philip Fisher, "Democratic Social Space: Whitman, Melville, and the Promise of American Transparency," in *Representations* 24 (Fall 1988), pp. 60–101.

50. On the exclusion of women from the "fantasy" of the frontier myth, see Annette Kolodny, *The Land Before Her: Fantasy and Experience of the American Frontiers* (Chapel Hill: University of North Carolina Press, 1984), pp. 5–6: "Having for so long been barred from the fantasy garden, American women were also, at first, wary of paradisal projections onto the vast new landscape around them. Their imaginative play, instead, focused on the spaces that were truly and unequivocally theirs: the home and the small cultivated gardens of their own making."

51. Henry Nash Smith, *Virgin Land: The American West as Symbol and Myth* (Cambridge: Harvard University Press, 1950). Offering this work as a sort of Christmas present to American literary studies in 1949 (see his "Preface"), Smith begins and ends with a discussion of Turner, as if the text of *Virgin Land* itself would enact a "settlement" of sorts—"the present study"—which, he says, "traces the impact of the West, the vacant continent beyond the frontier, on the consciousness of Americans and follows the principle consequences of this impact in literature and social thought down to Turner's formulation of it" (p. 4). Even as Smith distances himself from Turner with phrases such as "[w]hatever the merits of the Turner thesis," he clearly relies on a logic of vacancy manifested in other phrases such as "vacant continent" and "untouched natural resource," thereby once again exposing the reliance of U.S. "history" on making invisible—one way or another—*earlier and ongoing* inhabitants.

52. Thomas Jefferson, see *Notes on the State of Virginia*, "Query XIX."

53. For an important discussion of the relationship between yeoman farmers and the wealthy plantation class in the construction of "race" as an ideological discipline that emanates from the class-inflected social pressures of slavery (and not slavery as a function of a pre-existing condition that we might call "race"), see Barbara Jeanne Fields, "Slavery, Race and Ideology in the United States of America," *New Left Review* 181 (May/June 1990): 95–118.

54. Fisher, *Hard Facts: Setting and Form in the American Novel* (New York: Oxford University Press, 1985), p. 12.

55. Smith, *Virgin Land*, p. 3.

56. This essay is the first stage of a project whose primary concern is precisely to articulate a more complicated vision of the construction of "America" as it rushes headlong into Du Bois's "twentieth century." The fact that I don't discuss cultural attitudes about the "place" of women in the landscape ought not to be read as a lack of awareness or indifference about those issues. I am currently at work on an essay on William James, W.E.B. Du Bois and Harriet Monroe that deals with issues of personal and national health, or "sanativity," and the problem of the color-line as it relates to issues of gender and aesthetics, all concerns which were, originally, very much a part of this paper. Time and space constraints dictated addressing those concerns elsewhere.

57. The other candidate I might offer would be Martin Luther King Jr.'s "I have a Dream" speech, delivered on the steps of the Lincoln Memorial on August 28, 1963, just slightly less than a year before the passage of the Civil Rights and Wilderness acts of 1964.

58. I cite from what Garry Wills calls "The Final Text" in his *Lincoln at Gettysburg: The Words that Remade America* (New York: Simon and Schuster, 1992), p. 263. I have stressed the phrase and clauses that Kennedy is clearly citing.

59. Slotkin, *Gunfighter Nation*, pp. 1–4.

60. Clearly, the legislators are implying that no additional monies will be needed to protect these areas since the system for administering the enactment is already there. In this way, the legislative desire to protect the very notion of "free land" whose demise Turner had lamented, turns on the promise that it will, indeed, be as near to "free"—of people, entanglements, and of new tax burdens—as possible.

61. Sigmund Freud, *A General Introduction to Psychoanalysis*, trans. Joan Riviere (Garden City: Garden City Publishing Company, Inc., 1943), p. 325, emphasis added.

62. Cosgrove, "Habitable Earth," in *Wild Ideas,* ed. David Rothenberg (Minneapolis: University of Minnesota Press, 1995), p. 35.

63. Something on the inferential order of De Morgan's Theorem occurs, whereby the "meeting place of savagery and civilization" (conjunction) is rhetorically transformed into a negation of conjunction, "It cannot be the case that I am *both* savage and civilized," which is logically equivalent to the disjunctive "either I am not savage or I am not civilized"—where "either/or" occupies the historical "space," as Tim Dean refers to it, of "versus." At this point, our singular first-person frontier subject, by way of what Dean calls "inversion," or blaming the victim for the violence that victimizes him, naturalizes the inference "I am not savage." Thus the disjunctive meeting of the binary opposition savagery/civilization ("either I am not savage or I am not civilized") is transformed, by way of disjunctive syllogism, into the reassuring "I *am* civilized, therefore I am *not* savage." How would such logic look as narrative? Very much as Slotkin glosses it: "Although we were a people of 'the wilderness' we were *not* savages" (*Gunfighter Nation,* 11).

64. Hurston, "Court Order Can't Make Races Mix," in *Folklore, Memoirs, and Other Writings,* volume 2, selected by Cheryl A. Wall (New York: Library of America, 1995), p. 956. References to this text will be cited parenthetically.

65. Francis Paul Prucha, *The Great Father: The United States Government and the American Indians, Abridged Edition* (Lincoln: University of Nebraska Press, 1986), p. 355. Subsequent reference to this text will be cited parenthetically.

66. Cited by Robert F. Berkhofer, Jr., *The White Man's Indian: Images of the American Indian from Columbus to the Present* (New York: Vintage Books, 1979), p. 187.

67. There's a lot implied in Prucha's phrase, "unified Indian voices." Not only does the failure of termination strengthen the concept of tribe, but it also solidifies the concept of "Indianness" across tribal boundaries.

68. *Legislative History,* "Additional Views on H.R. 7152 of Hon. William McCulloch, Hon. John V. Lindsay, et. al." The war in the streets over race was viewed by many senators and members of the House as a foreign relations problem. Indeed, many who voted to pass the Civil Rights Act did so less out of concern *for* blacks as out of concern *about* blacks and how America's reaction would look to the rest of the world.

69. Taylor Branch, *Pillar of Fire: America in the King Years, 1963–65* (New York: Touchstone, 1998), p. 68. Branch is citing a *New York Times* article of April 6, 1963, p. 20.

16. Guilt by Association: Women as Participants and Victims of Lynching

Marilyn D. Lovett

There is a historical marker for what the town of Dodge, Texas, was to the railroad industry. Is there any mention of an entire family by the last name of Cabiness being slaughtered? Dodge Cemetery is down the road from the marker. Would they have been buried here? Were their bodies even buried, or were they thrown into the nearby Trinity River? Was the home burned down or is it still standing? Did every Cabiness leave town after this tragedy, or change the spelling of their last name? What did the entire family do to merit such treatment from folks who probably attended the local First Baptist Church weekly?

The railroad still runs through Dodge. A neighborhood watch exists, for what purpose I do not understand. There is also a post office along its Farm Road 405. The distance from this town to Elysian Fields is less than 3 hours. Along that route I notice 3 or more roads named after cemeteries. Traveling north on state highway 59, I notice a correctional facility exists in a town with a population of only 4000, Diboll. Further up the road, around the town of Appleby, the clerk drops the change in my hand from a 4-inch height when I stop to get a soda. I see my first Confederate flag a few miles from Garrison, not long after the interaction with the clerk.

Around Carthage, I take route 79 north that leads me to Elysian Fields. It is on the edge of Harrison County, sitting next to Panola County, and reminds me of other small towns I have visited. It seems that Blacks live on the outskirts or on the other side of the tracks from Whites in many of these places. I wonder from which tree Mary Jackson was hung in this area. The questions I have about the Cabiness family, I have about Ms. Jackson, as well. There is a post office here as well as a bank. One historical marker on route 31, off of route 79, which curves through Elysian Fields, concerns the town of DeBerry, named after a Confederate soldier. "Pioneers" are buried in the Bracken Cemetery, named after the Bracken family who "settled" here in the

1830s. I am not sure whether Blacks are included in this number or not. Someone in a big red pick-up truck with a large dog on the back glares at me and slows down as I prepare to cross the street back to my car after reading the marker. On the way back to the main road, someone in a black truck waves at me. Here, I see Blacks; maybe it is due to the early evening hour. Yet, there is no marker for Ms. Jackson. I visit these places hoping to secure the answers to my questions.

In Texas, 500 Blacks were lynched between 1870 and 1930. A small percentage were women, the focus of this paper. Harrison County leads with 15 between 1900 and 1930 (Glasrud, 140). Panola County borders this county in the northeastern part of the state and is the site of Mary Jackson's death. Walker County was 1 of 8 counties with 5 or more lynchings (Glasrud, 140). This is where the entire Cabiness family was killed. Between 1900 and 1910, Texas ranked 3rd among the states in its number of lynchings, over 100 (Barr, 136). In some cases, the media in Texas did not cover lynchings, so the total number may be under-reported. It is even more difficult to determine how these Blacks lived before their lives were snuffed out by mob violence (Glasrud, 156).

When we talk about lynching in this country, the focus is usually on men, but women are the forgotten victims. Women were usually killed because they were perceived as having protected the accused in some way, shape, or form. This paper attempts to put a face on these forgotten victims and delves into the way that women encouraged lynching as a collective behavior.

In Claude McKay's poem "The Lynching," there is a line that reads, "The women thronged to look, but never a one—Showed sorrow in her eyes of steely blue." Many people recognize the role of women in lynching. Anywhere from ⅙ (Zangrando, 117) to 23 percent (Hall, 17) of lynching cases were attributed to a Black man having some sort of alleged contact deemed improper with a White woman. So, not only were women victims of lynching but they were participants as well.

Lynching, as defined by Tuskegee University, one of the earliest institutions to keep records of this phenomenon, involves an instance in which the "person must have met death illegally (by a) group of 3 or more.... The group must have acted under the pretext of service to justice, race or tradition" (Ginzburg, 245). The term is derived from Charles Lynch, a farmer in Virginia, who was known to tie thieves to trees and whip them, thus taking the law into his own hands (Cutler, 24).

One of the earliest studies related to the collective behavior of mob activity was completed by Meier, Mennenga, and Stoltz (abstract). 35 percent of those who participated in an experiment on crowd behavior and its motivating factors would have stayed away from a lynching. This category consisted of women overwhelmingly. Yet, there is a discrepancy between the laboratory and what actually happened. Lynching as a collective behavior involved participants who were overwhelmingly White men, but women and children were known to have been present at a hanging or burning as well.

Women as Participants

Women participated in lynching directly as well as indirectly. In some instances, women goaded men into taking a person from jail, suggesting that they were not brave enough to do a "man's job." During the New Orleans riot in 1892, White prostitutes encouraged would-be lynchers in search of a man accused of killing police officers, saying, "our best wishes, boys" (Wells, 26). Law enforcement officials were less inclined to use deadly force to keep a lynch mob away if women were present and they brought their children with them at times (Raper, 12).

At other times, women "contributed" fuel for fire and looked for "souvenirs" after lynchings (Brundage, 38). There were cases in which women actually participated in the lynching process. In some situations, White women who encouraged lynching cried rape when their crime of intimacy with a Black man was discovered. For example, sometimes a baby would be born who was obviously biracial.

The notion of children at lynchings may be appalling but was not abnormal. When a man in Paris, Texas, was lynched in 1893 for allegedly killing a 5-year-old, children were allowed to miss school. An acquaintance of Ida Wells Barnett told how while traveling in that area a year after the lynching, an innkeeper's wife discussed the event as if it were nothing. The 8-year-old daughter interrupted her mother while they were talking and said "I saw them burn the n— —, didn't I Mama?" Her mother replied, "Yes, darling, you saw them burn the n— —" (Wells, 84–85).

An incident in which a biracial baby was born occurred in the case of one woman in 1899 in Darien, Georgia, who named her neighbor as a rapist. He was moved for safekeeping, after Blacks mobilized to protect him, and was later acquitted (Tolnay and Beck, 209).

Men, women and children were also part of a mob who had lynched a Black man, identified as a killer because a White woman was found dead in Cairo, Illinois. Some of these women pushed baby strollers as the ringleaders dragged the body to where the dead woman was found, cut off his head, stuck it on a pole, and burned the body (Wells, 310).

In Chester County, Pennsylvania (August 1911), 4000–5000 men, women, and children participated in taking an alleged killer from his hospital bed and burning him. Although the ringleaders in the lynch mob were brought to trial, they were exonerated. The widow of the White man killed supposedly by the Black man remarked that she "wanted to apply the match" (Murphey, 27).

In May 1937 in Georgia, although the police killed an alleged rapist/murderer because he tried to escape, a mob took his body to burn it. Women took part in the procession to the field and assisted with the practice of cremation (Ginzburg, 231).

In Loudoun County, Virginia, a woman shot into the dead body of a man accused of raping her in February 1880 (Brundage, 42).

Many may ask how women could bring their children to watch the atrocities against people who were lynched. Brown (16) suggests that when people were members of lynch mobs, they did not necessarily lose their identities but they did become less self-attentive. For women, being a member of the White race was more salient than being female as participants in these groups. As well, because they did not pay as much attention to themselves as they usually would, they did not think about how a lynching would affect the children in the long run.

Women as Victims

The numbers of women lynched vary. Between 1882 and 1934, 94 women were lynched, according to Zangrando (117). These numbers may be an underestimate, but all but 17 of the 94 were Black. Cutler (173) documented the number of women killed by lynching between 1882 and 1903, reporting 5 Black women and 5 White women were reported lynched in 1895.

The reasons for women being lynched were numerous. Cutler (173) reported most of the time women were lynched for murder. This may speak to these women trying to protect themselves from White men. The second most common reasons for lynching according to Cutler (173) included minor offenses for Black women and unknown reasons for White women. The minor offenses included slander, self-defense, gambling, making threats, resisting arrest, and race prejudice (Cutler, 167). In many cases, they were killed because they were guilty by association. They were related to the accused or perceived as obstructing justice, which was also a minor offense.

Lynching was not endemic to the South. It was typical in the West as well, where Whites were more likely to lynch Whites (Murphey, 17). In Sweetwater Valley, Wyoming, the most infamous of those lynchings was that of Ellen Watson and her husband. She was also known as Cattle Kate after the lynching because she had been confused with a prostitute by an identical name in a nearby town; however, they were not one and the same (Hufsmith, 44). It was believed that she and her husband rustled cattle and illegally branded them in July 1889 (Hufsmith, 180). The men who lynched them were politically connected enough to have a trial go the way they wished.

Because an essential witness to the lynching disappeared, or was possibly killed, these men were tried and cleared (Hufsmith, 282). It may be that the accusation was just a ruse for one of the men who wanted Watson's land and was repeatedly refused its sale (Hufsmith, 307).

The lynchings of a Black postmaster in Lake City, South Carolina, Mr. Baker and his baby daughter, Julia, galvanized the country's Blacks in February 1898. Mr. Baker's crime? Race prejudice, a minor offense because no other reason was credible, even that one (Cutler, 168). Whites in the South were hard-pressed to explain the reasons for shooting father and daughter, who was in the arms of her mother at the time, as they attempted to escape their burning home and post office. Newspapers declared the actions of the mob spineless (Carter, 3).

In one case, Ballie Crutchfield was lynched for being the sister of a man accused of stealing. The mob had taken him from the sheriff; he eluded capture so they came after his sister. She was shot and thrown into a creek near Rome, Tennessee, in March 1901 (Ginzburg, 38). In another instance, the Ms. Barringer, the 16-year-old daughter of a Black farmer, was killed when she answered the door to the Ku Klux Klan. They were after her father for ensuring Black employment in Shelby County, Kentucky. A $9000 reward was offered but no one ever stepped forward (Wright, 31).

There were cases, which seem to be the exception rather than the rule, of women being lynched who were accused of some "legitimate" crime. For instance, Jennie Steers in July 1903 was accused of poisoning a 16-year-old girl's lemonade, who died as a result, near Shreveport, Louisiana. It seems that in many cases of lynching, the mob coerced a confession, I would think, to assuage any guilt. They did so in this case but Steers refused; she was still hanged (Ginzburg, 61).

In Doddsville, Mississippi, in February 1904 Mrs. Holbert and her husband were lynched when he was accused of killing a plantation owner and another Black. Before they were burned, their fingers and ears were removed. This instance of guilt by association left a motherless (and fatherless) child (Ginzburg, 62–63).

In Okemah, Oklahoma, in May 1911, Laura Nelson and her son were executed. Mrs. Nelson's son was accused of shooting a deputy when police searched their home for stolen meat, but she took responsibility for the fusillade. Mr. Nelson was taken to the state penitentiary while she and her son went to jail. When 40 men came after mother and son, the jailer tried to protect them by denying their existence. After being threatened, however, he told the lynch mob where to find them ("Without Sanctuary," 1).

Marie Scott, in March 1914, was hanged in Muskogee, Oklahoma, after being taken from her jail cell. She was accused of stabbing a White man who had visited the "Black" section of town with some other White men (Ginzburg, 90). What is interesting about this case is the question of what those White men were doing on a Saturday night on that side of town. Most likely, they were looking for Black women to be with sexually and that White man approached the wrong one in the wrong way. Additionally, at that time, it was not all right for Black women to refuse White men; after all, Black women were not viewed as females with virtue. This characteristic was assigned to White women exclusively (Collins, 71).

In November of the same year, in another state (Mississippi), Mrs. Sullivan and her husband were accused of burning a barn. They were taken from the custody of the deputy sheriff and lynched (Ginzburg, 92). The KKK lynched Mrs. Hawkins, her husband, and her oldest daughter in November 1872 near Fayette County, Kentucky, for registering people to vote (Wright, 51).

December 1915 saw the lynching of a mother, Cordella Stevenson. Her son was accused of burning a White man's barn. She was questioned by police about his whereabouts and they released her soon after. A mob broke down the door to the home she shared with her husband. They grabbed her and threatened her husband, who went to the nearest town for help. It was too late (Ginzburg, 96–97).

A man who tried to defend his mother, Mary Conley, in Arlington, Georgia, in October 1916 ended up killing the person who had slapped her. Her son escaped but she was held in jail. A mob took her from her cell, and shot her repeatedly, leaving her for dead (Ginzburg, 110).

The Rosewood incident in Florida, in which eight or more Blacks were killed by White mobs from a nearby town, included the lynching of at least two women. Sarah Carrier was killed in January 1923 for having a son who refused to leave town when he was "ordered to," and attempting to shelter Blacks who had to hide out and defend themselves before her home was burned (Jones et al., 14). She had also worked for Fannie Taylor, the married White woman who days earlier accused a Black man of attacking her when, in all likelihood, he was her lover. It was said that Mrs. Carrier's son might have said, in reference to the attack on Mrs. Taylor, that it "was an example of what Negroes could do without interference" (Jones et al., 15). The other Black woman killed was Lexie Gordon (also a Rosewood resident), who was shot when she escaped from under her house, which had been torched (Jones et al., 17). Restitution was made by the state of Florida for those who lost their property and for their descendants. The Rosewood Claims Bill, passed in 1994, gave $150,000 to nine of the town's survivors (Halton, 2).

In July 1892, a man in New Orleans was accused of killing four police officers. Law enforcement officials, as well as others who wanted to retaliate, could not find him. Mobs took out their wrath instead on every Black person they saw, beating men as well as women. While the mayor of nearby Kenner went to New Orleans to endorse mob action, the mayor of New Orleans called for peace to no avail. Hannah Mabry was killed while she was sleeping, as a result. Her son, daughter-in-law, and grandchild disappeared mysteriously afterwards (Wells, 17).

Bertha Lowman, her brother and her cousin were accused of killing the sheriff of Aiken County, South Carolina. It was expected that after her brother was acquitted, the others would be as well. Nevertheless, a mob took them from jail and shot them in October 1926 (Ginzburg, 175).

Marie Thompson was accused of killing a man and lynched in Lebanon Junction, Kentucky, in June 1904. She claimed self defense because she was breaking up a disagreement between a White man and her son. Black men guarded the jail initially but she was taken by a mob and hanged from a tree. Miraculously, she cut herself down, attempting to escape, but was shot. She did not die without a struggle (Wright, 116).

In some cases, women accused of arson were lynched. For example, Emma Fair and three other men were accused of setting fire to a house. They were jailed when a mob went there to shoot them in their cells (Wells, 75). Louisa Carter and Mahala Jackson were lynched as a result of being related to a man accused of arson in Jackson, Mississippi. Mother-in-law and wife were set free because their role was not as clear in the misdoing; however, a mob hung them as well soon afterwards (Wells, 49).

Dorothy Malcolm and Mae Dorsey, sisters and newlyweds, were killed with their husbands near Monroe, Georgia. A mob seized their husbands from their new employer, who was taking them to their new job. The men had been accused of stabbing their former employer. The lynch mob also grabbed the women because a member of the group thought one of the women could identify him. They were shot so viciously in July 1946 that their bodies were barely distinguishable (Ginzburg, 238–239). Once again, because these women were associated with the men, they, too, were lynched. In a recent ceremony (1998), the memory of these particular victims was honored by Blacks and Whites alike in Walton County, Georgia. There was a different name given in the dedication for one of the women, Dorothy Malcom Dorsey. It is now unclear whether she was married to Dorsey or Malcom; she was buried near Mr. Dorsey and separately from Mr. Malcom (Shearer, 1).

The most deplorable lynching of a woman occurred in Valdosta, Georgia, in May 1918. In no way does this overshadow the other women who were killed. However, the brutality involved in the innocent was horrendous. When Mary Turner's husband was lynched, she made statements alluding to the possible prosecution of those responsible. For speaking out, she was hung upside down from a tree and set afire. Hundreds of men and women were in the crowd and witnessed the killing of her baby as well. When a man cut her stomach open, the eight-month fetus fell out and cried before being stomped to death (*Barutiwa*, 1).

The following is a partial list of reported lynchings of women. It is limited in the number of years and only includes lynching in the South although it occurred all over the country. It does not include the women whose murders are being discussed.

Name	Place	Month/Year
Mollie French	Gallatin County, Ky.	May 1876
Eliza Lowe	Henry County, Ala.	August 1891
Ella Williams	Henry County, Ala.	August 1891
Mary Deane	Greenville, Ala.	April 1895
Martha Green	Greenville, Ala.	April 1895
Alice Green	Greenville, Ala.	April 1895
Harriet Talley	Petersburg, Tenn.	March 1895
Mollie Smith	Trigg County, Ky.	July 1895
Hannah Kearse	Colleton County, S.C.	December 1895
Amanda Franks	Jefferson, Ala.	May 1897
Molly White	Jefferson, Ala.	May 1895
Rose Etheridge	Phoenix, S.C.	November 1898
Eliza Goode	Greenwood, S.C.	November 1898
Betsy McCroy	Carrolton, Miss.	August 1901
Ida McCroy	Carrolton, Miss.	August 1901
Laura Porter	Monroe, La.	August 1910
Hattie Brown	Graceville, Fla.	September 1910
Belle Hathaway	Hamilton, Ga.	January 1912
Stella Young	Newberry, Fla.	August 1916
Rose Carson	Elloree, S.C.	July 1914
Mary Connell	Leary's, Ga.	October 1916
Emma Hooper	Hammond, La.	March 1917
Alma House	Shubuta, Miss.	December 1918
Maggie House	Shubuta, Miss.	December 1918

Some of the previous cases mentioned included the lynching of women and their relatives. However, there are cases in which entire families were killed. In September 1892, a mob met at the home of Hamp Biscoe in Arkansas. They believed he had killed the local law enforcement official who visited him because he argued with a White man who was on his land. Ms. Biscoe was pregnant when they shot her as she held an infant. They robbed them of $220 before they set fire to the house (Wells, 23). Night riders set fire to the home of the Walker family in Kentucky for having a disagreement with a White woman and supposedly bullying a White man who tried to settle it. They shot the father, mother, and four other children, one of whom was an infant. The mob claimed that he shot at them first and that they only wanted to whip him. Governor Augustus Willson offered a reward and sent troops to the area for a year. He also insinuated that anyone who killed a night rider would not be prosecuted (Wright, 124).

Texas Lynchings

An entire family by the last name of Cabiness was lynched in Dodge in June 1918. The U.S. was in the middle of World War I and drafted young men on a regular basis. George Cabiness, the son of Sarah Cabiness, resisted and was said to have threatened with a gun (according to the *Light*, 5) the sheriff and his family, or (according to the *Express*, 10) A.P.W. Allen. If Mr. Cabiness did intimidate either, it was for the purpose of avoiding the draft. It was said that he refused to register for Selective Service and refrained from addressing the Walker County Exemption Board. Although Black men were only 16 percent of the state population in Texas, they made up 25 percent of troops from the state (Barr, 115).

It is likely that the second newspaper account, dated June 2 (the *San Antonio Express*), may be more accurate than the one dated June 1 (the *San Antonio Light*). The story continues with the shooting death of Mr. Cabiness when law enforcement officials attempted to arrest him for "pulling a gun on A.P.W. Allen" (*Express*, 10). The day after Mr. Cabiness' death, one of his brothers went to the Allen's house armed and was shot. His family members took him back home that evening. The next morning, a mob encompassed their home and an exchange of gunfire ensued. The house caught fire and Sarah Cabiness carried out her sons until she was shot. Surprisingly, none of the White men in the posse were injured.

A total of 6 died in this encounter; the women were Sarah Cabiness, the 55-year-old matriarch, Bessie, the 27-year-old daughter, and Lena, the 17-year-old daughter. Their ages are based on the 1910 census. They owned the farm on which their house was burned. If I were a member of the Cabiness family, I would certainly consider leaving town or changing my name at this point. No member of this family is listed in the directory for Dodge or even nearby Huntsville.

In February 1912, Mary Jackson was lynched for supposedly supplying the gun that murdered a wealthy White man. Tennie Sneed shot Paul Strange; it may have been because he took a pair of shoes and he was on Mr. Strange's "bond" (*Messenger*, 1). Mr. Sneed was caught and sent to Longview jail. Law enforcement officials told groups of men who had visited the jail throughout the day that they had taken him to the state penitentiary. They did this in order to protect him from being lynched.

Mr. Sneed implicated Ms. Jackson and George Sanders as equipping him with the gun and some of the jail's visitors found out. They were bloodthirsty enough to go after Ms. Jackson and Mr. Sanders, who lived together with Mr. Sneed, who was separated from his wife. They were hanged in Penola County and found by Mr. Strange's brother. I do not think it would be a stretch to say he might have been involved. Ms. Jackson, about 40 when she died, is said to have known what Mr. Sneed wanted the gun for but tried to explain that Mr. Sanders knew nothing about the exchange. Mr. Sneed was moved to the Rusk Penitentiary after this event.

A grand jury was called to investigate 4 deaths, among which Ms. Jackson was included. They deliberated and indicted no one in her lynching, citing a lack of evidence; however, Mr. Sneed was indicted.

Legacy of Lynching Women

Several scholars are in agreement that one of the most influential reasons for the Black migration to the North and West was lynching (Ginzburg, 171, Jones et al., 3). The South lost over one million Blacks to migration between 1900 and 1930. Specifically, by the end of 1910, it was nearly 200,000. 20 years later, this number had more than tripled (Tolnay and Beck, 214). The legacy of lynching women is evident in the discontinuity in many Black families currently living in the North who have raised their children without knowledge of their Southern ancestors. Those families who migrated, after having heard of or experienced the lynching of women, were probably even more reluctant to look back.

Women who were eliminated obviously left motherless children. Those children failed to receive the emotional support one's own mother could provide. Additionally, those children had to heal from the psychological scars of having a loved one killed whose only crime was guilt by association, in many cases. The lack of financial resources seems to have been evident for these children as well. Some of the sons, brothers, and husbands had to bear the sorrow of their unintentional complicity in the lynching of their mothers, sisters, and wives.

I have asked several people if they knew of any cases of women being lynched. They usually say that is something about which they have never thought. We know about the men being lynched and the reasons behind them. We would be remiss if we forgot about the female victims.

Bibliography

Allen, James, J. Als, J. Lewis, and L. Litwack. *Without Sanctuary: Lynching Photography in America.* Santa Fe: Twin Palm Publishers, 2000.
Associated Press. "Six Negroes Dead after Battle with Citizen's Posse." *San Antonio Express,* 2 June 1918, 10.
"The Bloody Lynching of Mary Turner." *Barutiwa News Service,* 28 June 1999. <http://www.barutiwa.com/bns/bio11/html>.
Barr, Alwyn. *Black Texans: A History of African Americans in Texas 1528–1995.* 2nd ed. Norman, Okla.: University of Oklahoma Press, 1996.
Brown, Rupert. *Group Processes: Dynamics Within and Between Groups.* Oxford: Blackwell Publishers, 2000.
Brundage, W.F. *Lynching in the New South: Georgia and Virginia, 1880–1930.* Urbana, Ill.: University of Illinois Press, 1993.
Brundage, W. Fitzhugh, ed. *Under Sentence of Death: Lynching in the South.* Chapel Hill, N.C.:
University of North Carolina Press, 1997.
Carter, David. "The Lynching of Postmaster Frazier Baker and His Infant Daughter Julia in Lake City, South Carolina, in 1898 and its Aftermath." Department of History, Duke University. 7 August 1998. <http://www.usca.sc.edu/aasc/lakecity.html>.
Chadbourn, James. *Lynching and the Law.* Chapel Hill, N.C.: University of North Carolina, 1933.
Collins, Patricia Hill. *Black Feminist Thought: Knowledge, Consciousness, and the Politics of Empowerment.* New York: Routledge, 1991.
Cutler, James. *Lynch-Law: An Investigation into the History of Lynching in the United States.* London: Longmans, Green, and Co., 1905.
Ginzburg, Ralph. *100 Years of Lynchings.* Baltimore: Black Classic Press, 1988.
Glasrud, Bruce. *Black Texans, 1900–1930: A History.* Dissertation, Texas Technological College. Ann Arbor: University Microfilms, 1970.
"Grand Jury Convened." *Marshall Messenger,* 19 February 1912, 1.
Hall, Jacquelyn Dowd. *Revolt Against Chivalry: Jessie Daniel Ames and the Women's Campaign Against Lynching.* New York: Columbia University Press, 1974.
Halton, Beau. "'No Resentment, Rosewood Survivors Say: Reception Focuses on Racial Healing." *Florida Times Union,* 20 October 1997. <http://www.jacksonville.com/tu-online/stories/ 102197/2b3rosew. html>.
Hufsmith, George. *The Wyoming Lynching of Cattle Kate 1889.* Glendo, Wyo.: High Plains Press, 1993.
Jones, Maxine, Larry Rivers, David Colburn, R. Tom Dye, and William Rogers. "A Documented History of the Incident Which Occurred at Rosewood, Florida, in January 1923." Florida A & M University, Florida State University and University of Florida. 22 December 1993. <http://www.tfn.net/doc/ rosewood/txt>.
McKay, Claude. *The Lynching.* <http://www.cyberramp.net/kb2iqs/the lynching.html>.
Meier, N.C., G.H. Mennenga, and H.J. Stoltz. "An Experimental Approach to the Study of Mob Behavior." *Journal of Abnormal and Social Psychology* 36 (1941): 506–524. PsycInfo 0096–851X.
"Men Were After Sneed." *Marshall Messenger.* 13 February 1912. 1.
Murphey, Dwight. "Lynching-History and Analysis: A Legal Studies Monograph." *Journal of Social, Political and Economic Studies,* monograph ser. 24. Washington, D.C.: Council for Social and Economic Studies, 1995.
Raper, Arthur. *The Tragedy of Lynching.* New York: Arno Press, 1969.
Shearer, Lee. "Lynching Victims: Dedication honors those slain in 1946." *Online Athens,* 14 December 1998. <http://www.online athens.com/1998/121498/1214.allmoores.html>.

"Six Negroes Slain for Alleged Plot to Wipe Out Entire Family." *San Antonio Light*, 1 June 1918, 5.

"Sneed Is in the Pen." *Marshall Messenger*, 16 February 1912, 1.

"Strange Is Dead." *Marshall Messenger*, 1 February 1912, 1.

"Tennie Sneed and Will Whitten for Murder and James Carroll for Burglary and Assault at Harleton." *Marshall Messenger*, 23 February 1912, 1.

Tolnay, Stewart and E.M. Beck. *A Festival of Violence: An Analysis of Southern Lynchings, 1882–1930.* Urbana, Ill.: University of Illinois Press, 1995.

"Two Negroes Were Hung." *Marshall Messenger*, 15 February 1912, 1.

Wells, Ida. *Crusade for Justice: The Autobiography of Ida B. Wells.* Ed. Alfreda Duster. Chicago: University of Chicago Press, 1970.

Wells, Ida. *A Red Record: Tabulated Statistics and Alleged Causes of Lynchings in the United States, 1892–1893–1894.* Chicago: Donohue and Henneberry.

Wells-Barnett, Ida. *Mob Rule in New Orleans: Robert Charles and His Fight to the Death.* Chicago, 1900.

"Without Sanctuary." Postcards collected by James Allen. <http://www.journale.com/withoutsanctuary/pics_33.html>.

Wright, G.C. *Racial Violence in Kentucky, 1865–1940: Lynchings, Mob Rule, and "Legal Lynchings."* Baton Rouge: Louisiana State University Press, 1990.

Zangrando, Robert. *The NAACP Crusade Against Lynching, 1909–1950.* Philadelphia: Temple University Press, 1980.

Many thanks to Joe Cabaniss and Dorothy Meadows for assistance with researching the Texas lynchings.

About the Contributors

Amir M. Abdurahman is a doctoral candidate in African American studies at Temple University.

Steve Andrews is an associate professor of English at Grinnell College.

James Chambers is an associate professor of public administration at Florida Gulf Coast University.

James L. Conyers, Jr. is director and university professor of African American studies at the University of Houston.

Malachi Crawford is a doctoral student in the department of history at the University of Missouri at Columbia.

Otis B. Grant is an associate professor of law and legal studies at the University of Indiana at Gary.

Maulana Karenga is professor of Black studies at California State University at Long Beach.

Marilyn D. Lovett is a visiting professor of African American studies at the University of Houston.

Emerson Mungin is a community historian in Omaha, Nebraska.

Tanya Y. Price is an assistant professor of anthropology at the University of Missouri at Kansas City.

Sharon Pruitt is an associate professor of art history at East Carolina University.

Elice Rogers is an associate professor of adult education at Cleveland State University.

Larry Ross is an associate professor of sociology at Lincoln University in Jefferson, Missouri.

Saadi A. Simawe is director of Africana studies and associate professor of English at Grinnell College.

Andrew P. Smallwood is the coordinator of the African American studies program and an assistant professor of African American studies at Austin Peay State University.

Alonzo N. Smith is director of the African American history program at the Smithsonian Institution.

Index